My Dear Wife

My Dear Wife

The Letters of
Pvt. Charles H. Prentiss
1862-1865

NANCY N. JORDAN

authorHOUSE®

AuthorHouse™
1663 Liberty Drive
Bloomington, IN 47403
www.authorhouse.com
Phone: 1 (800) 839-8640

Published by AuthorHouse 10/27/2015

ISBN: 978-1-5049-2593-8 (sc)
ISBN: 978-1-5049-2592-1 (hc)
ISBN: 978-1-5049-2590-7 (e)

Library of Congress Control Number: 2015912180

Print information available on the last page.

This book is printed on acid-free paper.

INTRODUCTION

Dedicated to the men of the North and South who gave up their familiar lives and struggled through travails and hardships to fight for their country and the cause they believed in.

This is a compilation of diary entries and letters written by Charles Holbrook Prentiss detailing his experiences while serving in the Union Army during the Civil War. Charlie was my father's great-uncle by virtue of his marriage to Roena Camilla Clark, the daughter of Hosea and Lydia Maretta Whitman Clark. Hosea and Lydia also had a son, George Spencer Clark, who was married to Laura Anderson. They were the parents of Elsie Irene Clark. She was born in 1861, and her birth was recorded in Charlie's pre-war diary. He was very fond of her, and she of him.

The deep affection between Charlie and Elsie eventually led to Charlie and Roena taking my grandmother, Elsie, to live with them as their daughter when she was twelve years old. She was never adopted and, indeed, remained on very good terms with her parents. For example, both her children were born in her father's house. After George's death in 1912, Laura made her home with Elsie until her death in 1914. When Elsie married Arthur Newton Nevins the couple made their home with Charlie and Roena, who were like another set of grandparents to my father, Archie Prentiss, and his sister, Marion Irene, when they were growing up.

At the time of Charlie's death in 1924, Elsie allowed her sisters' children to go through the letters and take any that they wanted. The rest were given to my father, along with other mementos of Charlie's war experiences. In later years copies of the letters which were taken, and, in some cases, the letters themselves were given to me and my father, and so the collection is complete, or nearly so. One of the diaries and parts of a few letters are missing. Dad gave me the collection of papers before he died. These papers include a diary kept by Charlie detailing farm life before the start of the war and letters written to Charlie by Roena and others during his time of service. This book is a compilation of Charlies' letters and diary entries while serving in the Army from August 1862 to June 1865

There are references to the extended family in the letters especially to Laura's brother, David Anderson, who enlisted with his good friend Charlie and is referred to often.

There is much discussion of singing in the letters as well. Hosea had a very pleasant baritone voice and held singing schools in New York state and Michigan, even when the only instrument available was a tuning fork or a pitch pipe. He continued to do this most of his life, and the whole family was in demand for singing at special events as well as for church services. Charlie and Dave evidently possessed good voices and enjoyed using them. Singing was an important part of the family life, and in later years Elsie and her two sisters were called on to perform at various local functions.

Charlie had never known a secure family life as a child. When he was quite young his father, Stephen Turner Prentiss, a reed organ builder, abandoned his family and was never heard from again. His mother, Henrietta Holbrook Prentiss, was sent to prison for stealing, perhaps for food to feed her family. The four children spent some time living with his Prentiss grandparents until more permanent arrangements for their care could be made for them. In Charlie's case, his uncle Jonas Galusha, who lived near West Almond NY, took him. He thought there was bad blood in the boy and that it should be beaten out of him.

Charlie told my father about two instances in his life during this time. At Christmas, when his cousins got candy in their stockings, he had a rotten potato. Then there was the family gathering to attend the wedding of his aunt Narcissa to Marcus Whitman in 1836. They were leaving that day to go through unknown territory on a route, which became the Oregon Trail to be missionaries to the Indians in Oregon. The family members were crying because they knew they would never see the couple again. *{This was right; they were all massacred in their mission at Wailatpu in*

Oregon. NNJ} Charlie was too young to understand, but he knew he would be whipped if he didn't cry. Thinking quickly, he went into the kitchen, made tear streaks down his cheeks with soot from the stove, and put a piece of onion in his handkerchief so as to appear to have been crying and thereby escaped one beating.

The only schooling he ever had was part of one winter term during this time. He went for about six weeks until it was too cold to go to school barefoot. His grandmother, Clarissa Ward Prentiss, who offered him love and consideration, had read to him from the Bible, and her affectionate attention had helped him learn to read. Her loving care gave him a strong religious faith as well as a passion for books and reading which lasted the rest of his life. Because of this he was an educated and literate man, as is evident in the letters. He never cared much for fiction, but he was interested in history, natural history, biography, religion, and science. He had an aptitude for drawing and architecture, and, well after the war, he drew the plans for the new Methodist church in Otsego, Michigan, which opened in 1888 and is still in use.

When he was nine years old he was bound out to a neighbor who treated him worse than his uncle had. When he could stand his life no longer, he became a criminal by breaking his bond and running away to the nearby city of Rochester NY. After wandering the streets, cold and hungry, he was befriended by a boy who took him along and introduced him to a man, who took him in. There were other boys living there, and all were trained to steal in return for board and room. Because of his interest in books, he was encouraged to steal them. In the course of time he stole a Bible. When he realized what he had done, he was shocked, and because of his memories of his grandmother's affection and interest in him, he went to the shop and returned it. The bookseller became interested in him and offered him in exchange for janitorial duties, his board, a bed on the floor, and permission to read every book in the store - which he did. He later served as an apprentice, both to a blacksmith and then to a marble cutter, an occupation which he enjoyed very much, although he eventually gave it up, thinking, correctly, that breathing the dust was bad for his health.

He worked for a marble cutter in Dansville NY, and it was there that he met his first love, Harriet Young, while he was living in the temperance hotel run by Hosea Clark and his wife, Lydia. Harriet was the daughter of Lydia's sister Candace. When Harriet's mother and step-father, Darius Fenner, decided to move, Charlie planned to follow them to Martin, Michigan and work to establish himself and marry Harriet. It took all his money to buy a ticket to Detroit via the Erie Canal and boat across Lake Erie.

He arrived in Detroit in 1854 with no money but was willing to work at anything that offered. On arriving in town, the first job offering he saw, just as he was leaving the docks, was for an opening with a tombstone carver. He went to work there until he had earned enough to establish himself, acquire some land, and marry Harriet, which he did on January 1, 1857. The marriage was a happy one, but it ended suddenly on September 13, 1858 when Harriet died in childbirth and her twin sons with her.

In 1854 the Clarks had also moved to a farm in Pine Creek outside of Otsego, Michigan. This was fairly near Candace and her family, who lived in Martin. Candace and her sister were very close, and so Hosea's family settled near her. The rest of the Clarks, including Hosea's parents and brothers, also went to Michigan and settled in the area around Adrian. Two of Lydia's brothers also came west and settled near Niles, Michigan. The families kept in touch, both by letters and infrequent visits.

After Harriet's death Charlie and Roena Camilla {why he often called her Millie} Clark were married on July 4, 1859, rather sooner than Candace's

family thought proper. After Charlie and Roena were married, he was happily engaged in a stable home environment for the first time in his life. He had a family and greatly enjoyed being part of it. But the clouds of war and the imminence of a draft were on the horizon, and it became evident that someone from the family would have to serve, since they had no money to hire a replacement. Charlie, even though he was born October 1, 1830 and was almost 32 years old, had decided that he should be the

one to go rather than George, who, although seven years younger, had one child and another on the way. This is referred to in a letter from Lydia's brother, Lorin Whitman: "It seems that after mature deliberations and prayer that your Family have mutually come to the conclusion to lay a sacrifice on the Altar of our common Country in the person of one of your number....As you say in your letter, Charles is making the greatest sacrifice, and, next to him in true patriotic sacrifice, is Roenna."

Charlie makes it clear that he chose to go. But when he talks of his longing for home, he is speaking from the heart and is well aware of the value of the comforts he has left.

Charlie wrote entertaining and informative letters in a conversational style. He was careful to keep his accounts as accurate as he could. He had a high regard for the truth and would not knowingly deviate from it. He often says that his version of events is to be trusted and that he can be believed without reservation. *{I have been able to verify their accuracy on more than one occasion.}*

Many of his letters were decorated with drawings and pictures. He had considerable talent along these lines, and this stood him in good stead during the latter part of his service in the army. Due to his lack of schooling, his spelling was exceedingly erratic, and his sentence structure almost non-existent, especially since he was writing to an uncritical audience. The letter he wrote to the church is much more studied and correct.

For clarity's sake I have tried to improve spelling and sentences, but I have left as much as possible as he wrote it. Sometimes his mind went faster than his pen and a necessary word was omitted. The omissions are infrequent and quite obvious, and I have been bold enough to insert the missing word, or words. Any comments in parentheses marks were made by him. I have occasionally made comments, which are in italics and enclosed in brackets.

This collection of letters was given to me by my father, who had grown up in Charlies' house. Because Dad knew the people. He did not feel comfortable reading them, but he felt that they were too important to be discarded and so he decided to give them to me. I have thoroughly enjoyed them, as have the groups with whom I have shared some fragments and hope you will as well. Reading these letters is as close as we can now come to listening to a Civil War veteran recount his adventures. My father had this pleasure first-hand when he listened to the "boys" reminisce in Charlie's store. Fortunately, these letters are almost as good. Enjoy!

Nancy Nevins Jordan April 2015

CHAPTER 1

AUGUST – DECEMBER 1862

Dawagic Aug 28 1862

Dear wife

While I am takeing my nooning I will write a few lines to you all though I have no news to tell you when you were here I toled you that I thought we should be mustered to day. It so happens that we do not. Our last company came in to day (27) yesterday they have to examined first. Dave went home yesterday, If I make any mistake you must excuse me for the boys are singing homeward bound & a crowd is gathering around the tent we have a good time giveing concerts we have a plenty of listeners I expect to have a dulcermer tomorrow. I cant tell when I shall come home. I may not / Charles Owes interupts to tell me that he sends his respects./ Orders to drill. I must stop. Aug 29th. Last night I was wanted to beat the bass drum on eve. perraid. I took it you now then after perraid they told me to keep it. The Capt. & Lieut says to that I shall have that place in the Reg. I have a good drum & have to pay $15. for it. They all seem to be suited with my playing. we have an old drum Major from the Mexican war. we have lots of fun here this morning, we have in the gaiurd house 13 men & 2 weomen, they (the weomen) were taken into a waggon & drumed out of camp to the cars & sent off. Also we have a prisoner to be courtmarshaled to day, the same man that we had on the ground when you were here, he was on gard in the night, stuck his gun in the ground & run away, he was caut 4 miles west on the railroad asleep. what will be done with him I cant tell the rest that run gard has to carr a large stick of wood (weight about 60 lbs) on their sholders 1/2 day & the Reg. all laghing at them so you see that it stands in hand to behave him self. I am interrupted by haveing to & go to the Capt tent & be measured, my height is 5 ft 10 1/2 in. they are getting ready to muster. I cant think of anything, or news to write to you, How do you all get along. How is Geo. & Laura, I hurd they were sick, & how is little Elcy I want to see you all, My love to all, be sure & git your share, Pleas write as soon as you get this letter. Excuse all mistakes, I cant write very well when there is so many talking & carring on Direct your letter to Charles H. Prentiss Dawagic Cass Cty. Camp Willcox Care of Capt E.B. Bassett then I will get your letter Your Husband Charley Scince writing the above I received a kind letter from you. Rather sad news from Geo. & Laura. There is 11 of our Comp agoing home to night & it so happened that could not get a furlow now, & I dont care to before were Mustered. My time is limited so I must close. Now my Dear wife be of good chere I think I shall be with you again. I have got the posesion that you long to have get.

Your Dear Husband Charley

A little more, pleas mark my wolling sock by working in letters

Camp Wilcox
Aug. 31st 1862

Dear Wife. I will send you what I have copyed from my diary, haveing nothing els to do at preasent. Tues 19th This morning Geo. & Laura, Wife & myself came up town to see me off to camp, put my trunk in the waggon, bid my friends all good bye & started off. A sollom time for me. We stoped at the junction & eat dinner. then off to Kal. arrived there 1/2 past 1. Marched to the cars got aboard, then off to Dowagiac the company arrived at D. about 4 P.M. Marched to camp 3/4 mile from the villige, detailed our cooks got supper, went to the village with Dave & Hubbard. Back to camp at 1/2 past 8. 22 men loged in our tent Wed 20th got up this morning at 4, eat breakfast at 5, the company came to town & was examed. put a new lock on Hubbards trunk. 112 men came in our company. Rather tuff living just now. Three company came to camp yesterday stayed in town untill noon, came to camp eat dinner. Drilled this afternoon, had a good time, Living is getting better, through a mistake we had rations /delt out {crossed out} for only 60 men drilled after supper. Wm Starks was here from Otsego & tented with us. Thur 21 I got up at 5 washed & prepared to eat, after eating the Company marched to the Capt tent to choes officers Darrow was appointed for Lieut. to fill Lieut Wm Williams place, Autustus Lilly Orderly Sargent, Company dispursed, Gard chosen from our Co. for 24 hours, did not drill this fournoon. Large No of people are Cleaning & sweeping the campground did not drill this afternoon. Layed around done nothing, good living now. Fri 22 this morn. at 2 oclock I was taken with the Disentary in great pain, better at breakfast time, at 9 Co. met at the Capt office & finnished electing the officers. Last night one of the soldiers of in Stirgis Co. got fighting & was put in the gard house Kept there all night this morning he was taken on the camt ground & made to stand all day with out eating & relieved this eve. The names of the officers 1st Sgt. Alx. Duganne, 2nd Sgt. P.A. Hager, 3rd S. Geo. L. Clark, 4th S. J.C. Bixby, for Corp, 1st John Dewell, 2nd Rob. Patterson, 3rd D.R. Anderson, 4th P.A. Putman, 5th G.L. Bard, 6th D.O. Brown 7th Elye, 8th Youngs. This afternoon My wife Father & Mother came here, they were on the way to Niles, I got a pass & went to the village, at 4 they went on to Niles. I in a small squad drilled 1 hour. Sat 23rd. This morning early I was taken sick again, quite sick all the fournoon. I took a dose of Doct. Hopkins meadicen & cured me rite off. I was excuse from gard to day. Co. drilled some this /. & after supper the holl Reg. come out on dress peraid. The Cor. named this camp Camp Wilcox. Sun 24th. This morning got up at 5. roll called, eat breakfast after this washed & shaved dressed up for meeting. I went to the Congregation church this fournoon. About 3 this afternoon we the Co. went to the creek to bathe. This eve. 8 Companys came out on dress peraid, dismised at 7. The street that we live on is called Allegan st. Our tent is Concert hall. The Reg. behaves very good except a few gets shut up in the guard house for running away from guard duty. The camp ground is cleaned off evry morning. Here evry morning their is 96 men drawn from the Reg. for gard. Mon 25th This morn. at 5 the revellee was beat, evry man must be up & wash & prepare for one hour drill before breakfast at 9 we commenced drilling & drilled untill 11 & from 2 to 4 in the afternoon. Dress peraid this eve. we once in a while get a prisoner for disobeying Orders. I feel very well now with the exception of a cold. Dear Roenna I dont know wether this will be interesting to you this is just as I have it in my book. Their is a good deal of sameness to it. we have had some hints of our going to washington to drill before long. I did not go to meeting to day I had a lite chill last night & dont feel firstrate. I thought of home last night when I am sick Dave stays by me like a brother. I should like to here from you, how is Geo. & Laura to day. I feel sorry for them. Kiss Elsie for me, my love to all. Pleas tell me all of home. I cant tell what day I shall start for home. Pleas write the same as though you did not expect me home I wish I could get a letter evry day I have my paper most full & will stop

Your dear Husband Charley

Camp Wilcox
Sept. 3rd 1862

Dear Wife, I received your kind letter but a few minuts ago & was glad to here from you, but it filled my heart with grief to hear such news. I stated the facts to Lieut. & he to the Capt. I wont go untill we are mustered. that will be Fri next. And Fri night at 11 oclock I think I will start for home. You must not think that I dont want to come home because I dont come. The reason is that I am under strict orders. we have not mustered yet. we expected to last tuesday & was disappointed Byron Baloo came here this afternoon I asked him how you was & he said he saw father not long ago & sayed that you were a little better but how long ago I dont know. I want to come home & stay with you but I cant. O if I could get out of site a little while & give vent to my feelings it would do me good, but I cant. but Dear Wife be as cheerfull as you can & make the best of it. I trust I shall be with you again. it is the opinnion of Our highest officers that this thing will soon be settled so we will not have to stay long. tell Geo. & Laura that I remember them. I shall send this to you by Byron Bauloo. I must close it is getting late, so Good night my dear. I have you in my mind all the time. I am sorry that I cant come to night, but I cant. I am bound. I am well at preasent Love to all, especially to you. From you Charley to my Roenna

Dave sits at my left a writing a letter to Sophronia, we are in the Capt. tent alone. The capt has gone to see the Cornel for me. I think I am coming next Sat.

Charley

Camp Wilcox Sept. 14, 1862

Dear Wife.

I will drop you a few lines. I am in a great hurry, we are packing up our duds to leave at 4 oclock to day for Cincinnatie I have sent my trunk to Kal. to Milo Pierce the key inside, you will send & get it & send money to pay the charges it wont be much Father coat is in it. I bought the drum. the Lieut. has started a subscription to pay for the drum. I have advanced the money but I will get it back. I will send you the money by & bye. I arrive here safe & am well as I ever was. you neednt write untill you here from me again My Love to you

Charley

I will send you my Certificate of enlistment. Save it

Gravle Pit
Sept 17/62

Dear wife I have taken the oppertunity to write you a few lines. I am 18 miles west of Cincinnati, we started from Dowagiac last sunday evening at sundown & landed in Cin. Monday evening at 8 oclock. we were marched about one mile up in the city & stacked armes then marched to a building I think about 800 ft long & tables in this building the holl length & there we had a good supper then a part of the Reg. was marched to the Commertial Chamber & put up for the night. This chamber is a splendid hall about 150 long & 50 wide 30 high, we stayed in the city untill Tues. at 4 oclock, we was not wanted there so we took our back track 18 miles a place called gravel pit, to keep the rebels from crossing from the river, a very shallow place we have a very pleasent place the railroad on one side of us & the river on the other. steem boats are passing up & down all the time we have 2 ten pound connons & expect more. I have seen Kentucky but have not been in

- 5 -

it yet, we have about 140 thousand of union troops in this vicinity & the rebels are about 25 or 30 thousand strong. I have seen a little in the war line. Or army they are from 6 to 15 miles in Kt. a crost the river from the City. Cin. City is a durty black looking place but some splended buildings, the country is some like the Allegany cuntry in N.Y. very hilly stoney & clay soil. our water is not very bad to drink. better than that at Dowajac only it is not very cold, we can bath. evry day, are but a few rods from the river when we came we was heartly cheered & I over hurd a number say that we was the nicest Reg. that they had seen. We carry a good name wherever we go. Last night I slept on the ground in the open air for the first time. The weather is very warm. Mon. night murkery stood 83° at 9 oclock & yesterday we marched 6 miles in the hot sun, & swet so that I could ring out a quart of water from my cloths, at least I had to ring my shirt so as to have a dry one, my bage was pacted and I could not get it & I was wet as I could be & slept on the ground & slept good & did not take cold I am tuff as a nut at preasent & dont have any pane in my stomach now. I am the bass drummer for the Reg. & dont have any knapsack to carry on my back, that goes with the Company baggage. I dont have but little to do, the rest have to pitch tents.-- Last night at 12 oclock the boys got a little scart, while we was asleep the call was given & evry man was supplyed with 10 cattrages & had their guns & sayed the rebels was just acrost the river. I dont suppose there is one with 20 miles of us--I hurd some good music this morning. it is what is called the Caleope or steam organ on the steem boat as it pass by us--I found a wallet this morning with 11 dollars in it which belongs to some of my brothers. I have not found the owner yet but I think I shall before night. I report to each Capt. & he enquires of his men, so I think I shall find the owner. I am very glad that I brought my spyglass--Dave & I got one likeness taken yesterday in the city but come away to soon to get it finnished we get 6 for a dollar I will send it you when I get it. I have not got the money from the Reg. for the drum yet but hope to send you some soon they have been very bisey--I want to see you very much but cant & dont know when we can. dont feel bad dear wife for the time will soon come when we shall see each other again I hope, The people all think that the war will soon come to a close now If I cant be with you my heart is with you, I am constantly think of home. I dont fear the rebels here any more than I did at home, dont think there is any more danger. I enjoy myself very well. you may write to me as soon as you get this if you will. I have not much news to tell you yet, you must excuse all mistakes & pencil writing my ink stand gave out & I throughed it away. Dave & the rest of the boys are all well. I will stop now & find out where you want to direct your letter, I dont know yet. Thur morn. Sept 18 Dear wife now I finnish,--Perhaps it will be interesting to you to know my rought here. you can trace it on the rail road map & see exacly where I am, from Dowajiac to Niles to Michigan City to Lafayette, to Indianapolis to Shelby Vill, to Lawranceburg and to Cincinnati. Then from Cin. back to Lawranceburg. This Reg. is guarding the rail road between Cin & Lawrenceburg, 18 miles we have one very large railroad bridg to gard over a small river at Lawranceburg, it is some 6 or 8 hundred feet long 30 ft high I dont have much to do, 55 of Co. B went to Cin last night to gard a battery, will be gone about 8 days. Jim Bachelder has come with some ink, we had a little fun last we had 2 larmes last night. it was done to try the men. the bugle was sounded & the long roll was beat to armes, to armes was the cry & form line of battle, just at that time a great many was sick, some lame, some one thing & some another, it was laughable to see the performance, It is very lively about here this morning it is now 9 oclock & there has beenn 24 steem boats up the river, & about as many trains of cars by here this morning, they are loaded with horses, muskets, soldiers, provision &c, all for the war, we shall not go into action yet, awhile Direct your letter to Charles H. Prentiss Lawrenceburg, Indianna Co. B. 19 Mich Infantry & I will get it.

write soon Charley my love to all,

Camp Gravle Pit, Sept. 17. 1862

Dear Brother

I take this opportunity to pen to you a few

lines, I have writen 2 letters home & received no answer, I am getting somewhat anxious to here from you all, I have no news to tell you, but will try to say something, This is a hard looking country to me, the timber is principaly here the wild & honey locus, buckeye, once in a while an oak, black walnut, maple, paw paw, the woods is compleetly tyed togeather with grape vines like the wild locus & grapevine togeather makes tuff clearing, the bodeys of the locus very in size; from 6 in to 24 in through & covered with thorns from 2 to 6 in. long, the soil hard clay. after a shower it is almost impossable walk or stand up. The weather is very warm & cool nights, It is a lively & buisness place here, not but 6 or 8 dwellings in sight, last Monday 24 trains of cars pass here between sun & sun, the Mich 13th pass here this morning on a steemer. I had no chance to speak to them, they are on their way to Louisville, we have to stay here & do nothing but to drill & practice & gard the river & R.R. 18 miles we have a splended martial band. I suppose you have hurd of the fight we had here the 2nd night we were here, for fere you have not I will tell you all about it, & disscribe it as well as I can, The night was dark & rained, the wind blew hard, all most took our tents over. Our tents being strained very tight & the wind made the tents rower when inside like cannon a little way off. There is a valuble bridge 2 miles below us where we expect the rebels might cross. the bridge is in our care, the roer of the tents started an alarm & was called to armes twice supposing there was fighting at the bridg, such a bussle I never saw before, Capt. Duffy while getting his Company togeather was so skart that he {word scratched out} his britches at the same time the gard was going around to relieve the old gard one man was so scart that while they were advanceing him he ran from his post shot at them, they went up to him & he could not speak. This that I write you is true, The report has come back to us from Mich. that we had a fight & was all cut to peaces.-- I will send you a list of our clothing & price. Knapsack 2.57 Haversack .48 cents, Canteen .34, Cap .57, Over Coat 7.20, Straps .12 (to strap our coat on Knap sack) Dress Coat 6.71, Pants 2.15, Blanket 2.95, Blouce or fategue Coat 3.03, Shirts .88, Drawers 2 pare 1.00, Socks 2 pare .52 Shoes 1.94, Shirts & shoes I did not get we are allowed $46, the first year for clothing Dave is at fort Jones one mile this side of the city & about one half of the Company is there. There is not a great many sick, S. Knapp has the measles. & a few others has them, the general complaint is Desentary. I am tuff as a bear, or the only complaint is that I have, is I cant here from home great many others has received letters from home. we are haveing a good time here, Pleas let me have a letter from some of you once a week. My love to wife & all, tell wife to write if she is not sick & can. How does all get along. give me all the particlars. all for now. Truly Yours Charley

Direct to Lawrenceburg Indiana Mich 19 Infantry Co. B. and I will get your letters.

Camp Hooker Oct 12 1862

My Dear Wife. I will try and write you a few more lines to let you that I am yet alive. I received two letters last Wednesday evening one from you & one from Geo. also a paper from Geo. & was glad to here from you. I suppose you have got my last letter by this time that I mailed Oct 3rd. Oct. 8 I mailed a letter to Father. we still remain at gravle Pit, I dont know when we shall leave, I hope we will not have to stay here this fall & winter, we are affraid that we shall have to, we want to go where it is warmer or els go home. we are haveing very easy times. There is about 200 sick in the hospitals both here & Cin. 2 has died in Cin, we have a good hospital in the city. The main trouble or the cause of our sickness is the water that we drink, I use but little & I am very healthy & will be as long as will take care of my helth, there is but few that does that, Last Sunday I took a walk, went North of the camp 1 1/2 miles over the hill, (you see we are located in the valley) & see some pleasent cuntry, all at one sight, about 2,000 acres of corn, The Pawpaw apples are very abundant, & very good to eat, they tast very much like the mandrake, The game is very scarce, none here as I can here of but the red squirel, Turkey Buzard, screech owl, Hickry nuts are very pleanty, there are as large as blackwallnuts, the largest I ever saw, the butter nut, & blackwallnut, are very plenty. I took awalk into one of the cornfields to see the corn I think the stalk will everage from 10 to 12 ft tall. one stalk we found was 14 ft tall & 8 1/2 ft to the ear, it was out of my reach, it is planted 4 ft one way & 1 1/2 foot the other way, & think it was plowed but once during the seson but one way, the weed was tawllr than my head. I have an ear in my tent that I wish I could send you, It is plump 10 in long & 2 1/2 in Diamiter. It is the yellow dent that growes here. The miseltoe is some thing very curus, it is a bunch of evergreen sprouts that grow out of the boddy of the branches of the Elm, Oak, & one or two other kinds of trees, it has a small green & thick leaf resembleing the snow drop leaf in shape & a green burry the shape & sise of a curant, it is a curiosity to me. I have seen only 2 kinds of snakes, the black snake & the blow snake, the latter is a short thick chunked snake with a ugly looking flat head, with a very dul motion. on the hill back of the corn fields we have a splended view of Miami river & flats. we can see perhaps about 6 miles up the vally & there you see splended farms & in the distant can see a village the name I dont know, Also the river handsome winding its way through the larg corn field. we cant see down the vally a great way on account of the hill on which is an old fort Harrison, These flats are very rich. clay soil, when in the cornfeild we picked few ears of corn to carry to camp with us, in the woods on our way to camp we (Jim Batchelder) chance to meet some cows, we naturally coaxed her a little, but she was rather shy, so we put our corn to a good use, after coaxing a while I succeeded in getting up to, & Jim milked each of us a canteen full, you better believe that I fatted one inch on the ribs while that milk lasted, Now we will skip a few days, David & I took a walk yesterday went west of the camp 1 1/2 miles, went up on the hill where Harrisons fort was, it was built in 1812 I think, there is not much to be seen there now, only the entrenchment it is a nice plesent place, we can see, many miles evry way, their is 3 villages in sight, one is Lawrenceburg, one up the Miami river, & one in Kentucky, we can see up & down the Ohio 2 or 3 miles, also the rail road, & R.R. bridg which is 1,600 ft long & 50 ft high in some places we can see thousands of acres of corn. All to be seen at one sight, the fort ground is covered with blackwallnuts & hickry trees & aplenty of nuts. Oct 13th I shall have to close my discorse, & write about something els. I have hurd this eve. that we shall to leave here tomorrow morning for Covington Near Cin. I entended to write you a good long letter so I shall wind up the wosted, No saying that I will send you my picture & 21 dollars in money, It is about all that I have except some change that I made by marking knap sack, I have had to use more money than I expected to the oficers have not been paid off yet so I havent got my money back for the Drum, I shall get it, my vest cost 3.50 & some other things I had to have, we are not yet to go in to any danger at Covington. I have got your last letter dated Oct. 5, write when & as often as you pleas & direct the same as before, they will follow the Reg. I will tell you when to change the directions. I have not time to write, because it is all excitement here & in the tent. From your Dear Husband Charly Prentiss I shall write soon again, but dont wate for me to write, I am well & have good liveing, we have but little fruit, Charly, I guess that Is all now,

Camp near Covington Oct 15/62

Dear Wife

I this opportunity to write to you a few lines to let you know where I am (If I make any mistakes you must excuse me for there is a dozen around me talking & gabing & put me out) I am 2 1/2 miles from the river & one mile Covington city, one mile & a half through the city, quite a place, some splended buildings, where we are camped is a very pleasent place, wright in a beach & maple grove, we have a fine view of Cin, City & Covington & hills avound us & splended mansions on them, we started from Gravle pit yesterday noon, got in Cin, at 8 oclock then marched to our camp ground at sundown, stacked armes, eat our chips (hard bread) layed down under a beach here, went to sleep, & slept good all night, I have got so hardened that I could go into any of your fields with my blankets, & sleep good when it is cold enough for a frost, so you see that I am getting tufened some, my health is as good as it can be, now dont you worry about me when you here that I am doing as well as I tell you. I am hard as a brick, we have around us about 32 thousand men, there was 2 Reg. came here from Cumberland Gap, The hardest lot of men that I ever saw, they are the 33 Ind. & 18 Ky. many of them are bare footed, raged, durty, some with nothing but drawers on for pants &c, but were the tufist, hardist looking men I ever saw, & they say that they are well clothed compared to the rebels they look ten times worst than we do, I dont see how the rebs, can live if that is the case, man can get hardened to most any thing, so I am good for it, why they came to come here, they were in the gap & the rebels cut of their supplies & starved them out, their was 10,000 of them (union) & could hold back 100,000 if they should as many attact them, so they cut their way out, without any loss, the rebels followed them some 50 miles, they started 18 of Aug & arrived here today, a part of the time half rations, & the other part 1/4 ration, while on the march they took each man a blanket, piled up there knapsacks & clothing set fire to them then went on {fut} before they started they burned all ther tents & bageg, they have been one month with out a tent, there will be 4 more Reg. of the same Brigade here tomorrow, They give our Mich battery a good name, they say they fight like tigers, ther was a battery came in this afternoon, I have been at work most all day putting up hospital tents, which is the duty of the band, I think I have very easy times, it may come tuffer by & bye if so let it come, I dont care, I will tell you where to direct your letters tomorrow if I can find out. Tell Geo. the folks out this way drive their teams with one line & wride the nigh wheel horse, for haw is a steady pull on the line & for gee 2 or 3 little jerks, the line is only fasened to the nigh leader, & have a spreding stick one end fasened to the hame ring of the nigh horse (of the leader) to the outside bit ring of the off horse. a horse is driven the same way, we have with our Reg 78 muels & 12 horses, 13 waggons drawn by 6 muels each, each waggon weighs 1,600 I will cloes. I will write again soon. write soon as you can My love to you, my dear wife. give my respects to all. I am in hurry, be a good girl Charly Prentiss

Falmouth, Oct 21ˢᵗ 1862

My Dear beloved Wife

I take this opportunity to drop you a few lines to let you know where I am. The space between us is growing longer evry day now, we started from Covington last Sat at 3-15 oclock P.M. & marched 11 miles to Florance, We rendersvooed in a larg round building 200 ft in diamiter, this is on a fair ground a splended place. We were very tired, had a good place to sleep, up the next morning & on our march at 4 oclock, The country is very hilly & rough but had a splended mecadamised road they tell me here this same road leads to Washington, it passes through the Cumberland gap & so in, The soil is clay I would not live here if they would give me the state if it is all alike what that I have seen. The secend night we encamped on a secesh farm, an old home to, we burned up about 40 rods of rail fence for camp fires & another Reg. that camped with us, burned as much. I live as well as I want to. we have fresh beef, sheep, hogs, yes, hens, fruit &c, all rebel property remember & honey, too last night we confiscated about 25 sheep 100 gees & hens, 6 or 8 hogs & I think 8 horses, & so it goes all through this state we caqn tell a secesh as soon as we see them we come a cross a union family once in awhile we will see them with a pail of water or cakes, apples &c the seem so glad to us, but a secesh will hang back, keep out of sight, scowl, look cross & so on, it is easy telling them, we pass through one battle ground on our way here, saw one large brick house that was burned & an army waggon burned layed side of the road, the spokes all choped off, fields & gardens all lay to the commons, looks desolate, 4 Reg. in company with, we arriving at this place at 12-15 oclock P.M. yesterday the rail road bridg was completed that was burned by the rebels about 6 weeks ago, here we found about 12000 men or soldiers, a larg city of cours, we are crawling on towards the rebels, we are on our way to Lexington. Dear Roenna how I would like to see you, I get lonsome once in a while but it wont do. I am well & tuff as ever I enjoy good health as I ever did, The health of the Reg. is improving, Let Baird is sick with the measels, all the rest of our Otsego boys are all well. Dave sets by side flat on the ground writing to his Father & Mother I have not hurd from since Oct. 8, dated Oct. 5, Pleas write as soon as you can if you have not. I have no more time to weite I want to mail this tonight, tattoo will in 5 minuts then lights out, we march in the morning from here. I will write again, Your Dear Husband, Charly

Direct to Charles H Prentiss

Co B. 19th Mich Inft

Covington Ky.

I am in a great hurry

Wed morning Oct 22nd I will fill this sheet seeing that we are not a going to leave as we expected to last eve. The General thought it prudent for us to lay over one day & rest. we have march 45 miles in a little less than 3 days. I went down this morning to see the R.R. bridg. the ruins lay there yet, it was a splended bridg 200 ft long & 50 ft high covered with Iron it croses the Licking river on the south and are rifles pits. they are dug in circles, 30 ft in diamiter so that they come to the front & fire pass on & load while going around It is on the peak of a revolver on one side they are load & on the other there are fireing. there was a nomber of Reg. went from here to Lexington this morn. & cavelry we are makeing a clean sweep of secesh this time while at Covington I saw a larg number of cannon & parrot guns & howitser, a parrot gun is for throughing canister shot. A canester catreg is composed of a tin can filled with small round ball & power for shooting a short distance very much like a shot gun & grape shot are about the same as canester only for a little longer distance, & out of the same kind of gun. these guns are 4 1/2 in calabre & smoth, The guns for throughing shell & balls are cut the same as my rite arm. Cast iron 3 1/2 Caleber, the shell is not the same bom shell they will not explode untill they strike /something {crossed out} A bom shell explode by a fuse atached to the shell, for a shell that travels 40 secends has a fuse 10 in. long. I will give you a more minute explanation of these things after a while, I cant give you a correct idea of all now. It is very lively around here, troops coming in & leaving all the time. I think by what I here that we are under General Baird. I saw him this morning. we are the 2nd Reg. in the 3rd division of some Brigade. I have not learned how it is exacly, when I find out I will tell you. I am afraid that we are not a going to get in our pay in time for your payment I dont think we shall be payed in 5 or 6 months from the last pay day in Dowagac. I have had to use more of that money than I expected. I payed 15 dollars for drum, 3.50 for vest, Oil cloth blanket &c. I have but 1 dollar now, I sent you 21.00 dollars by Mrs Baker, have you got it. 40 men out of Co. B has gone out scouting after forrage & provision. you may think where dont have any thing to eat but hard bread & bacon, that we fair hard, but that is not so I feel better after eating it than I would to set down to a table & eat a great veriety of food when I am well & that is what keeps me well, I buy a chuck of cheese once in a while at 15c per lb this is all we have when on a march except what we confiscate. I must say that I like a soldiers first rate when I am well & if I could have my with Wife me, we have one of the fineist looking Reg. that I have seen, we are all jus like Brothers all through the Reg, there is good singers in the Cor as well as ours & we all get together & have a good time a singing. But Oh, after all, home is place that I had rather see. Pleas write often if you dont say much, if I could know that you are well It would seem better. It seems hard when Dave gets many letters, he has had from 12 to 14 & I have had but 3 It must be that you write oftener Dear Wife keepup good courage, I am in hopes to see you befor long, Pleas tell me the date of the last letters you receive from me, then I can tell if you get all that I send you. I am afraid that I am a going to have soer eyes I have the information in my right eye now & troubles me much, It commenced yesterday It may be nothing but dust, I never saw land so dry as it is now, I think it has not but 2 little showers since we came in this country. This Bridg I spoke of was burned 30 rebels 15 of them were killed by 7 men & 2 boys, I dont have any form to my letter because I write as I think of it.

now I will send my letter to you & let you correct the mistakes. I have not red it, I wish you could see this army of men that I here, It looks splended.

From your husband Charley, to my Dear wife Roenna

Oct 24/62

Dear wife we start on our march this morning at 7, I received your letter yesterday & Marys. Direct your letter as I told you in my last & when you write pleas send me the receipt of the Diphretic power, I mailed a letter to you the 22nd we are all packing & I have no time to write Good bye Dear Roenna your letter come very excitable, my eye is very sower. I dont use but one eye Charley

Camp Gravel Pit

Oct 2nd 1862

Included with the letter is a small slip of paper which is labeled "Read this first" and reads as follows: I will explain how to trace this letter. On the sekend page evry other line, also the 3 & 4 then at the bottom commence & read right back again evry other line I think you can follow it with any trouble, Charley

Do what you like with these Pictures {the pictures are lost}

My Dear Beloved Wife. It is with pleasure that I can set down to my drum which is my writing desk to write you a few lines again. Your letter was kindely received the 29 Sept. dated the 24th & mailed the 26th. I have no news to tell you now, but will say something if it would be any comfort to you, There was never any thing come so exceptable as your letter did the other day. It seems that it takes more time for a letter to get to you than it does for one to come from you to me, I mailed my first letter to you Sept 15th & according to your letter, you received mine the 23rd Sept. you say you will hasten to reply for fear I may be ordered away, there is no danger,

It is the oppinion of our officers that we shall winter here, so you need not be scart about that, I will gurrentee that we will not see a single engagement, we are getting good news evry day most in regard to our National affairs, we have the Cincinnati daly evry day to read--The reception of a letter may come good to you But I dont want you to get excited so as to make you sick. Yes I do suppose you was glad to here from me. I dont want you should worry about me, because I have Dr. Hopkins meadicen with me I shant be sick more than 2 days at a time, I was sick yesterday & getting well today, night before last I was taken with the Disentary & vomiting the same time, when daylight come I took one dose of the checking drops & have been getting better ever since & feel first rate now. Stephen Knapp has been quite sick with the mesals, he went to the hospital most 2 weeks ago, came back to the tents today, Mr Higgins son in law Baker has been sick ever since he came here, home sick I guess. Their is some 7 or 8 sick with the mesals 2 are not ecpected to live, I dont know what Co, they belong to, the general health is not very good at preasent, It is so warm & dry, we had a little shower a few minutes ago & the air smells good, we have had no frost yet, The leaves are turning yellow. It looks like fall now. You can see that I have taken your letter for my text & am preaching from it. you say you feel like the Ague. If you dont feel well you must docter yourself as I do, if ever I take care of myself it is now & I want you should do the same, I expect to see you before many years. yes before many months, The Cor. was hurd to say to day that we should remain here untill winter then move to Cin. Oct. Fri. 3 Now I will proceed withh my scribbleing, I am glad to here that Father & Mother is as well as useal & also Mary. Tell Father that I think of his prayers evry morning that is what I dont here out here. Evry day is alike out here, Our chaplin is not with us yet. Perhaps will be next sunday. or next. Tell Mother I think of her when I dont feel well, & Mary I have not forgoten. I am sorry that Geo. does not get well you must be very badly behind with your fall work, I think I shall be able to help you this fall in regard to money matters. I think I shall send you $50. by express, by the time you want to use it. I am sorry to here that Laura does not get along any faster than she does, I am looking ahead for a better time to come than we are a haveing. You say that Elsie is sick, what is the matter with her, the little bird, I wish I could see her, kiss her for me. I never shall forget the time & feellings that I had when I left you in Kal(amazoo). it was a solem time with me, It would not have been near so bad if I had left you at home, I was glad to here of safe arrivel home, You say you felt entirely alone, you are not, my heart & mind is with u all the time, It pleases me 2 have u say that the people use u well. Father went 2 Kal & got my trunk, was all the things safe in it I did not lock it. Corn is not all cut up out here yet & have not had any frost, the weather is very warm & dry, I have not seen any wheat sowen here yet, this is a cuntry I dont think much of. Dont say any thing about peach pie or any good to eat if you dont want to make me homesick, I have seen the time scince I have been here that I would have given 50 cents for a good drink of your well water, when I feel well I can get along very well for food & water. the water is good tasting water but it is soft & warm. Dear wife you must keep up good spirits & not be sorrowfull feeling, give away. No, I dont wonder at your mistakes for I dont see any. I am not good at finding mistakes aspetchely in your composition. you say u would be plesed with my pictures, I dont think you will, they are not good, I am shamed of them, they are troubled to take good ones in Cin. on account of the black smoke made by burning coal, I will get it taken again after a while, I have only 2 with me now, I am intitled to only 3 pictures, Dave & I went in for 6 he has 3 & I 3 Dave with 1/2 of the company is at ft Jones yet, I have not seen him very lately. I would like to share with you the peaches on our little trees. I would like to take a peek on the other side of the creek. I presume it would look like home. some sunday afternoon take a walk will you. you say it reminds you of me. Yes I think it does. But what reminds me of u, when I go to my knapsack & see my shirts & socks hankerchiefs & more than of the rest is your likeness which I carry clost to my heart all the time both night & day if I cant stay with you I think what I carry in my side pocket. I think some of geting the likeness put in a small case or locket it filles my pocket so much, the case is to bulky, I dont sing a great deal now because Dave, Hubbard & most all the singers are up to ft Jones & they have the books I am glad you like the new singing book.--I will write to all after a while. I mailed a letter to Geo. Sept 27th & I mailed a letter to Cosine Ira Kenney Sept 29th I wish Geo would write me & tell me all about the buisness how to does the cows, hogs, hens, sheep dogs, cats & crops get a long. what would seem silly to u would be interesting to me, dont be afraid to write all the particulars I think you are getting the particulars in my letters at least I tell all I know. You say, I hope you will try & do right, I will all about that, my word for it, I hold a good name here both on duty & honesty. I told you that I found a wallet with money in it, I reported myself to the officers, & they made enquiers and found the owner. the hole Reg. knows me now, some are honest, some sayes it is lucky it fell into my hands &c. now I am trusted to do buisness for any one of the Reg. That is the name that I have so fare, you ask if I ever expect to come & stay with u. I answer yes. if we are not cut off by sickness very soon. I know of no danger here than at home, I know your anasious Dear Wife. I feel in my heart for you, your lonely feelings, but we must look on the bright side, you say again. Good night my dear & may you have pleasent dreams dreams. I surely did the night after I received your kind dreamed of seeing you & being with u. I have followed your letter through & answered it as near as I could write, dont care what u call it. We have a little fun here once in a while. yesterday morning we had the pleasure of druming 2 laydes out of camp & set them a drift on the rail road. Day before yesterday we moved our camp to a better place than we had, it is moved just acrost the R.R. track north from where it was, on ground that is about 50 ft higher. the ground which we first occupied was to close to the river, the water is getting lower evry day & smells bad. I wish you might here our band play. we have a good one, we are talkeing some of getting up a brass band, we are not agoing to have anything els to do. I am haveing very easy time of it. when I am sick I have the best of care, not a quarrel has been in Co. B yet but in other Companys they quarrel some & would fite if they dare. I have hurd that Dr. Hopkins & wife is both sick. is that so, & hurd that Dan Arnold is dead. you may tell Doct H. that when I get some money I shall send for 5 or 6 doz. bottles of his checking drops. It will sell rappid. If he is aminded to trust me, he may send me some & I will forward him the money as soon as I sell it. or enough of it pay him I dont suppose there is 200 in the Reg. but what has the Disentarry & that I had seems to be the best to cure. he can direct it the same as you would a letter onely by express to Gravle Pit. I dont think of any els to say now & think I will close Now Dear Wife, another word to you. Keep up good spirits, be cheerfull & look for the best, for there a good time coming. write evn as you can & a long letter, Cant u all turn in & write, evrry one of you, & make a long letter & it wont be so teajus I dont care what you write This to my Dear beloved Wife Roenna From your Charley

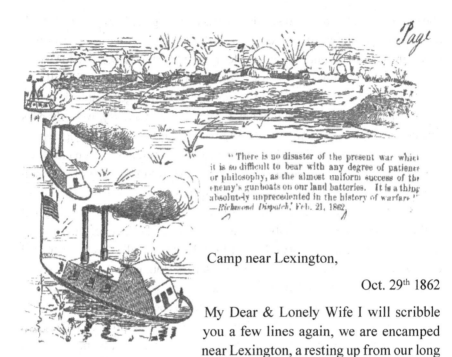

" There is no disaster of the present war which it is so difficult to bear with any degree of patience or philosophy, as the almost uniform success of the enemy's gunboats on our land batteries. It is a thing absolutely unprecedented in the history of warfare "
—*Richmond Dispatch*, Feb. 21, 1862.

Camp near Lexington,

Oct. 29th 1862

My Dear & Lonely Wife I will scribble you a few lines again, we are encamped near Lexington, a resting up from our long march, we have marched about 125 or 30 miles since we left Covington that is scince the 18 of this month, the first part of our journey was the worst looking contry I ever saw, the land is rough, the hills high & steep & made the travleing slow & teagous, we have had hills to clime very much like the hill you have to climb up by the dam, the steepest part of it only they are from 40 to a 100 rods in length, such places we have to double teems 12 muels to a waggon. remember the rocks are laid so it is the same as climbing a flite of stairs, when we came to Paris the land & cuntry begins to look handsomer & so on to Lexington, the last 15 miles we came I see the pertist cuntry I ever saw, level, smoth rich soil (clay loam) good fences & stock I have never have seen finces untill I came here the rail finces are (on an everage) 8 ft high, In travling the last 15 or 20 miles I think I have seen more than 100 miles of stone wall fence & higher than I can see over when standing close to it, large quantities of wheat & corn. These nice farmes are owned by slave holders, they have from 10 to 40 slaves each & as good looking negroes I ever saw, these are the union slave holders with few exceptions, they have some splended dwellings, but I have not seen a barn as large as 30 x 40 in the state, they scarsely have any thing but hovels. The best cattle & horses that I ever saw, you dont know any thing about cattle, when you coud see the cattle, very large & heavy, I dont think that I will run down the state of Ky. any more When we came through Lexington I saw the monument of Henry Clay It stands clost by his body. It is a splended thing, it is I think about 75 ft tall & his statute is full sise on the top, I cant tell you what it is made of I did not go clost to it. It is a yellowish collar, I cant give you any description of the citty, we only pass through it. I dont get chance to go any where, The factory that makes our Kentucky jain is about 80 rods from our campground, it is a large building. we are camping on the same ground where Morgin took 150 of our men week ago last Saturday, he also had possesion of these mills that I speek of to make cloth for his men, rather thin cloth for this time of the year, that is the best they have, the nabours say that some of the rebels are almost naked, they have no uniform, have all kinds & sorts of clothes we have a chance to find out a little about the rebels, they dont have enough to eat & ware they say themselfves that all they get to eat, is out of this state. A letter was got hold of by some one near here from a rebel Gen. had told his men to work up into Kty, Ill, O, & Indianer to get their supplies or if they did not their families would have to starve & then we have got them very clost to the southern line of this state, The story will soon be told in this part, How it is in Via I dont know we dont get papers any more, we have quite a nomber of darkeys with us. In answer to your letter. when I received your letter I was in a great hurry. I got it just at night, & were to march the next morn. & just before I got your letter I mailed one to you, so just before we started in the morn. I mailed a little line to you to let you know that I got your letter O you dont know what a relief it is to me to get a letter from you & from home, (The train that I march in is about 2 miles long, 6 reg.) I forgot myself There is so much noise here I cant write nor think, 5 & 6 thousand men around me all the time. last sunday morn I got up & {here 2 pages are missing} Oct 30th Dear wife I will say a few words more if I can think of anything to say. Their is a rhumer a float that peice is declared for 60 days, Cant believe it, & another thing, they have given a chance to enlist in the regular servis 10 out of each Company. & some other things are indicated to lead me to believe that this trouble is drawing to a close, There is something a bruing, Another the Major agrees to give evry man 50 cents per day after 50 days as long as the war will last if they will give him 6 cents for the first 50 days. no one will take him up, this all showes to me that something is going on, evry thing quiet as far as I know, I dont know but I am wild to think so but all talk just as I do. if that is the case we will soon be discharged, & I hope it is, I am tuff & healthy as ever except my eye, I suppose I have lent my spy glass to some sore eyed person, & I have taken it from that, I will give you a little idea of the prices of things out here, sugar 50c lb tobaco 1.00 lb a small corn cake baked in a common round pie tin 25c pie in the same tin 10 & evry thing els the same rate, Milk 10 qt &c. I have hade a talk with Doct Bennett he is most to much for me he feels his posision to much he may be a good man &c but feels his oats. Dave sends his love to all, Let & Ansel Baird is at Cin. sick & Knapp, Ike Kinney is uder the weather some & the rest of the Otsego boys are all well. Capt. Bassett is very sick, he was taken sick night before last, I dont know what the matter is, Our Lieut is promoted to agitent & Hubbard acts as first Lieut. Our march was most to much for us, when you write Direct your mail to Covington & the rest as before, I think I will close, My love to Father & Mother, Laura, Geo, Mary, & Elsy & to my Dear Wife, from you Husband Charley

Camp near Lexington Oct 30 1862

Wal, Brother I will say a few words to you I have told all of my story to Roenna so I not much to say in regard to nuse, I will send you a plan of a hay rack & you can see how you like it, first there is 2 bed peaces 4 x 4 the shape of a sled runner, with 3 peaces fraimed crost (fig 2) projecting beyond the wheel, with a thin hard wood board bent over the hind wheel (fig 3) & a streight board over the front wheel (fig 4) this is fraimed sollid together, brings the load very low on the waggon, I think you can understand it. Another nice little thing is a latch to a larg gate (fig 2) is a lever attached to the baroe latch, projecting up above the top of gate (fig 3) is the bar & (fig 4) is a spring fasened to the bottom board, made of wood, Another is a land roller whis easy on a teem when in opporation, The top of the roller is all covered so that all the roll is covered above the fraim & the toungue is put in with a joint clost to the fraim, & a chain fasened to the corner of the fraim to the end of the evener with about 3 in slak chain, so in geeing about the nigh horse will draw it around & this makes it easy for the teem, the only object in Covering the roller is to make a place to stand & to keep out of danger of the roll. I think that I have discribed this so that you can understand it if not you can ask what questions you want to in to these or any thing els, there is things that I was a going to find out & tell you when

I came out here & I have forgoten them, my eye pains me & I must stop writing, Pleas write soon & give me the news, Yours Truly Charley

{This letter is illustrated with sketches, very clearly showing the first two plans which he describes.}

                                        Camp near Lexington Nov 5/62

My Dear & Lonely Wife,

I will try & write you a few lines again to let you know how I am, I received a letter from you to night & was glad to here from you, but am sorry to have you feel so lonely & bad, I dont think you can help it, You say you set down in the old home to write to me, & a lonely home it is, My Dear, I can sympathise with you, It is hard to be sepperated so long, it seems that the three years is more than gone, But. I honestly beleive that I will eat dinner with you next 4 of July, & I think sooner I hurd a good sermon last Sabath, from our Chaplin he. I will give you a little disscription of my house this evening. to begin with we all set flat on the ground like somany Taylors, my big drum at my right hand, me next with my portfolio writing a letter to my wife, & Dave at my left writing to his Brother Juleus, 3 or 4 scratching around in the straw a makeiing their bed like so many boys. V. Rose writing a letter to some one, Ike Kinney, Tim Dagget Ed. Baird, & John Duel haveing a gaim of cards & the rest telling storys, the center of the tent is a stack of guns, & our Candle sticks is a bayonet stuck in the groung, but a little whiel ago Hubbard was in here & we had to sing. & the weather is howling out side it has been a fine Indian summer day all day, & towards night the wind raised & commenced getting cold,--I dont think that we shall go much farther south than we are now, even if we do, our communication will not be cut off now, dont borrow any trouble about that, we are just as safe there as here, I prefer going father south wher it is warmer than to stay here, The ground is as try as can be here, we have not had any rain scarsely scince I left Mich. we frequently have little spots of rain, but not to amount to anything, we think some of puting up about here for winter quarters but I dont know how true it is, Their is a armistes out, not a man is allowed to fire a gun or pistole, even to the Gen. is not allowed to, And it the opinion of all here, that the fighting is done, & I think so jusging by the movements of evry thing arround me, no marching is going on, no guns are to be fired, & Reg. are settleing down for winter, enlisting out of our regements for regulars, for standing army, The rebels are starving out, 5,000 rebels layed down their arms, &c. All these things goes to shhow to me that Peace is clost by, still more, Our officers are trying to speculate out of the poor soldiers by saying that they will give them 50 cents a day after 50 days as long as the war will last, if the soldiers or any one else will give them 6 cents a day the first 60 days, It seems to me that the officers must know that thire is something up. what does that look like, I dont think that I immagin all of this without a cause, A great many make their brags of being at home to eat a christmas dinner, this is a little to soon to believe, Now Dear wife dont be discoraged, think for the best, dont look on the dark side, I guess it will all come out right in a long run.

I am glad to here that you are all well, that comforts me more than all the rest, I am well & tuff as buck, my eye is getting well, I got a flax seed poltice & wore it on my eye 2 days, & scince that it commenced getting better, am glad that Geo, & Laura is a getting better, You gave me a disscription of your sunday eve. fireside of the 26th I cant tell you of ours, the fire came up missing but the side was a chilly one, evry evening is alike to us, I wish that I could have the privilage of playing with Elsie. I dont suppose that I would know her now, Does she walk or talk yet. I tell you what it is, I can tell how you all look in the house, I can immaging just where you all set when in the kitchen, what you are reading, what you are talking about. how the stove stands, how the butry looks & what you have in there to eat, evry thing around you looks natureal to me, yesterday when come from Lexington I immagined myself on my way from town (Otsego) agoing home, I was buisey thinking about something a travling alone the roads look some alike on looking up I was lost, but when my thought came to me, I found myself in Ky. in the army, Dear wife I want to come home I frequently loose myself in thought, then again & find myself some where els. I dont fair hard here I want you think, but I am away from home, A boil on Geo. noes hay! that is a mean thing if I were in his place, I would not be guilty of carring such a thing for it is a nasty thing to have around, It is in a good place, write before his eyes, he even see to take care of it, wall I wont abuse him any more Thursday eve. Nov. 6 Now I will write a little more to you. we are all spralled out in our tent as useal Pleas tell Elder Buck to write & not wate for a letter from me, The more letters, the better, I would be glad to here from him, I think of the prayers that are offered for us, & I am glad to have it so, I think we need prayers, it is the wickedest place that I ever saw but that is no excuse for me, I try to do my duty & pray for myself, I hold myself in readyness for any emergincy. But still desire your prayers, The fact of the buisness is, I wish I could be at home to some of your good visits, I have lost 2 good visits when Charley Franklin & lady. Uncle Henry came to see you. I under stand that Charley is sick yet, or is not a going to get well, So Vernon says, If Geo knew all he would wish himself at home agin. I will admit that there is some things very pleasent in a soldeirs life, anyway a musician, we are get up a brass band for the winter occupation, You need not be scart there will not be much drafting done, now I think that is all over with. You say that Mother has got a cheese saved for me, I shall be right glad of it But dont send any thing to us untill we settled down for winter, if we should get a box of goods then have to march we would have to leave it & that would be to bad, When you send a box to me I would think it best to go in with the rest of the nabours, such as Mrs Anderson, Mrs Kinney, Mrs Dewell, & others of Otsego, it would better for me & the rest, to come in one box, I will let you know when to forward it to me, The fact of the buisness is those things you have mensioned would kept as choice as gold, I am glad that you are going to do so, In regard to shirts dont send me any white shirts, some colared cloth of some kind is better, I wish you had these that I have got & I had some other kind, I would not care if they were wollen, I have nothing but cotton to were next to me now, I toled dave your erened I here some funny stories about Hubbard & Addie I suppose you knew all about them I will not mention them, It is most time for tattoo, & my fingers are very cold, & will try & finnish tomorrow, you see that it fare weather & we have tion a good deal of the time so I dont have much time to myself just now, A kiss for you do good night my Dear Nov. 7 Fri evening, Now I will try to finnish my letter I have been at work buisey makeing a fireplace in our tent so as to keep warm, Mr. PA Hager got news last night that Wm. White died in New Orleans about 2 weeks last Sunday of Congestive fever he takes it hard, The Our Capt is not much better, he has sent for his wife, S. Knapp, Let & Ansel Baird is at the General Hospital Cin, the rest of our Otsego boys are all well, Oct 30th I received a letter from Father, Nov 5 I received your Letter of the 26th. Nov 5th I made a visit to Lexington Cemitary, To commence at the beginning, wright away after Gard mountin I got a pass

{Next page is missing}

Dear wife I received your kind & punctual letter today, dated Nov. 5 The date of this letter will be Nov 10th, This heading is some of my sunday evening's work, Seeing that I had nothing els to do, I think that I have from 2 to 3 letters on the road to you all the time, I have no news to tell you tonight but will try to write this sheet full of something, I wish you would give me the date of the letter you answer, then I can tell how many there is on the road, I must close for tonight, & will finnish tomorrow, Nov 11th Just 3 months ago today since I put my name to the enlistment roll, It seems as though it was 3 years, & I am sorry a thousand times for I am not doing any earthly good here & havent since I enlisted & dont think I shall, nor this Reg. we all want to come home, I was toled yesterday that we (the Brigade) is to be left here to gard the frontier of Indiana & the rest is a going to move on, we are under Rosencrans & our Brigadier Gen. is Baird. It certainly is a great comfort to me to read letters from home, as you say, all the comfort that I have, If you will answer all the letters I send you, you will have your hands full for it is great pleasure to me to write home, I want Uncles Henry address so that I can write to him, Cosine Ira has not answered my letter yet, perhape he did not get mine or I not his, In regard to my sore eye. It is most well, I cant see as well as before, but is getting along first rait, It is very week, I think that I poisened it some way, my left eye is well enough, you must not be alarmed about that, It layed me up from duty some 3 or 4 days, you must not think that such a little thing as that will let me come home for we have some of the worst, hard hearted, Doctors you ever saw he says that he had rather burry 150 men than to furlow 50 to go home. The boys are quite up about it, yesterday he was cortmartialed he has got to carry him self or hhe will get a P... O you know what. Doct Bennett is the likelyest of the three, but. I am not as well as common today. I cought cold a day or two ago, but I will get along. You know when I left you that I told you to go whenever you got a chance, I want you should go & mak your self as contented as you can, If I had the means to send to you you should have it to use at your pleasure but I have none & dont know when I shall have any. All the money is spent & sent home in the company, their is some oweing to me but cant get it, If you get a chance to go, improve the opportunity if you can go perhapse you had better go when slaying comes I think I shall have some money by that time. I am very sory that I lost a visit with Uncle Henrys family, I lotted a great deal on a visit with him I am sorry that I have not kept up correspondance with him, he may think that I have slited him. If I can get his address I will write to him. I dont know Aunt Almira's address, I will write to her too, But I dont know about Uncle Henry Kissing you so much, I should not allow it if I were at home, -- I should like to step in & here you & Mrs Knapp talk over your troubles. indeed I should, you would not get me in the army again, I have not hurd from Stephen in a long time I dont know whether he is dead or live, we left him at Covington & he was go back to Cin. to the hospital. Also Ansel Baird, we left Let Baird at Falmouth to go back to Cin. they are getting better, I hurd of Old Low before you letter came to hand, A good job done, how comes out the tater crop how many did you have, About how many acres of wheat have you sowed &c. I would like to have a shar of the sugar cain sirup, Just this minit (Nov 11 7 oclock PM) Mr. Hager brought in a letter for Stephen Knapp the same letter she wrote when she was at youre house, & Mr Kinney has got some 8 or 10 lettrs for him, Yes I remember Old Atkens, wal, wal, wal I suppose he feels better if he has got a girl to sleep with, hell want some body to tell him how to go to bed to her &c, &c. &c. I will pospone my writing untill the morrow. I must say one thing more scince I stoped writing a particion came in the tent to have our old hee Doctor removed from our Reg. His name is Clark. A brother-in-law to the Cor. he has been drumed out of 2 other Regements before this. we have 76 names in Co. B. their will be about 800 names in the Reg. Woe be unto Doct Clark & Cor. Gilbert if we ever get into action, you know what I mean. I dont know as I shall have time to write to morrow because we are a going to have a Division drill, there will be some 10 to 12 thousand, It will be a splended site, one Brigade is a beautiful site, with only 4,000 men. Dave was very glad to here that his folks got come, he has borrowed a great deal of on their account. Im glad to here of the majority on election, we are haveing the nicest kind of weather as you ever saw, Nov. Thurs. 12th after dinner Our grand Division drill is all nocked in the head. It is a misty wet day & has broke it up, The news in camp is that we shall move tomorrow to winter quarters 15 miles from here to Nichelosvill, I will enclose you a peace of music that we think is very good, but you may think it is not very good, I forgot to say to you that I got a peice of Henry Clays monument, I broke off a peice of the corrner stone for a keepsake, it is to large to send to you in a letter, & when I was at Lexington I went into a hemp factory & have lerned how to spin hemp. By all means send me Elsie picture & as many more as you are a mind to send them in as small a compass as possable. any thing that comes from home will be kept sacred. I want all of your picturs, the whole of you, not one excepted, but I suppose you are short of means. Dave wants I should put Geo & Laura in mind of his letter. Tell Laura to write to me, what I have writin to all.

Camp Nicholsville

Nov. 11th 1862

My Dear Lonely Wife. Yours of the 3rd came to hand the 8th. & was kindly received. also a line from Dear Mother I am glad to here from you. I thought it would be a good plan to write you a letter to day because we expect to move to morrow to Dandville, I dont want you to feel so bad because of my poor fare, I am living on the shelf scince I got my box. I dont ask for anything better, you have been very kind in doing what you have. I think the glove might to go on the other hand. I aught to do more for you than I do, but my hands are tied, the only thing is to hope for the best. shure enough I had one of my new shirts on when your letter came. & could not be bettered all the boys want them, I am well clothed you think that I am struting around as big as life, you are right. It hapened to be a warm day so took of my coat to show my red shirt, we have nice pleasent weather here, not a bit of snow in the contry. the dust flyes in the road The weather seems like spring 2 days ago I hurd a robbin sing, that brought the tears to my eyes what do you suppose I though of. In regard to them stories let them drop before they make a fuss. Sophie is not the only one, Miss Foster is another that has a hand in. I have done you earand to day. You must write him You must manage to get to Uncle Henrys this winter some way. I wish I could help you, I mailed him a letter yesterday morn, I dont get any letter

Elder Buck yet, I wrote him some time ago. I will receive all the advice kindly that is sent me dont be afraid to talk. say what you are a mind to, Dear Millie I received a few lines from your hand that pleases me again. I did not expect you could wright of course I know that you have been sick great deal & will make allowances. I can see just how you all look in your good old home when I lay down to rest I can all the cattle in the barn, hens in coop, but the sheep I cant tell where they are, the work bench, stands there in its old place, the waggons to, the wood pile about half gone &c. but it would pussle you to give a discription of my place, & I will not attempt to disscribe it to you for I have no time, I have not been very well for a few days back. I have the yellow janders, not very bad & now I have got over with that, I have had my old complaint some, but not bad, the worst of all is my eyes, they are better, I use them to much a writing..I must make my letter short this time on account of my eyes. Dear wife yours of the 4th came to hand the 9th. when I opened your letter I was surprised to find $5 enclosed in. I never had tears brought to my eyes so quick as when I saw that money. I did not intend to have you pay the fraight on the box & send money two, I am thankfull that I have friends at home, I may not use it. I would like to have Elsie likeness. & all the rest of you except yours. I have 2 of yours, one in a locket that was gave to me, I got a picture taken from the one I brought with me & put in the locket & tied that too my cloths so if I lose one I will have one left. Our Capt arrived here night before last, The boys dont get their box yet, they are all whining around like a dog with a soer head. I dont blame them when I see what was in my box, what a gift that was to me & dave. Now Millie keep up good courage. I write soon again, I still remain your husband & want to see you, I dreamed of seeing you last night A kiss for you. From Charley Direct your mail as before this to the butternut grove, to a lonely wife Fred Nelson is going home & I will send this letter by him you cant beleav all he says. he is a strong sesesh good night, Charly

Nov. 17. 1862

Dear Wife I have a few woords to say to you I received a bundle of papers the 15th & found lots of good reading, we read /out {crossed out} loud to the squad, & it is very interesting & pases away time. found a receipt in the bundle, them powders is as good as anything to stop the Dysentary, I would like to have you send me 2 boxes of my kind of pills, if you send a box to us, In regard to shirts, I shall weir them for an out side shirt, or I shant were but one shirt & want it made with collar some kind of boosun, Geo can tell you I think how to make it, & I want side pockets with triming, you have seen them, make them as you are a mind to. I dont think of any thing els that I want to send for, but if you can think of any thing that I want you can send it, it will come good, Pleas mark what you send to me. I dont know as it will be convieniant to box mine sepperate or not, some say that barrel bulk will come cheeper & better than a box. the boys all say that the butter better be all put togeather then divied it when it comes here, It would be nice to have a box to keep the things in when they get here. I have no news to send to you at preasent, I think I have done my share of writing scince I inlisted, this letter will make 12 letters that I have mailed to you beside a number of others, I dont get any answer from Uncle Ira Kenny. I think that I shall send your letters home for safe keeping. I am well. My love to you Dear wife, Make your self happy as you can, write as often as convieneant So good bye my Dear, From your Husband

Charly,

                                                    Camt Nicholsvill, Nov, 22/62

My Dear Lonely Wife,

I take the pleasure once more of answering your kind letter Dated Fri. Eve. Nov 14th which afforded me great pleasure to peruse, If I was deprived of writing or communicateing to my Friends I dont know what I should do, I am well as useal, While we were laying in camp near Paris I weighed myself, & weighed just 150 lb day before yesterday I weighed again on the same scales & same cloths just 162 1/2 lbs leaveing a ballance in my favor 12 1/2 lbs, you can tell whether I am gaining or loosing, My living is composed cheifly of hard Pilot Bread, salt beef, & fresh beef, bacon, some times soft bread, & fruit eternal slathers of it, onely we dont, Appels 2 sometimes 3 for 10 cents, that is cheep, Salt 1.00 per pound, & other things in the same propotion, The Union familys in this state of Tenn. will have to have help or starve to death. Ancel Baird came home to the regement last eve, from the Hospital. he started 2 weeks ago yesterday from the hospital he was miscarried & went to Nashvill Tenn. & he says the people are destitute of provision & evry thing els. The reble army has striped them of evry thing, he went in a house to get something to eat & they commenced to cry thinking that he (& the rest with him) was a going to take what they had left. As soon as they found out that they were Union soldiers they offered to do what they could, they would cook for them, but could not give them anything to eat, So it is through the Southern states as far as I can here, I dont think that I fare hard when I think of them, we have fared well in comparison to them, I will tell you how our bed we have red cedar bows, layed on the ground (of which I will send you a peace of) & the fether bed is a little sprinkling of wheet straw, for sheets, is an indian ruber blank(et), layed over the straw, then 2 blankets layed over us, then our over coats, this is our bed, Dave & I nests together, when we are all nested it looks like so many hogs, I sleep first rate, but when I thhink of the bed at home these cold nights I ! It seems to me you are haveing a great time a makeing up your sugarcane, I would like to step over to your house & help you some, It makes me think of home when folks come to your house a visiting. A great many thoughts runs through my noddle, I have had many a pleasent visit at party wedings, &c.--Mr Hager takes the loss of Wms death very hard. (What I have said about Mr. H. pleas keep it to youirself. All there is about it H. tryed to use to much athority, more than belongs to him) Our Capt is getting better he made us a visit this morning for the first time scince the first day that we arrived at Lexington Oct 28. He will resume his dutys about a week. He & his wife came to Nicholsvill yesterday from Lexington.--I cant here a word from S. Knapp, A. Baird dont know any thing about him. I think that he will be sent home if he dont get well, or if he lives, just pleas to come home & spend the sabath with me, hay! I reckon that would sout me very well. thats a right smart chance, no so good news as that just now, but be patiant & you will see me before many years goes by, I would like to help you sing next saboth if I could, In regard to them stories Sophy wrote to Dave that when Hubbard was in Dowagiac that he wrote back or somehow there, was some gounds made for H. & he did not get them, & that Addie Hop. was useing them &c. & that Hub. was the cause of Addies sickness, I have forgoten most all about it. Sophy can tell you all about it. Anyway the boys joke H. a great deal about the night gounds. you wish me to give you an account of my clothing. I have one Good over Coat, one dress coat but it is too small. I would send it home if I could get a chance A blouse coat, A vest 2 pare pants use one pare for drawers which is very comfortable 3 pares Socks, one pare I have not worn yet, one shirt I have not worn yet, the other 2 is very good. I am sorry that I brought fine shirts here. I have to wash them in hard cold water & you can guess how they look. I have 2 good towels & hankerchief. all that I care about your sending me is 2 wollen shirts & one pare socks, you see that I have one pare of good new socks you let me have. All I want is a change & not to much to carry around it makes me to much load. I have my mittens yet, Dave wants I should tell you if you see any of his folks to send him a pr of wollen shirts. you send me little serup if you are a mind to. but sont send to much weight, Chease & butter will be the greatest treat to me, Chease is worth 25 cents lb butter the same I wish that I could send you some of these large hickry nuts they are very planty this is all the luxery that we have you did say whether you got any that I sent you or not I sent you 3 or 4 the largest hickry nuts that I ever saw they make us very good living if I new that they would go through safe & did not cost to much I would send you a bushel of them but I am affraid that it will not pay. 3 or 4 days ago I saw 2 prisoners blindfolded & brought into camp. I dont know what was done with them. we have had quite a row with our old Doct. we have got up a paper for names & circulated it through the regement to have him put out. we got 840 names one of our Capt. had his soard taken away from him & he was arrested & put under a gard also an Orderly was arrested. They kept the Capt. a while then offered him his Swoard he refused it, & demanded a trial. I dont know how it will end. I cant tell you the text of last sunday because I did not go to church. Our meeting was held in the meeting house in the village Our Chaplin is a smart man but dont care anything about religion he has not visited one of our tents as I can find out, he is working for money & not for the good of his soldiers. He has the charge of the Post office. I think that we shall stay here this winter or some where near here there is a heavy force a head of us & all around us the land is purfeckly allive with soldiers. It is the choice of me & all the rest to be on the march. rather than lie still here & do nothing. It is drery buisness & lazy buisness to be a soldier. Our band is a thriving first rate. we have the best band in the Brigade. How my eyes will come out I cant tell. I am bothered a great deal to see. ifis in the eyes now. I think that we shall lose Capt. Bassett He will be our Major for the Reg. such is the report. for my part I dont care much. I think that I will manglle this sheet any more & will come to a close I Still remain your affechonate Husband Charly My Love to all

Camp at Nichlosvill Nov 28/62

My Dear Lonely Wife.

Have received a letter from you last night bareing dat of the 21st from you & will hast to reply, you need not expect a long letter from me this time because it is very cold indeed, I set raped up in blanket & overcoat a writing & my fingers so cold & numb that I cant feel my pen but will try to answer your questions, I find by your letter that it takes 9 days for my letter to reach you. & the letters you send me come in 3 days. In regard to the box & things, you need not send any boots. but you may send what you are a mind to, If you can go to Bye Ballooe's & get some flanell for me some shirts they would do me more good than any thing els we are haveing extreem cold weather, & have no stoves yet, we expect some evry day. I saw a box that came to this Reg. from Cold Water yesterday, the size is about 2 ft long 1 ft wide & 10 inches deep. came here by Express & cost only 75 cents. As for money, my Dear, I am out entirely & dont expect to get payed off in 2 months, their is no money in the Reg. the most of the officers have sent home for money for their own use, & growl a great deal because they are not payed off. It will better to have the freight on this end of the rought, at Nichlosville. I wish you may lone some 8 or 10 dollars of some friend & I will pay it when I am payed off & send about 4 dollars & use the rest your self, if you send me any be sure & send Sothern mony in one dollars bills, our northern money is of no account hhere, the green backs are good as gold. if you new all you would not blame a soldier for spending his earnings when he has nothing but salt meat & bread to live on, some beans cooked on our stile &c. I will tell you how things cost, postage stamps 5 cents each, apples 5c. stick of candy 2c. A three cent paper of tobaco 10c. letter paper 35c. a quire, small ginger snaps such as you make (only not so good) 15c per Doz. butter 30c, lb cheese 25c. tryed beef large as you 2 fingers 10c, & so on, & so it goes. when our officers get chickens, turkeys, fresh pork & meets of evry kind, & the privet is punnished if he take anything of the kind. This garding rebels property is not what is cracked up to be in our minds, their is more swering about that than any thing els. I have told you in another letter how to conduct the box. that is Dave & I togeather, but dont say any thing I have no objection of Mrs. Wakefield puting in with us. Send the box the same as a letter, only send it to Nichlosvill Ky. if you can get any money for me send it to me by male, & forward the box as soon as posable I am not very well at preasent but not bad off, my fingers are cold & will close I still remain you afficanate Husband Charley

To Butternut grove Roenna C. Prentiss

Camp near Nicholasville
Dec 3rd 1862

Friend Rowena,

As Charley can not write on acct of his eyes he wanted I Should write a little for him. his eyes are not very painful but it makes them werse to look Steadily & they blur badly. He is not well nor has not been fro Some days. he is not So bad he is able to go out around, he has got a touch of jaunders & he wants you to See the docter Hopkins & ask him the best mode of doctering them. He thinks that the docters here do not know much & I guess he hits it at least I reckon So. We have got us a Stove in our tent now which makes us quite comfortable, especially those that are not well. Charley do not eat very much. We got Some fresh pork last night & I fried him a piece & he thought it was good. to day we have had Some liver & that was very good indeed he Said. I also made him Some tea & one of the boys & your humble Servant went last night in the night & got a little extract of Cow which I put a little of the same in his tea which was quite a rarity. to night he feels some better. Mr. Hager got a letter yesterday Stating that there was a box on the road for us. we Shall be looking for it now Soon. Still we expect to hear from you before we get the box. There is not much news tonite. We were in brigade inspection last Saturday Maj Gen Wright & Gen Granger were present. with their Staff. I could not See that they were more than human I got a letter from Sophie day before yesterday. Shall answer it Soon. also got one from julius he was well. & one from Marcia this week. Charley says he would like to have the docter Send Something for his eyes he says it is the regular infllamation but not very bad. he has been washing his eyes in Sugarlead that is all he has done for them he says pperhaps he can send it by mail. in a vial or Some way I Suppose the taxes are rather high this fall. What are yours Charley wanted I Should ask. Tell Father & mother Clark I Should like to hear from them I like to hear from the old people as well as the young & one from my father & mother is received with more pleasure it may be than from any other perhaps you think it is no So but it is truly So. Lester B came to the regiment night before last. he is quite well It rained very hard Sunday night nearly all the night but we were cozy in our tent but I must Stop good night please write Soon I expect to hear from Geo. & Laura next Spring excuse all mistakes to this line from

David

My love to all the friends I hear that Chandler Eaton is 2nd Lieut in a cavalry company I do not know whether it is so or not.

Onward to Victory!

Camp Nichlosvill Dec 6th

Dear Lonely wife. In reply to your letter in a red shirt pocket without date, I will let you know that the box arrived here yesterday It would be amuseing to you see the ansious eyes that watched the contence as we overhalled it. only 20 in the tent 16 ft in circumferance. It arrived here safe except one thing, that is the honey box sprung a leak & run through the box some. my shirts was not dobed very much. the box was mark rong side up. I never had anything come & looked so good as the contence of that box. I would like to know how much the charges were, you need be scaired I shant eat it up to fast. I shall string it out as long as we can. Those shirts are tiptop no fault to find. Dave likes mine the best. when we get our pay you will have some money to pay for this job The fruit cake we will not cut yet a while that has got to last also the butter, when we cut it I will tell you how good it is. That pillow is the nicest thing yet, that has got to go with me where ever I go. I layed awake most all night last night athinking of what you know, you cant imagine how a fether pillow feels under my head, The butter we shall leave in the can. I can keep it frose farther than that we have nothing els to keep it in. I will risk it, the cakes was passed around this morning in the squad. (our squad consists of 16 men) & the tast of them allmost brought the tears to their eyes, put them in mind of home, when the boys get their box they will devide I am sorry that I did not send for a pare of boot taps. I dont care how large a cheese we get, we can take care of it, Chese is a great treat to have to eat with our army bread, that dont get cut wright off. I am satesfied with the tobaco I did not think it was so high. It will be the last that I shall buy. this will last me untill I get home If it would send me the tribune evry week after you get done with it if you can pay the postage. I dont know but I am asking to much of you, but you must excuse me for begging so much. Dave & I received a letter from Geo. yesterday & it was quite interesting, I shold like to have had a hand in the deer scrape, also those toothpicks, we think a heap of them I would like to have Geo take good care of my rifle & use it all he wants to, the can of serup I have not opened yet, I shall try & send you one or two cuts of good Cane seed in the spring or bring it to you, Tell Father & Geo not to pay one sent towards the $1,400 bounty for the 14 men that are to be raised. I have hurd all about that. That is outrajus. let them draft if they want to You must excuse my bad writing my eyes are quite troublesome. I must close & not use my eyes to much at one time. I will write short letters & offen, my love to all the family, & to you

From Charley to the butternut grove Wife Roenna

Tuesday morning Nov 7th {sic} One word more I want to say that is I want you to apply to Mr Chichester & see if you can get some money, if you are in need of money or means to live he is obliged to help you, tell him that I cant get my pay of the Goverment before spring & you are in want of means to live tell him the money I sent you is payed out on your land to save it now do as I tell you there is others that do it & it will not be any worst for you I have a little as for the rest, but after all, if I had the money you should have it. I feel bad to have you without money. if you can get any of any body els get it & I will pay it some time, I want you to go to Uncle Henrys very much Dave & I has just enjoyed a good meal out of our box. Dear wife I wish that I could be with you & stay over sunday so that I may know what sunday is. evry day is just alike except one thing, we have a surmon insted of Batalion drill. just now some 28 or 30 loads of wood came into camp & evry thing is Hurrah boys, fifes & drums Brass Bands &c. a part of our squad has gone to church & I stay in my tent on account of my eyes. I am not doing them any good while I'm writing, they pane me some. but I must write to a lonely companion that is so far away. Be cheerful Dear wife & all will come around right, all of our Regiment is cheerfull & feel well with a few exceptions, we have had 11 death in the Reg. scince we organised Mr Baker is the laughing stock of our Company he is so homesick, playing up sick & evry thing els to go home. he got discharged from the hospital & put in the ranks now that goes against the grain with him, Roenna I think you would be ashamed of me if you should see me. I have not shaved nnor trimed my face scince we saw each other in Kal. we are haveing very cold nights & pleasent days. the ice frose hard enough last night to bare up a mule Lieut Hubbard, Cap Anderson, Ancel Baird & myself has just been singing a peice on the 144 page 2nd piecce of the new Lute. It put me in mind of home. I dont know but think that I am homesick by my writeing. I am not but who can help thinking of home once in a while. show me the man that wont, show him to me. I have not had my pant off to sleep since I left home, it is not a healthy way to live, I am quite well now except a coald, I am troubled some with my old complaint, while I am finnishing this letter I here the fuernerl durge playing at the funeral in the 33 Indiana. I must Close my. Dear wife so good bye I will write soon again Charley Ike Kinney just tumbled down with an arm full of dishes. (later) Pleas send me an Alminac for 63

Camp Nicholsville, Dec 15/62

Dear Wife

It is with pleasure that I write you again a few lines, I did not know but you had hurd that we have moved from this place, The Reg. has gone to Danville & I dont know but farther but Co. B. still remaines at Nicholsville. we are left here to guard the rail road & commissary stoers that supplyes our army south of us. we have a large force within 30 miles of us & one mile west of our camp the Mich 2nd Cavelry is camped, they are armed right up to the noch, they can fire 15 times without stoping load, & their armes cost $65. we are haveing a good time sance the rest of the Brigade went away. we have all the pies & cakes, Turkeys & chickens & milk we want, & we mix in a little honey & cheese & butter that you sent us, I had breakfast this morning some first rate coffee bread & milk, fresh beef, bread & butter & honey, & some fride cakes & some beef tong. So you see that we live well well. that is not all, we have 2 turkeys & one chicken to cook for dinner, just come over & dine with us if you pleas, I dont know as you will like our style of cooking, that I cant help, I would like to you come & see me, you need not be affraid of any danger here all though we have rebels all around us, yesterday morning after breakfast I went over to the Depot where Dave was on guard & stayed untill meeting time. then we went to meeting, it seemed like home. the church bell sounds just like the Otsego bell, we got there just before sunday school was out, after the school was out I made myself acquainted & got a singing book & sung a spell, then we had to sing in church, the way they do here is to stand up to pray & set down to sing the rest is the same as at home. We had a good sermon, the text Heb. 12, 2nd. there is no baptest meetings here the one we went to yesterday was the presbeterian church. then in the afternoon Dave, Ancil Baird, Henry Blakesly & I went out in the cuntry 1 1/2 mile to Mr. Ballard's a good union folks & had a good time there was 2 girls, 2 ladys, & 2 older laydes & 3 men they have a good piano & play good. they gave us apples, & treated us first best. they invited us to come to night & would not take no for an answer, so we agreed to come, they are very much surprised to see such people as we are from the north, they expeced that we were saveges Tues morning Dec 16th Now I will continue my letter. We did not go on our visit as we expictege to last evening. It rained very hard yesterday afternoon & eve. so we were obliged to stay in our tent & play checkers & other tricks, we got up this morning & found very little snow the ground hardly covered, Now I tell you of Daves fun that we had this morning. Dave & I & 4 others of our squad took a notion that we would have some milk for breakfast At day light we started for a real genuine secesh farmer 1 1/2 mile from camp & just as we arrived than we saw a wench with a bucket of milk on her head, we met her, halt, was the command, ground arms was the command, the bucket of milk was set before us, the next we was to fill our canteens, some 15 or 20 appeared to us from the house but dare not day a word, we were buisey filling our canteens we saw the old he one coming from the lot on horse back with a gun in his hand. he road up to the gate dismounted came storming in with his gun, thinking to scare us. I drew my revolver & cocked it, & stood before him, He soon cooled down we got milk & piked to the camp & had a good breakfast be side a good bunch of fun why he had his gun in the lot, he was in his sheep lot where the dogs had killed a lot of his sheep. The secesh are affraid of the Mich. soilders. we make them do just as we want them to. they dare do no other way, if they refuse down come their goes shanty. dont you worry about me I am perfect safe when I have my trusty companion with me. I dont go out without him with me, it cost me $14 dollars & it may save my life I have a plenty of chances to sell it. Dave & I came a crost a hand car near the rail road the other day on the track the car was lifted & away we went in spite of men, their is complaints entered against us to our officers but the officers dont know us just then. no rectelections of seeing any such men that thats all the satesfaction they get. It is now now 10 oclock & I will tell you what our squad is doing. Ike Kinny riting a letter to his father 5 boys cracking hickry nuts some 4 or 6 gone out in the cuntry a fectctting coffee, soap, candles, rice, sugar &c thas been confiscated during the night. somehow evry thing that comes in reach of a soldier it freeses to him; & very often he has the cramps in his hands especially when they get theyr had over a turkey head. some are down to the depot at work unloading cars. when they come in they will come in with a bag of sugar or some els, or a gallon of molases in canteens, this is the way we gard secesh property. let a dog come out at us & the next thing he knows he knows nothing I never saw so many dogs in one place as there is here 8 to 10 to each farm. savage hounds. I wish you could manage to send me 1/4 lb of fine powder.. the powder that we use in the army is very coarse, to coarse for a revolver it is not to be had here. the boys dont get their box yet. I think it was sent us common frait. they feel very much worred about it I tell you what it is Dave & I are living on the big side. I traided of one of my shirts (my old fine shirts) & got 9 pies last saturday I have 2 more to sell at the same rate. will you bye these common roudy hats sell here for $10 a hat. & other things in propotion. I am comfortable clothed & have pleanty to eat so you need not trouble yourselves about us. we have a stove in our tent so we sleep warm & we are all hunk on the goose question. 2 oclock P.M. I have been up town & found some Powder & the train has just come in & 2 boxes has come for Mr Hager & one for Baird. we had yesterday or the citiscans of this place a auction sale of negros. & they had one a week or two ago & it was stoped, I did not attend it so I cannot give you a discription of it. we have got attached to our Regiment a battery of howitser which is a savage machine to fight with, it is composed of 6 small guns weight 222 lbs. mounted on small low carrages drawn by one horse. the gun & carrage can be taken to peaces & all packed on horses & carried over rocks. & mountains & through woods & other impassable places for waggons, this battery is designed for clost fighting. they are use for shel & shot the distance from 40 to 100 rods. Refugees are constantly passing through here from Tenn. they that their familys must starve & they are compeled to leav them or be pressed in the rebel survis. My Dear friends at home, you dont know any thing about hard times, their homes are desolate & nothing to eat. the same with the rebel familys & well as the union. this seems hard. This is Tenn. that I speak of there is plenty here. I must draw my letter to a close you see my sheet is most full I shall not compell you to answer evry letter that I write. I have more time to write than you do. I am not doing anything now days, the Reg. is gone & I dont have to drum any now, my eyes are not much better I cend a letter to you by Fred Nelson last week I suppose you have got it I have not broke the bill yet that u sent me. I wish you had kept it I am well at preasent I have been a little under the weather for a week or two but am all right now except my eyes I cant write but a little while at a time Pleas tell me all about evry thing about home how are the cattle have you all of them yet, & the horses &c. The boys are unloading their boxes now & I must close From your Dear Husband Charley

Camp Nicholsville Dec 18ᵗʰ 1862.

Dear Wife,

Seeing that I have nothing to do today I will write to you a few lines. I mailed a letter to you 2 or 3 days ago & will try to write another. I have nothing of any particular intrest but I must buisey myself about something. The health of the Reg. is very good at preasent, we have burried but 2 in our company scince we organised, one is John Howard of Allegan, & the other Norman Wilson. he lived one mile south of Franklins, he done wrong to enlist in the army where he could not get any liquor, Taking away his bitters is the cause of his death, The janders is the main trouble in our company it dont make us very sick, but makes feel mean I have got over my janders so I am well again except my eyes, they trouble me much, we have lost our best snair drummer, he died the 13 of this month I am very sorry to lose him. his name is Charley Bort of Coldwater, I think that I am have very easy time of it now, the band has gone on with Reg except what belongs to Co. B. we, the members of the band is exempt from duty, I told you of an invite that we had to one of our good neighbors, we did not go untill Tuesday eve because it rained & stormed so, I shall have to give you a little history of their stile & fashion &c. as for visiting it is the same as at home they are good singers & players on the piano & guitar at 10 oclock they got us a good Oyster supper we all set around the table, they passed around the oisters soup. we all eat & I supposed we had got done eating supper & shoved back partly, then they pass around beefstake, buisquet, butter, sausage, cabbage & coffee we all eat untill we got done again, & (we had a glass of water with oisters) I shoved back again, then they passed around the persurves & catsups of differant kinds, this time we was releived from the table, we went back in the parlor. they showed us all the pictures they had, then of course I had to show mine, in the parlor is a piano guitar, nice spring bottoms chares & 2 sophies spring bottom of the nicest kind & evry thing in the most splended stile, when got up to go home they wanted to know where we was a going to spend Christmas, & give an invite to come & spend christmas with them, that is the kind of union people to find.

Dec. Sun. 21st

Now I will try it again. I write as long as my eyes will let me then I have to stop. Last Fri. I went over to the Mich 2nd Cavelry & on my way home I found laying in the road a good gold pen worth a dollar, so I have 2 good gold pens & silver holders, the holder is worth 50c. Yesterday I went to Lexington with 5 others, & took 9 priseners of war & delivered them to the provose marsial of Lexington, they went along without any trouble, they are hard looking pets, we went a foot to Lexington which is 12 miles & came home on the cars we got home at 9 oc. we had a good time to. This is just such fun that I like, all soldiers boys are like brothers we are well acquainted at first sight. The Mich 18th & 22nd are at Lexington to stay this winter. Mr. Hager, Mr. Kinney, Dewell, & the Baird boys & 2 or 3 others had 3 larg boxes come last week & it cost them 25 dollars & some cents & it makes them feel rather soer, they thought it would not cost more than 4 or 5 dollars untill they got a letter from B. Balloo, he sayed it cost $5.50 per hundred now I can tell what Daves & my box cost. I guess about $5.25 we are haveing very nice weather here the farmers are doing their plowing now. we have a little rain & a snow squall once in a while but nothing that looks like winter to me if you should happen in our tent just now, you would think we had a writing school, their is 6 of us writing to our homes & 4 takeing a knap. I dont get my mail as regular as I useto because the mail all goes to the regiment & they are 22 miles from us. Our Co. is in very good health & spirits. I think there is but 4 sick in our Co. We had quite a joke played on us last week all the Otsego Boys got a box of stuff made up to send to otsego then Mr Hager got a letter from Balloo & scairt us out of that, we had some shoes, drawers, coats & other trinkets to good to through away, & If we sent them by freight, you would never get it.

Sunday eve

I have just come from evening meeting, Dave & Ancel are writing & I thought I would, The text tonight was Acts 5, 29 to 32 we had a good sermon. Delivered by the presiding Elder to day was quarterly meeting. & our covinent meeting yesterday, I did not know it this afternoon & I should of gone this afternoon to communion. They have the worst singing that I ever hurd When we go in & sing it makes them stair. I wish you all could come down here & show them how to sing. when they sing they make a noise all over the house. I believe I must tell you what the boys got in their box, Each one had a pair of boots, & gloves, socks, honey, chese, but very little dryed fruit, not as much as you sent us, maple sugar, about 2 bushels of cakes & cookes, lots of bread & boiled poark, we have all the pork than we want & more too we get soft bread, the did not like that much & a lot of butter, we have use up about 1/4 of the butter you sent us & most all the honey, the fruit cake is not cut yet & the can of cane molasses is not opened. we have eat 1/2 of the chese as I have said before we live heigh. yesterday morning when I got up I found a patent pail of milk. we had corn meal on hand, & we have some mush & milk of coars, we shall live well as long as we stay here seperate from the Reg. I think we shall stay here this winter, it is left with the capt to say I do wish that Geo. could stay with us this winter, it would be fun for him, we have sport here evry day or two a huntting the line backs that clime our legs & back they are so large that we ketch them & tame them & yoke them up & do od teem work. they are not very pleanty yet, as soon as we found out they were in camp we commenced scershing for them, the boys that has been in hospital brought them here, & when we camp on the same ground that the rebels have camped on, we get them their, (Mon morning) I will close my letter & I want to mail it this morning, keep up good spirits & carry a stiff upper lip, so good bye my Dear wife, my love to you all. from your Husband Charley

Nicholsville Dec. 26th 1862

My Dear Lonely Wife

I embrase the preasent opportunity to drop you a few lines to let you know how I am gitting along in the army. I have no news to tell you at preasent. We still remain at Nich. & I presume we shall week or 2 longer & perhapse all winter. Our Regiment left Danvill this morning for Momfordvill. The Reg. going off makes it bad for us to get our mail, the mail goes to the regiment then we have to send to reg. when it is not to far off. John Duel went to the Reg yesterday & back to day & brought back a pile of mail but none for me, I have not received any mail from you scince Dec 9 except a tribune, that I got last Monday. Their is a considerble excitement all around us & dont know what is going on. Our troops are all on the move we mistrust that their is something a brewing. I hope their is, because I have got tired of laying still so long in one place. I dont find any thing to write about. O, I forgot. I wish you a merry christmas. I had a good christmas breakfast we had in our squad 7 chickens well cooked with dumplin. We came in about 4 in the morning then Mr Hager & Mabbs got up & went to work a dressing cooking, so you see that we had a tip top good breakfast, for dinner & supper we had a oysters, rice puding &c. so you see that we live well on the secesh. mind you it dont cost us any thing. I cut our fruit cake yesterday, that cake cant be beat, it has kept first rate. Our chese & butter is about half gone, we have not opened the can of syrup yet wate untill the honey is gone. The boys are all so fat that you would not know them. we are very healthy, my health is good, my eyes are the greatest trouble to me, they dont pain me much only when I use them to much I dont know what to think about mail, I dont know whether you dont write, or it is miscarried, time seems like a great while scince I hurd from you. I dont know but you are sick. it seems to me that you are, but I hope that I am mistaken, we have (our company) got our little 2 dollars to day for enlisting, payed to us by the Capt. scince I have commenced this letter we have hurd that our Reg. has only gone to Lebanon 50 miles from us on a forced march. Sat morning Dec 27 You can see by reading my letter how uncertin our stoping are, we do not know to day where we shall go tomorrow or where we shall be at night, I scarcely know what to write to you that would be interesting to you. I will say that I stood gard last night for the first time at the commisary at the Depot. Dec 29. Yesterday morning, our company struck tents & at 11 oclock we commenced our march to the Ky. river bridg

8 miles from Nicholsville we arrived to this bridg at 4, oc. we cleaned out the bridg, got seder bows for our beds, eat our supper. then after this Dewel, Dave, & I took a walk up on what is called Boons Knob, the sise of this knob is about 60 rods long, & 30 rods wide & to the top from the river is 300. ft heigh. The side next to the river is all most perpendicular rocks, this is the place where Boon pushed the indian, it is a frightful looking place, the shrubery on this knob is red ceeder, these trees groes on the bare rocks seemingly, we went back to the bridg. spent the evening then went to bed. I will give you a little discription of the place where your writer is sitting & writing this letter. about 3 oclock this afternoon I went up on a ledg of rocks which 350 ft above the river, & seeted myself on a shelving rock hanging one foot over the rock & my right foot in a tall tree top, the rocks are most streight up & down, when I came up here I commenced sketching the boons knob & this letter which was partly writen slid out of my portfolio & went down below me 25 ft & lodg then I clambered down & got it, a frightfull place to go. Now the bridg. This bridg 270 ft. long. 40 ft wide & 100 ft from the water suspended on 2 butments, it cost $80,000. 2 tracks runing through the bridg, we occupy the west side the tool on this for 2 yoke of oxen & wagon is .75c the water in river is very mudy & runes very slow & is not navigable here. This morning we arose in good season, eat our breakfast then a nomber of us started off on a tramp for Boons cave & another cave called big mouth cave, which is 1 mile from the bridg. following the pike 1/2 mile we turned to our right, then we had climing to do. the rocks from top to bottom is 400 ft. we commenced traviling on the shelving rocks 1/2 mile, came to the big mouth cave, this has an enterance of about 10 ft. squir & can pass in a larg room & other creveses larg enough for a man to crawl in 8 or 10 rods from the mouth, the room is 12 or 14 ft. high nicely orniment with presems made with water constantly droping & forming a transparent iceal, after visiting this cave we then climed down the rocks to the extreem end is one mile, but we only went in 68 rods. from the mouth we crawled on our hands & nees some 3 rods & found a large room, then to get out of this room crawled up the rocks some 18 to 20 ft to another small room where their is a small basin made of this sement filled with water, it will hold 3 pt. of water, & a crevice over this room 40 ft high where we saw names smoked on with candles, these are frightful places to clime, we left these rooms, took another direction took a small passage in which we had to crall on our hand & feet 25 rods I should think then came to a room & in this room is an orniment that I would $25. if it were at home,

it is the shape of a stand, with a cloth throne over it & a lam on the top, this is made by droping water, It is allmost dark & I must stop. so good night, Dec 30th Tues 3 oclock. Now I will go on with my story dont know as it will be interesting. in this room on the backside we climed up on a ledg of rocks 10 ft. high found another small passage just large enough for a man to squeese through, went about 10 rods & came to another room nicely ornimently with prism. we backed out of this room & took another passage that led to more rooms, we could have went a mile from the mouth & see the same that we have seen, but we got tired & our candles were gitting short so we concluded to retire from Boons cave. We crawled & climed down to the foot of the pressa--water, cross the creek, made our way to camp, eat our dinner went up on the rocks that I mention in the fore part of this letter to sketch & write Now in answer to your letter sent by fred Your letter of the 21 was gladly received, I have sent you a number of letters scince I got letter from you by mail. I am quite well at preasent. & tuff as ever. I toled you that I weigh 162 lbs. I weighed myself the day before we left Nicholsville. I weighed 172 lbs. Now what do you think a bout my being sick & poor we are haveing very easy times, my eyes are not well yet but are getting better. I got all the things you sent me by Fred Nelson. I am glad you sent me those taps, I have a plenty of stamps. I am sorry to here that Geo. is sick. if he would join the army he would fat up. Only think of 172 lbs for me. I want you should go home with Mr Wilson. I pay all damiges after a while, we may get out pay within one month, but dont know I wish you would send me some of your pictures, No Hubbard does not show Addies letters. Dave & H. jokes each other & have fun between themselfs, Laura Foster, there is nothing said that was out of the way, I am very sorry that I said a word. Pleas not say a word. I should like to have a little fun with you, at the sining school Yes I pitty your stiff neck, we shall have to detail a gard over Friend Higgins, it seems to me that he is doing a stiff buisness is he not, I am very thankful for Mother's letter. I would say more in regard to mother letter but my sheet is most full & I am in a hurry, /& my sheet is most full {crossed out} & I want to a good deal About one hour ago I received a letter from you bareing date Dec 10 the answer to Daves letter. In regard to the jaundice I have got over them & entirely well. Dont borrow any trouble about me I am doing well, yet I dont blame you for feeling bad. I am all right except my eyes I am glad of the receipt for my eye wash. The box & money from you. I did not expect you to send me money if you pay the freight on the box. I have had $5.00 worth out of that box & more than that. I cut the fruit cake christmas & it was first rate, none better, In regard to Mr Kinneys, you can do as you like, you know better than I you have seen him, I am perfectly willing that you do as you pleas Yes I am. There has a battery & 5 company of infantry come here to night, we expect an actact here by Morgan, we dont fere him, we are strongly fortiffied we can hold back 5,000 Cavelry & inft. with the force that we have we are ancious for a fight, This bridg is a important place. if this bridg is distroyed, our supplys would be cut off, I think that we shall move in the morning to another bridg on Dicks river. I am so nere blinded I cant hardly see to write, candle light hurts my eyes. Excuse all mistakes & bad writing. My love to you all good night From your Dear Husband Charley to Millie

CHAPTER 2

JANUARY – JUNE 1863

Camp at Danville Jan 4th 1863

My Dear Lonely wife

Yours of 28th came to had yesterday also a bundle of papers. & was very glad to here from you I must make my letter short because I am in a hurry. We marched from Ky. river bridg to Dick river bridg, 8 mi. from Ky. bridg, & stayed there untill yesterday noon. then we marched to Danville & joined our Reg. they was glad to see us, we have about 12,000 troops here, we did expect a battle here but Morgin is so cut up that there is no prospects of it now. The news came to camp a little while ago that Gen. Bragg was killed. I dont know the particulars, In regard to my visiting the laydis is done with there for we have moved from there. I hope you will not be jelous ofe me, I am not very intimate with them, My thoughts still remain at home, every time I comb my hair & put on my neck tie & all those little choers that I am use to have done for me. The boys are makeing up a barrel of things. so I thought I would send home some things that I dont want to carry. A pare of pants to small for me now, my bible & your letters, 2 pencils, 2 pr. socks most worn out, what I send to you, I would like to have you keep untill I come home. The barrel of goods will be sent to By. Ballou. Your letter is very interesting to me to read. We have got back to the Reg. & I will get my mail more regular than when we are sepperated, we are haveing very warm weather. Our Reg. is drawing their pay to day. & I will soon send you some money. I have put in a small stone in my pants pocket that came out of Boons Cave, keep it. & my mittens. I have got a pare of Gloves, that Gold pen is the one I found, I have put in some hickry nuts, & a gun lock that was taken off of a rebel gun. Jan. 5th/63 when I commenced this letter I thought that I should not have time to write much because we was very buisey yesterday & to day I was detailed on picket & now I have all day to write & read. Perhaps you think it strainge that I am on picket. I will tell you. When the regiment left us at Nicholsvill I was not able to march. (at least I pretended so) & I did not want to leave the Company. & if I stayed with the Co. I would have easy times & be taken care of if I was sick while with the company I went on picket twice & I like it. this is such work as I like because it agrees with my health. I have not felt so well in the last 3 years as I havve scince I joined the army. you would not know me now if you should see me, while I am so fleshy & my long beard, & all the rest are just so Vern Rose is so fat he cant hardly see. now we have come to the regiment & found my drum smashed up & I was chosen to go on picket & I went. I like it better than druming, & dont care whether I take the drum or not. When we are payed off the regiment will get me a new drum so I shant lose any thing on that, a part of the regiment was payed yesterday & will finnish to day. we only get our pay for the months of Sept. & August, they keep two months pay back The Otsego boy will put their money togeather & send it by express I think I shall send you all that I can spair. I have to pay Rose $14 for the revolver I bought of him, I dont know as I shall have any use for it, but I dont like to be without it. It is not at all likely that we shall go into battle. Our brigade is the rearguard of this army. all of our army trains rail roads, storehouses, & evry thing els has to be garded for thousands of miles & we have to help to do that, we have a good place here to stay. Danville is a handson place, some like Kal. & about as large, One oclock P.M. I have just eat my dinner, & I now I will proseed with my letter. What do you suppose I had for dinner! I will tell you. some tea, bread & butter & cheese Who would have thought it when you was makeing that cheese that a peace of it be eaten way down in Ky, under a elm tree in the woods, also some of the butter, what do you suppose it makes me think of. I think of the cows the cow yard. milking stools, the pails that I use to carry in full of milk, the cheese press & the those that market it, then to think again I am way down in Ky. watching rebels in the woods & other places, & sitting under trees writing letters to a fond wife 5 or 6 hundred miles from me, it is sad to think of, You may think that I am homesick by what I write, I am not, but I want to go home, & see my friends that is so far from from me. No it would not do for a soldier to give vent to his feelings. he would be laughed at. would call him a brave man, think him a baby like Baker. I would not have the Co. run on me as they do him for all I would get in 5 years, they dont ketch me whineing & playing up sick like Baker. (Baker of Allegan) he is a poor stick, the hole Co. hate him & all around the hospital I have nothing against but I dont like to see a man act like a fool, Now Dear Wife, beleave me, & put your mind at rest, I dont fair any worst

than you do. that is to say I feel just as well, just as safe, & dont suffer any
more here than I did, than when I was at home, to be sure it seemed tuff at
first, but I have got use to it, we dont have very cold weather here & I am
well clothed. Take good care of yourself & we shall meet each other again
before long, my hopes is as strong as ever that I shall see you the next 4th of
July. I am well & harty as a brick my eyes are getting better, but I cant use
them by candle light. Isaac Kinney his barrel of things in a day or two by
express to By Ballou, there is a budget for you. there will be no charges on
them I will pay it. My bible I am sorry to send home, but I cant carry it evry
thing a soldier has, has to be carred on his back, the socks will do to foot
over & perhaps you can send them back to me by & by. tell Geo. & father
that I cant find any cane seed here. I saw great deal of it in the northern part
of this state when we were on the march. you will see some tall darning on
them socks I send you. take pattern & learn how to darn. I am very glad
of my boots taps. I have them on, cost of me only 15c to get them put on &
now I am riged for boots. Dont forget to send me them pictures. The one
that have with me is a great comfort to me. That stays in my brest pocket
close to my heart both night & day My love to all be sure & git your shair,
I must close. I will write again. Direct your letters as before & I will get
them. Now Millie be of good spirits, dont worry about me. I am all right
the rebels dursent keep around here. This from Ky. soldier Charlie This to
a soldier wife Millie good bye Tell Father & Mother I dont forget them also
Geo & Laura, Mary & Elsie & all the rest a good shair of my letters are
for all of you. You can pick out what you want & let thee rest have what is
left C C C C C Milly I am to I have put in the package of money $12.00. It
will go to By. Balloo. I will start in the morning.

Danville Jan. 5. 1863

Friend H. Kinney

I received a short note from you in my wifes letter & was glad to here
from you, allthough we are straingers but hope that I might chance to
enjoy an acquaintace with you. I have hurd Father Clark speak of you
great many times, & have been ancious to see you, I am thankfull for
your kind advice & wishes. It seems very hard to be so far from home &
among strangers to be exposed to the dangers of the enimy who is seeking
for our lives. I have not seen very hard times yet & perhaps I will not.

to be sure Camp life is far differant than home life, but that is nothing when we get use to it. I think that I am ggetting tuff & enjoy better health than at home. I would be happy to here from you again When you write Pleas send me your address & I will endever to answer it. Truly Yours Charles H. Prentiss

Union for ever is my motto Charley

Camp at Danville, Jan. 9th/63

My Dear Wife

Seeing that I have a few leasure moments this evening I thought I would drop you a few lines to let you know where I am & what we are doing. I am useal well at preasent & enjoy my self very well considering where I am. but would enjoy myself better if I only could go home & see my Dear lost companion. that is so far from me. we still remain at Danville, garding this town & the country around us a looking out for the enemy. but see no signs of him. I received a letter from you the 7th of Jan. Dated Dec. 14th & enclosed in it the Miss Brown song, it must be that it was miscarried. I have news to tell you, only an accident that happened her in the Reg. yesterday, one of our negroes was killed by the bursting of a shell that they undertook to open to see what was inside of it. This shell was sot at the mark the day before & did not explode & one of our men picked it up & brought it in. layed it on an anvill & commenced to pound it. the darkey was holding it, with both hands on the anville it exploded, taring off both arms, tairing his bowels out, brrakeing his thyes, he was a hard looking sight, the soldier that was pounding it was wonded in the thick of his left thye & cutting his face some, but not very badly hurt, another man stood 4 ft from them was not marked at all but nocked him down It is a wonder that all 3 of them was not killed, I sent you $12.00 by express, which will find at By. Ballou, sent it last Fri. You can do with it what you are a mind to, there is 2 months pay dew us which they kept back. Sunday Jan 11th I have made a mistake & got the rong sheet of paper. I have not finnished the sketch & have no time now to finnish it, this is the sketch of Ky. River bridg & Boons knob, you can get some kind of an idea how it looks perhapse. I have not much to write to day. we still remain at danville Not much to do. It seems very dul buisness to lay here not do anything, no signs of our fighting I will try & do better next time From your Husband Charly to Millie When you get that money perhapse you had better get ready to mak Uncle Henry a visit We dont live quite as well here as we did at Nicholsville we have very pleasent weather now

Charley

Cam at Danville, Jan. 14 1863

My Dear Beloved Wife

    I take this opportunity to pen you a few lines to let you know that I am yet alive & well. Yours of the 8th came to hand yesterday (the 13th) & was glad to here from you. You say that it has been a long time since you received a letter from me. It is singular that you dont get my mail because I write 2 letters a week evry week & that goes to show that I have not forgotten you, for I have not, As soon as I get a letter from you, I answer it immediately. I mailed a letter to you yesterday, You need not be affraid of our Reg. a going in any battle. We still remain at Danville & doing nothing but to drill & eat our army rations. Dave says he dont get any from Sophie, The fault is in the mail cairiers, I think not me. I am glad to here that you are all well & kicking The weather is very nice but have few cold rains, dont have any snow. The boys had a great time a cheering over the Otsego Draft. Stuck & Whitcum. I think Otsego has taken a good puke.--You say you are in debt a conciderably, I would like to know how much. I will try & send you money after a while to streighten it up if I get my pay pay. I have sent you $12. a few days ago by express, to By Ballou I presume you have it before this. We dont call it steeling when we confiscate, for instance a cesesh comes in to camp with a lot of eggs or some butter, & charges 30c per Doz would not you snatch? & charge 50c for a little lump of butter what would you call it, when the man is rich 30 to 40 cows, & 3 or 4 hundred hens & a reble at that. No we dont steel we snatch, thats right, fool old parker much. its all on acct. of the war ha. ha.--I tell you what if is this war will come to a close, Dont be scart. its the darkest just before day, The big wheel begins to move we can here it squeek The proclamation begins to grind the rebels bad. I dont want you to borrow any trouble about me. I am well & comfortable & feel all right. It is a very wet rainy day. & our tent leaks some we all have a large gum blanket so we can cover ourselfs all over. I want them pictures very much if you have them.. We are a going to lose Capt Bassett he has resined & will go home in a few weeks. The Co.

feels very much worked up about it, he agreed to stick by untill the last & now backs out, that meen. he is the best Capt. in the Reg. Our squad is all in the tent some writing, some playing checkers, some cards. & some asleep & some gitting supper out in the mud & rain, thats the way we live. but I dont play Cards. It is getting dark & I will draw my letter to a close. I have no news to tell you, Pleas write again My love to all

Yours as ever

Charley

You may direct to Danville Ky insted of Nicholsville

Thur morning I will say one word more we are have the worst storm now that we have had since I have been in Ky. It commenced yesterday morning & has hardly stoped raining since & it is now near noon. It is now fine hail & rain & sleet, & we are all confined in our tents. Now a little about this state. This state is behind the times more than 50 years, in buildings, farming tools, & evry thiing els. the houses are of the oldest stile & no Barns. Old fashion plough. for an ox yoke is a streight stick with iron bows. Old stile waggons just ready to fall down. &c.&c. No schools of any kind & the best they have here very poorly educated. It rains down on my paper & I will stop writing & mail my letter. I have nothing to write about any how

Charley to Millie

Danville, Jan, 19th 1863

Dear Lonely Wife,

I again take this opportunity to pen you a few lines, to let you know that I am yet alive & well with the exceptions of a hard cold, that is caused by the suden changes of the weather. We havve had a very bad storm which lasted 48 hours of snow & rain, which made it very disagreeable for us to do our cooking that has to be done out in the weather. I am very sorry to here that you do not get more of my letters I write as often as once in 4 days on an everage, so I think I do my shair of writing dont you, Last Sat. evening I received an Alminac & a Tribune from you & som stories in side of the paper. We still remain at Danville, doing nothing but to drill,

There is nothing going on here now days. The rebels are driven a good ways from here. We have the daly news evry day, & we find that the rebels are loosing ground evry day.

It is mow evening & I will write a little more. Perhaps a disscription of our tent would interest you of this evening. I have been making a cup of tea for Dave & myself (seeing that we have a hard coald & feel rather dumpish) & a peice of tost which makes our supper without any thing els to eat with it but Corn Beef) 15 minuts leter we have got done our supper I take my pen & paper go to righting, Dave has gone out & Let. Baird is at the stove tosting a peice of bread & makeing fun for us, his bread has fel in the stove, cant get his bread, shut's the door, lets it rost a spell, then digs it out & is eating it, & keep us in fun. The gard for 7 oc. is caulled & 2 are going out on gard. Ike Kinney, John Duel, & Vern. Rose is rolling & tumbleing in the straw & haveing quite a play spell. Some are writeing &c O we enjoy ourselves first rate. The weatherr is very miled this evening My eyes are most well again. We have 16 in our tent, we frequently get to talking (There the Cin. daly Commertial has come) over what we will do /when {crossed out} after we /go {crossed out} get home. One resolution we have pass, that is, to have a aniversery visit at each of our homes. I mean jist our squad, if we all should live it would take us 16 years to visit all around, we are to invite each our families. It would be surprising to you to see the feeling that we have for one to another, we all seem like brothers, except one, he lives at Allegan. when one or two is out on pickit in the stormy nights, their names are mention often. Their is so much going on here I cant write any more to night. good night. Tues. 20. This is a very wet morning. it has rained most all night but it is not very coald yet. Last evening after I had gone to bed the mail came to us, the first we have had for most a week. The reson /is {crossed out} that we did not git our mail, was becaus the heigh water has carried off the rail road bridg at Falmouth. This was a temporary bridg that was put up after the rebels had burned the first one. I was very much disappointed not to get a letter from you. I am satesfied that there is 5 or 6 letters on the road belonging to me & there must be some on the road to you, because I am writeing a great deal of the time to you. Dave has had but one letter since we have been at Danville. This makes the forth letter I mailed to you since we have been here. If you dont here from me as often as you would like dont give yourselves any uneasyness about me. I am doing well, we have not been in any battles yet & are not like to. You have had rurmors that we have been in battle & all cut to peaces, that is all faults. I think that Capt. Duffie had better undergo another change of linnen, he is a laughing stock for the Reg. We are haveing very good news from war, evry thing is working right. I should not be surprised if you would see Lieut Hubbard in Otsego before long. The Col. thinks some of sending him out to recruit for this Reg. I am not certen of this but this is the talk. We have used up the last of our butter & wish we had some more, we miss that part of our liveing Think some of sending for more. Now Dear Wife dont be discouraged if you dont get all of the mail. Direct to Danville the rest the same as before I still remain your affectionate husband

To Millie MillieCharley

We have a New bass drum for the reg. cost $20.00 which belongs to me, it is a splended drum, cant be beet for /goo {crossed out} quality. I will write again soon Millie!

Camp at Danville, Jan. 22nd 1863.

Me Dear Beloved Wife,

Yours of the 16th came to hand this evening at 8 oclock & while the rest are at bed I thought I would commence a letter to you, seeing that you take so much pleasure a reading them. It seems by reading your letter that you have the blues. is that so. Am I not right my Dear companion. I am sorry, but I cant blame you. Be patiant I shall see you soon again. I should not think that you would not feel bad to see something that came from me, it aught to make you feel better, In regard to the Bible we have 3 in the tent all the time, & you know that evry thing helps to make a load, I have to much load to make the best of it, the load that we have to carry will weigh about 43 lbs. let him carry that all day without stopping & eat our grub on the run, a man will naturly get weary when night comes, this we soldiers have to do & think it nothing more than an ordinary days work then lay down on the wet ground & sleep first rate all night & get up in the morning feeling fine as silk. O shaw a man dont know what he can do untill he is forced in to it. But above all, I beg of you not to worry about me. I am not going in any battles, & my health is good, my eyes are well now but some weak yet for the candle light. Dont feer Dear Wife I dont neglect my bible dutys. I pray for you evry night & for myself. I should have geathered more hickry nuts & sent you if I had a little more time before the barrel was sent away we barrel was got up with a jirk to it. Thats the way we have to do. If I remember right I sent you a little stone as a memanto of Boons Cave. but am not certin. I find a great many little things I would like to keep, but I cant. Yes the little red covered book I sent to Mary, sorry to here that she is sick. Tell her to write again. I am glad to here that you all are usealy well, I have expected to here that some of you were sick before this time. We have been haveing some cold stormy weather for the last 10 days, but little snow, it makes our camp ground very muddy, the soil being of clay we will come out all right in the spring. If Dick & Mage are to unruly you had better sell them at $70 if you can get it & get more if you can. You can do as you see fit, I will not complain. I expected that beef would be low when I came in this state & see so many head of cattle & swine without nomber, There is provisions enough in this state to keep the hole army one year this preasent day. The rebels regreted very much to leave this state, but we have cleared them out & they dont get here again. We have about 100,000 troops in Ky. according to reports at headquarters, & some will be removed to Vixburg soon I think by what I here, I would advise Father & Geo. to lead old granny into the woods & give her a blue pill, I think it will be the cheapest for you all, The money I send you if you get it, is at your disposal. I have $2.00 I would send you which is all that I have, if I dare risk it in a letter I can get along without it. there is no use of spending money here & pay such prices as we have to here, Citisans come in camp with pies that is not fit for hogs to eat, I will disscribe one, or give you a recipt to make them, Take on lb. flower mix to a consistancy of {its} thick enough to roll out with a rolling pin thin as a case knife, put in a plate, then spred over one thickness of dried applesauce thick as a window glass without any sweetning than upper crust like the first, then bake in a quick oven, then you have a Ky pie worth 10 cents, Good night, most midnight Fri. Morning Jan 23 Now I will go on with my letter, you say to me come home if I have any mercy on you. how can I, I have my hands & feet tied, I suppose you know that cant do as he would like, I find that the best way is to just come under & do my duty, & mind my officers I will com out all right. But let me undertake to run away see what the consequences will be, they will take 6 months pay from me, confine me in the gard house 30 days & live on bred & water & dress me in womens cloths then marched up & down the lines on dress perade followed by the band a playing the rougs march. that is the way they do it, you would not have it said of your soldier husband would you. Dear wife, I will come as soon as I can Ill warrant you, I dont think that Lieut Hubbard will go home as he expected to. Col. Cobern has made out his list before Hubbard applied also Capt Bassett cant get his resignation, so he will have to stay. Yes it is idle talk of coming home before I get a discharg. I never have got my pay for the drum & never will, I have another new drum worth $35. when I go home, my old one is all smashed up & we have the other here now, we got it for $19.50 I wish you could send me a peace of the hog that you have been dressing, it seems to me that it would taist good, I dont get the liveing here that I had Nicholsville. but remember the dinner I spoke fore next 4th of July Our Govenor is makeing us 9 month men & our time is most up I spose you know. To day is as nice a spring day as I ever saw I can here the spring birds in evry direction they make me think of home. O if I only could be at home I would give all, it seems as though I would. I want you to send them picturs soon as you can. I have spent a great deal of time a looking at your picture. perhaps that is what gave me sore eyes, it has been a long time scince I could see to read my bible, untill now, Dave or Mr Hager, or Mr Mabbs read most evry night, I never have had time seem so lost as since I enlisted. evry thing seems to be lost. time passes very slow with us take good care of the little lambs, perhaps when you get this letter you will get over the blues. because when you have the blues I have the blues so milly both have the blues together. then when you & I have the blues Father & Mother will have the blues. I guess you are out of ink aint you, if so I will bring you some by & bye. I have but a few more stamps or I would send you a lot. they are hard to be got now when I was at Gravle pit I sent to Cin. & got $1.00 worth & now their most gone...I think of nothing more at preasent & I will close give my love to all be sure & get your shair

From your Dear Husband Charly Direct your mail to Danvill & it will be all right.

Camp Danville January 25th 1863

My Dear Absent Wife

Seeing that I have a little leasure time I thought I would commence another letter to you. allthough I have nothing to write about that will be interesting to you. There is some prospects of our marching from here in a few days to Louisville, & from there I dont know where, We are all enjoying good health at preasent except 2. Tim Dagget & Ancel Baird they are sick with a coald, I think some of sending home some more cloths, it is now comeing on warm weather. I shall have to through them away or els carry them, so I prefer to send them home & when I /come {crossed out} go home I can were them I send my dress Coat because it /was {crossed out} is too small, the vest is all right except too warm. Now dont you feel bad when you see them as you did when you saw those other things. I want to reduce my luggage much as possable, it will be the easier for me, we are feel perty well now, I worked very buisey all day yesterday. we had no drill & I had some marking to do, so I went at it. I marked knapsacks & blankets to the amount $1.50, that is clear gain. I will send you 50 cents of it & 50 in the next, so if the letter gets lost I wont lose but 50 cents, today I am willing to divide as long as I have got it. I think I shall have more to do after a while. I am perty well off for clothes now. I am ready for any kind of a storm. I have 1 large gum blanket, 1 pr. of gum leggins, & a gum {havlock}, 1 large woolen blanket, over coat, blouse coat, 1 pr. drawers, 2 good pr. socks, 2 good woolen shirts, 1 towel & my pillow, & one pare of pants, one of the towels you gave me is lost in Ky. river. I am sorry to lose it, but one is all I want at once. Do you remember the ring that you put on my finger when I was on a furlow, I toled you that should not come off untill I see you, I have kept my promise yet, it has not been off, since you put it on. Sunday evening I have packed up my coat & vest, you will find in the bugget a Harper paper & a book for you & my marking ink, tincil plate that I dont want to use in the army, & the canvis the holl package is done up in that belongs to me, want you to get it, we have orders to march in the morning also the Division to Louisville, The freight will be paid on my things. You will here from me again when we come to a stopping place, the mail that is now on the road will be sent on after the Reg. Now Dear Wife be of good cheer, we shall see each other soon I think. My love to you, be patinet, From your

Dear Husband Charley   To Millie

                                        Cam at Louisville, Jan. 30ᵗʰ 1863

My Dear Wife,

    Seeing that I have a few leasure moments I thought I would drop a few lines to let you know how I am &c. We arrived here to day noon (Louisville) all feeling very tired after our march, We started from Danvill last Mon morning & just arrived here, /to at {both crossed out} the distance of 85 miles. we call that perty good marching, dont you? I feel good for another such a march. I dont know where we shall go, or when, some thinks to Nashville & some to Vixburg. The game is to go to Vixburg, & cut off the rebels supplies & starve them out. I have just this minute received a letter from you. I think you write as though you was discouraged, I am sorry to have you feel so, it makes me feel discontented & uneasy, I am bound here & cant get away. but I cant blame you It is hard for you I know but I am into it & cant get out. My wages are small & I cant furnish you what you want you want & pay debts. I will send you some more next pay day (I forgot The date of you letter I just received Jan 23) I am glad you have got red of the old cow. I am sorry to here that you are sick & the rest of you you must come down here, where it is healthy. I sead in my last letter that the charges would be paid, we could not they were so buisey at the express office that they would not attend to it, your propotion of the charges will be small. I am sorry you are haveing such bad work with the lambs. I shant need any cottne socks I dont think, as for yarn I can get all that I want, I am now supplied, if it did not cost so much I would send you my picture. it will cost me 2.00 the cheapest that I can get, I thank you very much for your compliments on darning, I think we shall get our pay is less than 2 month. I dont see why Uncle Henry dont write to me, & the rest I wanted he should help you some to go to his place, Since I commenced this letter I have hurd that we shall go to Nashvill Tenn. I have no time to give you the history of our march, we have had some snow, but none to be seen now the weather is fine at preasent, we are all perty well now except some complain of sore feet, & legs a marching on the pike roads, perhapse you had not better write untill you here from me again but if you do Direct to Louisville & they will follow the Reg. it is a very direct rought for mail where we will go & we may stay here 3 or 4 weeks. we dont know what morrow will bring forth, I will enclose you 50 cents again, make your figure 19 as plain as you can on the direction so that there will be no mistakes as to the Reg. My love to you my dear & keep up good courage From your Husband Charley to Millie

You will here from me soon again
Evening 8 oclock. we leave here in the morning

Feb 7th 1863
Camp on Steem boat on the Cumberland river

Dear Wife

I will try & write you a few lines, to let you know where I am & that I am yet alive & well, one week ago to day we marched from Louisvill to Pourtland (distance 4 miles) went a board of a steem boat (Ohio No 3) & remained there untill Mon night 4 oclock, then started down the river. It took some time for our fleet to get loaded, we have in our fleet 64 steem boats & 11 gun boats, the largest fleet ever was known in the west, The water is very high in the rivers, the Ohio river is one mile wide in some places, we arrived at the mouth of the Cumberland river Wed night, stoped there & took on a new suply of coal, & while there got word that the rebels had attacted fort Donelson, A detail was made to help load on the coal & hurry on to the fort, we traveled or sailed all night, Thurs eve. at 4 we arrived at ft. Dolonson, The fight lasted 1/2 day Tues afternoon. Our Col. gave us a permit to go ashore & see the battle ground when we arrived hurd that the rebels had left, there was of the union forces at the fort one Reg. 83 Ill. numbering 550 affective men & of the rebels 9 Reg. or 7,000 affective rebels, the rebs had 11 peices of artilery & we 6 & 1 large siege gun. Our loss 13 killed & 40 wonded including one Capt, one quarter master & one orderly sargent, & of the rebs 240 killed, dont know how many wonded, but the rebs took 2 of our men prisoners & they got away the same night & the rebs told them that they was over 500 men out, kill their Col. McNair & some others oficers, I saw quite a nombr of the dead rebs & lots of dead horses, we captured one large gun Sunday morn Feb. 8/63 The rebel commander is Gen. Forest, I presume you have hurd of him This fight was not in the fort, fought in a little town called Dover 2 miles from the fort, the rebs had our men surounded, they attacted on 3 sids they got so badly whiped that they are ashamed of it, they went that night 2 miles back & calculated renu the attact in the morning but it so hapened that one of our gunboats arrived there that eve. & commenced throughing shells in their camp & roughted them & killing a great many of them. /Thur {crrossed out} Weds. night when we got our boys thought they had burried all but 3 supposing to be all which was 120, /Fri {crossed out} Thur they commenced to find them by waggon loads, all through the woods & bushes, it is supposed the gunboat killed a larg nomber. The intention of Forest was to take the fort, & hereing that our fleet was coming up the river, unbenone to us & give it to us as we come up, but they miss there figure that time, Our boys had reenforsements from fort Henry, but they arrived to late, a teligraft from one fort to the other, they are 12 miles apart 2 Reg. & one battery of artilery, & they went back Fri. morn. It dont seem possable that 550 men will hold 7,000 at bay, this is true. We had all day Thur. to look around & see the fort & the old battle ground, which was fought most one year ago the 12 of this month, it was not very pleasent that day, it snowed, & snow about 3 inches deep, I saw 5 larg rebels guns and they are monsters too, Fri. morning our fleet prepared for battle, lashing 2 boats togeather, & the guns boats go ahead & 2 in the rear of the fleet 75 boats in one fleet, a splended sight, we moved up the Cumberland river very slow expecting to meet the rebs, or they to attact us from land, 11,000 rebs along here somewhere, under Gen. Forest, we in our fleet over 60,000 troops & a larg amount of artelery besids the gun boats, we could gobble them all to one mouth full I recken, we arrived at Nashville Sat eve. at 5 P.M. I have a very inconvineant place to write & have but little time to write, we are getting ready to leave the boat & it is herrah boys. I will write as soon as I can again, I received your letter last evening with Geo. & Lauras pictures in, I cant reply to that letter now but will soon. I saw Whit Mansfield last night, he came on board, the 13th Michigan is at Murfeesboro, Dear wife, be of good cheer & be patunt untill I come, pleas excuse all haist. From Your Charlie Direct you letters just like this, & I will get it

Mr. Charles H. Prentiss

Co. B. 19th Mich Infty

Gen Bairds Division

Army of the Cumberland

Via, Louisville, Nashville

Dont think because I am way down here that I wont get your mail. I am well & tuff & fair very well. I expect to see the Mich 13 in a few days Pleas excuse this letter I will do better in a few days I still remain your Dear Husband

Nashville, Feb. 8ᵗʰ 1863

My Dear Lonly Wife,

Seeing that I have a little more time to write, I will & enclose it with the rest. This morning when I was writing I expected to move from the boat, I have been out a part of the day helping unload some waggons & put them togeather I think we shall stay on the boat to night then in the morning we march 2 or 3 miles out to guard the railroad, & perhapse we may go to Murfreesboro, dont know which, I here the rebs are begining to owne up whiped. Your letter of the Jan 25ᵗʰ arrived at Nashville before I did. It dont seem to make much difference where you Direct a soldiers it will find him, I dont expect to here much news from home for it a poor place to get news. If I can here that you are all well I call it good news. I like to here what you are doing & what is going on at home your letters are as interesting me as mine are to you, its true that I have more to write about than you do. if you can tell me all about the stock & farm it will be interesting to me, I have got over my coald & will now, Dave is well & fat as a pig. Dave sends his respects to all he says he received a letter from Geo & Laura, Ike Kinney we left at Danville sick with rhumetix we have had some very bad weatherr scinse we commenced our march, I know it is dull buisness to stay at home all the time, Luit Hubbard will not go home now, that is all fell through with, I should be glad of your butter & cheese but there is no use of talking. you ask me what I suppose I would be doing if I was there. I think I should be telling you some awful stories about the war &c. I can do that. I wish I could have some of your nut cakes & hulled corn, that makes me feel bad when I think of such, but I feel contented with what I have, Dear wife I want to go home once more. but not yet, I am bound to shoot some rebs first, we dont think no more of shooting a reb, than to shoot a skunk. Tell Father & Geo. to cut up a good pile of wood, for I want to help burn it next winter. I glad there are agoing to try the machine, I sold one of my shirts for 9 pies, through one away, & have the other on & that is good for Nix, that other picture is gone up. it was not worth having, when I can I will get another taken for you. I am sorry to send you them back again so soon. I shall expect some more soon. O wouldent I like to take a peek in that room once more & I think I shall. tell mother to put on her specks & read the 11 commandment again I think she made a mistake. pleas all write. it is now dark & I cant see I am up on the deck of our boat a riteing, this letter from your Dear Husband Charly

Camp 3 miles S.E. from Nashville, Feb,10,1863

My Dear Wife

Haveing just received a good letter from you, (I hardly know how to express my mind & feelings) dated Feb. 1st with you enclosed in it, which does me so much good, now if you only would talk, it would /do me {crossed out} be all right, O if I could get out of sight a little while I believe I should let loose to my feelings. but when I have 50 or 60 thousand men around me, it is best for me to keep my eyes dry, A person at home knows nothing of a soldiers life, being deprived of a companion's care, of a Mother love, & of the good living, to see men /dragged {crossed out} shot down & dradged by the coat coller to the grave or hole in the ground they call a grave, as you would drag a log to the heap to burn, thousands of men have been piled up like cord wood & rails piled in with them & set on fire & all burned up togeather, & many other things that I could mention that a soldier has to see & do, I saw at the fort them burring the rebels, they dig a hole 6 ft long 2 ft deep & 10 to 12 ft wide then geather them togeather with the waggons, draw them to the hole tumble off like unloading wood, then take them by the coller & dradged to the grave & tumbled in & the dirt thrwn & piled on them this makes me think of home, & of a companion, a union soldier is not burried in this stile, they all have a coffin or box of some kind as far as I have seen it enough of this, I am affraid that I will make you thin that I have hard fair, but to see your pictures puts me in mind of all these things, it is far differant than home life. I want all of your pictures, it does me so much good to look at, I was sorry to send back Geo & Laura's it was your request, I suppose you intent send some more back to me. The Baird boys got a lot of pictures from home today as well as I did, & Dave got Sophie picture last night sent to him most 2 months ago. I will try & get my picture taken & send you if possable. I wish you would come in person so that you can talk the next time you come. I dont feel dispoised to send you back yet a while. when I do I will come with you. Yes I am glad to see you & more than glad, I will make it manifist by some way {a small self portrait is sketched here} I am sorry you have a sore throat, you must be careful my dear & keep well, Nothing does me more good than to here that you are all well. I have hurd of quite a nomber of cases of Diptheria about Allegan & Otsego. In regard to that bundle, it was left in such a shape that

I shant warrent it to go to you, it is not much account if you should not get it. I could use them when I go home. we sent it by Express or left it at the office to be sent & being in such a hurry to go away that we could not pay the fraight on it it may come after a while. The bundle was to By. Balloo to Otsego, you will not have to go to Kal, after it. I shall look out for myself for money. I have not much use for money out of the Reg. I dont pretend to buy anything butter is 50c per lbs. Coffee $1.00, molasses 3 dollars per gall. & evry thing in propotion, Do what you pleas with the money I send you, I can trust you. I am affraid you dont like my receipt for Ky. pies, I am ansious to have you try one batch. I think a great deal of your picture, it is a good one. I notice that I have seen your uniform before, allso the flat lying on the stand, it all good, pleas send me Fathers & Mothers, Geo. & Laura's & Marys, & the babys I shall be choice of them, You must go to the parties if you have a chance, & make yourself as cheerfull as possable, Dear wife, I know how to pitty you, It is lonesome I know, I glory in your spunk not wanting me to desert, it would be a disgrace to us both, We have had 3 desert with the last 2 weeks, Mat Jones. Eldridg Morry & Henry Wilcox I think all of Allegan. Mr. Baker wants I should ask you how his folks are getting a long & if they are well &c. he iis a busting man, he amounts to a big sume in this army, just as much as Mary does at home, O the poor man, I think Mr Hager is not a judg whether I am fit or not, I am better that I have been for many years, to be sure I have my {duinping} spells or pain in my guts. that is not very often. I like to have you all write to me, I would write to each one of you individually but I should have to repeet what I have writen, it may be the same with you, I am well, the health of the Reg. is good, I will tell you what our Gen. Baird tells us. he says that this Reg. is the largest & best in the south & behave better. & says that we stand No. 1. & also says that we keep the cleanest & the cleanest camp grouwnd &c. We are frequently visited by the Generals & Major Gen. & all of the big Gen. & they all call us No. 1, we had a very pleasent voig from Louisvill to Nashvill, I do wish you all could see our fleet When we was under motion it was a splended sight & to see the poor blacks rejoice to see us come they would clap their hands, wave their hankercheifs & evry other way to express their joy, poor fellows, how I feel for them. I cant begin to tell you all about them. Millie! do you remember 5 months ago today when I left you at Kal, how slow time does /go {crossed out} pass it seemed like one year, I think it will be 5 months more before I shal see you. they begin to talk 6 weeks will close the fighting, so the rebels say, I dont hardly belive that, although I have no reason to disbelieve it when I see the situation of the rebels, I must tell you a little more of our trip down the river. Sun Feb 1st was a cold, wet day it rained most all day, we are laying at Louisville, Mon. 2nd we layed at Louisville untill 4 this afternoon, the weather is coald & lowry, the boat runs down the river at the rate of 15 miles an hour. our boat is the largest boat on the river except one, we had a considerable more than our own Reg. & we were very much crowded, we had to sleep in open air, Tues. morning the 3rd when we got up our beds & clothing was all white with frost. the collest night I have seen this winter, we have no fire to go to to warm us, we had to keep hopping. The trip was very cold one to fort Donelson we stayed there untill the storm was over, the snow fell 3 inches thursday /while {crossed out} I saw the residence of Hon John Bell, the union canidate for President, the rebels has layed his iron works in ruins It was a splended peace of work & macheniry. evry thing looks desolate around here, can see ruins most evry direction. we have some union men about here & the Gen. has placed a gard over them, their fences are not tuched, but when we come to a rebels residence his fences are burned to keep us warm & do our cooking & when the fences are gone they commence to pull off the siding from the houses & misc. buildings too. Wed morning Feb 11th Do you remember dear Millie just 6 months ago this morning when I first put my name down to serve our country, how long it seems. this morning is one of pleasentist mornings I ever saw. Dave & I has gone out in the field to write, 1/4 mile from camp where it is still, except the drums & bugles that can be hurd a great distance. O this beautiful spring morning No one can tell how I feel where I set I can here the blue birds, meadow larks, ground birds & robins & evry other kind of birds that I use to here at home I am tired of a soldiers life, I dont want you should be alarmed thinking that I am going into battle, we are kept back to guard the railroads & other property, I am not one of that kind to makie my friends think that we are going in to battle & do some awful thing when we are as safe as you are at home, Many has done it to make their folks think are brave & do something smart when they are same ones are cowards I tell you just as it is, but after all I dont fear the battle, to tell the truth I should like to go in a battle & fight. I dont fear it at all, /evry {crossed out} a man that leaves a home as I have feels as though he wanted to do something then go home, I dont know but you will think that I am homesick bu the way that I am writing. I must confess that I am this morning when I am out in the field alone & to see this beautyfull warm day & evry thing to put me in of home.

If I had no friends at home I should not feel so I dont think. we are haveing very good news on our side of the army. I was reading a few days ago that a rebel corespondent of the Richmond that if they could not rase 100,000 more troops in one month, they are gone forever . this is taken from a rebel paper. & I here from other papers simular stories I have a good reason to think that I shall get my discharge before the forth if I live, when we are discharged we shall go to Dowagac & be mustered out as we we were mustered in. I will draw my letter to a close, for I have writen all that I can think of. I have writen you most 7 pages I will try & write again before long. I dont know as you can read my letters when I write them this way, can you {letters are written, then inverted and interlined}. Paper is very scarce here & heigh, I have a good supply on hand now but stamps are getting scarce with me. I hhave 5 more then I shall have to frank my letters to you & send you the money. From your Dear Husband Charley, The same bird marked my letter above a small yellow spot near the middle of the page. the same one that I have speek of. Now I will stop writing & go & do my washing. I have to wash one shirt, one pare drawers, one pare socks, my haver sack Charley

Camp at Nashville Feb. 17th 1863

My Dear Wife

I have a few moments to spend in conversing with you, all though I have no news to tell you, I have not been very well sence I arrived here, our voyge on the boat has a bad effect on us all, most all of the Reg. was taken with the Diarhea whhich reduces a person very quick I have had it & got over it & feel quite well now. this is no more than we expected. I have used up all of Doct. Hopkins meadicen. & it dont mater much, it does me no good down here. it requiers another kind of meadicen for this kind of Diarhea. I have it frequently & get over it very easy I am all right now, The Fusileer Reg. are encamped about 1 mile from us & are getting out timber for a R.R. Bridg at Franklin 14 miles from us I want to go & see Charlie Straton & some others but we cant all go, cant more that 2 get a leave of absensen at a time. I feel more & more encuraged evry day that this war is comeing to a close, the rebels talk enough & cry enough in Braggs army there are deserting from 3 to 5 hundred evry day, a day or two ago one hundred deserters came to our lines & gave them selves up

& were brought to Nashville. they tell us that Braggs army /was {crossed out} is very much demoralised & on the decrees evry day, I cant begin to tell you all by writing but I will come & tell you all about it before long, you must brighten up & hope on you will see me soon if we both live. it is surprising to see how the troops are comeing in to Nashville, another fleet arrived here to day of 30 steemers, cant see any thing but soldiers in this regun, this is a very healthy contry, we have good water but evry thing is very high, letter is worth by the quior 60 cents, potatoes by the bush. worth $4. Chese 50c butter 60c Sugar 30c Eggs 40c &c. &c.. & other things in the same propotion. The news is to day that we march tomorrow to Franklin 14 miles from here, dont know what we are agoing to do I suppose to help guard & build a bridg, you will find all the places that I have named to you on the map & can trace my rought where ever I go. when you direct your mail put on the same directions that I sent you in my two last letters, & you may continue to do so untill I tell you differant, The more I look at that picture of yours, the more I think it is the best you have had taken, it is perfectly natureal, I want the rest of your pictures, I will tell you what I do want, I want some of your sausengers, head cheese, dish of milk, a cup of tea, some hul corn & some good bread some good sweet pork, some nut cakes, & some other things that I could mention. just pass some out this way, I think I could eat some, I never want to see any coffee while I am in the army, It is a poor drink for me I have lived more than a week on raw baken & hard bread, & stinking meat at that, rather tuff, but it is better now, Never mind that, all on account of the war, many a rebels families dont get as good as that. I dont complain of such small faire as that when some families are starveing to death, last saturday we drew some new guns the Enfeeld improved they are a splended gun to shute. Pleas write soon as conveneant & tell Father or Geo. to write & tell me all about the stock & how you get along & evry thing, dont care what you write, say something. I like to read letters from home. & the neighbors, Dave is well. Mr Hager is most sick to day with a cough. Let. Baird is under the weather some, the rest of the squad is usealy well. I got 8 stamps to day you nead not send me any now, I may send for a bunch of envelopes by & bye I have planty of paper now, I think I will close & will write again soon, from your Husband Charlie

Camp at Nashville Feb 19th 1863

My Dear Wife,

It is with pleasure that I set myself on the ground to pen to you a few lines, to let you know a little more about myself & how we are getting along way down in Tenn. I am well & enjoy myself very well, we have nothing to do but to drill, the same I got out of this afternoon, we have a Brigade drill this afternoon, the 4 Reg. drill togeather, it is a handsome sight to them that has not seen such, but I hate the sight of it, am geting sick of it. I ran off when drill called & dont know what they will do with me & dont care. John Duel & Lester Baird is laying in the tent & are some sick. What did you have for dinner to day noon, see if you can tell me, I have made a guess, I guess a good boiled dinner & some milk &c. I had hard bread & beans, thats all, I have no news to tell you so I shant make this letter interesting this is a pleasent day & very warm & the mud is drying up very fast, we have good healthy water to drink but it very warm, we have a large spring near us that we use from that flows about 2 barrels per minute & is very warm, fools cap paper is selling down here for 60c a quior, one bunch of envelops & a small ink bottle cost 60c that is the way that they tuck it to us. It takes all of a soldiers wages to live comfortable & suffer at the best, I have traveled on the march all day without /any {crossed out} eating anything but that infarnel hard bread & it seemed as though I could put one foot before the other, & so it went day after day & then to of the cause that brought me to such useagekit would make the most tender harted person fight to the last, & occationaly think of home what is worst is that they will keep us guarding rebel property to a certain extent, we do finally have some pribalages such as burning rails &c. to do our cooking & to keep us warm, however this is not a going to last a great while longer. Our big rosea (as we call him) will make a strike soon, when he makes his way to Chattanooga with his 200 thousand (which he has got) which will cut off all of their western supplies & cut the rebel army in two, we think it will tell the final story. It is impossable for the rebels to hold their men from deserting, they know that their famileys are starving & they are going home to provide for them, they knnow if they let this spring pass & not sow nor plant they are still wors off, therefore this spring will tell the story. I think & evry one els in this contry, we have but 3 points to gain that is Vixburg, Chattanooga, & Richmond, & that will be done soon. I have good reason to say what I have & have proof to back me. There may be some big battles fought at Chattanooga & we have the force here to do it & they are comeing all the time How does your fodder hold out will you have enough to last you through the winter, how does the stock look, & how does Fred & snip look, what are you keeping through the winter, how many cows give milk, which one do you milk, send me Milk in the next letter. how many hens do you keep how many eggs have you got, how many acres of what have you on the ground, how did those potatoes turn out that Geo & I planted in the fence corners under straw. tell me all about your farming, I would like to here, the sheep, how are they, & how many is there by this time, perhaps you think these questions answered would not be interesting to me, but they will. I would like to know how you are all getting along. I think I can speckulate some if you can fernish me what I want. As letter iis selling for 60c a quior I could make something, if you could send me a ream of letter paper the size of this sheet by mail & not cost to much. I sell it for 40c a quior & envelops at thhe same rate you can cosult with the post master, if it dont cost more than one cent an oz. you had better send me one ream & as many envelopes, but if you cant get any let it go there is a great many out of paper if you dont think it will come through sage dont undertake to send it. I wish Geo. or Father was able to bye up a lot of butter, dryed beef, chese, paper candy &c & come here & sell it, you could a larg prfit A part of our Reg. went away this morning (Feb. 20) & some expect that we shal go in the morning, going south about 8 miles, I would like to send Father & Geo. some whittleing timber, we have lots of red ceder rails to whitle & burn, To day is another of those beautiful spring days This green leaf I send you is an ever green, it is a beautiful arnimental tree, this came from a rebel door yard in tenn, I think I will close & try it again some other time. I am well, my eyes are week yet cant use them by candle light. This better is for all of you, as I have said I can talk better than write, I dont want to send home any white paper with I have scribled over it. So good bye for this time, From your Old man Charley to Millie

Brentwood Army of the Cumberland
Head Quarters of the 1ˢᵗ Brigade, 3ʳᵈ Division
Feb, 24ᵗʰ 1863

My Dear Lonely Wife of the butternut Grove

Yours of the 15ᵗʰ with a new dress came to hand last evening, & was heartily glad to hear from you & to see Elsie's likeness, this is the first that I have received since the 7ᵗʰ of Feb. I tell you it seemed a long time, but you obeyed my orders I suppose, I told you not send untill you learned where to direct, I have news to write you but will try to say a little, & will commence by saying that your picture is the best one that I ever saw. I think it is perfect, I had a good notion to cry but dare not, I must wate untill I get out of this, that wont do here you know I call that a good one of Elcies. I can see something there that I am acquainted with. her looks has not altered much. O how I want to see you all. but there is no use of talking. I think you have got a beautiful dress, you did not tell me what cost, I want to see you with it on. & go to meeting & other places with you. glad to you are getting fleshy & feel well, for me to know that you are well makes me feel more contented, but if youre were way down here amagst the rebs I should not feel so contented, there is some danger here if a man stroll away from camp, he is liable to get poped over if he isent carefull, but let them rip, I dont feer it, I have no reasen to complain of your writing a blue letter for I think I have writen some blues in my letters, but dont mean to. I know it is a privilage to have some one to talk to at such times, you can write as you are a mine to. I am glad you went to the Donation party & wish you would go more & make your self as contented as possable, I dont know but my faith is to strong, but we have the news here & at Nashville that Vixburg is ours with a great loss of life, we dont hardly believe it is true, but hope it so, I dont credit all that I here. The letter from the steem boat, with a lock of my hair, I wrote untill dark then out with my jack knife & sawed off some hair, if you know how it hurt, you would not ask for many such locks, it is not the hair I care any thing about plage on it all, it hurt. seeing that you have got it, it is all right. No Ill warent you that my hair does not get oiled, you oiled it the last time. Who have you got to saw your wood. If the wood sawyers confuse you what you do if you had from 3 to 4 thousand men around you as I do when I write. I am getting use to it. I use to be easely disturbed, but nothing will disturb me now. I am glad you have got them things, what is your shair of transpotation, I suppose you know the frait is to be rated between 5 of us & Dave & I had the smallest packages in the lot, our (Dave & mine) was of a size. Did you get the canves the things was done up in. I want to save that, I shall look for some more pictures before long. I glad you have them, they are a great comfort to me. You tell Mr McKee he need not trouble himself about you When you apeek of washing, I have a shirt to wash. I tell you what it is I feel proud of our Leader Gen Rosecrans (dont know how to spell him) I & we all have confidance in him, No traitor about him. If I go into battle I want to go under him, he is my choice, we had some speaches yesterday on the sniversery of Geo Washington birthday. I have just got done eating my dinner & will try to finnish. Capt Bassett is bound to sine & have us && that is not all I nor we dont care, he dont prove to be the man we thought he would be, he is a hard harted & little feeling man, has no feeling for the sick, & if he does go home & leave us, he will never here the last of it if we ever come home, what a fool a man can make of him self if he sets out. Our Company is down on him & he can go double quick, any thing but a coward, that whats the matter, When I come home I can tell you all about it, I dont you to understand that we are very badly abused & have suffered but has used us mean, I am well, Dave is most sick with a coald, but not very bad off, Mr Hager is well & most all the rest, some are grunting some, I dont here from Knapp do you if you do pleas tell me about him, there has 5 men died out of our Co. & 3 deserted I gess I will stop for my sheet is full. & I must save some for the next time. Never mind the paper I spoke to you about you need not send it. it may be lost, send me a news paper once in a while & do up some tea do it up stout From your

Dear Husband Charley   Millie

Brentwood March 2nd 1863

My Dear Wife,

Yours of the 22nd came to hand last evening, enclosed in it Mary & Fathers likenesses & was glad to here from you, I have nothing new to tell you, but will make some reply to your letter, I should have not written to day if Mr Hager has writen home & told his wife that I am in the hospital This I will not denigh. 4 nights ago I was taken with Ague & fever which lasted all night in order to get an excuse I had to go to the hospital. I will commence a little father back in my story. To begin with, we have one of the most unmercyfull Capt's that is in the union army, he is a hard harted old seed if half of his Co. lay dead in the hospital it would not be him to go there to see them. he never has been known to visit one one of his sick, & while I lay here the Capt of the other Co. to visit evry day Thank the Lord Capt. Bassett leaves us in a week or 10 days for home. All the Co. except one or two is very glad that he goes. he is going home. here I have to stop. we have marching orders, Mar, 4th This is the way we are jircked around, only one hours notice & just at night too. Now I will go on with my story, if Bassett is a minde to he can excuse a man or use his influance to get an excuse for him, he has made men come into the ranks to drill when I new he was not able to stand up alone, & it has been the case with me, & I have set down in the ranks & let them march away from me. I took a notion I did not want to do duty, did not feel first rate, but not sick when the morning came, I pretended I was very sick, the Doct. gave me a bunk in the hospital, & now I will get a resting spell & recruit up some, have better living too that is something. I expect the boys all wrote home that I was very sick at the hospital, you dont suck that do you? I am heartily glad to here that you are all well yet that I call good news. we had not hurd of the death of Mr. Kiney untill you told me, he was left at Danville Mrs Kinney must very bad. also a great many others, you cant tell any thing about it untill you come in the army A mans dying grones are not headed no more than the winds blowing. I noticed some men quite sick in the hospital, they would speak to the nurce, /he {crossed out} for some meadicen, or some water, or some little nottion that he wanted, he goes bye, dont pay any tention to him, no more that he want their, let a sick man say that I am worst they say how can I help it, evry thing goes just like this. O there is many a poor widow that is to be pittyed. I have not seen Mr Stratton yet, hope he will come around & see us, have not seen Charlie yet, he is clost by us but there is so many men here I dont hardly look at a man Harrison Whitlock is clost by us, I have not done your erand to Mr Baker yet, he iis transfured to the Ohio 9th Battery in our Brigade Mar 5th Tell Geo. not to fiel to large over my cloths, for he can get a suit any time that he wants them, just hire out to Uncle sam you will get blue close enough. The coat I can wair without buttoning it up. The cloves I did not want nor anything els in the pockets except the toothpick. I thought I lost that. who sawed your wood you must have quite a lot of it. It was a blue jay, the nasty bird. I thank you very much for them pictures. I want some more. Father has a piece of chese in his fingers I see, I want he to give me some, but he wont I am very much obliged to mother for her letter, I like to have you all write a little--I think it is too bad that I am not out with the Reg. they are out about 3 miles haveing a fight, they went out yesterday morning left their things in camp except 4 days rations & their blankets. I have hurd the guns howl all the forenoon had a little brush yesterday & scatered them, killed 14 rebs. & none of us Fri Mar. 6th To day we have very bad news we got whiped very bad, we fought with our Brigade 4 of the enemys. Our forces are composed of the 19 Mich. 22 Wis. 85 Ind. 33 Kt. infty. Mich 2nd Cav. Penn. 9th Cav. Ohio 9th battery this is all that we had in the fight. while the rebs had just 4 times as many. The 4 Reg. of infty are all gobbled up, all the boys are gone, dont know whether they are dead or taken Prisenors. I am safe yet. Capt Bassett played out & got away so he is with us. Our Col. is killed. There is nothing left of the 19 now, Ancil Baird is with me & Sid Brundage & John Hogal are teemsters so they escaped. It seems very lonesome here. we have a plainty of reinforcements that came last night & Rosecrans is on the other side of them & we will have them yet, This fight was at Spring hill 8 miles from Franklin. My love to you all. I will write soon again From your Dear Husband Charley Millie Sat Mar. 7th I have hurd a little more, we sent in a flag of Truce yesterday, & get very faverble report of the battle, insteed of all of our Reg. being killed, as was reported. Our loss is only about 75 killed out of the holl Brigade & 250 wonded, who is wonded I dont know we shall get a list of them to day from the rebel Doct. The rebels act very manly about this, the rebel loss 150. I Brigade is all taken priseners, Dave has gone with them if I had not been sick I should have been with them. There is only 150 of our Reg. left I will write in a day or two when I get all of the particulars, I am on the gain we expect another actact soon dont worry about me, one thing more the rebels had 30,000 & we had about 5000. now we have enough for them Charley

Brentwood Mar. 10th 1863

My Dear Wife

Yours of the 3rd Came to hand Yesterday & was glad to here from you. It seems by the looks of your letters that you have no ink If you would come down here I will lend you some ink & a pen. We are haveing very wet rainy weather which makes it very unpleasent for us. we dont have much snow down here, I dont like it down here very well & want to get away from here

There is some very nice looking land here & beautiful springs & some very pleasant places, But O the improvements on buildings & farming implimints. One hundred years behind all the Northern States. Dont see a deasent looking waggon, use a streight stick for a ox yoak & iron bows, drive them with a roap, & great many ride the near ox, have not seen a drag, nor a plow that I would take as a gift, I have seen one thrashing machine. No straw cutters, No reepers nor No nothing but a few negrows, Some parts is good land, but thousands of acres is so stony that a sheep nor a rabbit could get a living. the landis covered with rocks. Most all the wood land is cleared or under brushed so that it makes the woods very pleasant. & have some beautiful Parks, in these parks we Union Soldiers have our Camping ground & the timber is badly cut up, & spoiled, We have no regard for beauty nor any thing els even human life we shoot at most everything that we come to, evry sheep, evry hog & pig & roster, evry hen, rooster, chicken pacock, Ginney hen, has to die even oxen & cows are killed privately, & calves, there is one calf hanging near my tent door most dress, thats the way that we guard rebel property now. Our Major sys to us /it is {crossed out} the great secret is to hide. then all is right. dont let the officers see any thing. all is right. I have seen officers when they mistrust any thing to go out of sight, they must do their duty if they dont their comnashien is taken away & reduced to the ranks. but this contry is perfectly desolate, & many a poor family's do suffer for want of provision's. all on account of the war, It is enough to /make {crossed out} brake the stoutest heart of a soldier & make him weep to set down think & then get up & look around him. It is horred, to see men drawn up in line of battle, then to stand & be shot down like so many black birds, & the one that kills the most is the best fellow, then burred like a dead dog or through up in heeps & burned. that is the way this war is carried on. And what is still worst is to have our own Doct. (Doct. Clark) say that he had rather burry 100 men than to furlough home 50 to recruit. That man was very carful not to go on the battle field the other day. That old Doct. has left our Reg. & gone home, we are glad I tell you. Doct. Bennett is our Surgeon now & appers to be a fine man, he is not the man he was 6 months ago. The condision of our Reg. is in rather a feeble state, we have but 229 men. & 74 of the 229 able to do duty. we have 2 officers left. Capt. Bassett. & Lieut Leasaleer, one Doct. one Quuarter Master Chaplin, heard up are we not? There has been a /rick {crossed out} requition made to Gen. Blair to send us to Detroit to recruit. I think we shall go, we have been reported unfit for duty All of our Reg. was all in the

battle except Co. D. which was left at Brentwood to guard a R.R. bridg &
a few that was left behind at Franklin that was not able to march & some
that was in the Hospital. I hapened to be one of the nomber that was left.
perhapse you was glad but I was not, but after the 2nd day I was glad I never
wanted to go into battle worst than that time. only 19 of our Co. is left. the
rest of the poor boys I know nothing about. This parole buisness is played
out, They will have to stay until they are exchanged, but the officers, we
shall not see again untill the close of the war. the revolver is lost with the
rest. I never shall see that again. I lent it to Lieut. Hubbard. I am very glad
to here that you are all well, I am not very Sick neather, I am so as to be up
& go where the rest do. I wish I could go to church with you. It seems to
bad not to go to meeting, we hardly know when Sunday is, evry days labour
is alike, & most allways when there is any marching to do or any reviews
to go through with it is sure to come on the Sabath day, I am glad you have
a good Minister after a long time. I wish you would drive the Sam Leighton
Cow down here for me to milk this summer. I think I live first rate on hard
bread & milk but never mind I will have the better apitite when I come
home. It seems that Father & Geo. has at last made a rose of some plaster.
I am anxious to here the result of the plaster on that land, if you can traid
off some of your cows & get some choping done in the South East corner
of the farm, in connection with the rest of choping & the wheat field, & if
you can get some pairs & cherry trees, & some other trees I wish you
would, such trees can be set in rows E. & West parilel with the peach trees
South of the peach trees one rod apart I will draw you a Diagram if I can,
Make all the improvements that you can, if you can see Mr. M. Warrent
about that note, & if you can spare some money (if I get it for you) I would
like to have you pay it. Tell him I am sorry that I did not pay before this. /
also {crossed out} Uncle Sam is owing me $52 dollars. dont know when
we shall get our pay, I suppose you are makeing prep to make sugar O if I
was with you this spring, I think that I can brag over you some, you say
that calico is 3/, per. yard, Calico is not to be had we tryed to get 15 yds. of
ticking in Ky. & they wanted $12. for it, A hat such as I wair at home cost
$10. & Salt $1. per. lb. I can bye 2 sticks of candy for 10c I can bye 4 ginger
snaps for 10c, A 3 cent paper of tobaco for 20c. if you wont give up I will
tell you some more. I can get a peace of Cheese 1/2 inch squir & 2 inches
long for 10c A drawing of tu for one man 10c. pipe to smoke in 50c, & 75c
to look at a piece of butter as larg as a peice of chalk a small slice of dried
beef 10c. will this do. I have not lied any for the sake of braging. I could

tell you of some more butits of no use. I dont want you to send me any paper nor envelops. I have a pleanty. I shall have to look out for peddlers, It seems that there is many that wants me to get killed, I dont mean to die if I can help it here You may tell the beddler that he may not come again, for I am soon comeing home again. I risk you, It seems that Jim Steel means to stick by you yet. I wish such fellows as he would enlist. he must be makeing money to pay $2,000 for that farm. Geo. Otto has cut a gut..I sont thank our folks for carrying of them pictures, what pictures I have got I am very well satesfied with what I have got only I want more. If you can do me up a little tea in a newspaper, you may, be very careful in doing it up. No I have not got to always live so thank the Lord, there is a better time a comeing. if it was not for hope, the heart would break. I am not discourage yet, the remainder of that lief I through away. I will send you more when I can get some. I think we shall get in some place where you can send me some, beef & butter. & some other eattables. I was very sorry when the contence of that box was gone, that cyrup was good I wish I had more, your wish did come to pass in regard to my being sick. If I was not sick I should have been a prisener with the rest. The place for the Musisians ia all amungst the battle a picking up the wonded just as much exposed as any, I am not a drummer any longer. & dont want to be. It allmost killed me to carry a large bass drum on my brest all day, I prefer the gun as things is shaped I shant have to go into battle again untill our Reg. is filled up again. I did not suppose you sent me off. I went because I thought it my duty, who says you sent me off. I thank Mr Wolfe very much for his kindness. Ill endever to do any duty as a christian & as a soldier. Mar 11th Now I will proseed with my letter. I dont want you to make too much calculation on our going to Detroit to recruit. we may go & we may not, it is not certin, there is so many rhumers in camp that there is an excitement all the time. Now I will tell you what I know about the fight at Spring Hill. Mar. Mon 2nd Our Brigade had orders to march from Brentwood to Franklin at 4 oclock, in great haist, the sick at our hospital was left at the hospital of 85 Ind of our Brig. to be sent to Nashville the next day, I was with the rest to go to Nash. but when morning came I found my self on the road to Franklin to the Reg. if I was sick, distance 8 miles, I took my time, stoped at the neighbors on the road & got a good dinner, which done me much good, On the night of the 3 Gen. Colbern received orders to prepare to march early in the morning (4th) with 4 days rations each Co. took 3 tents. No body new what was going on, They went off, & at 10 oclcock heavy firing was hurd, lasted 2 hours our forces found the enemy 8 or 9 miles S of Franklin at Spring Hill. we had one man wonded & one horse, & we killed 14 rebs & put them to flight. Our boys encamped on the battle ground that night, Mar. 5th: The enemy came on with a large reinforcements 30,000 strong, at 9 A.M. the fight commenced, it lasted untill after noon. after fighting a spell the center of the enemys line gave back. Our men followed up then their right & left closed around our little handful of men & captured the 4 Reg. we lost no guns nor Cavelry, we captured 12 priseners, killed 250. I dont know how many wonded. The 6th we sent in a flag of truce to get permision to burry our dead, The rebel Doct. told us they had burried all of our dead which is between 50 & 75 & of our wonded 250 I told you that our Col. was killed, he is not dead. I think we lost but one field officer, that is Capt. Smith of Co. A. I may here more of the particulars after a while & I will tell you, But O the feelings of the few that was left, it would have made you cry to see us wandering around after we got the news, like so many lost sheep with out a shepard, Our officers all gone & our comrads all gone, Only one of my squad left. that is John Duel. what remains of our Co. all occupy one tent, when before that hapened we had 5 tents full, what a chang, This makes me homesick to have all of my mates taken, dont know who is killed or priseners, will now find out. I will give you the names of those that are left Peter Gordan, A. Lenard, H.C. Pratt, Jim Batchelder, Norton, from Martin, Otsego John Duel, C.H. Prentiss, Sid Brundage, John Hogle, Allegan, Jobe Kingen, B.F. Chapin, Stephen Lampman, (Cleafman (from the colony), Milo Barker, J.B. Nelson, Thomas Kincade, John Young, Geo. Martin & Baker in the battery, Fred Nelson & the Capt., Fred Nelson is soon going home & I will send you my memmorandon book home by him, I have it full, I presume that will be enteresting to you, In reply to Mothers letter, I have not received any letter from Elder Buck, nor Cosine Ira Kenney nor Uncle Henry, why dont they write to me, I have writen to all of these, & I want Father, Geo. Laura & Mary all to write, I wish I had a nip of the cheese you just cut. that would relish with my hard bread first rate. I wish that I might exchange some of my hard bread for a couple of your fride cakes for my dinner, I hope you will be kind a sppareing of your cheese, I may send for one after a while, if you want to spare one of the smallest. I allways think of you when I set down to my meals. I suppose that I might as well close my letter, for I think I have writen enough for one letter. be sure & all write. My Love to you all, be of good cheer I think I shall soon return to you Put your trust in God for he is allways with us, he will do with us as he sees fit, So Good bye Charley To Millie Mar. 12./62 I have found my other picture. We have got 2 geese for dinner C.

" He who noteth even the fall of a sparrow will have some purpose even in the fate of one like me."—ELLSWORTH.

Brentwood, Mar. 14th 1863

Dear Wife,

It is with pleasure that I drop you a few lines again to let you know how we stand, Fred Nelson intends to go to Otsego next Monday, & I thought I would send home some things, what I send you my paint knife, molds & screw driver to my revolver, some brushes, a bunch of letters, my memmorandom book & Daves memmorandom book which I would like to have you send to his folks he spoke of sending it home before he left, tell his folks that Dave is all right not killed nor wounded as we can find out, 2 men from each Co. was detailed to examen the battleground after we drove the enemy back, we found but one of our Reg. Co. C. & we found only 32 killed on our side ensted of 75 we found all, & reburried them, we suppose our boys are gone to Vixburg, we have put all the boys things in bails & send them home to their friends, I will make Geo. a preasent of a fine tooth comb, I found it. I would like to have George take good care of my rifle if he will & not let it get rusty inside, These things I send home I hope you will keep for me untill I come home, we still remain at Brentwood, no news at preasent. I am quite well, we live a little better than we did. I had some hokake & milk for supper last evening, want that good! Doct. Bennett is a fine man, we all love him, things go a little different scince Old Doct. Clark left, Dont expect he will come back to the regiment again. I have all the letter paper & envelops that I want but you may send me some stamps, I am most out of stamps & money I have 5c left, write often, Send your mail as you have before, to Nashville My Love to you all, From your Husband Charley To Millie, March 16th. This watch belongs to James Batchelder & he wants it sent home the first opportunity   Charley

Headquarters Camp Brentwood Comp. B
19th Mich. Inft. March, Monday 16 1863

My Dear Lonely Wife,

Seeing that I have nothing to do, & it being so pleasent, I thought that I would try & compose a few lines. I have no news to tell you or in other words I have nothing to write about, time passes so slowly that I want to buisey myself about something, This day is one of those beautiful days that I tell so much about & I have gone out in the woods alone to write & kill time, The ground begins to look green & the wild woods flowers begin to show themselves through the leaves, the insects humming about me, & I here most evry kind of birds in the branches above me, & it seems that evry thing was trying to make me happy, & I do feel happy. I should feel still happyer if I could only take a look into your house again & stay with you. what a pleasure it would be to us, to meet again wouldent it? but No that cant be so now & when I dont know, but time will tell. I hope that it may not be long when we shall meet again, but if we shold never chance to meet on this earth again, I hope that we may meet in that happy home where parting never shall be, no troubles shall molest us. there will be no war, no battles to be fought, but all calm, quiet, piecefullness, & happyness, that is the home that I am fighting for now as well as for my earthly home & Contry. Dear wife I hope this is your ame, trust in God, do his will & he will comfort you in your lonely home, I can say that if I am taken sick & die in the hospital or fall in the battle field, Thy will be done, I am ready, what a pleasure it is to me scince my comrads have been taken away from me. I have no one to talk with me on the subject of religion, Mr Hager, Mr Mabbs, Mr Gunsaul, Dave & myself use to have some good talks togeather, they were all in my tent, we took turns in reading the bible evenings & sundays. The Chaplin depended our squad to sing for him, Now they are all gone & I am left alone to a certain extent, When overhalling the knapsacks the other day, I found bibles & testements in a large nomber of then (of our company) that would sware & drink. I felt much surprised some of our worst men. I thank God that I am not of that stamp. My health first rate now & the health of the Reg. is improving fast evry day, Doct. Bennett is a good Docter, he seems to take a gread deal of pains to restore our healths, & is getting better food for us, gives us exercise, wants we should play ball, pitch quaits & other play to content ourselves, There is some 30 or 40 men that will get their discharge through his influence that Old Doct. Clark would have kept here to die, he would not discharge them to save there lives, I understand that he is in the Nashville hospital very sick. I nor one in the regiment has no sympothy for him, all say that it a blessing to the regiment that he is gone. he is mixed a little with rebleism I think, has been turned out of two other regiments, & would have been out of this if he had not been a brotherinlaw of the Col. I dont here any thing more of our boys yet. I expect they will soon be parolled & go home /soon {crossed out} Last night I stood picket & had some fun, some rebs undertook to run our lines & they sliped up on that job, did not ketch us asleep we fired into them & they returned the fire & then skedaddled, no one hurt on our side, dont know what we done, the long roll was beet & all in camp was on hand when the alarm was given, all ran is the stockade & pickets went to camp, all but Peter Gorgon & my self & another man who stood all on one post, we stuck to our post, there is a good many garilees in these parts, they want to burn the bridg that we are guarding, but they cant do it, we have driven the rebels back acrost Duck river from spring hill where we had the fight the other day, we are enough for them yet. Mar 17th Now I will go on with my letter I have taken my old post inn the woods to write, I will commence by saying that I had some mush & milk for dinner, I'll, asure you that was good, Coffee is a very scerse article here with the rebels so we traid coffee milk, pay 10c a quart & traid coffee for meal & other things so we make out to live very well for a soldier, but I dont suppose you would think it was fit to eat, neather should I if I were at home, we have no convieneant way of cooking in the army, we have nothing but sheet iron kettles made like an ash can & we have what we call mess pans made of sheet iron, cant cook any rice nor beans with burning it & so on. We have a very pleasent place to camp, we are in a nice little grove onn the bank of the Little Harpath river which makes it handy for bathing & a larg spring & with good water to use, & the rail road runing in front of our camp about 10 rods from my tent, we may stay here some time & I have a good notion to have you send me something good, you know what I want, but I think I will wait a few days, for it has been hinted that we shall go to Louisville, yet I dont know any thing about it. I hope shall & stay a spell, I expect to see some very warm weather way down here, the sun is uncomfortable warm today, The cars are somming & I will go & see if there is a letter for me before I write any more. March 18th I received no letter yesterday & was much disappointed, it has been some time since I have hurd from you & I am very anxious to her from you & the rest of the family it seems as though I write a great many letters & get few in return. I sent to you by Fred Nelson a little package for you to save for me, I would be very glad of some newspapers to read, I have nothiing to read, & have no money to buy the daly, & if I had I cannot afford to pay 10c a peice for papers, cant you afford to send me one paper a week, which will cost you only one cent a peper or do 2 up togeather, I want something to buisey myself with time passes very slow. I understand that the rebels have vackuated Vixburg & consentrating their forces on Rosencrans & try to flank him, this let them do, the Old Rose has a trap set for them, General Grainger makes a stand at Franklin & is fortifing there, some large seage guns pass here on the cars yesterday & you have no idea how savage they look, when they speek it sounds worst than any thunder you ever hurd, it fairly jars the earth, they are from 10 to 12 ft long & almost large enough to stick my hand in, at our last battle the rebs had one & the report could be distinguished above all the rest they are used for long distance with a slug ball & with great acricy. shell are used in them to. I dont like to be near them when fired, it seems as though they would tair a man a to peaces, I shall write a letter to father & to all of my christian friends in Otsego & now I will draw your letter to a close, you can see by this letter that I am out of any thing to write about & I dont duppose it will be very interesting to you but it is the that I can do, You may say to those who has friends in captivity that it will do no good to write to them untill they are within our lines again that seems hard but it can not be helped, we are in hops that they will soon be paroled or exchanged, we dont here from them any more only that they are at Shelbyville Tenn. Pleas all write as soon as convieneant, I have some notion to join the 1st Mich Engineers formaly called the Fusileers as a macanic to get $14 a month, a building bridges &c. to get better liveing. Truly yours Charley Millie

Headquarters, Camp at Brentwood Company B
19th Mich. Inft. March, Wed. 18th 1863,

Dear Father & to the Baptist Church in Otsego, Mich.

Dearly beloved Bretheren

In the midst of the trials and privations by which I am surrounded here My heart often turns back to the old home circle and the christian associations by which it was surrounded and if I say I sometimes sigh for the society of my christian bretheren, now will wonder who have experienced what it is to be a soldier and surrounded by the influences that prevade an army, Particularly does the christian man remember his home when the Sabbath appears In the army the Sabbath is an accident whether on the march or in camp it matters little there are a thousand things which grate harshly on the feelings of a man who has been accustomed to regard this day as Sacred to God and the purposes of religious improvements. It is not necessary to suppose that military commanders seek to and require Subordinates to violate the day, there are many things pretaning to the security and conduct of an army in an enemy country which must be done on the Sabath as well as any other day such as standing on guard, doing picket duty and often the obtaining of supplies for subsistence, and if there is added to this the annoyance to good men occasioned by cursing and swareing card playing and other vices there is surely enough to cause the man whos heart is set on things above to turn away and cry for strength from him who is able to save. But amid all these trying scenes dear bretheren I am trying to live as a christian ought to live, To let my light so shine that others seeing my good work may glorify our Father in heaven and while I am thus laboring and striving I rejoice to feel an assurance that I still live in the simpathies & prayers of the church, Suffer me still to hope that you will still pour out your earnest petitions at the Throne of the heavenly grace that I may never bring a reproach upon that sacred name whereby we have been called. By the recent disastrous battle of Thomsons Station Near Spring Hill Tennessee in which about 475 of the officers and men of our Regiment were made prisoners many of those whose companionship I prized have been torn away and he who knows the end from the beginning can only tell when we shall be reunited yet still I shall press on hoping to rejoin them and the friends in my far off, but much loved home on these lower shores. But if the master should otherwise decree if amidst these changes of earth I or the friends so dear should fall to rise no more in time, I still will join those faithful ones where /sickness & sorrow {crossed out} toil and trial--wars and rumors of wars where sickness and sorrow and sin and death will never come, there my well beloved bretheren I hope to meet you and indulging this hope my constant prayers shall be for yours prosperity and success in your christian calling,

I am Dearly beloved, yours for the caus of Christ

Charles H. Prentiss

Dear Father

you may read this to the church if you pleas, so they may know my thoughs and mind as a christian.

Headquarters Camp Brentwood,
Company B. Mar, 23rd 1863,

My Dearley Beloved Wife

Yours of the O it does not come yet, I am ansiously looking for a letter from you & it dont come. I am somewhat inclined to think you are sick or your letters get miscarried, I here a great deal of the Diptheria in your section & you spoke of haveing a very sore throat, leads me to mistrust that you have it. But I hope not, I hope that we may be spaired untill we meet again & live in a quiet little home that we have toiled so hard to get. I have nothing new to tell you, yet evry thing seems to be quiet about here. Dont here anything of the boys yet, I dont want you to believe anything you here in the newspapers, we have had quite a nomber of papers & evry one have lied about the battle of Tompson station, The second day after battle we detailed 2 men from each company in each regiment, went out on the battle field & dug up evry man that was burried & found but one man from our Reg. & he is from Co. C. You have undoubtly hurd some awful stories about that battle & what you here differant from that I tell you is false, one of the boys of Co. E. came in the day of the battle in great excitement & says that he saw 6 men fall from on his right hand & swore by all that was good & great that he saw one half of the regiment fall, when he was not in the fight atall, the cowardly scamp ran when he hurd the first gun fired, now if hhe is a good righter or composer & send it to some editor & have it published, many a poor womans heart will be broken, Our paroled prisenors say that they are used well & full as well as we use their prisenors, It is true that we know not who is wonded & if they wonded they used them as well as we use our own wonded so they are as well off their as they would be here & better off for they have no guard nor pickit duty to do nor driling. Now I beg of you all, friends & relations not to borrow so nor morn untill you know for certin that they are suffering or dead, to be sure they are deprived of the privilage of convercing with their friends. That is very bad, to keep their friends in suspence. Now I beg you not to borrow any trouble about me, as long as I am live & well & you can here from me dont feel alarmed, we have garrilla bands prowling about us, what of that, They dont scair me any, we are safe where we are located & the way we manage it is purfictly safe. They cant get in upon us before we know it & have time to get in the stockade, With 200 men we could hold back & fight & whip 4,000 of infantry or caverly or mounted cavelry. This is the ground plan of the stockade {drawing of a square with a gun tower on each corner} this about 100 ft squair built of logs set up end ways 12 ft high above the ground 3 ft in the ground & a good trench on the out side 3 1/2 ft deep, we have imminition enough to fight a week. their is a small port hole in each log, just large enough to stick the musle of the gun through so you can see how safe we are situated, And standing picket is rather dangerous so some would think, there is the place to test a good soldier you can pick out the cowards there, some will get scarte at near nothing, we sometimes have a little fun a scareing the collard people, I dont suppose you believe all that Fred Nelson says do you, we all call him our secesh, allways on the of side, allways telling some big yarn about the rebs &c. dont believe him, he told you some lies when he was home before & I am afraid he will tell you some more. I went out with a forageing train last Thursday to get hay & corn &c. I saw on my way lots of peach trees in blossom, evry thing looks like spring if you dont believe it I will send you a couple of blossoms, went out 7 miles & found an old reb way back in the woods & found corn fodder & 2 stacks of oats, so we got what we wanted, found a crib of corn with 2,000 husk in it, went back the next day & got 8 or 10 loads of corn, found lots hams, the hams & sholders from 25 hogs, we naturely helped ourselves to the hams & some sauseges put up in the big guts of a hog I should think they are as large as your arm, The poor old fellow could only stand on his door steps & see us d---d yankees carring off there stuff, & they dare not say a word, The way we do is to take from 5 to 100 teems, & on an everage about 8 armed men to a teem, & 1 or 2 peices of artilery then waid in as Uncle Henry says, when we leave their primices you can make up your mind there is not much left, we allso found some 4 or 500 bush. of potatoes, I recken that I got some of them, I eat at the first meal about 27 I dont want you to think that I am a hog but I could not help it, I some thought of sending some to Father & Geo. for seed. I could send you 10 or 12 in a letter & would not cost more than 3c I think they would be an improvement to cross them with farmers delight potatoe, they will everage in size as large as a good size cherry. The largest one I found was as large as a small size blackwallnut with the shuck off, I suffer very severely for the want of sleep, a setting up nights a pealing these potatoes, dont take me as I say but as I mean, These potatoes are strong enough to so that 3 or 4 might carry a man, O yes I am in the capt tent a watching a hen that I have in oven to bake, (the Capt. has a small stove) came into camp That wont go bad, will it; I wish you would come over & help eat it. If I dont have but little I am willing to divide, we do have a little fun to mix in with our hardships after all the fus, so dont you morn to much, I am getting a head of my story, when we drive up to a rebels premices we through out our pickets all around the barns stacks & teems untill we get loaded then march of in good order, that's the way we do it, Uncle Sam dont have to support us all the time you see dont you, the rebel living is the best some dinner, I grow poor on Uncle Sams living & fat on rebel living, so on an everage I fair about middling, I have not made up my mind to have you send meany things to eat yet, when I do John Duel will go in with me, he is my chum now & a good fellow he is to, Dont suppose you are acquainted with Mrs Duel, we may go farther north after a while, that the way the thing looks now. March 24th Tuesday morning, Now I think I will finnish up my letter, I am out of stuff to write & dont know as I shall find enough to fill out my sheet, I dont like to send off white paper, & dont like to receive white paper, I dont mean to complain of you. I think you do first rare, The cars just passed here with 2 batteries or 16 large guns, going to Franklin we expect a big fight before long, soommer the quicker, The rebs will get most awfully whiped I have no mail up to this date, I begin to feel bad about it, I must draw my letter to a close & mail it, Pleas write soon & often you will here from me soon again, My Love to you my dear wife, & all the rest From Your affectionate Husband Charley To Millie Direct to Nashville as before

City Point Va, Sunday morning Ar 12th 1863

My Dear Wife,

Hallo! Here I am again right side up as useal, Bin down in Dixey, See lots of um, Look like hogs, Bin a prisener I recon, Had a good time down dar, Seen lots yaller gals, Dont suit me, Had a long ride Jeffs expence, clear from Tallahoma to Richmond & to City Pint, the latter place lays in ruins where old Mc. gave it hail Columba bout a year ago, The fact of the buisness you know on the morning of the 25 of March 2,500 Texican Rangers & a battery, attacted & took us all prisoners (Commander Gen. Forest) or gobbled us up, wal thats nothing, had a good time any how, Ill tell you all about it some time, Lost one of my red shirts & my piller that's mean, I am well & have been well scince you hurd from me before, tuf as a knot, got so that I can march 48 hours night & day without rest & food, aint I tuff, Lots more just like me, 750 I recken, right smart hall at that, 210 of the 19th Mich. the ballance of 750 are the 22nd Wis, never mind that, I tell you the rest some day, when I got time I am lousy now & have something to do, that I dont care anything about, mark my word rebeldom is a bout played out, When 5,000 woman rase in a mass & threten to hang Jeff. Davis if he dont give them something to eat, Yes, their's Longstreet you have hurd of him, haint you? has sent to Jeff. if he dont provide some provisions for his army he will give up his command, sent in 3 times, let her rip, who cares, its all working right, I been to Richmond, wrode in a stilish hog car, O, I dident know but you would like to here from me, So I thought I would write a word or 2 before the rebs get another clip at me, but couldent hit, rather nerves I recken, I shant tell what I done, I dont expect to here from you untill I am located some where, perhaps in Detroit Darn the rebels, take evry thing that a man has got even to a needle down to his blanket & overcoat, never mind, I pay um. Needles are only worth 5c a peice with them & matches a penny a peice, one dollar greenback is worth only 5, confederate scrip, they have no confidence in their own money, I tell you what it is, I never had the stars & strips look so good to me as when it did when I came to city point & looked way out in the river & saw the Old boat standing & waiting for us with the stars & strips at one end & the white flag at the other, seem to becken to us to come & I will receive you from bondag, The James River is about 3 miles wide at City Point, we are going from here to Ft. Monroe, I am writing this letter on board of our boat while we are a weighting for the train to come in with some more of our prisenors, & will mail it the first opportunity, so you may here from your old man, O, how I want to here from you, I dont know whether you are dead or live, but I hope this will find you all right. we have not found the other boys yet, but find their names writen in the prisons where we stop, I presume you have hurd from Dave, I think he is all right Dont borrow any trouble Dear Wife for all is right now, you must not expect a long letter from me now, I will make it up some other time, April, 14ᵗʰ 63 Today we arrived at Annapolis Maryland, from the Chesapeek Bay, came up on the black hawk, we was gladly received, got a good chance to wash, the first good wash we have got scince we were taken, drew a suit of cloth throughout, got a good supper, then I finnish this letter, we shall (we think) leave for the West the last of this week, You will here from me soon again I still remain your True & affectionate Husband C.H. Prentiss Prisenor of War

Annapolis, April 22ⁿᵈ 1863

My Dear Lonely Wife,

I again improve this opportunity to drop you a few lines to let you know my whereabouts, We still remain at Annapolis waiting for transpotation West, I dont think that we shall remain here long, we expect to start for camp chace, Ohio, evry day, My health is good with the exception of a head cold & a sore mouth, my cold I got on my travels through Dixey, after the rebs took away Over Coat & Blanket, When we lost these we suffered very much with cold, I think it will be the best way for me to coppy from my Diary. I shall not be able to get it all in one letter, so I shall make more of it, I have no stamps to pay my postag, nor any thing els, except I have a new suit of cloths, these cost me nothing, I will commence back to Mar 23. Brentwood Mar. Mon. 23ʳᵈ 1863. Up this morning at 5, I stayed in my tent most all day, not very well to day, commenced to write a letter to wife, this afternoon, went to cook a chicken by the Capt. cook stove & done some writing their, We drew soft bread this evening. We drew 53 loves for 16 men The weather is cloudy & rainy, rained quite hard this afternoon & most all night. Brentwood Mar. Tues 24th 1863, Feel perty well, Up this morning at 5, washed & combed, eat breakfast, then help draw 5 days rations, 2 batterys passed here on the cars going to Franklin where we expect a big fight their before long, I finnished & mailed a letter to wife. I am derailed to act as corporal of the picket to night I stand the latter part of the night from 12 to 5, Brentwood, Mar. Wed, 25th 1863, This morning early a negro sliped into our Camp informing us that the rebels were taring up the R.R. track south of our camp & prepareing to attact us soon we made ready for them, at day light we could see that we were surrounded on evry side by Gen. Forest with 4 Brigades of Texicans Rangers & had a battry planted on a hill one mile south of camp which we could do nothing with at that distance with our guns, if they had kept away their battery we could have fought them a week with perfect safty, but the commenced throughing shells at us, so we knew of no better way to save our lives than to surrender, when they got a good ready commenced closeing on all sids, the same time sending in a flag of truice & demanded a noncondisitial surrender, we hesatated a spell, they shot shell amungst us which struck a tree in the rear of my tent & bursted, done no harm, it came so clost to me that I could feel his breath, This brought the surrender to a close, at the same time we were exchanging shots on the East side of camp in good earnest. A part of their forcers went to Brentwood Station attacted & took about 450 men of the 22nd Wis, started them off then made an actact on us at 7, they would not give me time to eat my breakfast. after the surrender was desided they came in llike so many hungry & commenced to plunder camp, our tents & our knapsacks &&c. We layed down arms & got ready for the march, while the rebels set fire to our tents & the R.R. Bridg the bridg did not burn a train passed over it the same day, We are now prisoners of war, I filled my haversack with bread, The only one of the Co. so you see that did not last long, my canteen with water, took my blankets & a few little notions (most of which I lost on the way) from my haversack, we formed a line then were marched off through the wood, crost fields, & over hills, in a westward direction, They also took our tram which was loaded up last night with the boys things to be sent home, They felt rich over our guns & amunition (but will see how this came out) we marched about 4 m. where we hawlted to rest, here knapsacks were striped to lighten their loads, After about 6 m. march we came to the Little Harpeth river, This we had to waid, water up to my knees, now I have wet feet, from this on the rest of our marching we all have wet & galded feet, my feet was not so bad as some of the rest but I have a lame knee, 2m. more brings us to the Big Harpeth River, we had to waid this too, water up to our arms, Now we march with wet bodyes, the air quite chilly. When 6 or 7 miles on our journey, The rebs were overtaken by our Cavelry & had a fight, we were under a force march for 4 ms. one man of the 22 Wis gave out & was shot dead on the spot, because he could not run & keep up the way of our men, I dont know how many was killed & wonded, but most all of the rebs were taken prisoners, Gen. Forest acnolagers this was the dearest job that he ever under took, all of our train was retaken by our troops, many of us came very near going for it on this march, after the chace we march untill dark, layed down on the wet ground 2 hours to rest, the night very cold & our cloths wet, & no supper, my 2 loves of bread did not go a great with 20 men through the day, we had eat nothing since last night, At 10 we started again cold, wet & stiff & hungry untill 4 in the morning, here we were permited to lay down in the road & rest untill daylight, The rebs soldiers were very good & kind to us but the officers, woe be unto them if any of us gets our eyes on them, but all are not alike, I overhurd one of the tender harted rebel Capt say I wouldnt be officer of the rear guard for 2 thousand dollars at the same time the tears come in his eyes & saw another rebel soldier cry, they have to fulfill their commands, I cant blame them the soldiers. March, Thur, 26th 1863, At 4 this morning we haulted one hour because the roads are so bad & the night so dark, At 5 this morning as soon as it was light we started again hungry & tired, we traveled all day without any thing to eat, at 3 this afternoon we haulted & got a little bite, a peice of corn dodger about 2 in squir & a peice of raw pork in the same size. here we rested 2 hours, from here we have to march 12 m. to night so lame & tired that we can hardly move our cloths wet & heavy, at 5 off we started again on our march only 12 m. miles more to Duck river, We arrived at Duck River at 1 1/2 mid night set down in the mud on the bank of the river & waited one hour to be furyed acrost, the night was cold, dark, & foggy & we was all swetty warm & wet, Duck River, Mar. Fri. 27th 1863. At 3 this morning we got acrost & found some good fires which seemed good to us, here I made me a cup of Tea, (some that I sliped into my pocket before we started) layed down by the fire & slept untill day light, then I got up & washed up, rosted me an ear of corn & eat it which done me much good, at 7 we drew another small of corn bread & bacen the same as yesterday, I dont know as I blame them because there is nothing in the country to eat, we had as much as their soldiers to eat, this little ration must last us 2 1/2 hours, we must go to Columbia which is 15 m. we arrived at C. at 5 & here we was imprisoned in an old filthy Court house, hardly fit to put hogs into, here we some expected something to eat but did not untill morning, I planted my self on the dirty floor & slept good untill morning The weather cloudy & chilly. Columbia, Mar Sat 28th 1863, Up this morning in good season & found it very cold, The first thing this morning commenced paroling the 22 Wis, we are so confined that we have to ease ourselves in our rooms & this made it very filthy for us, we had but one meal to eat to day, The ration for 10 men is not more than 3 men could eat at one meal. Weather very cold. Columbia Mar. Sun 29th 1863, we arose early & found it very cold. The first thing this morning the 19th was marched to the parole office in Companies & paroled, it took untill noon & at 2 we drew our little ration again, which was hardly a taist for us, At half past 2 we started on our march to Shelbyville, Marched 10 m, Marched untill dark then camped in the woods, built our camp fires & seated ourselves around, many droped aslepe so tired & wore out, & at 10 we drew a ration of corn meal, (unsifted) & made us 2 corncakes by mixing the meal with cold water, no salt nor any thing els, eat this & curled down & slept untill morning, The corn meal & brand gave most all of us the Dysentery, this helped to weeken us, I will send you a coppy of my Parole,

Parole of Honor, I the undersigned, Prisoner of war, C.H. Prentiss Co. B. 19th Mich Inft. captured at Brentwood Station hereby give my Parole of Honor not to bear arms against the Confederate States or to perform any military or garrison duty whatever, untill regularly exchanged; & farther that I will not divulge anything relative to the position or condition of any of the forces of the Confederate States

Mar 29th 1863   Charles H. Prentiss

Witness J. W. Sims Capt.

This is the shape of the parole made on sunday

Shelbyville, Mar. Mon 30th 1863, Up this morning at 5, Poped some corn to eat through the day, we eat raw corn to say our stumech After a while rations come & had a good supply, the best we have had scince we were captured, We started on our march at 6 1/2, Marched to Farmington, the distance of 15 m. Camped at 3 just through the town, a little Union village, here for the first time we were permited to burn rails, The afternoon &

evening was very stormy, rain & snow, we traveled over some of the roughest & rockyest & mudyest road I ever saw. through a red ceder woods & swamp, We are very tired, sore & lame. Farmington, Mar. Tues 31st 1863. Arose early, got ready for our march, did not rest good last night it being a stormy night, & we had to set up & stand up by the fire & keep revolving to keep warm & dry. We started on our days journey at 5 1/2, we had a very hard days march, the rain & snow last night made the roads very bad, traveled 19 miles to day we passed through Shelbyville at 2 where we expected to take the cars, but was disappointed, at 3 we started on & went 4 m. farther & camped on the bank of a river, went to camp at 5, when we stoped the first thing I done was to drop under a ceder tree while the rest geathered some wood & built a fire, I tell you a man wants to be made of iron to stand such a march, We are bound for Tellehoma, The weather pleasent & very cold nights Near Shelbyville Apr. 1st 1863, Off again at 6. had a very rough & mudy & stony road, going through woods, crost lots & climbing hills & mountains & evry other obsticle you can think of to tire a man out. Arrived at Tallehoma at 2. Marched 18 m. to day, here we found a very strong rebel force, about 40,000. The strongest force they have, We had a very bad camp ground here up on a blekey hill, the wind blew strong & cold all night, we had some green oak brush for fire wood, we suffered much with cold, we drew a ration of corn meal unsifted & made us a little of mush, for supper & bought a cake about one foot squire & paid 10.00 for it, in confederate scrip the cake sweeted with honey, the bees left in, I layed down on the ground & went to sleep in spite of the cold air & wind, we were so tired out. As long as I keep my health I can stand it, but it is a wonder that I am not sick being so exposed as we are. Tallehoma, April Thur. 2nd. 1863. Arose early annd marched to the Provose Marsials office & was striped of our over coats & blankets, then marched to the Depot & joined into some cattle cars & started off for Chattanogs, we started at 7, the train ahead of ours ran off the track a few m. before Andersons station, no damage done, all of their railroads are in very poor condition & they have not a deacent car to ride in, evry thing is rack & ruin, you have no idea of the condition of the South, Rebelism is about done out, The first thing when I meat a rebel is /what {crossed out} doea the north say anything about Piece, Yes, I tell then when you come to our terms. Many a rebel has told me, if they dont give me what I want to eat they dont keep me, They are deserting by hundreds all that we need to do is to hold still & the rebel army will die out in time of it self. I am not at tall sorry that I have been taken a prisoner of war, although I dont want to go through the same again. I have seen a great deal of the cuntry, see the shape of the & the condition of the rebel army &c. we have traveled a thousand miles or less & not cost me nothing. If I could be with you I could tell you better than I can write, I will do the best I can, I have told you just as bad as it is, I have not keep nothing back. Now I want you to take it all in good part & not feel bad. I care nothing about it now. I am alive & well with the exceptions of a hard cold & cankersore mouth, I learn that the rest of our Reg. is at Camp Chace Ohio, we are not exchanged yet, it may be 3 months befoe we shall be, we are all enjoying our selves very well on the banks of Old Chessepeek, we have our liberty to go where we are a mind to. through the City & go fishing. I will draw my letter to a close, My Love to you all Charley to Millie

You may send me a letter & Direct it to C. H. Prentiss Co. B. 19ᵗʰ Mich. Annapolis Md. jist write a little so that I may know how you all are I may not get it any way, Dont know when we shall go from here Charley

Parol Camp Annapolis, Apr, 26, 1863

My Dear Wife

It is a pleasure to me to write to you, & I suppose it is to you to read them, I am very sorry that I am so situated & so far off that it allmost impossable for you to get a letter to me, if I could be located is some place, it would make a differance but now you know that our Reg. is so broken up & scattered that it makes bad work with the letters to soldiers from home, It makes it very unpleasent for me not to here from home, I dont know how you are, weather you are dead or live, but, I have a good notion to say as the rest do, that Ill go home before I am exchanged, but I think that I can get a furlough, to run away, it will cost me so much, & a furlough will not cost me nothing for transpotation, I dont know when we shall get pay, they dont use us very in regard to pay, many of us is suffering for the want of money, I am not contented here I want to get away from here, Annapolis is not such a place as I supposed it was, it is a small stinking place, not as large as Kal, & many of the buildings look as though they were 200 years old, The old State house that Washington resined his commition & made his fairwell speech, the same table, the same chair he set in is here, The brick this building is built of came from England, it all looks old, We have a good place to stay & sleep but our board is not first rate, we have hardly enough to eat, & I think it is better for us while we are laying still & doing no exersise. Wed. mor. Apr. 29th, Now I will try & write a little more. I am perty well to day, we do not get away from here yet, we expect to travel evry day but dont seem to get started yet, I understand that Dave & Mr Hager & others are at their homes, I wish it may be my luck to get home once more, but never mind I will come by & by & perhape to stay, I wish that we will get our pay, I am out of money & stamps & evry thing els. I have to beg my paper & envelops that I send you, We are haveing a very easy time here now, nothing to do to pass away time, Their is some talk of our being mustered for pay soon, I wish I could here from you, if I could I should be much more contented to stay here. I will fill out my sheet from my Diary. Apr. Fri 3rd. Up most all night, so cold we could not sleep a small supply of fuel was furnished us & no clothing to rap up in, so we had to grin & bear it. We stayed on this ground untill 2 a wallowing in the dirt & the wind blew hard, the dust flew so that we could hardly see 2 rods from us, Took the cars at 2 from Chattanuga, 6 or 8 miles out we passed through another tunnell through the mountain. At 5 we arrived at Cleavland. stoped one hour, then on we went, traveled all night, I slept some, we suffered very much with cold, Weather chilly. Knoxville. Apr. Sat. 4th We arrived at Knoxville at 5 this morning. Left the cars went out a little ways from the Depot & camped & cooked ration untill noon. Drew rations of soft bread & fresh beef & bacon. We rosted our meat over the fire on sticks &c. Eat our dinner, then started off at 12 We traveled all this afternoon & all night 110 ms. Bristal Apr. Sun. 5th 1863. we arrived at Bristal this morn at 3 left the cars, laid violent hands on the neighbors woodpiles & built some fires & stayed untill 9 then march out of the City one mile & camped untill morning. The weather pleasent but cold. The night very cold, a hard frost, we stayed up all night by our fires to keep warm, Bristal, April, Mon. 6th 63. We took the cars this morning at 3 from Bristal, suffered much all day with the cold. Our train run very slow cant keep up steem, & got behind the other train 12 hours. Dont have enough to eat, wrode all night Weather cloudy & cold. Linchburg, Apr. Tues 7th Up on the move at the peep of day found ourselves, cold & stiff & hungry wrideing all night, we arrived at Linchburg this morning at 9 1/2 marched to the fair ground one mile distant & stayed untill morning, no transpotation here for us. here we got no sleep so cold, got a small ration again, a ration for 24 men no more than 8 men would eat at one meal. & it has to do us 24 hours, hard bread & bacon, a man of the 22ⁿᵈ Wis. Died on the train last night from exposure & the march, The weather cold but pleasent...I must close my letter I still remain your Dear Husband, you need not write for I dont think I can get a letter from you. good bye Millie from Charlie I here this afternoon that we shall leave here in the morning for the west

Camp Chace, May 5ᵗʰ 1863

My Dearist Wife

I again take this opportunity to inform you my whereabouts. I dont here from you yet & feel very ansious to, it has been a long time scince I have Not scince the 3 of Mar. I hope you are alive & well, this remains unknown to me. We left Annapolis May 1ˢᵗ & arrived at Camp Chace last Sunday evening at 10 here we found but 10 of our Company left all of the rest have taken a French furlow home, some were brought back, Lester & Edward Baird & Vernon Rose was brought back & put in the bull pen & are to be tryed & Court Martial because they had on Civilian cloths on, this is how detected them. The Capt says that nothing will be done with them, the rest of the officers are gone & will be relieved, We have a very nice place to camp, we have shantys, I should think that there is about 1,000 buildings in the camp, first rait water & very good board for Uncle Sam to {unreadable} I suppose you have made lots of maple sugar this spring. I want you to save me a hunk of it how do you all get along O how I wish that I was their & that I would be their if I had the means to get home. I dont feel as though I could walk home. It is possable that we may get our pay before long. if I do you will soon see my face in Otsego. time will soon tell, I have not a cent of money & have not had for a long time, I dont think that Uncle Sam does the fair thing in regard to our pay, their is many families suffering for the want of their pay, I am sorry to have to frank my letters, but we all have to do it, I write you but a short letter this time & will try & do better next time, I am well at preasent, My love to you all, Pleas write as soon as you get this. Direct your mail to Mr. Charles H. Prentiss, Co. G, 4ᵗʰ Parole, Camp Chace Ohio & he will get it. Perhaps I may not get the letter you sent to Annapolis, I am your Dear Husband Charlie to Millie

Camp Chace, May, 10th 1863

Dear Beloved Wife

Once more I take my pen in hand to write you a few lines to inquire after my Companion which I have not hurd from since the 2 or 3 of March, I begin to feel very uneasy or ansious to here from you, When I received your last you sayed that you was haveing a time with your throat, that makes me feel rather uneasy about you, Scince I received you last letter I have mailed 7 letters & no answer has come yet, it makes it bad for me to get your mail because I am moving about so much. I mailed a letter to you May 5th & have no answer yet, I am looking evry day for one, O how I want to here from you, A letter would do so much good, O how I want to see you, that would do me more good, I want to go home & fix up your flower garden, I can see how you all look there at home, if I could only be at home a short time to make you a nice little visit, This is not all, if we all live, I shall see you in less than 4 weeks if I dont get shut up in some bull pen, If I dont draw my pay I shall start out with money & foot it home which is 298 miles from you to me, & beg my way, I never shall go into servis again untill I see you. that is sealed, if they dont give me a furlough I will make a french one. This I dont like to do because then I am considered a deserter, have my pay stoped, & a subject to a punishment,, this I cant help, the boys are leaving very fast, 14 went last night. All of our company has gone but 24. Doct. Bennett is at Detroit a working hard for us, he has persuaded the Gov. to go to Washington to see if he cant get all the Mich. prisoners to his own state, when then furlough home, This we all think will work, he is a going to give a furlough untill we are exchanged, we may be exchanged in 3 months & perhaps not untill 6 months, if I have a furlough my pay goes on at the rate of $13 a month, & those that leav without a permit, pay is stoped & live in of officers & a courtmartial, I dont want to do this if I can get along with it, (to run away) I enjoy my self very well. I have enough to eat & a library to draw books to read. I am well My health is good. The worst of all is I am straped of all, & have no money to help myself, no hankerchief, no towel, no paper only what I beg & no tobac, I have good cloths, Pleas write immedeately Direct your letter this envelope & I will get it. My love to you & all the rest

Charley

how many apple trees are ther alive this spring

{The diary records the "Jack Knife Furlough":}

Camp Chase, May, Mon. 11ᵗʰ 1863 We hear to day that our officers are exchanged & will be with us in a few days & father more that we are exchanged & have no right to go home, Sid & I went out & milked some cows & again this afternoon. The weather very warm & pleasent Co. G 4ᵗʰ Parole drawing clothing this P.M.

Camp Chase Tues 12ᵗʰ 1863 I have a blouse coat, went up to the other camp, The boys 4 of them packed up their cloths & left on foot, Milo Barker & myself got aboard of the train at Columbus with the 33ʳᵈ Ind & arrived at Piqua at 11 P.M. got our lodging in the engin house. A landlord gave us our breakfast

Piqua May Wed 13ᵗʰ 1863 We got up at 5, went to a hotel & their gave us our breakfast free, then went to the cross road station to take the cars to Toledo, The train arrived at 10, got on board with out money, the conductor ordered us off the next station, we got off at Pontiac & footed it Sidney distance 6 m. on the way we stop at an old farmers got a good dinner & gave us 6,00, went on to Sidney We took the cars at 10.15 from S. arrived at Toledo at 3.40 in the morning

{He reported to my Father that when he stopped at one farmhouse for dinner as partial payment, he offered to fix their reed organ. When he opened the organ, he found it had been built by his father.}

Toledo, May, 14ᵗʰ Thur. 1863 This morning the landlord of a saloon gave us our breakfast, Our fair from Sidney to Toledo 7.27. We start for Jackson this A.M. 9.45 I got a ticket for Jackson, payed 3,00 for 2 of us, we started at 9.45, Arrived at Jackson at 12. waited until 2 P.M. got on board of a frait train came to Kal. Charges free, Arrived at Kal. at 10. Stayed at Milo Pierces all night, Weather pleasent.

Kal. May Fri 15th 1863 First thing this morning went to the barber got my hair cut, went back, got my breakfast, got on the stage to Otsego fair 1.00, footed it home, got home at noon & found the folks all well, & glad to see me Took them by surprise, Elder Wolfe was at home to work, the Weather cool & pleasent, Roenna had expressed to me 20.00.

Otsego May, Sat, 16th 1863 Had a good visit with our family, Weather fine but not very warm

{The rest of the month was spent visiting family and friends, doing farm work and getting a new pair of boots.}

Otsego, June, 1st, 1863,

This morning Geo & I went up town, went over to Mr Hager's & got 2 bush of corn, Came back to town got my boots at Mr, Reeds & to pay $5.25 when I am payed by the Govenment, Came home at noon, weather cold & windy

Otsego, June, 3 Wed 1863

This morning at 4 I got up & got ready to leave for Kal. & from there to Camp Chase, Arrived to Otsego at 6, waited about one hour for the Allegan boys when we stered off guns were fired, Arrived in Kal. at 11. Geo. Carried me & others out we left Kal. 12.40 on the cars for Detroit, Arrived in D. at 5 P.M. Stoped at a Hotel & had supper. At 9 this P.M. took the Steemer Morning Star for Cleaveland, The weather warm & pleasent

Cleaveland June, Thur 4th

The Morning Star arived in Cleavland at 4.30 Stoped at the New England Hotel eat breakfast & dinner. At 2.55 this P.M. took the cars for Columbus. Arrived at Columbus at 9 P.M. Marched out of the City one mile took lodging in an old barn, The weather pleasent & warm

Camp Chase, June 5th 1863,

This morning we started on our march to camp 3 1/2 miles at 6 this A.M. & arrived safe in camp chase & found evry thing all right, Commenced writing a letter to wife. Batalion drill this P.M. The first we have had in 4 months. The weather warm. This evening went to the Capt. tent & had a good sing with Hubbard & Dave & others. The number of miles we have traveled scince I enlisted is 3245

Head Quarters Camp Chace June 5 1863

My Dear Wife,

Here it goes again, A writing as useal, a notion that we soldiers have & a way that we have to tell our stories. We arrived here this morning safe & well, We started from Kal. at 12,40 M Arrived to Detroit at 5,40 P.M. put up at the Hotell, had a good supper, at 9 evening took the boat for Cleaveland got a good bed, Arrived at Cleaveland about 6 in the morning, went to the New England Hotel & got breakfast & dinner, Did not leave C. untill 2,15 P.M. Arrived at Columbus 8,55, marched out of the City about one mile, took up lodging in an old barn, Then this morning early we started for Camp. After looking around a while I run againnst Capt Bassett the sneeking coward, & he looks as sneeking as he feels, The report is that he has got to Tenn. for trial, On arriving here I find the Camp as full of rheumers as ever, The talk is to day that we start for Nashvill next Monday, but I dont believe it. Dont know whether we shall draw pay before we go or not. I think we shall, The boys will get a furlough home that have not been, so the talk is, I notice that Crops & vegitation is not so forward here as in Mich. had a pleasent time on our journey. I have sent to the city for that money by Capt Duffee & will get it this evening, I will not trouble you with a long letter this time, you may not write untill you hear from me again. I found the Baird boys & Vernon Rose all right. Sat. Morning 6 I will close my letter. Capt. D. did not get that money because I did send an order. I am going Monday to the city & will get. I think that we shall not leave monday. The prospects is good for pay before we leave here, perhaps to day, I have no news to write you. My Love to all, Be patiant Dear Wife, you will see me again before many months, It is hard to be sepperated from each other so much. My eyes are about the same as when we left home, I will send you that money as soon as I get it. I still remain your Dear Husband Charley

Camp Chase, June 7th 1863

My Dear Companion

   Seeing that I have nothing els to do to pass away time this pleasent Sabeth evening I thought that I would take my portfolio & go to some still place & compose a few lines to a sad & lonely heart that is far away from me, morning the absence of a Dear companion that is in the army who is exposed to danger & liable to be taken away any time, a fighting for sweet liberty which we hope to gain in a short time as I think that evrything bids fair for it now, but it is sad to think of the thousands that is slautered by the hand of the enemy & taken away in their wickedness, useing the worst profain language that can be thought of while standing in front of the cannons mouth & in the very jaws of death, Why it is so I cannot tell, I am sorry to see it. They must answer for their own sins, I shall try & do my duty, You can set your heart at rest that that is not my way of liveing in this wicked world of sin all though I may not do as I aught. It is dark to write & I must stop, June 9th Yesterday I got that money, & while there I hurd that we had marching orders to Nashville I suppose, any way we are on our way to Louisville, Yesterday noon we started for the City & soon as we got their we received our pay for 4 months only ($52.) I enclosed $55 in an envelope, & sent to you, Sent to B. Ballou by Express, in the evening took the cars to Cin, & arrived in Cin. 2,30 in the morning then marched to the boat & got aboard just day brake, Started down the river about 7 The boat trembles so that I will not attempt to write much also so much confution that it is almost impossable to write, I would like to have you write as soon as conveienant, & direct your letters to Louisville Co. B. 19 Mich. Inft. My health is good, I weigh 171 lbs, My eyes are better, We have very warm dry weather here, The health of the Reg. is good, About all of our Co. is sprawled out on the floor asleep, The Otsego Boys are all right, The Col. will try & give all of the boys a furlough that has not been, he will do all he can, My Love to all, I still remain your Dear Husband Charley To Millie

   Onward to victory

Nashville, June 12th 1863.

My Dear Wife

I again take this opportunity to pen you a few lines to let you know my whereabouts. I suppose it will be a pleasure to you to know where I am. We left Louisvill night before last by Rail Road & Arrived here (Nashville) yesterday at 4 P.M. & found evry thing looking just as it use to, aplenty of Soldiers, Oficers, horses, mules, waggons, cannons, & evry thing els belonging to war. It all looks natural, but I have got tired of seeing them, if I ever get out of this scrape Ill try & keep out, allthough evry thing looks encourageing on our part at the preasent time, The rebs begin to own up the corn, (or whiped if you are a mind to call it so) It is reported here that we have taken Vixburg in the Louisville Journal, if this is so, It is a death blow for the Southern Confedercy, I hope & pray that it may be so. O! the rebels must fall, their time is drawing near all though they will hold out to the last, Sat. Morning 12. While I was writing yesterday we were ordered to move out of the City 1/2 mile & drew our guns & harness & tents. We have camped here & I think by what the Lieut. Col. says that we shall remain here a week or tow. It is generly supposed that we shall remain here a long time & let some other Reg. go on. it takes a larg amount of troops to hold the place, Partys of Garrillies are scouting through the contry all the time, there has been another fight in Franklin & the rebels got badly whiped, they are getting whiped {at (crossed out)} evry time now & I hope {it (crossed out)} we shall continue to do so. I noticed that the people are doing their harvisting along the road. I say now as I have said before that I would not take a farm here as a gift, on the best & handsomeist farmes, their wheat the straw is but or not more than a foot long, also oats all headed out is not more 10 to 12 inches tall, & evry thing els in the same propotion, Cherries, straw berries are are ripe, In regard to our trip down here & our living the past week, we have faired no better than we did in rebeldom, The cars that we had from Louisville to Nashville, we had cattle cars not cleaned out & no seets, Never mind that, its all on the account of the war, Who wouldent be a soldier! I suppose that you have got the money I sent you ($55.) by this time, Pleas pay Mr. Read $5.25 for my boots, I think that we shall draw pay again the first of July. that is our next pay day. Rebels are being marched in here evry day, States Prison convic's are put to work on our fortifications. I am glad to see that, Our Camp is clost to the state prison, I think now that it is doubtful that the boys will get home. I dont know as I can get Geo. any shirts or not, I dont get any for myself yet, I have but one shirt now & care about any more I dont want to lug them about, the lighter my load the better it is for me, when I want to wash this one I can put on my blous. I forgot to tell you that the dame kind of guns that we had before, the Enfield improved, the best that is made, We are all well. My health is good, with the exceptions of a cold that I got by runing around barefooted in Louisville I have to write of any importance & I will close. I had a good old time a reading letters when I got here, there was 4 letters & 2 papers here for me, the one with the tea, I am a going to drink some of it to day One of the letters is from Uncle Lauren Whitman & the rest from home, My love to you all Charlie to Millie

Direct your mail to Co. B. 19th Mich Inft. Nashville via Louisville.

Franklin, June, 19th 1863

My Dear Wife

A few words with you now in regard to my valice, I have sent it home to you in B. Ballou's name. The charges are payed on it, I have sent in it my rubber B. Cap, Dress Coat, 2 Books, A likeness for Dagget, & a case with out a likeness, A satchel & 2 other garments for John Duel, The Reg. has drawn new rubber Blankets is why I send mine home, Cap & Coat we have no use for this hot weather One of the books, Peter Gorden sends to Mr Sheperd, The other is one that I had a reading when we left Camp Chase & had no time to return it. I thought I would keep it rather than to lose it, I have not got any Coffee yet to send you, There is a place in that case for your picture, how do you like it. We started yesterday morning from Nashville at 5 oclock & came to Franklin (our old stomping ground) got here at 5 P.M. here we find quite a larg force dont know how many, but I think 10,000 inftry & a considerable of cavelry. Dear Wife I have but little time to write now, but will try & do better some other time, we are all well, we have very hot weather. My Love to you Charlie

Direct you mail to Co. B. 19th Mich Inft, Franklin, C.

Franklin June 21st 1863

My Dear Lonely Wife

It is with pleasure that I take my seat on the ground to scribble you a few lines to let you know my whereabouts & to give you some hints of our shape & condition, We have got around the gool, we are now when we left off, It look here just as it use to with the exceptions of the forts & fortifications & brest works they are numerous & strong, the amount of forces I cant tell, the troops are scattered so. We have a plenty of guns, amnition & Commissary we are ready to meet the enemy 30,000 strong. We have 3 forts on 3 differant hills where we can command 6 miles each way from us any where within rifle shot of these forts the trees are fell the tops from us, so that it impossable for them to get to us. One company of men could slauter a Reg. before one of them could get to us from behind our brest works. I have no feers of being taken again while we remain here, & I think that we shall stay here a long time, Our Col. has been promoted to a Gen. & has command of this Post, & Major Shafter is our Col. We also have a signal Coar at this place, we can hand the news to Murfreesboro in a few moments, In the day time we signal with flags which can be seen at Tryune distance 15 miles east of us, Nights we use lights for Signals, a certain motion of the flag or light means a word or centance, So you see that we can get word from Roseacrans in a short time, when he is 34 miles from us, & we know the enemys movement all the time, At Tryune we expect a big fight we have a large force there. Mr Baker is at that place. All the forces here have to get up in the morning at 3 oclock & form a line of battle & stand untill daylight for this is the attact will be made, when in this shape we are ready for them, We have scouts & pickets out day & night all the time on the watch, If they get the start of old Rosea, they will have to be right smart he know all about his whole army all the time & what shape there are in by these signals both night & day. Our Cavelry pickets had a skirmish last Thur. evening, killed one of ours & wonded one, did not here what was done on the other side, It is a hard matter for me to think up enough to fill my sheet, for I have no news to tell you, We are haveing some of the warmist weather I ever saw. It does seem as though I should wilt down when I go out of the shade, Our camp ground is in a nice cool grove, & we have nothing to do through the heat of the day only to eat & lay in the shade, when it gets a little cool we go out & drill about one & have dress parade, so we can get along with the heat very well, we draw new soft bread evry day & have very good living,

& we have a first rate spring of water. We have a new kind of tents, they are what we call the dog tent, we carry them in our knapsacks, each man has one, there are a peice of canvis about 4 1/2 ft squair, 2 men sleep to geather, we just button the 2 to geather, set up our guns to rase the center & stake the bottoms to the ground when they are up they are the shap of a roof with the gable ends nocked out when it rains we button on our rubbers, each tent weighs but one pound I call it a nice arrangement for hot weather, It is much healther for 2 to sleep in one of these open tents, than to have 18 men in one tite sibly tent It warm enough in one of the siblys to almost smother a person with 18 men a breathing & in these we breath freash air all the time, we go in to them on hands & knees, we set them clost togeather so that we raise them up. thus & make a pleasent thing of it,--My eyes are about the same as when I left home. My health is very good with the exceptions of the Dysentary, which is caused by changeing water. Have you got that money yet, I have not received a letter from you yet & feel very ansious to here from you. I dont suppose that you have the trunk yet. All the rest of the boys are well. Now Dear Wife dont feel overmuch about me for I am doing well & feel safe, we are not agoing to have any hard marching to do. be as cheerful as you can for I expect to see you again before long Mr Hager has had his possition of Orderly Sargint, John Duel has that place & does well. I here from the Nashville paper the rebs begin to whine at Vixburg becaus they have to live on 1/4 rations & that Grant has give the enemy in his rear a good dressing out. I here to that Lee has made a brake up in Maryland, that is nothing very discoring, they will get caut in their own trap. I think of nothing more now, write often From your Dear Husband Charlie

Murfreesboro June 27th 1863

My Dearest & True Companion
Dispair thou not, droop not thy wing,
How ere dark thy fortune are,
Beyone the desert is a spring,
Behind the Cloud a Star.
C.H.P.
You are my true and honorable Wife!
As dear to me, as are the ruddy drops
That visit my sad heart.

Yours of the 14th came to hand a few minutes after I mailed your last & was glad to here from home once more, that letter found me at Franklin & now I am in Murfreesboro a weighting for further orders, When I wrote you last we expected to stay in Franklin, but I find that a soldier dont know to day where he will be tomorrow, that it the case with me, I am enjoying myself as well as I can under the circumstances, We came Franklin last Tuesday to Tryune, We arrived here last evening, so you see we have been scense Wed. noon coming here, we were guarding a small train through to M. some 520 waggons with supplies for Roses small army. I wish I could tell how much of an army he has but I cant, he is on the advance evry day, & is scattering the rebels in evry direction, A dispatch was brought us yesterday that Vixburg has fallen with 40,000 prisoners. I am affraid this is not true, I hope it is, We have trains of supplies that is 31 miles long. The train that we was with was over 12 miles long including the Cavelry & Infty, 2 Reg. of Cav. & 3 regiments. The cavelry would be all through the woods & fields a scouting all the time, both night & day, The first day we came only 3 miles, the roads was so rocky & mudy, It rained about all the time so you see that we was not marched very hard Such a road I never saw I could not tell you how bad it was, When we left Tryune, we burned 300 boxes of hard bread & something over 500 barrels of Beens, rice, hominy, some 2,500 bushels of corn, Why we done this is because we wanted the troops at Tryune to guard the train & did not have waggons enough to bring it along. Such a distruction of property you cant imagin, & I cant discrib it to you, Day before yesterday the battle commenced, our right wing drove back the rebels & whiped them bad. the rebs charged on the Lomis Battery 3 times 9 men deep, & Lomis was not but a little while a pileing up 500 rebels in front of his Battery, so they had to give it up. When they charge on Lomises battery, they will find that they are barking up the rong tree, There is hundreds of acres here covered with canvis, it is the largest camp ground I have seen yet. I can see tents as far as the eye can reach & the Old Gent. has more with him than there is here. I think that evry thing is working right down here, you will here that old Bradys army is no more. Dear wife, I dair say that you must feel bad to set a lone where we both sat enjoying our selves so well, It must be with a heavy heart that you do so, I can read you feelings better than you imagine, I can only think of it & write which is the only comfort that I take & the thoughts of coming home, We have had some of the warmest weather I ever saw. I am glad that you had such good times to Charlies. You must go again, I am very sorry to hear of Geo. bad luck I did not dream of his being so bad, I hope that it soon get well. Pleas tell me if you got the money & trunk. I suppose you have the sheep sheared by this time, how much wool have you in all, The folks have got their harvisting done, I cant tell you what a sight of corn & other crops has been distroied on my rought through from F. the Cavelry ride up & down comes the fences then from one to two thousand horses riding through then the Infty march over it, so there is not much left when we get by, & to feed all of these horses nights & mules, the old reb has to stay in his hole & dare not peep, if he does, he gits a blue pill, It is reported that Rosecrans has esued an order that the mail must be stoped for 10 days, I hope not, Pleas send me some papers to read, I am well, my eyes are not so bad as they was, give my love to all. kiss Elsie for me. I still remain your Dear Husband Charlie I saw my old friend Harrison Whitlock last evening. I also saw Ames that used to live on Otto place.

CHAPTER 3

JULY – DECEMBER 1863

> Guy's Gap, Head Quarters, Rosencrans Army
> Grangers Division Colburn Brigade, July 4th 1863

My Dear Wife.

It is with difficulty that I write you these few lines. I thought that I could not wait any longer, I will tell you on the start what the matter is of me, A few days ago I sliped down & put my rist out of joint, It is getting along finely, Last Tuesday evening I wint down to the spring to get a canteen of water, & filled my canteen & just started away over some rails that was wet (just had a shower) I stept on one rail that one end of it was elivated both feet steped forward quicker than thought, I fell backwards letting the hole weight of my body on the palm of my right hand acrost another rail, bending my hand back so that it lay on the back of my arm. I set it before I got up & heled it. went to the hospital & had it done up, It was a painfull thing for 24 hours, & now it is doing well. It pains me so I must cut my letter short, I thought that I could not let this 4th Annevercery of our wedding day pass without saying little something to you, I am not fit for duty now. Our Reg. is laying here to keep watch, guard the gap. &c. & guarding a signal core between Murfreesboro & Shelbyvill, Our army is advancing very fast, I am well, It rains evry day. I have not received but one letter from home yet. I am getting anxious. Excuse me to day & in a few days I will get so that I can handle the pen some better, My Love to you. From your Dear Husband, Charlie

Send your mail to Murfreesboro

Scince I have close this letter (not sealed) a sad acciadent happened here in our Reg. 2 of the boys was going through the performance of fiting a duel in fun and not knowing that eather of the guns was loaded, One happened to be loaded, one shot a Corpoal in Co. F. through the right eye, a takeing off the right side of his head & the ball passed on & shot an old rebel citisan in his arm & shattering it bad, so that

- 104 -

amputation will necessary, Another man in Co. E. shot 2 of his off last night to get his discharge. He dont get it so the Doct. says I am well, & doing well & we are out of all danger of the rebs. they are all beyond Tallahoma.

Your Charlie

Guy's Gap, Head Quarters Gen. Rosecrans
Reserve Army Core, Co. B. 19th Mich Inft
July 6th 1863

My Dear Lonely Wife

It is with pleasure that I write to you a few lines again, to let you know how we are geting along away down in Tenn. amungts the rebs, We see lots of rebs but they dont have any arm's, not far from here their a squad of Rebs 500 in No. gave themselves up. And we are comeing in most all the time to give themselves up. Yours of the 21 of June came to hand yesterday & glad was I to here that you are all well. Your letter was just 2 weeks a comeing through, you say you have been to meeting & hurd a good sermon & one poor one, I have none, I have just hurd one prayer by our Chaplin. I would be satesfied if I could here a proper sermon, We are in a heathen land (down here) & I suppose our Chaplin thinks that we must live as heathens, at least we do. If I did not keep a close watch I would not know when the Sabath come. All their was a going on in camp yesterday was card playing & swearing & our Chaplin sitting in his tent smiking his segar's that is all he amounts to. I wish Elder Wolfe could be our Chaplin, I think that he will do some good. It seems to me that Geo. & I are rather unlucy in regard to broken limbs. He has had a little worst time than I have because I have had no broken bones, I am sorry that his ankle is so bad, My rist is gitting very Slow. I can work my fingers but the rist joint is quite stiff yet, it pains me a considerable, I am excused from all dutys & have nothing to do. O how I wish I could be at home untill I get well, Yes untill I make up my mind to enlist again. Ill garrentee that I would wait one spell. We are haveing some unpleasant weather, It rains evry day & rains now. The cross roads are impassable, All the travle is on the pikes which wair like iron. Mr Hager has not come yet & dont here from him, I dont doubt but that Mrs Hager feels very bad, I hope & think this war is on its last legs. Onnly look at the shape of the reble army, look at Port Hudson, Vixburg, Gen. Johnston is calling for help, Braggs army is all torn to peaces & is calling for help, we have taken over 4,000 prisoners from him at Tallahom & is driven back to Chattanoga, & Bragg cant get one of his soldiers acrost the Tenn. River that belongs in this state (Tenn) They swere they wount go out of this state to fight, Yes, Look at Gen. Lee. he is calling for reinforcements, he has got into a nice trap, It is the oppinion of all down here that that was a good move for us to let him go up in their & stir up the Copper Heads. See how quick they raised 50,000 men in Ohio & Penn, I think now that we can just begin to see daylight. Dont you, It is confermed in the Nashville papers that Richmond has falen & that Foster is in their with 50,000 troops, to good to be true, So takeing all these things into consideration that their will soon be many hearts be made glad & a great many will have to morn their lost Companion, lost Father, lost Brother & son that has fell in battle, I hope this may not be your fate, Yesterday I witnessed a very solum funeral of the young man that was shot Sat. An only son of a poor Mother (a widow) The boys tell me that it will kill her. She was most crazy when he enlisted. O what a sad thing this war is, Many a heart made sad, Many a home made desolate, Who can call it back. The only hope is to look beyond this dark world into that Brighter world where there is no wars, no sin. While all is happy forever, God grant that we may all be prepared for that world, then trouble shall cease.

This makes 9 letters that I have writin to you scince I left you last, I have received back 2, I am looking for a letter from Elder Wolf, I wish some others would write, Dont you give your selves any uneasyness about me. I can get along very well. I dont suffer much even if I do go hungry once in a while that is not so bad as it would be to lay on a sick bed perhaps with a leg off or an arm or a wond in the head, or sick with some feaver, I dont mean to complain as long as I am well, I have not suffered any yet only with my rist & that is getting along finely, I think the sheep is doing very well, 6 ¼ lbs is a good yeald. Well how did you enjoy going to Battle Creek, I wish that I could have gone with you. I never shall forget the time we had a year ago, the Association held in Otsego, The tea you sent me in that news paper was not very strong. I have used it up & would be glad of some more. Tea is something that cannot be got here & it wont do for me to drink so much coffee, & it wont do to drink but little water & if I could have a little tea to drink once in a while it does my good when on a tiresome march, When we left Murfreesboro we through away a half bushel of good coffee, how I wished I could send it home, I could not. We are not allowed to send anything home from here, About 10 minuts the mail came in, & what do you suppose I got. It was a letter from you & Geo. bearing date June 28th & was glad to here from you again, I will write Geo. in a few days, You letter commences by saying, Dear Charlie, We have just finnished Supper, That word "Supper" puts me in mind of something good to eat. O if I could only be there & help you eat supper I would be much happier than to be way down here in this Barbarous country. But never mind it will all come out right, I aint got the blues yet.—I think the fire in Otsego has done some good as well as some damage, I am not sorry to here that Dany's nest is burnt out, & there is more such holes that aught to be burnt out. I would be glad to have Elder Buck write to me, I have writin to him & he dont answer them, I suppose you have got the velice, what did you find in it. My Love to you all. Be of good cheer & be patient.

Write to me very often
Write to me very soon
Letters from dear friends
Are like flower-buds in June
They are affections torches
Lighting of Friendships lamp
Flitting around the heart strings
Like fire flies in the damp
Write to me very often
Write in the joyous morn
Or at the close of evening
When all the day is gone
Then while the star's are beaming
Bright in the azure sky
When through the fading forest
Cold the wild winds sigh
Write to me very often
Letters are links that bind
Truthful hearts to each other
Fettering mind to mind
Giveing to kindly spirits
Lasting & true delight
If you would strengthen friendship
Never forget to write.

From your Husband Charlie
good bye

Direct your mail to Murfreesboro as before C.

Guy's Gap July 9th 1863

My Dear Wife

It is with pleasure that I take this opportunity to inform you my whereabouts & to let you know that I am yet alive & well. My lame hand is getting along slowly so that I can use it a very little, I am laying around & doing nothing & the time seems to pass very slow. My eyes do not get any better, they trouble me much. There is a great many in the rigement that is troubled in the same way, And the itch you hurd me complain of is the ground itch & most evry man is troubled with it. It is caused by being wet so much & laying oon the wet ground, It is nothing very serious but it keeps a man very buisy a scratching. Vernon Rose we left at Franklin sick (not very sick) & have not hurd from scince. Mr P A Hager is at Murfreesboro, I have not seen him yet. Dont know what keeps him their, Dave Anderson is well, John Duel & all the rest of the Otsego, Lieut Lilly came in sick from picket this morning. A part of our Regiment has gone out about 4 miles to get out ties & repare 2 miles of rail road onn the Shelbyville & Tallahoma R.R. will get done today I expect. We are haveing very buisey times now because our regiment is so reduced, the regiment is scatered all over the contry & dont have more than enough for a change of pickeets. I want to ask you what your opinion is in regard to my comeing home by this time, Dont you think that peice will soon come. Our Col. says in 60 days that Peice will be declared. What do you all think, When you here that Vixburg has fallen with 20,000 able bodyed men & 100,000 stand of arms & I dont know how many larg guns, & that Braggs army is scatered to the winds, & that Mead has almost ruined Lee's army by killing & wonding 5,000 & taken 28,000 prisoners & 100 guns, What is the use of the rebels a fifeing. I think they will find that we are enough for them after a while. I begin to think that our hard marching is about done with, & fighting also, It is generly suppose that we shall go any farther South. We shall eather guard this rail road or go back to Murfreesboro & guard them forts & magaseans Gen. Granger has command there now. There is two magazeans there, built under ground. One 30 feet squir & jamed full of powder & amunition. What an explotion that would make if taitched off. I have no news to write you, all that I know about war you here of before I do & there is no use of my writeing it, To day is the first pleasant day that we have had scince we left Franklin, heavy rains evryday & we have been wet most all the time scince. Our little tents are not much protection for us, but it has been warm both night & day. I tell you I am not sorry that I got my boots, The most of the boys have shoes & have suffered with their feet very much. We have had to wade mud most to the top of my boot legs & shoes are not much account, We have lots of blackbarrys some new potatoes, & green apples. The boys go out evry day, strap their gun on their back & pick baries. I presume that there is 5 or 6 bush. brought in evry day. Wal, how do you all get along at home & how does buisness go, I suppose that you are harvisting by this time. The rebs had most all the harvisting done & we have taken care of it, fed it to our mules & horses, Corn is silking out & soon we shall have some green corn to eat I recken, We are fetching in straggling rebs evry day, I guess this will answer this time, my hand begins to pain me & I will draw to a close. Tell Father & Mother to write & all the rest. I dont care what you write if I only get a letter. Be a good girl & be patient untill I come, My Love to you From your affectionate Husband Charlie To Roenna Send to Murfreesboro

Head Quarters of the 19th Mich. Infty.
Vol. Guy's Gap, July, 14th 1863

My Dear Lonely Wife.

Yours of the 4th of July came to hand to day. The first mail that has come to the regiment since the 6th of July, There seems to be a great deal of trouble in getting our mail, There was a larg pile of it came in to day, You had better beleive that I was glad to here from you once more, It has seemed like a month since I hurd from you last, It seems by the countanance of your letter that you are or was a little homesick, But Dear Millie I never have passed such a day as I did on the 4th It was a lonely & solom feeling, I should not have felt worst if I was sentance to be shot, I awoke in the morning with this same feeling, I could not give any reason why I should unless it was the aniverdary of our wedding day, I surely felt very bad, It only lasted that day, I do not doubt that you felt very bad, It was with great effort that I could write you that letter. How thankfull I am that there is a way provided for us to communicate to each other when we are so far apart. If it was with us as it is with the rebels I should give up, if I could not here from my family in 2 years as it has been with many of them, We did not do any fighting on that day, all was quiet on that day. But perhaps many others were fighting for the victories that we all are in sirch of, which I am in hopes to find before long, Evry thing is in our favor & working favorable for the past month, I have not forgotten 4 years ago, nor 2 years ago, nor even one year ago last 4th, My mind frequently is runing over the good times that has passed & gone forever, I dont allow myself to think of it a great deal. It wont do for a soldier unless he wants to make himself miserble, as many do. I find the best way is to look ahead & hope for a better time to come, & keep looking on the bright side, for we all know that it has been dark enough the past 2 years, if it was not for hope the heart would break. I am looking for a good time to come, It is true I may be disappointed There is a chance to be taken down by sickness or be death in a few hours. I feel that life is very uncertain in time of war, yes at all times, I do not fear death.—Little did I think 4 years ago that we should be so widely sepperated & that I should imployed in killing men, but it is so. Your heart is full I know, but look ahead for that world where trouble will seace & the weary at rest, Dispare thou not, droup not thy wing. How ere dark thy fortunes are, Beyond the desert is a spring. Behind the Cloud a star. How true this little verse is, So you have the trunk. You did expect to find me in it, did you? I got a doubble case so that you might get your likeness taken & put in it. The boys all tell me that it was the best picture on the job, I gave one dollar for the picture & the small case then I happen to thhink that would want a double case if I should never come back. I gave one dollar for that. If I dont speak to you there in the picture I will when I come home & that will not be a good while, We all had orders to box up our clothing & send them to Nashvill, but I chose to send mine home. The boys do not expect ever to see theres again. I suppose you know all about John Duel's in the front part, The express charges on the trunk was $3. It will be your best way to hang my clothing out of sight & forget all about me, then I will come in behind you again as I did before, You must go when you can & enjoy yourself as well as you can. Dont give up in dispair but be cherefull & make yourself as happy as you can, that is the way that I have to do. There is a great many things that puts me in mind of home. I think of home evry time I eat my meals. The family prayer time. The Sabeths, &c. They all have a tendancy to direct my mind homeward, We are about starting evening prayr meetings. We have made the efort & gave the Chaplin an invertation, it works well, We have some good christians in our Regiment, Pleas tell Elder Wolfe to write to me & some others of the church. All the mail I get is from you except one. B. Ballou has sent me 2 papers, I am glad to see them. I write him a letter, Do you have good luck with the bees. Do you remember just a year ago the forth what a time we had with bees in the top of the Butternut tree. I do. I do not blame you because I do not get any mail, the fault is out here, it takes a long time for it to get around. Uncle Henry & Laurin does not write yet. I guess that Uncle Henry means to pay me off in my own coin. It is true that Rosecrans army is in motion I think that I have told you about it in my other letter I is very likely that we shall stay here, being that our Division is the reserve core of this army. Gen. Granger has command at Murfreesboro & all through this region. He has promised to let us move over on the rail road to guard that when our men get it in repare through to Tallahoma where we expect to remain perhaps a long time, all though we are liable to be called a way at any time, General Rosecrans head quarters is in Tullahoma & our army is in advance over 30 miles beyond, Tullahoma is the place where the rebels misused us so. where they made us stand in the mud all night on a cold blecky hill with nothing but a few green redoak brush to burn to keep ourselves warm, here is the place where they told me that Old Rosea could not take, & that they was a going up to lake Michigan in less than 6 month. I told them that, we, should be down here in less than 6 month & it has proved true. We took Tullahoma with more than 4,000 prisoners, As I told some of the same men that held us captive a few days ago.

The shoe is on the other foot I never did see men so used up as they were. To gard some of the same men guard them through yankeedom that guarded us through rebeldom. July 15 one oclock P.M. Now I will try & finnish my letter, if you will be patient Braggs army is very badly scattired, he has gone for the Cumberland mountains It is reported here that we hold Chattanooga Our Cavelry cut off his retreat to that place by burning the bridgis a crost the Tennessee river & the last was seen of Braggs army they were climbing rocks & mountains & now U.S. Grant is working his way with a part of his forces in behind him, So on the hole I think that Mr Bragg is in the tights. Droves of pack mules are passing daly with their packsaddles on to carry provision's to the army as they advance in the mountains after Old Bragg. A short time ago Old Bragg pass a centance on one of his men to be shot. the young man grabed up a gun to shoot him &

cut a tassal off his bot, he was instantly shot, A reble deserter says Bragg has to keep 10,000 of his Tennesee in his front to keep them from deserting. He wont get much fight out of men that feel in that way. So you can see what shape our enemy is in. You know the fate of Vixburg & you will know the fate of fort Hudson, & Lee's army is in the tights, also Morgan. I am glad that he has gone up amongst the Copperheads, they want wakeing up a little. It is reported here to day that Morgan & all his forces is captured. This I dont believe yet. You see that you have something to encourage you, Here I have told you worst & the best. I wish you would save me a wing of that Turtle & a slice of beef stake out of him. They say they have nine kinds of meat in them. I dont care if you save me a pigs foot from it, also the tail of a fish &c. I think they will all taist good, Now dont be gready but divide with your old friends. If you want pay for it I will exchange with you & give you some fresh we have good fresh meat 3 times a day. The fresh that we have is what some folks call maggets about ¾ innch long when we take the cover off of the box they jump out, we take the hides of those that we have caught by chargeing bayonet them & make a lassoo, so when they jump above the box we let one of the best & expert men of the company through the lassoo over his head, then all get hold of the end of the roap & start for some good stout tree, he will pull so hard that he will soon choke to death, one or two will make us a good meal if we are not to hogish. some times we are in a hurry & cant wate for them to choke to death so we go at them & stone them to death with our hard bread. That is what makes me so healthy & tuff, I never enjoyed better health in my life. Well I dont know but I hhad better change my subject, I dont want to have you think that I mean to cast a slur on your mud turtle because I call that a good dish & would be glad of some turtle soup myself.—You want me to tell you where Bassett is. We supposed that he runs at home, if he is not at home you may find him hideing himself in some rocky cavern unnone to us all & it is well for him that he is not here. Bassett has a dishonerable discharge from Rosecrans & it is to be published in one of the most influential in your state. The order was on dress paraid to select one of the soldiers from the regiment place thhem in front of the regiment & he (the soldier) was to cut all of the buttons off his coat, cut off his sholdier strraps slit his coat all in strips, brake his swoard then drum him out of camp, that is what would been the matter if he had been here, He is a lucky man. Lieut Hubbard is our Captin John Shafter first Lieut. & Lilly seckend Lieut, We have one of the luxerys that you have at home, that is black burries I eat about 1 qt per day, we will soon have green corn. John Duel says that he did not get all of his things that were in my trunk. he had a sachel 2 pare of drawers & one shirt. I had none, my paper is most full & I must pull for shore. I am well my love to all (get your shair) & writ aggin when convienant Truly your Husband Charlie to Millie

Head Quarters of the 19th Mich. Infnt, Fosterville,
July 21st 1863

It is with interest and

It is with interest and pleasure that I take this opportunity to write to you a few lines. Since I last wrote you, we have moved from Guy's Gap to Fosterville, the distance of three & a half miles. We are a guarding the rail road & on the lookout for guerrillies & rebels &c. We are right amungst the real genuine rebels. Fosterville is a perfect sean of desolation & distruction. There was once some five or six stores & now we use them for stables, hospitals & prison or guard houses. We pass by the dwellings, look in & see the occupents of the house a hard sight to behold. I cant disscribe their looks & feelings, But it is awful, Some of the children perfectly naked & the mothers not much better, hardly clothes enough to cover her person, hardly a chair in the house, an old bed in one corner of the room, not fit for a human being to sleep on, no provisions to live on, the very features of these poor objects denote distress & poverty, These persons that I disscribe to you are the poor class of Union people & their husbands pressed in the confederate army. I shall never complain of the fair & liveing that I have in the army, when I see such poor suffering people as these are. I wish this war would come to a close for the sake of these poor people, The Depot is most all torn to peaces, the watering tank torn down & miles of the track torn up to get the rail used up for horse shoe iron, & so it goes all through the south. Our army has come to a standstill, Bragg is thoroughly roughted & no one knows where he is, It is reported here that Gen Rosecrans & Gen Granger has gone to Washington & Gen. Cobern has gone home on a visit, & evry thing is very quiet just now, It is supposed here that our Generals has gone to help talk up peice. I guess that they are surmising a little to much. I wish it might be so for we all want to go home,--(The cars are just a comeing & I expect to get a letter) Our men brought iin last evening 3 garrillies, that we caught 5 miles from here. one enrolling officer & 2 privits, two horses, 2 guns, they were loaded & caped ready for battle, A Capt of the 33rd Ind. was murdered about 100 rods from our camp last week by a family of rebels, we have caught one that was concerned in it, he is a Lieut, The one that done the deed has escaped, but we think we shall get him, (No letter to day Now I feel disappointed) I write about 3 letters per week & get one once in 2 weeks. Uncle Henry has answered his I received it last thursday the 16th. I have no news to tell you & can hardly compose enough to fill out my sheet. Dave, Mr Sampson J.J. Young, Chas. Southworth & myself wennt out a blackburring yesterday P.M. & brought back ½ bush. We have all the burries /that {crossed out} we want to eat. We allso have fresh beef butchered evry day for the past week, some new potatoes, & occationally some fresh mutten & pork, My health is very good at preasent, my eyes are a great deal better, & my rist is most well. I have had quite a resting spell. I stand guard evry other night now this is all that I have to do, When my rist gets entirely well I shall go out scouting after rebs, this is fun, July 22nd /63 we have good news in the paper this morning, it says that Old John Morgin & all of his forces is captured, I hope that this may be true, if it is we will not be troubled with him any more. He has been a perfect eye sore to us for a long time, I was well satesfied that when I hurd that he had gone into Ind. that he was a goner. We expect to move from here in a day or two to Murfreesboro, Tenn is perty well filtered from rebels. The 10th Ill. came here a little while ago & we shall leave here tomorrow, Some thinks that we shall go to Bolingreen Ky. But this is uncertin. I will tell you when we get to a stoping place, The health of the Regiment is middling good. The main trouble is what we call the camp itch, The Doct. says that it is a small inseck, smaller than a knatt, so small that they are visible to the naked eye, They do poison me very bad, I am in misery most all the time, I wish you would ask Doct. Hopkins what is good to take out the poison, It comes out in blotches, resembleing a flee bite, I think if I could have some kind of a wash, such as you had, or something els I dont care what, any thing to take out the poison. Perhaps you can send me something in a letter or by mail. I dont think it is a humor in my blood, Send it or tell me as soon as you can. Evry one of the regiment is troubled the same as I am, Well. What do you think of the rebellion by this time. I suppose you have hurd all of the news If I come home as the war stops, When will you look for me home. Give me your opinion. As Uncle Henry says the back bone of this rebellion is broken, & so I think. They are to work at Charleston & that will soon have to come, & Grant is a going down to feel of Richmond then whet will the poor Confederacy do, They will have to give it up, Be patient a few months longer all will come out right, I dont think that we shall see any more fighting out this way. Evry thing is safe in the west. I here that rebel Johnston is in a tight place. It seems that the blue bellyed yankees are most to thick for them. Write often Dear Millie, My love to you all. Direct to Murfreesboro.

I am well. From Charlie To Millie

Head Quarters of the 19th Mich. Infty, Fosterville, July 23, 1863

Copperheadism in verse & a reply

Some weeks since some verses were printed in the Pittsfield Sun & coppied in the Boston papers where there intense copperheadism attracted the notic of a lady in that vicinity, who thinking that Uncle Abe ought to have a chance to reply, allthough too busy to do so in person, made herself his Secretary for the nonce, in the verses which we print below prefacing them so that they may be better understood, with the original verses from the Sun.

A Plain Epistle to Uncle Abe,
From the Pittsfield Sun

1st

I have a message, Uncle Abe
For your own private ear,--
As I cant go to Washington
And you will not come here,
I'm forced to put it into type,
With circumspection meet,
As bashful members often print
A speech they dare not speak

2nd

My head is nigh to bursting, Abe,
My very eyeballs throb,
To see what pesky work you've made
About that little job,
Which you & Bill & Horace G.
Agreed so nice to do
In less than 60 days from date
Some twenty months ago

3rd

We gave you heaps of soldiers, Abe,
To help you smite the foe,
A string of warriors that would reach
From here to Mexico.
We pack them on with spades to dig
And trusty guns to shoot,
With haversacks to grace their back
And fifes and drums to boot.

4th

You saw their mighty legions, Abe,
And heard their manly tread
You counted hosts of living men,
Pray, can you count the dead?
Look o'er the broad Potomac, Abe,
Virginia's hills along.
Their wakeful ghosts are beckoning you
Two hundred thousand strong.

5th

We gave you several shillings, Abe,
To pay your little dues.
Enough to buy a dozen shirts,
And several pairs of shoes;

We gave you cattle, horses, mules,
And wagons, full a score,
And several cannon, with a voice
Loud as a bull could roar.

6th

Now what I'm after, Uncle Abe,
Is simply to find out
What you have done with all this 'ere
And what you've been about:
If unto Caesar you have given
All that is his concern,
The Mrs. Caesar wants to know
What you have done with her'n.

7th

I know you're young and handsome, Abe,
And funny as our Poll,
A peer, exalted, great and high,
A ruler seven feet tall
You're big enough, if only smart,
To manage all the gang,
And, though a little green, you'll rise
When you have got the hang.

8th

You told us that the Locos, Abe,
Were rotten to the core,
Because they made so free a use
Of Uncle Samuel's store
Full 60 millions in a year,
Now wasn't it a sin
For Generals to squander thus
The darling people's tin.

9th

Are you not deserving, Abe,
Both gratitude and grub
For having stopped the wicked leak
In Uncle Samuel's tub?
The sage who did this wondrous work
Is fit with saints to sup
It only cost two billions more
To blug the vessel up.

10th

You said the South had ruled us, Abe,
Some fifty years in peace
And that the time had fully come
When their evil reign should cease;
That you were sent to take the helm,
The sinking ship to save,
And put it on another track—
And I really think you have.

11th

You're out of luck entirely, Abe,
The engine's off the track,
The biler's burst, and there you are
A sprawling on your back;
The excise man is at the door
Contractors cry for help
You're blind and stupid, deaf and lame
Nor very well yourself.

12th

Your Cabinet is feeble, Abe,
And dull as any dunce,
And if you had an ounce of brains
You'd ship them off at once.

Send Stanton to the Fejee Isles
Give Welles and Chase the sack.
Swap Halleck for a Hottentot,
And send for little Mac!

13th

Now that's the very thing, Abe,
That makes this din and clatter;
You don't appear to see it, Abe,
And that is what's the matter.
The nigger's in the woodpile, Abe,
As shy as any trout;
You thought the Proclamation, Abe,
Would smoke the weasel out.

14th

I know you tell us, Uncle Abe,
This is a mighty war,
And that the job is rather more
Than what you bargained for,--
That you have done the best you could
To make the rebels rue it,
And if you knew what next to do
You'd go right off and do it.

15th

You want to free the darkies, Abe, At least so I construe it;
The difficulty seems to be
To find out how to do it.
The way, dear Abe, is mighty dark
And bothersome to see;
I fear you'll have to give it up
And let the darkies be.

16th

I tell you what it is, Abe,
The folks begin to think
This colored soup is rather stale

For victuals or for drink;
Our mothers love their absent sons,
Our wives their husbands true,--
But no one cares a mouldy fig
For Cuffy or for you.
Uncle Abe's Answer

1st

I've read your message, Northern friend
As printed in the "Sun"
But what you wanted me to do
I've straight way been and done
I "looked across Potomac waves"
Those ghosts I tried to see,--
They were not "on Virginia's hills
A beckoning" to me.

2nd

Those brave "200,000 men"
I gave to "little Mac"
To the Peninsula they went,--
But he never brought them back.
He marched them off with great display
With music, flags and pomp;
He gave them spades instead of guns
And left them in the swamp.

3rd

I looked a little further off
To see what I could see,
And Rosencrans whipped the rebels will
All down in Tennessee;
I looked a little further off,
And down in New Orleans
Ben Butler served the rebels so
They all know what he means.

4th

I looked to South Carolina, too
And there I saw Dupont
And Hunter, too, make darkies do
The very work they want
So, when I thought the matter out
And cleared my foggy sight,
I found a "nig" could pick and dig
As well as any white.

5th

They've picked and dug and fought and rowed
For rebels well, I see
And now I think it's time they did
A little job for me.
A "darkey's" just as good to stop
A rebel bullet's flight
As our dear sons and brothers' forms
Though not so fair to sight.

6th

I'm bound to put the rebels down
And if my boys can't do it,
They'd better let "the darkies" help
To make the rascals rue it;
I own I've been a little "blind"
In laying up Fremont
And "lame" in keeping back the help
Which my best Generals want.

7th

My Cabinet still suits me well,--
The "Fejee Isles" are far.
And unlike "Toucey" I shall keep
My ship at hand for war.

But when I want a "Hottentot"
I'll write the "Pittsfield Sun"
Perchance the Editor thereof
Can recommend me one.

8th

The war's expense you need not lay,
Oh, Copperheads, on me;
The war itself would not have been
But for your man, J.B.
Had he but stood by Sumpter's band
And hit the rebels hard,
None need have cared a "mouldy fig"
For Lee or Beauregard.

9th

But if my "engine's off the track"
My "biler's busted", too
You'd better lend a hand to help,
And put the matter through.
So, now if my advisors, North,
Wants this great job well done,
They'd better lay their pipes away
And shoulder each a gun.
Uncle Abe
Charles H. Prentiss

Head Quarters of the 19th Mich. Inft.
Murfreesboro, July 28th 1863

My Dear Wife

Your letter of the 19th (mailed the 20th) came to hand the 25th & glad was I to here from you and more. It was about two weeks since I had hurd from you. We have moved to Murfreesboro to stay I expect. We left Fosterville the 23 we started early in the morning so as to travle in the cool of the day. We are haveing some very hot weather now, & freequent thunder showers. Arrived here at 12, when we got here I found that we were perty tired & hot, The distance 14 miles, Co. B. was rear guard. Capt. Hubbard gave us a chance to pick & eat all the blackbarries we wanted. There is hundreds of acres of barries patches & the bushes are just black, there is so many & the largest I ever saw, Tenn. will beat Mich. for barries, When we arrived here we expected them perty good. I suppose that you have seen to go to Nashville or to Louisville, but now I expect that we shall stay here perhaps untill the war closes. I should think so, by the way we are fixing up the camps, Last Sunday we had to pull down all of our tents & lay out streets, dig ditches, dig off all the grass & weeds, sweep the ground all over clean. & arrainge our tents in rows & in good shape, & now we have got as hand some a camp ground as there is in this country. The health of the regiment is not very good at preasent. Capt. Hubbard, & Dave is a considerible under the weather, but not so sick as to be confined to their tents, Dissentary is the trouble. It makes them very weak. I have it very often but soon get over it before it runs me down. A man that is in the army must take a holt & docter himself & not set or lay around & wait for some one to do something for him, It wont do for a man to think of home, mother, wife, or friends when he dont feel just right, There is enough that do & many that sicken & die. I think that Dave is a little homesick, (Dont say anything) & I dont know but Hubbard is. Wm. Mansfield made us a visit the day. He wanted me to go & work in the Gov. sawmill with him, he has the overseeing of mills. Sawing lumber & timber for forts, Magazene, Bridges &c. He wants to sell me a water power in Otsego, at least I commenced on him first, He offers me the old pump shop at the end of the long bridg & a strip of land 20 ft wide & (length) runing from the race to the river & 300 inches of water for $600, (six hundred) & gives me from 3 to 10 years to pay for it. I kinds runs in my noddle that I want a plaining mill & sash & blind & door shop. Evry body that goes into that, makes money & if they can I can. Sargent Hager came to the Reg. last Sat. & last sunday John Hogle & 2 others came. Baker is transfered from the 18th Ohio to the 9th Ohio Battery, He is with our brigade, He is well & looks as tuff as a bear, Friend Duel is well. Quite a number of our company is sick. I am well to middling healthy for me. My rist is not well yet, I can do some light work but cant handle a gun. I dont expect it ever will get strong again so that I can chop or mow or cradle, nor pitch, on account of the weeping scince that is on my rist, late years it has troubled me to chop & now it is much more worst. We have fair living now, draw flower, fresh beef & pork. I call the pork fresh because it is yet alive. We have to tie it up nights, if we dont we cant find it in the morning, the maggets will carry it off. I have learned to day that Rosecrans left this place with about 200,000 men, There is but a few troops here now. 3 Brigads or 12 regiments & one battery & one Batalion of Cavelry. One of Gen. Rosecrans spy's came in yesterday. He has been in the rebel army 6 months. He went to the rebels as a deserter from the Federal army & enlisted in the rebel army & found out all that he could then deserted from them & came home. He says he has good news for Rose. & he says the rebels are worst off than we have any idea of. Before he can say much he has to report to Gen. Rose. I suppose that Old Morgan is captured shure pop. We are haveing good news now a days. Dont seem to have any down backs yet, All seem to be encoraged that the war is soon come to a close. I hope it will. I have an idea that I should like to come home. I expect we shall move our camp tomorrow or the next day nearer the spring where we expect to stay all summer, we are haveing good prayer meetings now. Our Chaplin is allways absent. Seeing that my sheet is most full I shall be obliged to pull for shoer give my love to all of my friends. I would like to have them all write. Tell Addie to drop a few lines some time when she is down to our house & the Doct. too. Friendship & Love. I will sent you these words for safe keeping. I call them perty good, I suppose that you have seen them before. Dont hide them. /If you have {crossed out} I must stop it is getting so dark, From Charlie to Millie

> Head quarters of the 19th Mich
> Infty Murfreesboro Aug Sun 2nd 1863

Dear Father & Mother

I think it your turn to get a letter frrom this child & here it is. Yours of the 17th of March /63 came to hand in time, (not due time) You letter I have to get out evry little while & read it. It is a good letter. It is with much pleasure that I take in reading & writing letters. It is about all the comfort that I take. I wish that I might get as many as I write. I have mailed 21 & received 8. I received two yesterday. One from Roenna & one from Elder Wolfe. They were good letters. I shall answer them soon. It would me good to receive a letter from the church & all of my friends. I will remain the same christian as when I wrote that letter, we are getting finely with our prayer meetings, we have started a prayer meeting & give our Chaplin an invitation to attend, he does not come. He can muster courage enough to once in along while to pedelle a few sunday school papers, & this about all he does for the wicked. we do not look to him for support or example, he is of no account, The Regiment hates him, I wish that Elder Wolfe could be with us to visit our tents, to set & talk to advise us, to set an example, here is the place we want such a man, You must think it is a bad place to put a soldier if a minister of the gospel cannot resist the evels & temptations to which we are exposed evry day. To day is sunday & I dont suppose that one half of the regiment knows it, while I set here & write I can see gambling, Card playing, here swairing of the worst kind & would be drinking if the Company could get it. I shall try to do my duty. It seems as though I could feel the efects of your prayers & of the many friends at their quiet homes. I hope & pray that this cruel war may soon end so that I may enjoy going to meeting with my companion once more. O how pleasent it will seem to get out of this war & have peice restored to us & our country. We have no sunday here, no preaching, A paying a man a heavy salery to preach to us & he keeps his mouth closed. This is all wrong. I want to see you all very much, I want to get out of this & go home about my buisness. As I sit here a writeing the swet drops from my hands for you have no idea how hot it is here. I do not suffer as much with heat here as I did at home. I lay it to wearing wooling clothing. It is much healthyer than cotten clothing. I may go out & drill ½ hour then I can ring a gill of water out of my shirt yet we do not mind it & feel well. (I must postpone writeing until a little cooler) This day the fearful reckoning comes to each & all, We hear amids our peiceful homes the summonds of the conscript drums. The bugle's call.—Dear Father It makes me feel bad to think how I am situated. So far from home, A spending the best part of my life, which will amount to near nothing, A laying around & doing nothing, here in the enemy's country, a suject to death knowing when, far from home & friends. Yet I feel hopeful of returning home before many month. The battels that have been fought are very much in our favor. God speed the time when peice shall be declared & that we may all be permitted to return to our quiet homes, It may be a long time yet before we shall here such good news. I dont want you to think that I am discouraged or homesick, for I am not. I feel as though I had augh to be at home. I have not hurd any news lately, All seems to be quiet, How do you get along with your work, How much wheat do you guess you will have, Pleas give me thhe outline of your farming, stock &c. Anything that you are a mind to write, will be interesting. We are & our Brigade all stationed at Murfreesboro, where we expect to remain a spell, Dont know how long. 5 oclock, the bugle is sounding for meeting. (6 Pet

6. We have a short discorse from our Chaplin this eve. The first that we have had in a long.) the boys are ualy well, except Ancel Baird is some sick. My friend John Duel is all right. I believe that Sarg. Hager is not very well he does his duty yet. we are on the ground where Gen. McCook had his winter quarters, We do not have very good liveing here, the trouble is in our quarter master we expect our pay in day or two, You will excuse this short letter, you go over to Charley Franklins & you will the rest of this sheet Direct your mail to Murfreesboro as useal. My love to all, Pleas write soon Tel Roenna that I will answer her in a few days. From Charley to Father & Mother

Army Core,
Murfreesboro Co. B. 19th Mich. Infty 3rd Reg.
1st Brigade, 3rd Division of Gen. Grainger reserve
August 5th 1863

My Dear Wife,

Yours of the 27th came to hand & was cheerfully received & read with much pleasure. It found me well, we still remain at Murfreesboro & I dont think that we shall get away from here very soon. I wish that we might leave this place because I dont like it here. It is just like all the rest of the Citys & towns in dixey, nasty, filthy, stinking place, buildings a great many of them towrn to peices, When we want a few brick to build us an oven of we go to a nice Brick house & pull them out of the walls, when we want lumber to fix up our bunks with, go & pull down a good dwelling, & so goes evry thing els in this country. I was in a store to day & I prised a peice of factory, such as I have bought for 8c they charge 45c (unbleached factory) 2c a peice for roasting ears of corn, 5c for 3 onion, 85c for a pick of potatoes, 20c for a cabbage head 45 a lb for butter, These are the prices that we have to pay for something good to eat, We are haveing rather slim liveing now days, we have rations of hardbread but the maggets carry off our meat nights & hide it so you see that we have to with meat a part of the time. Thur. Morning the 6th, To day is thanksgiving with us, No drills & nothing is to be done in camp. This day is held more sacred than the sabath here, because the Preasident has set apart a day of thanksgiving & prayer. But the day that our Savior has set apart, has no notice taken of it. We, the people, are in arms. What are we fighting for, The sweet liberty, the Union, the good old flag, & to put down slavery. The realitys of war, the horrors of civil war, is upon us. What has brought these calamities upon us. From the avocations of peace, we have been suddenly sommoned to the scenes of strife, Then we were sommond to leave our quiet homes, & companions & families & fight for the freedom of our country, homes, & fire sids. Was there no time for thought? Or was there no need, Had the people been thinking & feeling for years, Has the god of our fathers been schooling us for this blooddy war battles. Look at our soldiers. They are volunteers, patriots all, christians many, scholars, artists, capitalists, not a few. Why have such men deserted their buisness & left their homes, submited to the privations of a camp life & exposed there lives on the battle field. What are we fighting for, Evry one of us can answer this question. O, wont I be glad when this cruel war shall end so that we may all go to our homes, Yes, evry one of us. Dear Millie I have no news to tell you. The fighting seems to be quiet for the preasent, their may be something going on in other parts that I dont here of. I am glad to here of the good luck that Father & Geo. has had in getting up their wheat. I here that some are haveing trouble to get their harvisting done, I also here that corn is hurt bad in some parts, is yours hurt much by the frost? Elder Wolfe must be a horse to cradle according to your tell, Now while I think of it, I want you to send me a hank of black linnin thread, roll it up in a newspaper, & a pocket Diary, pick out one with good paper & muslin bound, like the one you see me have when I was at home, the glazing comes off of the enameled cloth binding, I dont like such, get one that is about 3 ½ wide & 6 inches long & good thickness, I do not want one that is lettered & have the alminac, get a plain one, One with about 100 leaves or 200 pages. A loop & tuck to keep the book closed. you had better take it to the P.M. & let him do it up & mail it, it may not cost more than 6 or 8 cents, A bunch of envelops only cost 2c from Allegan. I wish you see what a ream of good letter paper would cost to send it here by mail the size of this sheet. I may send for some. It sells for 40c pr. quior, many of the boys are out. I think you have done well on the contract, I wish you would find out how much more there is due on the contract. You done better with wool than I expected. If you want berries you must come down here where they are plenty. It does not take long to pick a pail full. I have had about all that I want to eat this seson. I dont know what to say about canning fruit. It is a very expensive way of puting up fruit. If you had the cans it would do, but the cans will cost money. You can do as you like. If you was a going to send me any fruit, it would be to send dryed fruit. I wish I had some now. Dear Millie, Dont make to much calculations on my comeing home next winter, for fear you may be disappointed, to be sure evry thing looks as favorable as ever, but there might something turn up that would nock it all in the head, I am makeing calculations on comeing going home before many months, I think the capture of fort Sumter will tell the story. The war commenced there & I think it will end their. Just send over one of your custard pies. I could eat one with a good rellish also some of your cookies, We have some flower & make some slap jacks, we take some water, salt it, put in a little vinnigar, some sallaratus, We call them good, you wouldent think they were fit to eat, Dave is quite unwell, Farther than that I believe we are useally well. Keep up good courage Dear Wife. My love to you I must go & wash my shirt as soon as I mail this so good bye. Charley We have not got our pay yet, expect it evry day, Be sure & get me a good nice Direa book. I have disscribed it as well as I can. We are haveing very hot weather, A kidd for you, good bye, Millie Charly

Murfreesboro Aug.7 /63

My morning report

It is some time before I can mail my letter so I thought I would scribble some more, We had no services yesterday. Our Chaplin has resined, I suppose that you have hurd that chaplins pay has been redused. This accounts for his resining. This morning we are a going to have a Brigade review by Gen. Whiticur, I wish that you could be here & see one of our reviews. It is a handsome site to one that has never seen it. We have our camp all cleaned & swept & looks as neat as a house, we have to sweep it evry morning, & all filth carried away. Dave is good deal better he is writing a line to some of you & will put it my letter, I am well, I have a clean shirt to put on this morn There has been 4 or 5 trains of cars passed here since I commenced writing this, we are in sight of the rail road & the village, have a good spring of water which I think a great deal of. We have an insect here called the galnipper, it is built just like the mosquito, but is as large as 6 mosquitoes, they are a powerfull thing to bite. I had rather be stung by wasp than to be bit by one of them insects of all discriptions are very neumerous here. They dont come in the camp where there is so much smoke we have nice cool nights to sleep. A great many of our boys talk of reinlisting in the regulars $400. is no endusement for me to enlist again, when I get out of this scrape, I think I shall keep out. Its the case with many others if I was single I would not. I wish the time of my discharge would hasten, I cant wait, If a man is sick its all the same each man has to do his shair, if he drops & cant go any farther, they come with a streacher & dump him in the Hospital if he gets well its all right, If he dies its just as well, As it happens I have not been the unlucy man I have got along well enough yet Charly

Co. B. 19th Mich. Infty. 3rd Reg.
1st Brigade, 3rd Division of General
Grainger's reserve Army Coar.
Murfreesboro Aug. 10th 1863

My Dear Wife,

Here I am again, purched upon a large rock, under the shade of a larg black Oak tree, where I find it very cool this hot day, answering your kind of third inst. which comes to hand last saturday (the 8th) while I was standing on my picket post. The sargent of Co. B. brought it to me. I was standing at head quarters of the picket guards. Ill warrent you that I did not wait for my tuer to expire before I broke the seal & read its contence. If the enemy had have come by thousands I dont know as I should have noticed them, I was disobeying my orders when reading on duty as a picket. The officer of the picket kept muttering at me but I headed him not. Nor I should not if it had been Gen. Rosecrans himself. Only think, I layed myself liable to a severe punnishment for that little act. As it happens, I know who I am with. Our rules are very strict & sivere, Last week a man set down while on his post. his orders was to walk his beat, he was reported & courtmartialed, he had to stand on a barrel with his knapsack, canteen, gun & cartrage box 2 hours on & 4 off for 48 hours under a guard in the center of the camp in the hot sun. This is millitary, Another spoke a saucy word to his sargent, he was reported, courtmartialed, & sentanced 10 days & nights in the guard tent & labour 8 hours a day with a ball & chain riveted to his leg. You can see that a man has to mind his buisness & obey orders I never have been brought up but once that was when Bassett wanted to make an example of me when I was sick. On the holl I think he has set a good example for himself. Wall, here I have strayed from my post & got to Allegan.

Your letter found me well & enjoying myself as well as can be expected. I tell you what it is, It is no easy job to stand two hours with a heavy gun on my sholdiers, standing at head quarters I have no beat to walk, but halt evry body & evry thing that comes along. A man or any person cant travle these grounds unless Gen. Rosecrans says they may. Now night comes, all is still, except the numerous swarms of insects, the galnipper & mosqueetos. (John Duel has just come & taken a seat by the side of me to write) which keep up a perpetual cerinade all night long, At midnight I hurd the clatering of 2 horses approching. Hault I cryed out, when at a proper distance (30 paces) who goes there. Grand Rosind with the Countersign. Dismount one, Advance & give the Countersign, he advanced & gave it. examed us, & found no one asleep & evry thing all right, then left us. Then all was silent again except my favorate music, That I use to here at home. The August bug, Caty did, grass hopper & crickets What do you suppose are the thoughts of a man so far away from home in the enemys country. This is a great comfort to here them sing then my thoughts again turn towards home. how quiet you can rest ina peacefull slumber & nothing to disterb No first relief nor second or third to answer too. Then again I look up to the moon and it roades silently through the heavens, the stars too are just the same as at home, resting myself on my gun, thinking how long must it be, when shall this cruel war end so that we may return to our dear ones at home, God grant that it may be soon. I must say that it is a serious place to put a person that is very fond of home a mile from camp in a larg field or in a peice of woods in the dead of night watching & waiting for danger to come. Let those that wants to be a soldier, be one. I do not. There is one half of our Regiment that will enlist in the regular army, $400. is no temptation to me. A call was read on dress peraid few day ago that any one who wanted to go as a commishion officer in the collared regiment 5 years might hand in their names. What does this all mean, Why are all that preparations being made, I think it sounds like peice dont you? I long for the time to come when I may get out of this & return to my peaceful home once more, Where I can breath the free air of Liberty & enjoy the society of my friends. August 11ᵗʰ 1, P.M. Now I will procead with my scribbleing. I have nothing to make a letter out of, so I dont think it will be very interesting. Last Sabath we drew our pay $52. & I will send it to you soon, you say that you have had advanced on the contract $171.73. Now allowing that there is just $200.00 to be paid $28.27. Perhaps it would be best to retain the ballance now due untill Geo. can give you a deed. I dont expect that he can give you a deed untill he pays the mortgage. But if you can get a deed now I wish you would. The remainder of the money that I send you, I would like to have you keep untill I come home. Take good care of it we have a great many things to buy when we go to keeping house. If I thought that I should not go home in 6 months I should be in favor of letting it out. I cant tell how soon I shall go home. Capt Hubbard will pay me for my pistol so that is all straight.—We have just returned from church & had supper (you say) what does that mean. Do you have a sabath or a church? we dont, that is something that I know nothing about. What does supper mean, is it something good to eat, If I remember right I think it is, we dont call it supper down here, We call it, Come to coffee, hard tacks, & maggots in the morning at noon come to coffee, maggets & hard tacks, At night Come to coffee & hard tacks, the other favorate dish left out, Dont you think that we live, Two or three maggets on my pllate does not turn my stomach one mite. Now Dear Wife I will hold on. I have misrepresented the thing or gone a little to far I wont wond yyour feelings. We have fresh beef 3 times a week & a barrel of flower once in 5 days for the Company, sody, salt, pepper, soap, candles &c. but the bacon is alive with maggets & this you see I have made a great handle of. You know if I did not write something you would not have anything to read. Do I understand that there is 5 swarms including the swarm that is up to Mr Andersons. It seems to me that one year ago to day I assigned myself over to Uncle sam, That was a sorrowful day to us & I wish that I may never see another sich a time again.

The Soldiers Dream
Beside the watchfire's ruddy light
A soldier slept one summer's night
And as he slept he dreamed
A cot embowered in vernal trees,
And flowers that scented the evening breese
He saw, & hurd the hum of bees, So natural it seemed.
But sweeter vision blessed his sight
A form of grace with eyes of light
And voice of music sweet
Stood watching in the open door,

Where oft she'd stood & watched before
For my manly form that never more
Her longing eyes might meet.
But in his dreams they meet again,
Forgotten were his hours of pain
And weary marches past,
He strained her to his throbbing breast,
And on her lips fond kisses pressed,
And they were both supremely blest,
For he was home at last.
Alas! that such a dream as this,
A dream of home & love & bliss,
And all that makes life bright.
Should never charm his dreams again
For in a storm of leaden rain
The dreamer fell among the slain
Before the morning light. "Charly"

Dear wife, I have had many a dream of home that would make me feel
bad all day. Only 365 days gone, & if the war should continue, It would
seem like an age to have to stay two years longer, Only one third of the
time gone, But the prospects look bright & according to all accounts they
will continue to grow brighter Gen. Rosecrans army (I here) has advanced,
I dont know where he is a going. It will be with him as it is with a muskrat,
You may scare one into the water & he will come up when you are not a
looking for him, He probably will make a dive for Old Bragg, The weather
is so extreemly hot that it is impossable to march a great ways in a day, We
went on drill one day last week & we had not been out but a few minutes
before the men began to faint & drop in the ranks, but they soon get over
it. Aug. 13th You may think by the dates that I have had a teagious time a
writing this letter, but if you want long letters you must wait. (Cotten). I
have sent to you $50. day before yesterday by express, to Hyram Manson
the Postmaster in Allegan, He will deliver the money to Otsego, I hope
Dear Wife, that you will be very choice of this money, for it is hard earned
money. Sargent Pascal A. Pullman left us to day for Allegan to get recruits.
He is one of our Co. He is to return in 60 days, Perhapse you would like
to see him, I sent by him a picture & he will leave it at the Otsego P.O.
We did not know that he was agoing home untill last evening. If you want

to send me any little notions, you can send them by him. I was on guard yesterday, The weather very hot & the mosqueetoes very numerous. The tattoo has beat one hour ago & I must stop. Pleasent dreams, Good night. Friday morning, 14. I have been to market yesterday. I got 12 ears of corn. Paid 15c. 2 loves of bread 5c a loaf, 1 lb of dried apples 15c. 4 lemmons for a sick man 50c. ¾ lb cheese 20c, potatoes 75c a peck It costs something to live here, but is is little that I buy, Cant afford it, I must have something for a change once in a while, I am well now days. There is considerble sickness in the regiment, It is the unhealthy part of the season, But I stand it first rate, Dave is under the weather some, he is complaining with a pain in his breast. he is not very bad off. I believe /all of our {crossed out} the Otsego boys all right except Jim Dagget, he is very hard up with the Carnis Diarea. I am a going to have for breakfast some green corn, beef stake, bread & butter, Apple sauce & coffee, that will do very well for the army living. The Col. is teaching us edicet & drilling us & wants to make us the best there is. We go by that name now in Coburns Brigade. He makes evry man keep himself clean & bathe often we have a good place to bathe, a good spring of water, & we have another spring that we dont use, we have to keep a guard over it all the time. The water is poisen. The neighbours told us so, so the surgeons took some of the water & analised it & found it to be poisenous. This worm you see crawling on your letter is one that was crawling on my knee where I was drawing the vine. Cant you afford me more letters The rest of the boys get 2 letters a week. I dont like to see the rest get so much when I get so little Seeing that my little sheet is most full I must draw to a close. My love to all, be sure & get your shair & write often No signs of leaving this place yet. You may direct your mail as before. From your Absent Husband Charley. To Millie

Murfreesboro Aug. 12, 1863

Dear Wife,

This morning I have sent to the express office $50.00 to be forwarded by express to Hiram Manson the Post master of Allegan he will deliver it to you. I sent it in a package of about 2 thousand dollars. I am on guard & in a hurry. I am well, I have a letter most written to you, Yours in haist Charley To Roenna C.C. Prentiss

Head Quarters Murfreesboro August 25/63

My Dear Lonely Wife

Your kind letter of the 9ᵗʰ inst came to hand the 19ᵗʰ & was kindly received & was perused with much intrest. It affords me much pleasure to read letters from home. The only fault I have to find is that there is not enough of them, All seems to be quiet about here at preasent, There are rumors afloat that Gen. Forest is near here with a force & intends to make an attact on us I hope that he will, It will be a soer job for him. He will find that he has got into a hornets nest, We have 5 forts about this place & they will find that it is not so easy a job to take Coberns pit Brigade, as Gen. Gilbert calls it, We have here now that I know of the 33ʳᵈ Ind. 85ᵗʰ Ind. 22ⁿᵈ Wis. 19ᵗʰ Mich. of infantry, 5ᵗʰ Iowa Cavelry, 9ᵗʰ Ohio Battery besids what is in the forts, & the forts are well mounted. It is rumored here to day that Our Cavelry is fighting now 6 miles from here. I dont believe it. I am not in very good trim for writing to day, I was up most all night & my eyes trouble me some, they are quite week. I was on guard yesterday & last night, Yesterday was a seveir day, Had thunder showers all the afternoon & after them the wind commenced to blow cold from the North & remained so all night & so cold to day that the men put on their overcoats, (those that had them) At last evening came, the inside of the guard tent all mud, the boys neglecting to ditch the tent so I spred my gum blanket on the wet ground, my catrage box for my pillow my gun by my side, then burried myself in my wollen blanket--& 10 minuts found me asleep & it raining all the time. I new nothing about the rain, & here I go in my pleasent dreams, The next I here is "third releif guards fall in" Eleven oclock, I raised up & digging my eyes open & soon went stumbleing along to my post. Soon all was still again, Here I sit on my post a think, of what, Of home? Yes, of home, of my Dear friends; My Dear Companion who is grieaveing at my long absense, wondering if I will ever return. What is the feeings of those Dear friends. No tongue can tell, No pen can disscribe, The stillness of the night is broken, The Old Town clock strikes 12. & as it dones die on the calm midnight breeze; what are my thoughts as I set on a bail of hay, with my trusty companion stands by my side, who says not a word only in a tone of thunder & the breath like lightning when leveled on the enemy. That natural voice of the Old town clock soon carries me back to our Old native town (Dansville) where I have spent so many happy days, The Marble shop, where I spent 3 long years to learn the arts of Nature, the traid that I love, Engraveing the names of those who sleeps beneath the sod, in their quiet resting place, The Baptist church where so many Sabeths I set & hurd the good sumond of Elder Smith & stood by Fathers side a singing Gods prase, The singing schools, the band meetings. Where first I met with Dear lost Harriet, Also with you Dear wife. Where your Father first took me in & showed so much kindness to me gave me as good as he had, And your Mother too use to come & sit by my side, & I use to tell over my trials & hardships; Twas there In that Old tavern that I first met you in fun with Barns, Do you remember it? Alas what a change. Those happy days are gone forever. Hark! Now I here some person a comeing. The officer of the day, a poking around in the dark to see if his trusty centinals are on the alert mind you, /that {crossed out} he dont ketch this chap asleep. He is gone & all is quiet again. I amuse myself by singing some of the songs that I learned with you at home Time passes slow but soon the clock strikes one. & my relief comes. Soon I find my stretched out in my bed on the damp & 2 minutes more will find me in the land of nod.—A few hours ago another of our boys have left us & gone to the spirit land, he died very sudden, was not sick but a day or two, He belonged in Co. K. Cant think of his name. it was when I wrote you last. Gen. Beard says that we have the handsomest camp ground in the country, It has to be swept over evry day. We have cats, & fowls running a round us as we do at home I makes it much pleasenter for me, we have another little inseck that seems very free to run amongst us that is rats, The country is full of them, they harbor in the rocks, we kill a great many of them. Tell Geo. that I will /get rid {crossed out} of tell him how he can get rid of his rats if he will follow our way of traping them, Lay with your back on the ground or where the rats is the thickest, lay with your mouth open place a peice of cheese on your tonge, then pretend to be asleep, then they will come & stick their head in your mouth, then close your mouth quick & you have em, If this fails after you have tried it let me know & I will tell you of another kind of a trap. It is nine oclock & I must blow out my light. Good night Wed. morning. Roenna. I wish that you would nomber each letter the same as you see mine. Commencing with the first one that you received after I came away this last time then where you answer or write, tell me what your last number is, The number of this letter will be 16. this makes 16 letters that I have writen you, You must have your wheat thrashed by this time, how much wheat did you have. & what is wheat worth. You dont suppose that I would buy property of any body if the have no good title. I prefer running a plaining mill than a saw mill, it is not as hard work & I have got employment sutible for my physical strength, Wm. Mansfield is not a going to fool me out of any thing. My rist gets no better very fast, my right hand is very weak. It is all that I can do to handle my gun. I suppose that you have got the money that I sent you, if you have, tell me all about it, & the picture I sent you. I would like to have you tell me all about the contract & mortgage &c, Hubbard has paid me a part & will the rest by & by, I will get a good drum when the Reg. disbands, worth a great deal more than the one I furnished. We are about to start a brass Band & if they do I am one of the member. I am glad that the contract is so near paid up. Say. I wish you would take some other time to write your letters when you aint in so big a hurry, I dont get any letters from any one but you, so I guess you are my only friend. I dont know but you think that I am getting to be quite an author, but I must write something, if I sent you little short letters, that you would not like, I will send you a clame guide, Pleas keep it. I received a letter from my friend Mrs Ballard, She sends her best respects to you. I must draw to a close & hand this over to my trusty bird, she will bear it safe to you, So here she goes. Charlie I am well, Dave is getting better he has been in the Hospital most 2 weeks My Love to all. The weather cold enough last night for a frost. Can you get the Diary book,

Murfreesboro, August 30th 1863

My Dear Lonely Wife,

Yours of the 21st yesterday & was gladly received, I will not undertake to write you a long letter now but a sort of buisness letter. Those packages that you sent to me by Whit; I received last Friday, I received ¼ ream of note paper (you did not tell me what it cost) a Diary book, a skane of thread, a song, a picture, & a letter. Now I will tell you what Dave got. Dried straw berries, dried cherries, dried currents, a large chunk of dried beef, I tell you they looked good, also a quiar of letter paper, & a package of envelops, I let Vernon Rose have 2 quior of that paper for 60c & I could sell all for 30 to 35c a quior. I did not expect you to send me the paper, but I am glad you sent it. Roenna, I want you to send me one of my small 3 cornered filles a small flat file & buy a small half round flat file, it will cost perhapse, 15c also a small mouse tail round file that you will find in the desk drawer, and a drawing pen, I think that you will find one in the drawer. The one that

I want you to send is an old one with a brass holder, & if their should be no screw in it you will find one in another old pen that belongs to a pair of dividers, be sure not to send it without the screw, You may send me dried friut, dried beef, & some cheese & what ever you are a mind to except green fruit which will jam up & make bad work, if you cant send the fruit by Sar. Pullman you can send the files. I my send for my overcoat before long. We, that have over coats will make out a barrel & have it Expressed to us. I send to you a Compy reckers, It cost $1.40. You must take good care of it, It aught to be fraimed right away before it gets soiled. Perhaps I shall come home soon & do it my self, You may wait awhile. I am Well Love to all, Onward to Victory Charley

   Roenna & Millie

                                              Murfreesboro, Sept, 3rd 1863

My Dear Wife

   There is a few words that I wish to say in regard to your sending me some things, Mr Anderson says in his letter to Dave that he was a going to see Sargent Pullman about bringing some things to Dave & there will be your chance, I wish that you will send me some dried fruit such as dryed apples & burries & currents, espetially Dryed blackburries, they are good for the Diarrea, that I am troubeled a great deal, A box of pills, & those other things that I mentioned. I wouldent care if you would send a ream of good letter paper, I can sell it at 40 cents a quior & if you do, take this sheet for a sample, I want the best or none, also a box of envelops, the best kind of buff or coullard, you can do as you like about sending these, be sure & send the best Also some materials for makeing some ink. 3 months to day scince I last saw you (Good night) Sept. 4th Good Morning. I am in a hurry & I must be as breif as possable. I want you to send me /1/4 lb. of soft Prussian Blue /1/4 lb. Exalic Acid,/ one oz of Gum Arabic/ to make blue ink of, it sells ready at 10c a bottle. We are a going to stay here & I can go into some spickulation as not, A little more/1/4 lb Extract of Logwood/1 oz of Prutiate Potash/for Black ink, The paper that you sent me is good, I think that can be got for $2.50 to $3.00. Now while I think of it, I got that paper with tea, & the tea I used when I was a little sick, evry thing that you have sent, I have got, Be sure & not send me poor paper, for if you do it will be a dead loss. I dont care if you send some nice guilt edg paper say ½ ream

besids the other & some envelops to mach, If this stuff gets to me, it will
not be money throughn away, I will make 50 per cent on it, nice guilt edg
paper sells for 60c a quior. You had better get these at Kal. I am well, Pleas
write Mrs. Ballard a few lines, her address Nicholsville, Jesimen Co. Ky.

Yours, Charley

Tobaco Quick sold at $2.50 per lb. That money you will find at Allegan.

Head Quarters Murfreesboro Sept. 6th 1863

My Dear Lonely Wife.

Your letters of the 15th & 21st came to had
in due time & was gladly received & read
with much intrest. Your letter begins like this,
Could you but look in upon us this evening,
I can see you all at any time & see how you
all look & what what you are all doing in my
own mind, but how much better it would be
if I could be with you & talk a while, I am
glad to here that you are all well. that is the
best news that you can send me, & hope this
letter will find you all well, I am not very well
now day, but have been able to be about all
the time, The Dysentary is the trouble & the extreem hot weather that we
have had, We are now haveing nice cool weather, Our hot weather is over
with this season & I am glad of it, I wish that I could step in & eat a dish
of berries & milk. O! how good that would be, Dried sweet Corn is quite a
treat, I wish that you would send me some. I bought for myself Yesterday
a peck of potatoes 25c 1 ¼ lb of butter 40c & you had better believe that I
will live while that lasts. The book is not hardly just such as I wanted but
it will do, I did not expect you to send the book in a newspaper, but send
a skain of thread in a paper & the book by mail. When you want to send
any such thing by mail it is the better way to get the post Master to do it up
for you, I have got the paper with tea in, so that is all straight. Sell Nelly
if you can for $25 or 30. I drew 4 months pay & sent you $50. If you have
not got the money, it is at Allegan, You may send me the full amount of

principal or give me the full amount of the mortgage, (I forget the exact amount) & when the mortgage was given & when it (mortgage) expires, Then give me each amount endoiced seperate & their dates I guess you will under stand me, I want to know for my own curiosity, & if you give it correct I will send you the true amount of intrest, I think that you may get B. Ballou or Edcil or Turn Day to figure up that intrest for you. In reguard to the value of the farm, I dont know whether land has raised (the price of land) or not. I dont think that I should be far out of the way to ask $1,200. You know better that I do what it is worth I would be willing to sell it for that & not more than $50 less. I am willing to be governed some by the price of Fathers land. I am perfectly willing to sell it, If you do sell it, You will have the buisness done up right If you do not get that money, you need not send any paper & envelops, But I must have one lb of tobacco, All of the Allegan folks have received their money from that package. My eyes do not gain much, they are not so bad as they were when I was at home, My rist is quite week, It dont seem hardly right to let Dave have that Picture it is so pretty, but I had to do it, My love to Elsie, Kiss her for me & take good care of her Tim Dagget wanted I should ask you if you gave that picture to his folks, What is the matter with Henry Divine, I guess the Brown Boys will get the worst of it, in going of to Origon, I would not carry the name that they will for nothing, they never will here the last of it, I dont intend to do any thing to get cort martialed. Buit if Old Doct. Bennet dont do a little differant there will be a chance to Court Martial. I dont calculate to be abused by him, He tryed to me work when I was hardly able to sit up. He did not make it out, He is gitting very much disliked in this regiment, has been takeing lessons of Doct Clark, Sorry to here that Ira Chichester is so sick. Dear Millie I am glad to here you say that you are well used, I hope it may continue, I am sorry to have you talk about the blues if it is getting fall weather, you must think of a good time comeing before long, we are a going to have another bag full of game at Chattanooga, the battle is expected to commence to day, Thousands of troops have pass here to day. We expect to move to Tullahoma the middle of the week, A part of our Brigade went yesterday, As fast as the main army advances we have to follow after, Our Brigade did expect to take command of these forts, there is 18 forts here in sight of each other insted of 6 that I told you, Now it is 2 oclock, & 15 minutes ago I got a letter from you & one from Geo. Anderson, Yours bears date Aug. 30, You will find by this letter that I am all right yet, All that has taken place we are kept very buisey a guarding &

picketing, & fixing up our camp ground &c. We are just a going into the style & I am glad that we are a going to leave. Dave is in the regimental hospital where I see him evry day, he is about the same, he is not very sick but very weak, Ancil Baird is rather under the weather now, I think that all of the rest are well except we all have the Tenn. Quickstep, Ogden Brown has the Ague to day, If we move Dave will remain behind, Dear Wife take good care of yourself & be patiant & keep up good courrage. I still remain yours as ever Charley If it is going to be too much trouble to get that paper & envelopes, you may let it go.

Murfreessboro Sept. 13th 1863

My Dear Wife

I take the pleasure of writing to you this pleasent Sabeth Day to write to you a few lines to let you know where I am & how I am. I am perty well but I am not very tuff this hot weather, I believe that I told you in my last letter that I thought that we should move to Tullahoma, we did not go & will not go at preasent, a part of our Brigade had gone about all the troops that is here is the 22nd Wis & our Reg. a part of the 4 East Tenn Cavelry. We are stationed here to take control of this town & Rosecrans Commissary an----
--tion &c. There is a great deal depending on this place & roads. Buisness goes very lively, & we are getting good news daly & we all feel very much encouraged in reguard to our affairs. Our Rose gave the boys a short speech before he made a dive into Chattanooga. Says he to his boys you shall all see your homes by New years, What do you think of that? I hope it may be so, he, Rosecrans is one fine man. he is love by evry one of his men. But the rebs dread the name of Rosecrans, He will visit his Soldiers individually & privitly & have a good sosiable chat with them that is the kind of a Gen. to have isent it? Well, I should have writen to you sooner if I had not been so buisey the past week, I will coppy from my diary the last week just as it is. You will see by that, that we have been on Picket evry other day. Sun 6th Murfreesboro Sept 1863. Our Reg. went out on picket this morning at 4 to relieve the 33rd Ind. the 33rd marches this a.m. to Tullahom at 7. I am sick this morning, Wrote a letter to wife, mailed it. I feel better through the day but not so well to night. Warm & dry weather & very unhealthy. It is reported that we leave for Tullahoma in a day or so, I received 2 letters to day, One from Wife & one from Geo. Anderson A large nomber of troops

passed through here to day bound for the front, Gen. Rosecrans is expected to make an attact on Chattanooga to day. Three boys got tite & commenced carring on & got in the guard house. I carried Dave his things, we expect to leave him at the General Hospital. Mon. 7. I got up this morning a feelling a great deal better, I went to work & got my breakfast, thenn went to work at my tent a pulling it down & building it over & better, worked at it all the fournoon, then orders came to move. We moved about ¾ of a mile in fronnt of the Depot. here we have a nice camp ground. Worked untill dark a setting up our tent. Mr Mabbs helped me some. While the regiment went to pick out a camp ground & lay it out. I stayed as over the things that was left. Weather warm & dry. Tues 8 I got up at half past 4 & went to work on the tent eat breakfast then got ready for Picket. At 7 ½ we went on the Liberty pike. Buisness very lively, A great deal of travel, 2 of Forests men deserted & came in at our post & gave themselves up. They say that all of his men are discouraged & are deserting fast. I am No. 5 of the 3rd relief & my post ¾ of a mile from head quarters. The weather very hot & dry. We had a good place to stand picket. Mosqueeters very troublesome all night. I stayed on my post all night because it is so far to headquarters. I bought 1 lb of butter paid 25c. Wed 9. I was relieved from duty at 8 & got to camp at 9. Broke ranks inn the village & to report in camp in one hour, Mr. Mabbs & I went to work on our tent & bunks, we had to move our tent about 6 ft, to make the ally larger. At 4 P.M. I had to go after hay & corn to the Depot, We got our tent fixed up in good shape. Very hot to day. Thur 10 went on picket again this morning, went on the Shelbyville Pike. I am No. 3 of the 2 relief, News today that Rosecrans has taken Chattanooga. Weather very warm to day. A train of 70 army waggons & 20 ambulences & one company of the 1st East Tenn Cavelry came in & camped near my post. Fri 11. Went in from picket at 8. eat some breakfast then went to work at my tent aputting in a little cubbard &c. Went to the Hospital to see dave this evening. Very warm & dry. News is that Old Rosea has taken 12. or 13,000 Prisoners near Chattanooga. Sat 12. Rep. in good season & got ready for Picket, We started out at 7 went to the Liberty Pike, I am No. 3 of the 3rd relief This eve. some signes of rainey night the winds blew, the lightnings flashed, the thunder rattled & the rain fell. I did not get much wet, At eve, I was taken with a dysentary & at midnight taken to vomiting & was quite sick all night, Sun 13 I was relieved at 8, we got in camp at 9. I eat a little breakfast then took a knapp got up & commenced writing a letter to wife see 1st page {the rest of the letter is written diagonally across the first page, making the original first page very hard to read} At 3 orders came to get ready for inspection, went to work & cleaned my gun & brasses, greased my boots &c & at 5 came out on inspection I drew a pair of pants & a haversack. Went to the Hospital to see Dave, he is not any better, Doct Bennett came in & had we had a good chat about home, he got a letter from his family & says that you have seen the folks, so now he will welcome letter, this eveninng I finnished my letter to wife. There Dear wife you have your letter to night, we have to go on picket again tomorrow, I dont think that I should go unless I am better than I have been to day. I here to day that Mr Baker has sent for his wife to come out here, if she comes perhaps you would like to see her. Daves trouble is the enlargement of the spleen. It is getting late & I must close My love to you all, write often, & tell me all, Your Dear Husband Dear Wife a few words more I did not go out on picket this morning I did not feel well enough so I bolted. I am some better this morning I have some more wants supplied. I want ½ pound of Tartaric Acid & one lb of Soda, for a drink Geo. Anderson sent dave acid & Dave gave me some I took some whenn I dident feel well & I felt better right off. The acid cost 50c per ounce litre. Send it by Mrs Baker if she comes before Pullman does, I cant get use to this Tenn water so but that it will Phisic me. We have good liveing now Yours with a rusty nail, Charley In Regimental Hospital

At the Hd.Qurs of 19th Mich
Infty Vol Sept 22nd 1863

My Dear Friend Roenna

You may think a little strange at receiving a letter from me & I do not know but come to look at it all round I do not know but it is rather funny for me to be writing to a married lady but circumstances alter cases Sometimes you may. At this time the reason why I write is that Charley is here in the hospital & sick & not feeling able to sit up & write he wanted I should do it for him. In the first place he has had the summer complaint for some time & has been taking medacine, but it wore upon him until he came into the hospital last thursday & has been having the chill fever but his fever is now broken & he is much better, but is weak his diarhea is checked & he thinks he will get right along. we have quite a pleasant & comfortable place, our cots are within reaching distance of each other & it is not near as lonely for me as before he came. misery likes company you know. I have been here since the 13th of Aug. had the diarrhea at first which led me into the intermitent fever which was broken in a few days but left me with a trouble in my back & left side, which sticks by me yet. It pains me the most of the time. The docter says it is the disease of the spleen & tells me that I cannot get up for a long time. but you know there is no such thing as getting out as long as a man can draw a breath cross ways. So I shall have to content myself as best I can by lying in the hospital Charley has red the last two letters written by you. date of the last is Sept 13th. he will be well enough to write in a very few days. Capt Hubbard has the rheumatism pretty hard he walks as stiff as a stake he contracted them laying on the ground out on picket. there is not much sickness in the regiment now. the weather is cool & pleasant days & quite cold nights have had some hard frosts. I would like very much to help make way with some of those new peaches you wrote about there is no new fruit in this part of the country. I cannot think of any news to write there is stirring news from Rosa to day. had a hard battle yesterday 8,000 wounded have now learned the particulars, good bye write soon & accept this from Dave My love to all Those pictures are just the nicest little things on record. Have not recd any letters from home since the 7th I write to them often write soon Dave Whit & lady seem to be enjoying themselves hugely. She was over to head quarters which is in the house near the hospital yesterday I see the Lt Cols & Sutlers ladies who are here having a romantic time, the Lt Cols wife ride the pickets with him on horseback &c &c now dont you wish you was the wife of a Col or some body hem hem hem Oh I wish I was in Dixie Hurra Hurra &c &c &c &c Yours with a rusty nail Artemus Ward

Murfreesboro Sept 24th 1863

My Dear Wife,

You have doubtless hurd That I am in the Hospital sick. I requested Dave to write to you a few lines, to let you know how I was. I am now getting some better, I am reduced & quite week, but think that I shall get along now, I am so that I can set up some, I must stop for I am getting tired. Fri. Morning Sept 25. Good morning Dear Wife, I have got up & washed & combed & find that I feel some better, I came in the hospital a weak ago yesterday, I first had the Dyarrea then the chill feaver, I have it all broken up now & am getting well, I have had the best of cair, The Doct gave me the best of attention & seem to take great deal of intrest in me, scince you have got acquainted with his family, he dont act like the same man, We have had very exciteing times here Yesterday & last night in the hospital, I have layed on my bunk & see one mans legs booth cut off, A hard site, but I dont mind it, He fell from the tram yesterday morning & the car ran over both feet so that he had to have them taken off. 6 inches below the knee, Last night a Lieut fell the same way the car cutting off both legs & was also struck in the head. He was killed instantly, he lays here dead, All the wonded have been passing through here & evry thing is uproar & excitement here now. It is a very serious time here, You must not expect a very long letter from me this time I here of the death of Milo Hawks, C D Fox, Harry Brundage who was shot on the battle field, I wish you could send my over coat & dress coat soon as you can. I am almost sorry that I sent for that paper, I hope you did not get it, I have got ketched again, here sick & no money. I expected to draw pay before this. But I am not suffering for the want of it yet. I will close this miserable looking letter & get it out of my sight. I am ashamed of it, hope you will keep it out of sight I Still remain your Dear affectionate Husband, Charley Millie

Head Quarters Murfreesboro,
Sept. 26. 1863

My Dear Wife

    I will again write to you a few lines to let you know how I am. You will see by my letters that I am not very bad off, if I was very sick I could not write very straight, I am getting along finely just now, I will tell you what I have to live on here at the hospital. For Breakfast I have toast, a baked potatoe, & butter, To day noon I had some chicken soup, potatoe & butter bread & Tea, For Supper, toast, boiled egg. So you see that I fair very well, I have a plenty of good books to read. So I think that you have no reason to feel bad or mourn. because I am sick. Doct. Bennett is doing just all that he can for me & is very kind, He has a great deal to do at preasent, There is a great many wounded comeing along & he has to dress their wonds The boys from the Front say that Old Rose is enough for them yet. They are haveing a tight time of it. This battle will tell the story we think & It will take all of their forces that they have to make any kind of a stand, The boys say that Rose will ride a long the lines when the bullets are flying like hail & cheer his men. A better man could not be found for that place. Sept 27 Sabeth morning, This is a beautiful morning & I feel first rate. I am on the gain, I received a letter from you yesterday bearing date Sept. 20 & was glad to here from you again, I am very sorry that you did not send those things in the junction box I would get it so much sooner, but I will get them after a fation, I shant trouble you any more in getting things for me of this kind. It is more trouble than I supposed it would be, You may not send more than 1 or 2 lbs of tobaco. I will not try to speculate on that, dont send any but what is good. I think that I shall be satesfied with the purchace that you have made. There will be no doubt but that I shall more than get my money back again, Before I can give you the exact amount of intrest I shall have to have the date of the mortgage. I have received a letter with Elsie likeness, I want you to number your letters if you will, Your letter of the 20th of Sept. as I have it is No. 14. Now you have a starting point. I am sorry to have to disturb Father & will not any more, O! them peaches, if I could get some of them, wall there, there is no use of talking. It seems as though I would give all that I had for what fruit I want & mellons, but No. War will soon end & then, & then, & then you know. Dave does not get any better, I think he would be if he would pluck up courage— (he is homesick.) Dont say anything, he looks fleshey & tough. Tim Daggett I dont think will ever get well, You had better keep this still, We have just had some Lady visiters. The Lieut Col. Wife & Mrs Champion the suttler Wife. I understand that Gen. Forest is captured & in Nashvill in prison. We are not haveing it quite so hard on picket duty, have been relieved by a darky Reg. They are fine looking soldiers & do there duty first rate, A few days ago some white folks undertook to run the pickets line they just stuck the bayonet right into them. They thought because they were Niggars they would pay no tention to them. Many of the citisans think that they can do as they are a mind to but they get brought up. There, I have writen all that I can think of & my sheet is most full & I will stop. I think it is singular that I cant get any newspapers from home. I still remain you Husband. Love to all. Charley   Roenna

Head Quarters, Murfreesboro, Tues,
Sept. 29th 1863

Dear Lonely Wife,

Thinking that you would like to here from me this morning, I thought that I would write you a few lines, I am getting along firstrate. I am most well again, but quite weak, Jim Daggett is quite sick with the Cronic Diarrea, he dont get any better, Dave is no better, he has the fever & ague now, Dave Stockwell came back to the hospital yesterday. he is troubled with the Diarrea & gravels I think, I wont be sure whether it is the gravels or not, It is getting cooler weather & I dont think there is quite so much sickness as their was. Wal. I have no news to write You & I dont want to send so much white paper, I hurd yesterday that Rosecrans has made another slaughter amongst the rebs. The rebs undertook to flank him in the night & it seems that Rosecrans had one eye open for them, It must be that he mistrusted that movement So Rosecrans was at work planting his batterys all night, & at day light he open on them, fought about 2 hours & killed over 2000 of the rebs. That is the way to do it, I tell you when they ketch Old Rosea asleep, they ketch a weasel asleep, If we have had a few more such men a year and a half ago this rebelion would have been put down long ago. Now we have the rebels complain worst than ever, These battles are a going to tell the story, We are to work in the very vitals of the Southern confedercy, which will soon tell the story, & then I hope to meet you all again. O! what a happy time where will be amongst the Soldiers when the word comes that we can go to our homes again. I will close this letter & write a gain in a day or two. My love to all, be of good cheer, From Your Husband, Charley Millie

Head Quarters of the 19th Mich
Inft. Murfreesboro Oct 1st 1863

Millie My Dear Wife

I take the pleasure in writing to you again a few lines, I suppose you will think because I am in the hospital that I am very sick but I am not now. I feel quite well again, The Doct. wants I should stay here & diet a spell & get my strength I am willing to do so because I have better liveing & dont have to do duty, I think that I feel as well as ever I did only week.

You will judge by my letter that I am not very bad off. This I do mearly for a pass time & do a great deal of such work for the rest of the boys, Dave lays here by me a trying his skill in drawing, I have a plenty of applications to learn others to draw, but I dont propose to learn evry body for nothing I have a nomber of scholers engaged to take lessons when we get home, Wall, Millie, I hardly know what to make a letter out of when I write so often. So if you dont get a very long letter you must not scold. I suppose that you hear all sorts of stories about us down here, but dont you believe any thing you here more than I write, for Ill garrentee that I will write all there is to write or tell. I very often hear stories that some fool has writen home to alarm their friends & for the sake of telling some big yarn, That is not my way. Peter Gordon looks perty hard up, cant tell what is the matter of him, Some of his inside riging is out of order like myself. The trouble is in the stomach, To day is one of those dark, gloomy rainy days, rained all last night & all day to day, the first rain we have had I guess in 2 months, we needed rain very much, A sad accident hapened in Nashvill in the same building that I stayed in when I came out here last time, The same building is occupied with rebel prisonerrs, As they were going down stairs to breakfast the stairs gave way (they were winding stairs, raising 40 feet) & let them all down in a pile, The report that we got was that their was 80 rebs killed, I think their was not so many killed, Bill Mansfield stayed there that night & said he saw it, we have his story for it. I have figured up the intrest on the contract, but I suppose that there is some intrest on the mortgage that I have to stand, thatis one half of the intrest that accumilated between the date of the mortgage & the date of the contract.

Aug. 14th 1862	principal	$189.50	interest
Oct. 16th 1862	first endorcement	$20.00	$3.16
Nov. 15th 1862	2nd do	$62.95	$1.41
July 29th 1863	3rd do	$88.75	$7.55
Oct 1st 1863	remaining principal	$17.77	$0.30
			$12.42

You will see that there is $17.77 remaining of the face of the contract, and $12.42 of the intrest. The total principal & intrest up to Oct. 1st, 1863 is $30.19. I think you will understand this, I cant make it any plainer I don't think, If you dont understand it ask any question you chose to, I forgot to tell you I reckened this at 10 per. cent intrest, News is so scarce & I guess I will close. Pleas give my love to all the folks, Pleas send me a bunch of envelops by mail. I am out, it will cost about 3 cents. Good night to all. I must away, Good night to all, I tune our lay, Charlie, A poor Soldier, &c Millie

Head Quarters of the 19th Mich..
Inft Murfreesboro, Oct 8 1863
Dear Millie

Here goes a few more leasure moments, a scribbleing to a Dear Companion far away from her husband who is in the army far away from home & friends, but feeling perty well now, I am gaining strength slowly, I am not sick now so you will not worry about me. Will you! I stay at the hospital yet. I dont care to go to my company yet, because I dont have quite so good a place to sleep & good board as I do in the hospital, The weather is cool & pleasent. If you have not sent my dress coat & over coat, you may let it go & not try to send them I will draw some new ones by & bye, but send on the rest of the things if you can, I should like to have them while we stay here, Dont know how soon we may move & go to some unknowen region, It is surprising to see so many troops pass here. some 10 to 12 heavy loaded trains pass here evry day & so many more to come. There is 3 army coars a going through Pensilvany as fast as they do this way, the Cavelry & Artilery go that way, I tell you, when Old Rosea makes another drive it is a going to tell, The rebels have got all of their army togeather & means to make a desperate struggle & I think it will be the last. I would like to have you send the files the first opportunity, also a peice of rubber that is in my drafting tool drawer I think there is a small dark collored peice there. send that, Dave is about the same, he is trying to get his discharge, Jim Daggett is getting better, Dave Stockwell is better, I am better, we arre all better &c. Dont forget to send me a bunch of envelops by mail they cost 25c here & I have no money to buy with & I have but one more, So you will have to hurry & send them or go with out letters, & that you will not like, We have no news to day, evry thing seems to be quiet with the exceptions of the troops that are going to the front to fight. many perhaps never to return & many will come back without a leg, some without an arm, some a hand, some a finger, This will make the poor fellows think of home, yet How true the thought,

& yet most dear, That memory has a silent tear, For loved ones, where so'er our lot Though absent, they are ne'er forgot! Dear wife you will excuse this short letter for I have nothing to write How does Geo get along with stump machine I expect he will get rich out of that, The mail goes out in a few minutes & I must close, Lots of love to you all, Truly yours, Charley Millie

Murfreesboro, October 6th 1863

Dear Wife,

Yours of the 27th of Sept. was received last Sabath evening & was heartily glad to read another letter from home, I would like to know how you hear so many stories about the 19 you have been missinformed about our regiment leaving Murfreesboro, Co. D. has gone 3 miles from here to guard a rail-road bridg, & 2 other companies have gone to guard the Duck river bridg still farther South, That is all that has left, We expect to stay here, no knowing how long, perhaps untill the war closes as you hoped for. As for Rosecrans being repulsed it is no such a thing He holds all the ground that he has gained, We have men here that was in the fight that knows all about it, So you can set your heart at rest that we are in Murfreesboro yet. This line of communication has got to be kept open, if it is not, what will become of Rosea army, In reguard to what Mr. Hager says of our not seeing another battle, he is mistakened, We are haveing a battle (not really a battle) but skirmishing all day yesterday & today, We was attacted yesterday morning by 15,000 rebs (some say 20,000 I dont believe it to be so many) went to Stone river rail road bridg where Co. D. was, fought them 1 hour & 30 minuts, gave the Co. 20 shots from their artilery, mortally wonding one man. shot off his lower jaw, they shot one reb dead The first shot cut down the flag. it soon went up again, but they had to surrender, under such a force of 4,000 & Artillery 4 peaces, The rebs robed them of all they had burned the bridge, In the corse of the day Gen. Wilder came on with a brigade of Cavelry, had 3 battles with them & whiped them evry time. The rebs lay out here now about 3 m we are a going into them as soon as they feed their horses & get their ration, We have the fortifications all man besids 1 brigade & 2 Divisions. Co. D. has just come in they say they killed 2 rebs & wonded 6, We are trying to work them in rainge of our big bull dogs, we have their ears well rubed & soon expect to hear them bark, we are strongly fortified & can stand a big force of rebs, It is 2 m. from here to town, All the women

& citisans came in side of our brest works for safety, had to take up with a soldiers life last night. It was a bitter cold night last night, had sleep on the ground & sit by fires all night I could crying all night, We intend to take all of this squad of rebs before we leave them. 4 oclock P.M. In reguard to that box, I am very ansious to see it. I will warrent you I shall enjoy my shair of its contence. I dont think it will come any safer with Pullman than it will with him, If it should come by Express he will not see it untill it lands to its journeys end, But let it come, You must pay the charges because I have no money, I am glad that you have went in with Mrs. Hager—You will exccuse me not saying any thing about Mothers & Georges letter, I have also received a letter from you & Father, I forget to mention such things sometimes. Yes! Yes!! I should like first rate to look in upon you this evening seeing it is a cold rainy night. I believe the first thing would be the buttry, or a dish of good bread & milk. I wonder if Father has his nap out yet & what was his dream, I dont suppose any of you dream of home, do you. I do very frequently, What did Mother about me, nothing very bad, I dont think, Laura is chewing gum you say, Wall that is all right, I believe that she has never writen me a word yet. If she dont I shall call on Elsie to write for her. If Elsie writes me a letter dont fail to send it. Mary is a reading some good story I guess she must write to me. She can do it, I know, Try it anyhow, What do you think of me, I write most evry other day, You can write about the dog, the duccks, chickens, calves, lambs &c. you can find wnough to write about, it will all be interesting to me. Yes! Yes!! I know what you are about. Yes! sitting at the table a makeing a few crooked marks to you poor Old man away off in the army who is wandering around like a lost sheep from the flock, Not exacly from the flock for the flock is large enough I know when I have some 3 or 4000 men around me all the time, Ill ketch you at it again some of these times perhapse not in the wash tub We have quite a nomber of hard frosts lately. The trees begin to turn there coller to a beautiful golden couller. Oct. 7 You did not tell me what you see at the fair. I would like a discription of it. You did not tell where that rail road acident hapened. Tell Cosine Ira that he has never writen to me yet. I suppose that he is getting rich. I wish he would write to me often. The letters that I get are very scattering. I am a going to stop writing to all but you. I dont get any answers, a friend in need is a friend in deed. I must close my letter, my sheet is most full. Dave is writing to Laura & puts his letter in mine to save postage. I am pretty smart now. I have the flying axhandles some. Yours in haist Love to all, Charley to Millie

Murfreesboro, Oct 9th 1863

Dear Millie

Yours of the 1st of Oct. No. (O the number has not come yet,) came to hand yesterday & as you said was not read with much pleasure because you was so badly scared, you wanted me to tell you just exacly how I am & thha worst of it, Now I will tell you. I have got the small pox, kind pox, cholara, yellow fever, ague & fever, black & red tongue, earreslipries, salt rhume, ich, janders, rheunitism, lice & gray backs, &c. &c., Now you have the worst of it, If this wont do I will tell you the best of it in my next if you want me to, Maybee there will be something rong about this letter, if there is you must tell me, I thought that I would get Dave to direct my letter this time because I have had my right arm amputated clost to my ankle & both eyes dug out by some large rats, I wish you fly away & come down here & see me. I would treat with all the good things that Tenn. can afford, & give you a nice place to sleep as you ever had. U can lay & star gaze all night & see the eclips on the moon evry night, & the stars as they shoot at each other & the frost perhaps will one half inch thick on your face, wouldent that be nice, I shall look for you in your next letter. My wants are many & I dont think u could supply them if u were here. I in the first place to go home, I want this war to cease, &c. I dont knnow but u will think that I am imposing upon u but I feel just like abuseing somebody to day. I am very apt to do it. but you will considder who it comes from, Yes it is true there is no one like a true companion to one that is so badly afflicted as I am. U must excuse my pen for writing so. It must be that it feels worst than I do. U say that u was afraid that I would get clear down, I get dlear down evry night most. some times 5 or 6 times in a night when I get the Tenn. quick step as they call it. (I dont know what u call it) I dont know as I have said anything about feeling of any well, for I have not seen one for more than 3 months I have not been real sick yet, so u are all right yet. What have u against the hospital as long as one can get all that he wants to eat & do no duty. I guess the Doct. means to keep me hear untill he cuers my stomach complaint that I have been afflicted with for the last 6 or 8 years, If he does I shall stay hear untill the war closes. I take no meadicen, but diet, Nothing bad about that I know. If I knew that you was a going to be so badly scared I would have writen that letter myself. I think u are over it by this time, if not I will get him to write u another one, It pleased Dave very much to have you think that u would rather he would be lonely than to have me in the hospital. As u say, I am cured & have endured it too, yes, these things do taist so good. I enjoy them first rate, I dont care how much wine you send to me, I expect to get drunk on it, & have a spree, Do not send my over coat nor dress coat because I am getting some new ones, As for reinforceing Rose. we have not, & dont expect very soon, somebody takes a greate of pains to tell news up north. It seems that u know more than we do. The prospects that we shall have a big battle before long. It is surprising to see so many men pass through. Artillery, any amount of it, Take it all togeather it looks as though he intended to do something. I wish I could be there when they get at it. The noise of such a battle can be hurd many miles off. Dave is about the same, Jim Daggett is better. The man with his legs off is doing well, This sargeant in Co. D. is alive yet that had his chin shot off took out all of his upper teeth most all of his lower jaw & a part of his nose, tongue is not hurt but badly swolen. Poor fellow, he sufferse much. Give my respects Cousine Ira & lady. I should be very happy to be there & visit with you. I would be pleased to hhave him write to me. Tell him that I will pay the postage if he is not able to pay it, I wish he would come to our regiment as chaplin We have none now, he has run away, You can do as you like about spending the winter with him, It will be a good place, In reguard to the map, I should hate to buy a thing without seeing it, but I should not object paying $6. if it is a nice thing. You may get one, Be sure & have that mistake made right. & not have all tthe 160 acres put down to Geo. because if it is my land I want it in my name, What do you think of the price I set on the land, is it too much or is it not enough. I have done my erand to dave. Yes I remember that you & your heart is flying about me all the time. I can feel you pull my hair once in a while. You must take to yourself the same precaution that you give to me, Take good care of yourself & be of good cheer & carry a stiff upper lip. You tell me to write often, I write most evry other day can I do any better? There I think that I have abused you enough for one time I forgot weather I told you that I got Elsie's picture or not. I have got it & thankfull for it. I wish I had told you to send me some green tea, I think so much coffee hurts me. & that is not all, I dont like it without milk, Mr Mabb & I paid 60 cents for a can of prepaired milk that goes first rate, but it is too expensive our camp prepaired milk will last one person about two weeks if he will use it prudently. I sell my ration of suger for 20c per lb to buy butter at 35c per lb. I had gave to me the other day about 3 qts of dryed peaches, it was a man of the 85 Ind when they left here & could not carry them. I have had many a good meal out of them. O how I ache to have my drafting tools, I would have them if I had any way to carry them, Dont forget that drafting pen I wrote for withh a brass handle, that goes through the pen, Dont forget to write often, you see I am getting cornered & must stop writeing. My love to all the folks. Father & Mother, Sister & Brother, & neice. Your Old man Charlie Millie I wrote a letter to Sophie Anderson the other day. I hope you wont be jelous of me. I must write to somebody. My portfolio is all the comfort that I take, that all

No. 28 Tuesday morning Murfreesboro
Head Quarters of the 19th Mich
Oct 11th, 1863,

My Dear Beloved, I am left alone in my tent, the rest out on picket, so I take this opportunity to write a few more lines to a poor lonely companion who is left far behind, one that loves you, one that would lay down his life for you, one that only lives for you. How hard it is to be seperated from each other O! what a blessing it would be to have this cruel war end, how many hearts would leap for joy, to know that they can return to their homes once more, It is in most evry soldiers mouth a time is near when our great Uncle will say you can all go home boys, ... How good that will sound. I can tell you that my trip home will be a pleasent one if I live to see that time. Who can tell when that time will come. God only knows. He doeth all things right & knowith all. I put my trust in him & keep up good courage, & you must do the same, -- I asked the Doct. to let me come to my company yesterday, he said I might. I am quite smart again. It is not very pleasent to stay in the hospital where the wonded are, it sents the tent so, when we moved the hospital it so happened that I got in the tent with them. What do you think of a man that has his under jaw shot off, all of his teeth nocked out of his upper jaw, a part of his nose taken off & upper lip. That is the condition of one man in our hospital & the Docter all says that get well. He is an awful looking sight. I have helped to feed him Doct. Bennett is the best Surgeon that we have about hear my way of thinking. This man that had both of his legs taken off Bennett took off one, & another took off the other. The one that Bennett took off is healed over I was done 3 weeks ago.—I tell you what it is, the boys have a very poor oppinion of Daves sickness ((A discharge)) say nothing, Tim Dagget is getting quite smart

again. I have just eat my dinner of hard crackers & salt pork & now I will
continue my letter, I dont know but you think my last letter was rather a
saucy one, but I did not know what els to write. I felt just as though I wanted
to write a letter in answer to the one that I got the night before that done
me good. Well, Now a little about the war, we dont get anything now but
troops are passing through Murfreesboro by the thousands, what a site of
artillery there is going through to the front. Perhaps you would like to know
what we have got here in our fortifications, we have 18 forts, Leumets, &
Roundels, We have 8 Magazens The smallest one has 30 thousand lbs. of
powder, I cant tell you the size of the largest one but I think it will hold
20 times more than the small one & that is jamed full of amunition. They
are built under ground cannon ball proof, A guard is kept at each one all
the time, All of these forts are built so as to form a circle enclosing about
1,000 acres, The hole is what we call the fortifications, The stone river runs
through them. Mon. Morning Oct. 12 You see that I dont write but a little
while at a time, by the date of my letter. Yesterday I wrote untill I got frose
out, then stoped, My hands are so cold now that I can hardly write, we are
haveing very chilly weather now days for this country & we have nothing
but these dog tents which we have to carry on our backs when we march,
I dont know but I shall have to close my letter for the want of anything to
write. News is all played out, I feel prety well this morning, I had a pretty
good breakfast this morning. I some very small potatoes & boiled & fried
some hard tacks & some coffee, strong coffee without milk nor sugar is
rather poor drink. We have a great deal of fun killing rats, A few of us went
at it the other day & killed 75 or 80 large full grown rats. They are very
numerous, go where we may we cant lay down more than a few minutes
before they will run over me, steel our rations &c. One night while out on
picket I had my haversack under my head for a pillow, had some boiled
beef & bread in it. The rats were at it & knawed a hole in the haversack &
carried off my beef off under my head & I asleep, Rats here are the largeist
I ever saw. They anoy us very much, much wors than the rebs, I saw Mr.
Baker last night, he is well, he says that he thinks that his wife will not
come out here, I think that she is wise for not comeing, for I think it is no
place for a woman. I wish that Mr. Box would come along, I am ansious
to see its contence & perhaps to devour some of it, The remainder of our
brigade is ordered back here to take command of this post, & if that is the
case we shall remain here for some time yet. We came very near shelling
this city a week ago to day, so near it that one seage howitser was loaded

& leveled on the town, The evening before we had orders from Gen. Rose. if the rebs entered the city to shell it 5 hours, but they didnt get in. They were scattered by Gen. Wilders brigade who came up in the rear of them. There was supposed to be 20,000 of them We have taken a pile of them prisoners. Their Millie you must try & get along with letter this time, It is cold & I will close. My love to all the folks, Be sure & get your shair. You will understand that I am not sick now I hope this will find you all well. From your Husband Charlie Prentiss to Millie

Head Quarters of the 19th Mich Inft. Murfreesboro

Oct. 13th 1863

My Ever Dear Wife,

Yours of the 4th No. 17 came to hand last eve, at 4 oclock & was very happily received. I dont know but you will think that I am writing to you all the time. I have nothing els to do while I am not able to do duty, Last evening I wrote a letter to Mary & thought that I would direct iit in her name just to pleas her. She wrote a good letter for her, I suppose you save all the old letters that I send back dont you, I want you should, I am a going to send you 5 little books that I think a great deal of, & I will let you pay the postage on them, Your No. on the lasst letter corresponds with my book (No 17) Oct. 14th As I did not feel very well yesterday I did not write much. We are haveing such nasty rainy cold weather it makes me feel rather dull, We do very bad news from the 13th Mich. & am sorry. I think that our regiment has been very lucky not to get in any more battles than they have. I hope it may continue so untill the close of the war, Oct. 16th Good morning Dear Millie. How do you do this morning. You write me to always to tell you the worst & so I will. I have not been quite so well the last two or three days, I think it has been on account of the bad weather, Yesterday & day before it rained steady all the time & last evening had a hard thunder shower. A hard rain in this country makes it very bad for soldiers, The soil is clay & when there is so many of us we soon make mud & awful it is too. We have very comfortable beds to sleep on. they are up high & dry from the ground, We have now a stove in our tent, I drew me an over coat & 2 pr of drawers this morning to keep myself warm. I am very anxious to get that box. I exxpect to have a good time when that comes, I take it that the box started last Friday by Sart Hagers letter, if it did it must be here or most here by this time. You must have had a sweet time with Mr. Felshaw a going to Kal. I dont hesitate to ask for anything that I want, I know that you are willing to do anything for me, I did not iintend to find fault, You will pardon me this time wont you. What do you here from Geo. how is he getting along, or dont you know. I should think that Fathers work must go very slow only one alone, I wish that I could help work up some of your cane, When you get to singing some time, pleas sing a peice on the 305 page of the New Lute & think of me, also a peice on the 88th page and peice "Remember me" There the mail is just distributed no mail for me. thats too bad. I think Pack Pullman has just showed his, according to what I hear from letters that come to the boys. I have no news to write you so you will excuse this short letter. My news box is most emty & you must wait untill I get a new supply, I dont get any of your news papers yet, Dont you take the Tribune this year? I will in a few days write a letter to Father & Mother Yours in Love, Take a streight forward course & carry a stiff upper lip From Your Soldier. Charley to Millie

Head Quarters of the 19th Mich Infty Vol The
12th Army Coar Murfreesboro October 18th 1863

Dear Father & Mother

I am thankful that I am again permited to scribble you a few lines to let you know that I am yet in the land of the living, but I cant say that I am entirely well. I am with my company now but do no duty yet, I am not quite so good grit as {Look out who you read this to} Dave is or I might get a discharge. I wish that I could look as healthy as he does, & act as cheerfull when he forgets himself & when the Surgeon is absent. There is many men in the regiment that does duty evry day that is worse off than he is. Capt. Hubbard has made out discharge papers & is a doing all in his power, Doct. Bennett smells the rat so does the company. Pleas keep dark. I could tell you more about this matter, but I dont think it will be prudent. I cant help but say something about it because it makes me vext to see such great babys.—I am very thankfull for your kind letter, & I want more of them. You know that beggers always want more. All is quiet in Tenn. at preasent. No news now days, I understand that we are brigaded with the 12th Army Coar that came from the Patomic & that this 12th Coar is to take care of the line of rail road from Louisville to Chatanooga & it is most likely that we shall stay here. Rosecrans is getting a very large army togeather by this time, but I dont expect that he will make a move this some time yet, Jeff has gone to take charge of his army so I presume that they will make a desperate squddle bye & by,-- Now Father how does the farming get along, How comes on the sweet potatoes that you had a growing when I was at home, How does your crops turn out, Have you got any nice squashes? if you have pleas put one good nice one into an envelop & send it to me, also a good cabbage head. I have not taisted of a cabbage since I enlisted. O, how I want some vegetables to eat, They are very scairce down here I get once in a while a little butter, when I had money but now I dont get anything but what Uncle Sam furnishes, & that is not the best I can tell you one thing, that is when I get out of this you will not get me in it again. I am looking with great anxiety to see this terrible, terrible & cruel war close. When will it be, I cant tell, but I wish I new. I want to help you work up your cain &c. I am getting tired of a camp life, laying around day after day, have no exercise, poor diet, it is no wonder that were sick, John Duel is quite healthy again. Capt. Hubbard has been layed up with the Rheumitism about 2 weeks. Dagget is getting better. Dave is about the same. Sarg. Hager is well & all the rest of the Otsego boy's. We are haveing a good deal of cold wet weather, A hard thunder shower last night & quite chilly & pleasent today over head & O! O!! how nasty under foot. I have just eat my dinner Now I will finnish. Perhaps you would like to know what I had for dinner. Some boiled fresh beef & bread. Then I took some of the liquor, put in some peper & crumed in my bread. This makes a good dinner. Mother or Roenna I wish you would get me 2 or 3 nutmegs & grate them & send them in a news paper, You see we boil our rice in water then eat sugar on it taists rather flat & if I could have a little nutmeg to spice it up a little it would taist much better. On thinking it over, I think you had better send it in an envelope, For I find that the postmasters are very indifferant about sending papers, they have so much mail, One day last week the paper stated that over 40,000 letters left Nashville in one day, I suppose that you all have been to meeting to day. I haven't, I am not blessed with that pribilage in these parst, but I wished we was, How I would like to just step in to your house some time when you did not know it. But no I must wate,-- Violence shall no more be heard in the land, wasting nor distruction within our boredoers. Isa. 60.18. This shall be the day of the gladness of Christs heart, wherein he will rejoice & all the saints shall rejoice with him. Who can conceive of the triumph which shall be sung on that occation? And who can express the fullness & blessedness of that peace? How sweet & holy & joyous! Then there shall be no enemy & no enmity but perfect love in evry heart, No string shall vibrate out of tune, Evry soul shall be as a note in some concert of delightful music, that sweetly harmonizes with evry other note & all togeather blend in the most rapturous strains in praising God & the lamb for ever. I hope you will remember me in your family prayers Father I still try & live as I true to our maker as I can, My fear is ever in the lord. I very often have a good religious conversation with one of my comrads, we have a good many praying men in our Reg. & I am glad to see it & a great many that is the reverse! Now Father & Mother do not grieve for me But look a head & keep up good cheer. I perhaps will meet with you again. Pleas write often. Yours in Love, I am well (perty near) Charlie

Murfreesboro October 19th 1863

My Dear Wife.

Yours of the 13th ult No. 18 Came to hand yesterday and was very happily received, I was indeed very glad to here from you again but I am very sorry that I hurt your feelings so. I was not aware of that, I allways supposed that you liked to see me enjoy myself. Then I did not know that you was sick. I am sorry to here that you are sick Roenna? I hope you will forgive & overlook what I have said I will be carefull after this how I express my joy & feelings, I must acknoladge the commencement of your letter made me feel bad, I will tell you as you do me be very carefull of your health. I keep just about on the ballance, I dont gain strength, am not very well & not very sick, I am just sick enough to be excused from duty & make poseys on your letters, I do that for a passtime. You did not say aword about Georges success, only said that he came home, how did he make do, Pleas give me a little history of his campaign or get him to. How are Uncle Henry folks he owes me a letter &

wont write to me. I find that I havent many friends, they wont answer my
letters, They can do the other thing, About all mail that I get is from you
& the folks, On an everage one letter per week while others get one most
evry day, I think that I will save my paper, envelops & stamps. It cant be
because they dont know where I am, that so,-- It is now the 19th of Oct. &
I have not heard from the box yet, I expect it is in Nashville, There is so
much to come through that it cant get along very fast. It may lay there a
long time, I am sorry for I have nothing but hard bread to eat & not a cent
of money. Under these circumstances you know the box would come very
handy to fall back on. You may tell Cousins folks that I remember him I
dont know as I shall stop to think of him when I pull the box to peaces, I
had rather think of the those who fixed them up. I am real glad you sent
some Onions & Potatoes. I was in hops that you would send a good lot of
Butter, That is a choice article out here I am sorry to have to divide the
Onions & Potatoes. I think as much of a Potatoe as I would so much, I have
bought some marino potatoes & paid $1.25 per bush & bought nasty butter
for 35c Onions 2c a peace. I would like to know where you find pears, I can
just show you how to eat apples & pears, Say nothing. If Dave goes home,
he is a going to let me have his things that is left when he goes. If you have
a chance to send more butter in some bodyes box, you may send some if
you have not sent much. You know there is a gread deal of the time that
we have nothing but bread & fried pork fat. This happens just before we
draw our rations, We draw evry five days, & the boys dip a little to deep
the first 3 or 4 days. 2 days out of the 5 we draw fresh beef, & 3 out of the 5
warm soft bread, 2/3 of a loaf to a man. I tell you what it is, I can sit down
to a plate of boiled Potatoes, pepper & salt & rellish it as well as I did our
wedding supper, I can say that I love Potatoes now, I like them better than
I do the sweet Potatoe, I get once in a while one, You may send me the
mouse tail file in a news paper, if you pleas, I want to see if I cant make a
clam shell ring. The reason that Pullman dont come back is because that
he has got the Captaincy in a Coullered Reg. I beleive that I shant mind
paying $6.13 for the box, I expect to take comefort eating its contense. Give
my best respects to Beach Hall, tell him that I remember him. He gave me
a pair of sissors the day I left Kal. He is a good boy. What kind of a stove
did you get & what did it cost. When you tell of any thing new you should
explain it. What makes you think that I have not any intrest to pay on the
mortgage when I agree to pay ½ of it, Does Father or George say so? if they
do then it is all right, if they do not you will find there is some intrest for

us to pay. According to your figures you have paid out of the $50. $26. that leaves you $24. on hand. Wall, I have got to Stop. Capt. Hubbard just come here & wants me to superintend the fixing up his tent & the mail goes out in one hour, so I will close. My love to you all, Write when you can, No news this time, So Good bye

McMinnville, Oct 26/63

My Dear Wife,

  I take this short opportunity to drop you these few lines to let you know where I am by this time. Last Fri, we left Murfreesboro for McMinnville, We left very unexpected I have but a few minuts to write, I am well, we are builting up our winter quarters, We have rather bad mail araingements, now I have a chance to send you a line, the mail has to be carried to Murfreesboro, I have not hurd from my box yet but the Quarter master is going to Mur. tomorrow & will get it if it is there, you will pleas excuse this short letter for I have no house to stay in tonight. & it is now getting late, You will here from me soon again. Yours in haist Charley to Millie.

Head Quarters of the 19th {Mich}
McMinnville, Tenn.

My Dear Wife

  Your letter of the 18th Oct. No 19 came to hand last Sat, & was gladly received, also the box came. It was in a very bad shape. About half of the letter paper is like this sheet, very badly damaged I recken. The honey can both top & bottom was out, the corks to the bottles of the can peaches were out, The pickle bottle was open, The pickled peaches can was open, & run all through one end of the box My things suffered the worst & Mr. Hagers the least, My cheese was very badly molded, it being between the

others. The cakes most all moldy & spoiled. I could eat some of them. My
Over Coat & dress Coat was soked through. If it had not been for the coats
it would have been much worst. Tobaco badly damaged. I wanted 2 lbs at
least, I told you in one of my letters to send my coats & in the next I sed
not send them. I had drawed me a new over C. but I soon disposed of the
new one. The pears was half roted, Dave will not get any of them. (We
left him at Murfreesboro, he clames to be no better and no worst.) & the
big apple is jamed half away. The butter is all right only not enough of it.
Butter is as choice an article as gold, rather have it. The dryed fruit is not
hurt much I did not find any tea for me. I sent for the dry Prutian blue, this
that you have sent is of no use, it is put up in Oil. (A Mistake) Pleas send
some in paper by mail, if they have it in Otsego, send a little at a time. The
rest of the ink stuff is must up rather bad, I have had some good meals out
of the box a ready, The envelops & fancy papers was not damaged any.
Dear Millie, I have not much time to write you a very long letter to day. I
have to work on the fort, repairing it we expect Forest will make us a visit
this afternoon. We have (Co. B only) a good strong fort in. 5 companyes
are placed in different direction from the town & 5 companyes in the town,
It is reported that Forest is comeing in from the south with 1,000 men, let
them come, we are ready, I hope they will not get my stuff that came in
the box, a squad of men have gone out to blockad the roads, we all rejoice
to have them come, I suppose that you dont, "But" I think its all a camp
ruse the fort that we occupy is suffitiently strong enough to hold 2,000 men
at bay 24 hours with our Co. & in 12 hrs we can get reinforcements from
Tullahoma. We are now in a country where about evry family are secesh.
The worst that we have found, I want to see them all cleaned out.. This is
great garrillis country,-- We have our tents fixed up first rate for winter,
some think that we shall spend the winter here. We have a pleasent place,
but it will be rather cold because we are so high up in the world. I have no
news from that front. Dont know what they are doing only that they are
fighting & that we have drove Bragg left wing back out of sight. We are
away from the main rail line & will not get mail more than once a week
& my mail will not go out any oftener so you must not look for so much
as you have had. Dont be discouraged if you dont here from me so often,--
You may tell Mother that I would like the bread & milk & cream but I dont
care any thing about the all (awl) I am usealy well, Geo. does not say how
well he has done with his machine, I guess he did not do very well, You
may tell him that I will not except his letters if he dont write more, about

½ a page you know is not much of a letter to send way down in Tenn. If you want to write to Dave Direct D.R. Anderson, Hospital No. 9 Ward C. Murfreesboro. Direct my mail the same as before, I wish Byron Franklin much, dont you? I hope he will have a good time. Did Cosine Ira say that he would write to me? Elder Wolfe owes me a letter. I believe that there is nothing more at preasent only that I had a first rate breakfast, perhaps you would not call it so I had some good bread (first, for army bread) & butter I boiled myself 2 potatoes & made some dryed apple sauce, that is all. I call that a tip top meal, when one has to live on hard bread sow belly & coffee. I cant say that I dont like potatoes now, I had rather have them than apples. My love to all the folks, & to you Yours as ever Charley Millie

Nov. 4. No Forrest has come yet. Its a big scare. These two lines is ink that I made last night

Fort Mutton McMinnville, Nov. 8th 1863

My Dear Lonely Wife.

Another Sabeth has come & it finds me writing to my ever dear companion that is far from me who I love dearly, It is now 4 oclock & I did not know that it was sunday untill a few minutes ago, it was not because I did not want to know, but it is because the day is so little heeded that I hardly the day of the week, O, how cruel it is to be cut off from all my liberties & priviliges, Who will be more thankfull to be let out of this bondage than I will as a soldier in the army. There is many hear that like it but I dont. If you could only see what beautiful weather we have here now, Evry verity of spring birds that I ever saw or hurd is here now seeming to try to make us happy, But I am away from home & nothing will make me so happy as home. I received kind letter dated 25th No. 20 the 5th & also one good from Mother, I had a good time a reading letters for one spell & they done me lots of good. I suppose you will why I dont write as often as I use to, the reason is the mail does not go out but once a weak & come the same. I guess that you can get along with about one letter a week, cant you? seeing that I dont get any news to write,-- Yesterday we had considerble excitement here, At 11 oclock A.M. 200 garrillies was in site of town, Co. K. exchanged a few shots with them also the Lieut. Col. shot at them, No one hurt, We packed our knapsacks & busseled about & got read to meet them, but they dair not come. The same hour 1200 was seen 6 miles North of us, they made no attact, we slept all night with my great coat & catrage box on, so if they made an attact I would be ready for them, one minute is time enough for us to get out in line of battle. We was very much disappointed & felt vext because they did not come. We had our train out the same day & expected they would pitch on to them. The train hurd of it when they were within 12 m. of here unloaded & went back to Murfreesboro & got some cavelry, then tomorrow we expect them in (the train) If they should get our train of supplyes we should be in a bad fix. It seems to me & us all that I had rather go in a fight than to get a meal of vittles, Woe be unto the reb that gets in range of my gun. Nov. 9th Great excitement here now. I kin hardly right, The train has come & brought a number of boxes for the boys & they are in the glee. Bottles of wine & jelleys & honey broke & run all through the holl makeing it look some like mine, but its all the same. You had better believe that I have lived high the last few days, Dont care wether war keeps or not long as that lasts. I would like to you tell me how much paper & envelops you took out of what you bought, because I have sold out ½ of the paper & envelops to John Duel, We go company. He pays me back ½ what it cost & say nothing about the damaged paper. I wish I had another box of envelops, I have 3 bunches of the colered, I sell them for 25c a bunch. We have sold $6.50 worth in our own Co. I have to trust it untill pay day, If you payed $2.10 for the guilt paper you got it stucked to you. You did not send me half enough dried corn. I think evry thing of that, I have some a cooking for supper,-- Wall, I must explain myself. "Fort Mutton" The secend night we came here few of the boys went our & killed 2 sheep & the owner complained to the Col. The man claims to be a union man, but we know better. The Col. arrested the boys, which he had not aught to have done, & we named the fort after him. I will tell you all about it when I get home, We have to keep wide awake here, we are in a nest of garrellies & bushwhackers, we hawled in 9 the other night. & 7 horses. The weather is quite cold today & the wind blows hard, I am makeing a little at sketching for the boys. I sketch their tent to send home, get 50c a peace, I have made 2 & have 4 or 5 more to make. You will understand that I have not done any duty yet. I am troubled with a weekness in my hips & knees. It troubles me about carring any load or travleinng I never have felt right scince my journey through Dixey, Dont know as I will get over it right off, Aside from that I feel perty well. Tell mother that I remember her letter also Marys, My sheet is near full & I must close soon. I would more only I want to mend up our shanty a little, I have a nice brick trowel tell Father & would like to send it home, Wall good bye Millie from Charlie Have you sent me that peice of rubber I asked you to if not, Pleas send me a peice to rub pencil marks out

Head Quarters of Co. B. of the 19th Mich. Inft.
Fort Mutten, Mc Minnville, Tenn.
November 15th 1863

My Dear Wife

Yours of the first inst. without No. came to hand the 13th & was much welcomed, when I received it I was writing to Mother, I have hurd of nothing new scince to tell you. I want to ask a few more favors of you seeing that I am so helpless. Joseph Stuck is a going to send John Duel a box & I would like some more Butter. Some tea, Nutmegs about 6 of them if you pleas, A peice of indian rubber for rubbing pencil marks, you will find it in the drawer of the Drafting desk, also an old pair of brass dividers, iron pointed, you will find them in the desk or tool chest. And you may send me 1 oz. of soft prutian blue (the dry powder) if they have it in Otsego You need not go to much trouble to Kal after it. Farther than these things that I have mentioned you can send what you are a mind to, Some more dryed corn would come good. Some body had to go & stick Daves name on the budget you sent me, so I lost one half of it, I had rather let anything els go than the corn. One thing more, I want you to send my box of water colars & brushes. Send all the colars there is & one peice of black crayon, & all of the small pencil brushes, see that all the paints are in the tin box, send the box all along. I dont know but I shall send for my whole kit, I think that I shall get a new position, That is as regimental draftsman, such as drawing forts, maping the country &c. Doct. Bennett is interceeding for me, I dont know as I shall be furnished tools or not. I wish that I had another box of Envelops I have sold most all out at 25c a bunch. A box of 20 bunches cost 2.50 & sels for $5.00 that pays well. That will buy my Tobackker, If you had sent me the tobaco that I wanted I could have sold it for $3.50 per lb. & quick sale at that. O yes! one thing more, I have got the itch & want to be cured. I wish you would ask Doct. Hopkins what I must do to get rid of it, Send me a perscription or send some meadicen. I would rather he would send the meadicen. Most all of the Co. has it even to the Capt. Give my best respects to the Doct. & Family, Yes, Yes, Just as I expected. I expected to here that you would get jelous of me & go with some man Nothing straing & I cant blame you much. I would go if I were in your place. That is right, Go when you can & when you are a mind to You cant get me mad if you do So go it while you are young & while your name is Clark Pleas tell Charlie Franklin to not mind the dates of his letters but send them along, What I have said You will take in good part for I was only in fun. They have done a good thing at drafting in Otsego. Its all right except the $300. I think that I am entitled to $300 as a man that is compelled to go by law. Nov. 16. Mon. Eve. I have been buisey all day a getting ready to go to drafting for Uncle Sam. So I did not get my letter in the mail bag.

I have just made up my mind to have you send me 2 papers of ground mustard to eat on cold meat, & more yet, The boys are trying to get my files from me. I have been offered 50c for the one you bought me. Now then if you will go to B. Ballou & get him to get them for you one Doz. & wait untill get my pay. I will send it to you & you will pay him. But if they are not easyly got or are not to be had, let them go. he would do better to send to Kal. than you will. I want the same kind of the one that you bought. Dont forget the mustard & nutmeg. I think that I am a going to have a good chance in drafting. I am well to night, & hope this will find you well, It is late & I must stop, the rest are all to bunk. So good night, I wish that I could go to bed with you Roenna Charlie This scrap for Father & Geo. Pleas save it.

Head Quarters of the 19th Mich
Infty Vol. McMinnville, Nov 19th 1863

My Dear Wife

As I have been sitting at my desk all day & drafting & a little tired, to rest myself I thought perhaps you would like to have me stop & have me talk with you a little while, allthough I havve no news to tell you, but I must you a letter. Pherps you would like to know what I am about these days, The first place I have been detailed from Co. as assistant ingeneer at this post, for the preasant. Dont know how long I shall surve. I have no commition & do not draw any more pay. If I should happen to suit I mite get a right smart chance & draw big pay, but this is all uncertin, The cheif engineer is very much satesfied with what I have done thus far & gone beyond his expectations. He says that he will do all he can for me, I have my office a nice pleasant room, furnished with a desk & chairs fireplace & wood brought in & evry thing done right up to the noch. But my liveing is just the same old thing. Sowbelly and bread besids what you sent me. My office is next to the Provose Marsial office. I dont have to work only as I have a mind to, I like it so well that I work most all of the time. I can thank Doct. Bennett for this chance. We are fortfing this place very strong. Shall build some 5 or 6 forts & Redoubts, 2 or 3 drafts has to be maid of each one & one nice one made to sent to Washington for examination to see how each one is constructed, I am at work one for that purpus. We {maine} "Vinyard Hill Redoubt" Then after all of these all built we have to make a map of the whole town & forts & their position, & all of the roads, hills, mountains, riverrs, Bridges &c, &c.. This will be a big job, The map will have to the Gen. commanding the army. I make the engeneers furnish me tools. You will understand that I am not with the Company now. I am under Capt. Bigalow (of Co. G. of our Reg.) command, a first rate man, rather rough, Been in the army 13 years, engeneering good deal of the time, He is also Provose Martial here. The Provose office is full from morning till night, The people, men & women takeing the othe &c. We have lots of fun a searching houses & picking up Uncle sams property. Wel It is getting late & I will wait untill another day. So Good night. Nov. 21 Good Morning Dear Wife. As the train is a going to start out with the mail. I thought I would close my letter & I have but a few minutes to do it in & it may be a week before I will get another chance to send my mail. I am well this morning. I am getting along first rate with my Draft. I know of no news to write you this morn. All is quiet on the Cumberland I believe I enjoy myself first rate in my new position have lots of Music, Violin, & Dulcemer &c I hope you will excuse this short letter. I think it is hardly worth 3 cents. My love to all, Your Husband Charley

Asst Engineer
Head Quarters of the 19th Mich.
Infty. McMinnville, Nov 25th 1863

Dear wife Roenna C. Prentiss

Your kind message of the 11th came to hand last evening with a cargo of nutmeg. I was very glad to get the nutmeg I also received this morning a letter from Father & Mother I should have got that last evening but did not. It contained some tea. You betterr beleive I will have one good cup of tea, I wish that I could swap my coffee with you for tea, I dont drink coffee once a month, we have nothing in the first place, to make good coffee in, nothing but greecy kittles, then no milk so on the whole I dont take any coffee I prefer T. A few days ago I traided 1 ¼ lb. Coffee for 2 ½ doz. eggs & this morning I eat the last of the eggs. Coffee is worth 50c. Eggs 20c, Butter 25c & so on. Tell Mother that I have not received a letter from her with nutmeg. If she has sent it it will after a while. I think that I have received evry thing that you have sent me as yet. Except that letter. Whist, Hark, be careful what you say, read to your self. I am a going to give Dave a blowing up. I got a right saucy note from him day or two ago a giveing me a slight tutch of my dishonesty. If I am dishonest I dont want to be twited of it, You know whenn the box came I was in McMinnville & Dave in Murfreesboro. Mr Hager & I carried the box in my tent, & there overhawled it. On opening it, we found the contence badly damaged. Now then who is to blame, The fried cakes were molgied through, The cookies saturated with vinigar, honey, juice & collered with the log wood & the poison acid I through them away, The larg apple was 4/5 rotten & the pares were most all rotted away. some dried peaches in a bag was all full of maggets or a little fruit worm & the peaches well soked, I cleaned them out, washed the bag, put them back & dried as though they were my own. Now I get cused for it. I took the cloth off of his cheese & washed it. dried the cheese which was very moist & moldy, I made a box with my hatchet & jacknife worked hard all one sunday when I could hardly sit up, havent done duty in 3 months, then get such a going over is what grinds. Now I calculate to tell what I think of him. In a week from the time I received my box I got a chance to send him his by the supply train. What do you suppose is the matter of him. When I go to him & talk his conversation is soon on the way home. He is home-sick & love-sick & settled to the bottom of his heart & it may have squezed his spleen a little, A healthyer & a more rugged man I never saw than Dave Anderson. When the Doct. comes around his breath is not more that half inch long. But when he is asleep his breath is all right. He can play sick but his looks betray him & the Doct. knows it. Cant fool him. He eats more than any other 4 patients in the hospital so the nurses tell me, He goes hobbleing around with his staff & makes more fuss than the man who had both feet ampitaded when I was there, He layes on his bunk from morning till night & can hardly muster ambition enough to wate on himself, I have proof of what I have said & can tell you more. Fri. morning, Nov. 28 I have got tired of lying abed I thought I would get up & talk with you a little while. Dont know what time it is. About 4 oclock I recken, We are haveing this minute a nice warm thunder shower, Weather is like summer these days. The birds sing like spring, & the grass hoppers & crickets sing all night. Yes, & so does the Musqueetoes plage on them, & evry thing seems to be pleasent, I am still a drafting & engeneering & expect to keep at it the remainder of the time that we stay here, I like my new position first rate, When I commenced drafting I hunted around & found an old waurthliss kit of tools & drew up a couple of drafts, the Capt. showed them to the Col. & he was so taken up with them that he sent off & got a kit worth $18, so I am pretty well riged. You say you wish that you knew all about my health. I can tell you, it is not very good & not very bad, I have taken so much meadicen that I feel it has all of my joints, Am troubled with the pain in my stomach as useal, The Doct has tryed to cure me but give it up as a bad job, My weight 155. This is my averaged weight when at home. The itch (camp itch) troubles me the most of any thing els. You need not trouble yourself about me. Old Abe Lincoln thinks the war will end in three months, Any how we saw in the papers that he said that if the war progressed the next three months as it had the last 3 weeks, it would close the war, I hope this is so, I know one thing that is that we are squezeing the rebels harder evry day. Their strong holds are going weeker, their soldiers are deserting evry day conciquently their army is getting weeker evry day, While at the same time we are gaining ground & our army is getting stronger Our forces have (so the news is) controll of Lookout mountain.

This Lookout mountain is one of the most sightlyest places in the United States, There are 7 differant states that can be seen at one view from the summit of this mountain, Virginia, North & South Carolina, Georgea, Alabama, Miss'p. & Tenn. also the Miss. River, This place is a hard place to take. Gen. Sherman has wiggled around untill he has cut off their supplyes. Now they have got to fish or cut bate as the old saying is, This mountain commands Chattanoga; I saw this mountain when I went through Dixey, but thought little about it, It is a splended sight Doct. Armstrong of this place says that the Atlantic Ocian has been seen from this higth in a clear day & with a powerfull glass. I tell you what it is Roenna! a man wants a heart of stone to stay in a Provost Marshals officce, to see the women & Old Fathers beging & pleeding for their sons who get caught bushwhacking. Death is the penelty of a bushwacker. Yesterday I witnessed an old Father & his son, the son was brought in 4 days ago &

was suspected to be a bushwhacker & the father supposed he was to be exicuted, The prisoner was brought in my office, then the father came in. The poor old man just stood & claped his hands, & shook hands & said not a word he was so overcome with greif. Who can disscribe the feelings of many poor old man & women, they both proved to be good Union men & were releesed. I just hurd the mail is a going out in a few minuts, & I will close. I intended to fill this sheet but I will not have another chance in one week I will try & have my letter ready next, so good bye for this time my love to all. This from Your Dear Husband Charley Millie Prentiss The No. of your Nov 11 letter is No. 22

Head Quarters of the 19th Mich
Infty. McMinnville Dec 10th 1863

My Dear Lonely Wife

Seeing that I have a few moments to write I will improve the time. I received a letter from you a few days ago bearing Date Nov. 24 & was glad to here from you again. Also one from Wm. Warrant & Dave from Murfreesboro. I am yet allive & kicking. My health has not been good scince I wrote you last, but I have been up all the time. I have had the Diarrea very bad. Now I have stoped it & feel pretty smart. I have been drafting all day. It is now twilight & I will have to stop a little while. Now after taking a delisious from a tip top cegar that I got from a freind & the second one that I have smoked scince I saw you. I will continue my letter. You must not look for any news from me this time for I have none. I still retain my position as Asst. Engineer & my work takes well, The officers say that I am foolish to stay here & soldier it for $13 a month when I can get $100. I dont suck that but I shall try & get more that $13 if I can. I want you to understand that I dont go in the ranks again if I can help it. I have another office now. The first one was to much exposed, to many runing in & now I have a better place. A good desk & good tools, Aplenty of wood & a man to cut & bring it in, & a first class boarding place, I board with Mrs. Gen. Roggers Gen. Roggers is at Memphis a geathering military taxes. A very popular man. His life has been saught for many times by the bushwhackers of this town. I am sorry that I sent for those things I sent for last, for I dont need them when I am boarding Soldiering is so uncertin that I hardly know what calculations to make, I have butter & potatoes most evry meal. Our

Reg. drew pay last Sat. I had to pay only $4.05 for thhe overplus clothing so I drew $47.95 for 4 months pay, this is much better than I was informed at first. Our officers had that order countermanded. The Col. would not stand it, to have us pay for clothing that was lost in action. The old Acct. & the Anapolous Act. was all through out & all the clothing drawn scince the first day of June was brought against us, & all that we draw over $3.50 per month is taken out of this last pay. I want to send home some money but I see no safe way. No express running in this country & I dont like to trust it in letters, I dont want to send myself short as I did beforee. I suffered for the want of money while I have been sick. I have offered to pay 2 dollars for the use of one untill payday & could not get it. Tell father that he had better let the ague alone. I think it is cold enough way up norf without haveing the ague, We dont have that down here. We have had but few flakes of snow this fall. The weather is very mild & pleasent, evry now & then a frosty night. I can see some times some snow on the mountains. If I were in fathers place I would not bother with the ague. I ed have something that is worth haveing. That is the Tenn. Quickstep, I suppose you know that when a man gets cornered, he can shoot both front & reer. Not act as though you was scared & stand & shiver. Wall, Wall..I guess I had better change my subject, Thanksgiving pass & I did not know it, did not know as there was such a day. But that chicken pie is what takes me down. Save me a plate full untill come & I will show you how to eat chicken Pie, Wall I must pull for a close, It bed time & my eyes will not allow me to write or read by candle light. My buisness is of that kind that I have peck close all day. I sent Cosine Ira a letter day before yesterday. Oh..have you got my last letter read through yet, if you have I will send you another, Good friends to all Charlie Millie

Remember me Soldier

McMinnville Dec. 11th '63

Dear Wife

Seeing that I have a little time to spare I will write you a few more words. This is a beautiful Spring morning the birds are singing sweetly, & I feel pretty well & who can help feel happy. I have not received any paper with rubber in. I have sent to Nashville for some & some other things, I dont want any Prussian blue, I dont think that I shall trouble myself with ink, only as it runs off the point of my pen. I finally dont want any thing I sent for only my water collars. But if you have sent them let them come & if you have not sent them, you needent. In regard to the wine & jelly, the jelly bottle had sprung a leak, but little ran out. The wine was all right. The can peaches was all gone, dont know what became of it, the works was press open by the working of the peaches. The juice of the pickle peaches all ran out, but the peaches were good. The Vinegar all out of the Cucumber pickels, they were all good. Now, I think I have told you all about the box. I have got my money back on the paper & envelops & if it was not soiled I should have got more. I have but 2 quior & 2 bunches of envelops left. {Whist, keep this to yourself Hark. Dave is grunting the same as ever, he clames to be no better, he wrote me a letter the other day asking my forgiveness for what he had said &c. & told me if I wanted money to let him know it & he would let me have all I wanted. I ask no odds. I want you to understand that he is not very well liked out here} & Good by for this time. so here goes your letter

McMinnville Tenn. Dec 18 1863

My Dear Wife

Your kind letter of the 10 inst. came to hand just now & how glad I was to hear from you once more. O, it just fills my heart with joy to know that you are all alive & kicking. I am feeling first-rate now days. I am getting fat again, I weighed myself twice just 10 days apart, my first weight 145, & my second 155 on the same scales. Now according to old dayballs that would make in my favor just 2 lbs per day wouldent it, I am haveing first rate liveing now days, I have my rations cooked in a sencible manner & so that they are eatible also enough to eat, so on the whole I think feel rather big over my preasent situation, at least you would think so if you could see me with my pollished boots & my new officers Cap, which cost me in Nashville two hundred & twenty five cents, I spect before I know it there will be something sticking fast to my shouders, The Major urged me hard the other day to take a horse back ride with him, but I could not go, I will though? When it gets pleasant, He wants I should do some sketching for him. I have just all that I can do at drafting for the Engineers, When I get done here I have to chances ready for me, The Post Commissary wants me to come & clerk for him, do all his writing & make out his monthly reports & returns, He says that he only wants me to write & figure, That you know is a very responcible place, The Post Quarter master is the same They both declare that he will have me, But, But, I guess I will go to Nashville if I can get a chance wouldent you? I think that I have all the drafting & writing to do that I want untill the war closes. There is no knowing when that will be, What would you think if I should tell you if the women in this country eat snuff & chew tobaco, well they do right smart I reckon both white & black. The people here use some quir language. The boys out doors are haveing quite a spree, they feel well, I dont know of a sick man in our regiment. We are very healthy, I know I never felt better in my life than I do now, with the exceptions of the itch & weekness in my hips & hands. I reckon you are haveing some loud times way up norf. I hope you had a good time eating your Oyster supper, did you save one for me? I love um & guess I will have some next Christmas, dont know yet. Now about that changing name dicker, how shall I dispose of that, I hardly know what to say, to say, I wish her much joy, is out of fashion, Give her my compliments & let it go at that, I dont suppose it will do any good for me to say anything now /scince she has {crossed out} (I wont say it) You may tell her that she must not be affraid to wrrite to me now, if her name Mrs. Warrent. Tell Mrs. Phelps I feel slited because she did not write me too. Well there if you havent sent me another box, You must think that I am hard up, I guess you did not get my letter countermanding the order did, But I think that I can take good care of it. O what would I do if I had no kind companion to think of me & to send such good notions, then on the other hand what would I do if I had none to think of & to write too. Hault I must fix the fire. You cant realise the value we put upon those boxes that come to the soldiers, thinking about where it came from & by whose hands put in the contence. I wish you could see one pulled to peaces or gutted, I am not sorry you sent it, but I dont realy need it now. still I may need it when I dont think I shall so it is all right. Well, what does Tim have to say, I am affraid that he will let the cat out of the bag. Perhaps not, maybe you want to know what coller the cat is. I will tell that when I see you. You will not find it a very large one, Yes, he tells the truth about Dave. I cant tell you much about Dave scince I left him at Murfreesboro, He write me that he is just about the same & says he cant get a furlough & wants Capt. Hubbard to save him the vacantcy of sargent, I think if he gets it, he will have to come to the Reg. I hurd some very singular remarks about him yesterday & I did not ask for them. I do not wish to meddle nor stur up a stinque, I did not want you to say a word to any of them for now there will be a muss about it. If there is, who cares, I dont, let her rip &c. I know my rights,-- Well how comes on the new roof & door on the shanty. Have you dug your sweet potatoes yet. I have lots of um to eat down here, Tell Father that we can beat the South raising the Irish Potatoe, what they grow down here are not fit to eat, very watery & mostly the merino. As I have said before, I would not live here for the best farm in Tenn. I dont like it here. Too hot hete in the summer very mild winters, dont cost a man all he can rase to keep his stock through the winter, They have not commenced to fodder yet. I had Mrs. Roggers make me another cup of tea & that was good, I cant get green T in this part of the world, Coffee I dare not use any more. The T in the box {a small drawing of a box of tea} I shall prize very highly. Well it is now X oclock & I must go to {small drawing of a bed with a following drawing of a man at midnight walking picket saying have you seen any chickens out this way I must have some for breakfast and followed by houses & chickens labelled see them run} Well it is Saturday night again, the 19 And I will try & finnish my litter letter. I wonder if that fellow has got his chickens yet I realy dont know what to write about, We dont get any news. The weather has been very cold to day & is freezing very hard, I have got my table drawn up in line of battle before a rousting fire in the fireplace, which I find is very comfortable this cold night, & I feel perty well myself. I have been buisey all day at my drafting & dont feel very tired. I found in your letter a little slip, "The loss of a Wife," & it was a good thing, how true a picture it is & how sad it makes me feel to read it, How many there will be to say "The Loss of a Husband" who has left home expecting perhaps to return again, as I do, I expect to return to my home some time, but when I cant tell, I still feel encouraged that the war will soon end & let us all go home what few there is left, I think that I have hurd that the papers say that the rebs begin to talk piece, They certinly cant do anything now & I think they begin to see it. The country here is just fluded with rebel deserters. Most all take the Oath, some dont, Such ones we slap in the prison & take care of them, We fetch them to turmes, We have about 35 here, the most of them will have to pull hemp for liveing, I will tell you how that is. They come here & take the Oath then go to steeling horses & go to bushwhacking, When they take the Oath, they pledg there lives. We play lots of Yankey tricks to ketch them, We dress ourselves in butternut cloths & when night comes we start out & go long the roads makeing all sorts of the yankeys, they soon will make themselves known & will tell us where there is a gang. We have other ways to ketch them,-- Has Mother got her letter yet, I mailed one a day or two ago a good fat one, I dont know as she can read all of it in one day, if not she must take 2 days, Also a letter to Mary, I wish you a merry Christmas. What are you a going to have good that day. You must save a peice for me, The boys are haveing a great time a cerrinadeing this To be continued {On a small scrap of paper} Dec. 18 /63/. This letter has been writen & ready for the mail a number of days. I think it will go out to day or tomorrow. I am well. I feel better nowdays than I have for the last 5 months. No news, Yours as ever, Charlie Millie

McMinnville Dec. 25 1863

My Dear Wife

I wish you a merry Christmas. Not receiving your last kind letter, I feel it my duty to scratch you a few lines thinking that a short letter would do you some good, I will say to begin with that I am well, & enjoying prety good health for the preasent. Last Tuesday & Wednesday I was quite sick with the Diarreah, I employed Doct. Armstrong of this town, & he cured me right up. Our Surgeons do not understand doctering in this climate. & that is not all I dont think there is a sick man in the regiment, at least I dont know of any, The 23 Mo. that is here with us has from 40 to 45 in the hospital most all the time sick with the Dont know how you spell it. Been with some nice city wemen I spose May bee you spell the word. Well what about Christmas, what are you doing this evening at 8 oclock, See if you can tell me in your next, I will tell you how the day has passed with me & the rest, I have set at my desk a drafting most all day, & in front of me out on the public squair the boys have been haveing fun with 3 Jacks & one Jenny that they picked up somewhere. You have hurd before now what a contirary beast a jackass is, Well they would go when they took a notion to, From 2 to 3 would pile on his back, then he wouldent go, All that could get around him & push & twist his tail, then he would not go. Then another methard is tryed, That is to get a large brier & put under his tail & press it down, Then he goes, Heels high in the air & men too, Some went tumbleing one way & some another. At one time the three men & jack all lay spralled on the ground. And so they have kept it up all day, We have brought in three bushwhackers to day, One of them is the notorious Capt Canton, we have him in irons, He is elected for pulling hemp in a few days, He was much dreded in this country, He was caught in bed last night 17 miles from here. Let me see. What was a going on 4 years ago about this time. I think their was some weddings about that time, Who would have thought that we would have been a thousand miles apart at that time. Little did I, How true the saying is, we know not what the morrow will bring forth, --The weather is beautiful, the ground dry & dusty, Cold enough to freese evry night. I am still at my drafting business, & like it well, I have a good place to board, Had a splended dinner, I had rost turkey, fried chicken, rost mutton, potatoes, cherry pie &c, &c, &c, &c & other things to numerous to mention, I had the honer of eating with Gen. Roggers, He is a real sosiable old chap & had lots of stories to tell, I have an invitation to spend an evening at his house. You will remember it is at his house is where I board. He is home on a visit. He stays at Memphis, The time of Wheelers raid here the rebels robed & distroyed 70 thousand dollars worth of property for him. He /is {crossed out} was very wealthy man. The rebs has about ruined him. He had to flee for life when he left here, Mrs. Roggers tells me that I seem like one of her own folks & wants me to stay. I give her my rations & 50c a week for my board, & get tip top liveing. She wants me to tune her piano. I have had one other application to tune a piano for a rebel lady. I have not made up my mind yet. Her Husband is in the rebel army. If she will give me $5. I will do it nothing less. There is more in town that wants tuning done but confound the secesh wemen. If they get me to do their tuning they will pay dear for it & ten chances to one if I dont spoil them. Ill show them a yankey trick,--Well I guess you have had enough of my nonsence & I will close. I hope this will find you all well. I expect to get that box by the next train. Keep up good courage Millie. My Love to you. Charlie to Millie

How Comes on the Sweet Potatoes
Did you send me some tobacker in that box.

McMinnville, Tenn. Dec. 30, 1863
Head Quarters of the 19th Michigan
Infty. Vol. Engineers Office Thursday
Morning 4 oclock A.M. &c.

Dear Wife

Your kind & interesting letter Dated Dec 16th came to hand last evening
& I tell you what lots of comfort I took in reading it I also received one
from Sophie, which was a good letter, Your letter found me well & spending
the evening with Gen. Roggers. He is a very kind & pleasent man. Has
lived in this country 50 years & a stout Union man. It is enough to make
ones blood run cold to here him tell how he & his family has suffered by
the rebels, As I have said before, you cant imagine the suffering there is in
this part of the country. He & his son has been shot at many a time but have
escaped yet. For more than 2 years he has not stayed with his familly only
a part of a night. He is or was a very wealth man & has lost scince the
rebelion over 150 thousand dollars. Tell Geo. that he is exempt from the
draft he has a sore thumb. I am sorry that he got bit, but he must learn better
than to ketch a savage hog by the mouth. Dont you think so, As I have seen
down here, men try to ketch a musket ball in their mouth, & get a sore
mouth by the means. In the battle of Thompson Station a man was shot in
the cheek & took the ball out of his mouth. We are haveing beautiful
weather. No snow has fallen here except a few flakes that melted before
they to the ground. I hardly know how snow looks any more, It freeses a
little nights & pleasent day times, How fortunate it is for the soldiers that
the weather is no worst. I dont want to see any snow while I am a soldier
for it makes it very unpleasent for us, to stand picket. {The following is
written in red ink} I will change my collars a little while, Well I am sorry
for Dave, to lay in the hospital unwell 5 or 6 months & cant get his discharge.
He dont know how to go to work to get his discharge. He must get up &
clean them out 2 or 3 times & talk turkey to them, then he will get it, I say
it is too bad to have to stay there so long & live on two meals per day. I
would not stand it. I would get up & leave for some place, I should rather
stay with the company. The boy are haveing a good time now days, first
rate time. Stand Picket evry other night & dig on the forts 8 hours per day,
first rate time, I call it, Dont you. If I am up all night I would like to sleep
a little in the day time, wouldent you. My candle has burned out & I will
wate untill day light. It is now daylight & most dark again. I have eat my

supper & been out to take a walk, I should like to help you eat those cookies & friedcakes & things that you have been cooking. What a terrible thinking I keep up most all the time about these days, what a good time we had 4 years ago now, O. wall! never mind. There is a good time comeing yet. Dont you say so. Yes. All that I can do now in the line of comfort is to take pen or pencil & paper & scribble & make pictures & sent them to you. If they pleas you I am glad for it is all that I can do for you while I am bound to my country. It does seem to me that my servises does amount to but little, allthough I am shure of one while at Brentwood & would shoot another one as soon as I would shoot a squirrel. The rascals, sneeking in the woods evry day trying to kill some of us, the same time with the oth in their pockets, The trouble is we cant tell who the right one is, & the Union man dare not say anything for of his neighbour. I am haveing a very good time now, but I keep at work most all of the time. No I do not take such comfort as I would at home I am in the society of officers. I had rather have the society of my company by all odds. Dark again. ha. ha ha ha ha ha ha ha ha ---Out of breath. My box ha! ha! ha! My box has come, ha ho ho oooo It is all right except one brush that had crawled through the tin box. Oh what a pleasure it is, what a luxery y you dont know anything about it, nor anybody els but a soldier. To over hawl the work that you have done with your hands. O, didnt I have a good time a pulling it to peices. Yes! I found some toebackker, a pound I recken, I have about a quarter of the other you sent me, You had aut to have explained the itch arraingement a little more, You didnt tell me wether to rub the mug or the ointment nor how often. But I think I shall rub the ointment on the itch evry night, then when I go to bed I can scratch it in. I calculate to have a good time eating crout. You couldent hit me any better. That T I wouldent take gold for it. I gave Capt. Bigelow & Lieut. Mc. a cake, didnt they smack their chops? ha ha ho ho ooo Dont foolish me, I will enclose to you Capt. Bigelows picture for safe keeping. He is the engineer of this post I am a makeing him a set of drawings of the works of this place & he will have my name on them as Draftsman & he says he will have my profile My work takes them down the banks. The Col. is a going to have a set of them & have sent away 2 set. There is 10 in a set. Wall, about the box, what did the envelops cost. The fruit I shall keep, untill I cook for myself again. The butter is nice & the fact of the buisness is, it is all nice, When will you get your pay for all of this. Wall! Well, I dont know about this peddling itch ointment, rather funny buisness for me I recon. I supposed that I wanted to take something to clense my blood first. Now maybee you think I have the itch that has legs, that lays nits, hatch out & crall & bite. I dont think I have. Off the track again. That box came in all right on the train this evening while I was writing this letter just at dark. Gen. Roggers payed me a visit to day. Dont you think that I am heighly commooded to have a Gen. come to visit me. He is a friend, I must have a nip at my crout if it is most bed time. Now about that blackwallnut lumber. I have but very little & that is most to the bottom of that large pile of lumber back of the granery. You may sell it if you can get it out, It will be an {here the letter is turned sideways and the following is written in red ink} awful job to pull all of that large pile. You can do as you see fit, but if you can get along without the money untill I can send you some, I would not sell it now. If something should turn up that I should never come home then you can sell all, wont that do Those are very nice envelops, Aught to have some paper to go with them. You stole out one bunch dident you. 20 bunches in a box. Its all right. I have sold all of that damaged paper but one quior and got 30c a quior. Talk to me about takeing comfort down here. when I have to fight lice & rats & scratch the itch all the time I cant write half the time I have to scratch so much. If I dont give myself a dopeing tonight Ill wonder. The band is just a playing Dixey for tattoo. The Gen. says that we have the best band in the army. Our brass band arraingement has all fell through. It costs to much. Major Griffin has no returns from Nashville in reguard to my position there, I think that I shall get in there to draft I hope so when I get done here, I have enough to do here for 6 weeks yet. Say you can tell that mister that I will be after him. He had better be careful. Then you took his arm and was willing to go. Thats all right I hope amongst all of them, that they will take good care of my Dear Wife. I shall have to come right home & have that thing straightened What els is there that you have not told of. I must tell you something. I came very near falling in love with a Molatto women. She is handsome too. There, thats all. I must quit. The Capt. wants my desk to make out his muster roll so good night. Good morning. The last day of the month. (Turn to 1 page) the last day of the year & I wish it were the last day of the war. I feel very proud of my new years gift that I received last night. that box. You have done better by me than I can do by you. You know beggers always want more. I would like to have you send me a calender for 1864. My old one has run out. Have you got over your cold yet. You must be careful as you tell me. I dont want to here that you are sick, That would make me feel discontented. I feel all right when I can here that you are well.

I guess your numbering letters has run out. You have sent all that I wanted, the Crayon is right. You may let the prussian blue go to pot, I dont want to bother with it now. The file too, you neednt send any. I wish Father good success with his Singing skools. I expect that I shall forget all about singing, I want you to learn a good bunch for me. O how I wish that I could step in to the school just as you get started on a peice. & have you all see me. What a brakedown their would be. I pitty Alvin Leighton if he has a cancer on his nose, It will eat off his nose wont it, I will pick up a little nigger for you soon. I am affraid that you will not keep him if I do, Will you pay the freight on him? This stamp act is something that I have not hurd of. I did not know as you had to pay a revinew. Have you had any sleighing yet, How much snow have you, What is pork worth in Michigan now, I dont know what it is worth here. I did not do much at sketching, made but 3 for pay, $1.50. 11 a.m. I have just mustered. We have to muster evry 2 months, seeing that my sheet is most full I will pull for shore. When you get this letter read through just let me know it & I will write you another. I dont suppose this will be very interesting for there is nothing in it that amounts to anything. I will try & do better the next time. I wish you a happy new year for tomorrow. Be a good girl & keep up good courage, be patient. The war will soon close, I think. I keep hopeing & look ahead for a better time. Has mother got her letter read through yet.

Yours in Love Charlie

CHAPTER 4

JANUARY – JUNE 1864

McMinnville Jan. 6th 1864

My Dear Wife

Now I will make an effort to answer your last letter, bareing date, Dec. 24" 1863. The letter was much wellcomed & was read with pleasure. The only fault I have to find, there is not enough of them. I am happy to find you in such good spirits. Your letters of late seem to bare a cheefull expression & I am glad to see it. I think you will find by the reading of this letter that my news box is empty. I dont take the papers & all is quiet about here, with the exceptions of a few rebs that we pick up occasionly. Buisness is not (Pleas excuse all good spelling) so lively with us as it was before the army went into winter quarters, I here that General Foster has give Longstreat a good floging & done it twice. I presume you have hurd of it before I did. I thought I would just mention it for fear you might forget it & become discouraged, I dont here as, Johney I wish you would shut the door. Its getting cold here, as they are doing anything down on the Potomac & General Grant has burrowed for the winter at Nashville. He is a little, inferior looking man. I saw him at Murfreesboro some 3 or 4 month ago, he is not much larger than Geo. Gen. Grant is a man that, stoke up Joney the fire is low, my hands are cold & num I can hardly feel my pen, that is not very well liked, dont joggle the table so, We have a regiment here that has been in battles under him & they tell some stories about him. Sy? give me a chaw of your tobackker, mine is in my knapsack & I dont want to get up now. they say that he was drunk as he could be & not fall off his horse, & his missmanagement was the cause of their being taken prisoners, I dont think much of him, I had rather have the old posy by odds. Yes, your letter found me feeling pretty well if I remember right. We are haveing some very cold weather & I guess as cold as you have. We have no snow except what we can see on the tops of the mountains, the ground is bare, dry & frose hard, I suppose you have fine sleighing up norf, What kind of a thing is a sleigh, we dont have any down here, have wheeles dont they, what are they used for, These are the questions that are asked us & a great many others, Many of the people dont know as much as a wooden man. You asked me the question if I could take something to stop the dysintery, I answer yes, Day before yesterday I had it hard & was quite sick, During the day I felt as though I wanted to be eating someting, I goes to my little box & takes out my dryed black burries dryed in sugar & eat quite a lot, they was good, & scince that it seems that the seeds have sprouted, taken root, & absorbed all the moister, conciquently I have not had a vacuation scinse, & now I feel better. I lay it to the blackburries that has filled up the channel, dont you? I have a good lot of them on hand yet, I cant tell you now how much I did make in my speculation, some rainy day I will call my thoughts togeather & sum it up. You know I sold out one half of the stock of stationarys to John Duel at cost & he & I went in pardnership, We sold the envelopes at 25c per bunch the paper for 30c per quior the guilt edg for 35c & the, thats all. I kept one quior of the damage for my own use. At sketching I made $1.50 Cash. I have not got all for the Revolver & wont get it. I got $10. & there is $4. back yet. Capt Hubbard thinks he had not aught to pay all. I have sold the butter, just 4 lbs. & 16 oz. Cash in my fist & here you have it. I will risk 2.00 you let me know if you ever get it. Capt. Bigelow got it. I told Mrs. Rodgers what you told me to. She said she would. I am a going over some of these days & tune her the fire is getting low I must stop & fix it. Fixed. Now I tell you just what it is. all the comfort I take is to scratch when I ich, You cant tell how I enjoy it. I like it so well that I lay awake nites & skratch, then think of that jar of Jenny Lind ich slav. Pleas give us farther details of that, I have rubed myself on the mug 3 times & now I, Well what about Fathers christmas preasent, Does it suit, will have to tie a string to it for fear he may swaller it, Thats the way we do, when tobaco is so costly, just let the box down & draw it up, that will answer for a chaw. Did you put any directions on George's segar? Perhaps he has smoked that rong end foremost. That will cause the smoke to go down into the lower reagons & he may become Did you say that you had one for me. Well save it. What kind of a collar have you got. Soldiers wair paper collers, mules & asses down here collars made of cornhusks lines made of roap or bark. some of the waggons has but one wheel & some has 2 some 4 &c. {The following is in red ink and crosses the previous writing.} I suppose you have hurd of things changing coller before now I am one of that kind. I think it is to bad that you cant have a preasent for christmas & New years

O, how I did laf when it came. I cant tell you how long I shall stay here, perhapse as long as the Reg stayes here. I am doing well now. I have a good comfortable quarters, lots of wood I dont let on haveing my wages raised. Then Lyman is spliced he dont know enough to chaw gum with a string tied to it & the directions on it, &c. Let him go I shant trouble him. It is 15 minutes to 11 & I will stop & I guess you will be glad to have me stop abuseing you. Luck to all. Good night, mail goes out early in the morning. Your Husband Stub & twist

McMinnville, Jan. 12"/64.

My Dear Wife,

Again I will pen to you a few lines to let you know that I am yet alive, & well as may be expected, my health is not first rate, but I am so as to be at my drafting daily. I still keep at drafting & dont see any signes of geting through, that you know I am glad of. I have another set of drafts to make for Col. Gilbert & a map of this town & all of the fortifacations to draw yet for him, I dont get any word from Nashville yet, The Col. has gone there to day & may find out something about it, The news is about the same as useal, lots of it, but I dont get any, I expect that our destiny is in Alabam before long. Our Reg. has been asigned to the 11" army core, One of of the best in the army. The most of the troops I have seen, & the best fighters out, I have something of an anxietty to go to Alabama but on the whole I had not ratherr go any farther north when hot weather comes. O how I dread the insects this summer comeing. They come very near eating me up last summer. The worst of all is the galnipper, The bite of them is as bad as a bee sting. Then there is another insect called the chigger, so small that the naked eye will hardly desern them, not half as large as a knat. they dig down in to the flesh & make a bad soer &c.--I saw a young man from

Murfreesboro hospital where Dave is, He says that he is not any better He wants discharge, He applyed to the Medical Directer & was examed. The Directer sent him back to his hospital & told the Surgeon to send him (Dave) to his regimennt to Col. Gilbert & have him put in the hardest labor. [That's great talk for a sick man] I think Reams told me that he looked as healthy as any person can. & he says the Doctors say that he is playing off. Peter Gordon is there & is pretty hard up. He has some kind of spam's I dont know what kind, but is getting better I think the rest of our company is well except a Dutchman who has very soer eyes, Our Reg. never was so healthy as now. How do you like the heading to your letter, I paint such a picture & furnish paper for one dime a sheet & sell enough to keep me in whiskey & get my washing done, Pay 5c a peice. The old darky comes evry monday morning & gets my cloths & brings them back Tues. & does it nice, Wall Millie you must this short letter for I am tired. have been sitting at the desk all day & now it is late & the mail is going out early in the morning, I thought perhaps you would like to here from me before I could get a chance to send you another, I was very much disappointed last evening when the mail come not to get a letter from some body, I have found out who my friends are, none but them write, I am done answering my owne letters If those that pretend to be friends & stay at home & enjoy themselves, cant do as much as to write a few lines to a poor soldier that has left their homes to suffer the hardships of war, they can go to hallafax & kill snakes for all me, About all the letters I get is from your house, You must not think that I am a whipping any of you over some ones back. I think you all do well, I take lots of comefort a writeing to my home. If Laura would write the whole family would be correspondents except the little one, & she would if she could talk & write. On the whole I am not disposed to find grumbleings on you. Sophia Anderson is the only one that has answered my letters prompt, I have writen her 2 & received 2, I hope you wont feel jelous of me will you? We have one company of Col. Shafters black regiment here & they are fine looking fellows & good soldiers Love to all, Get your shair, Yours as ever

Stub & Twist
Millie

My Dear Lonely Wife

Your kind letter dated Jan 3rd was gladly received & read with much pleasure. It found me well & I am well now & fat as a pig. I think that you would hardly know me. any how you never saw me as fat as I am now. I have very good liveing & dont work hard & am not exposed to the bad weather But if I should go back to my company I would get as poor as job's off turkey, I am still drafting for uncle sam, I shall send home a set of drafts by permition from the Capt. I have to keep still about it. This Engineer buisness is a secret. No one knowes anything about my work but the Engineers & the Post commander. That is, the plan of the Forts, We are surveying the town & vicinity & I shall soon go to maping. I dont suppose that they will let me have one of them, We are haveing some very cold weather for these parts, Colder than it has been in many years, so the people say. You must have had an awful time up in your country, according to your letter & others. I tell you what it is, this cold weather is rough on the boys, expecially those that have to stand picket, But I dont hear any grumbleing. The boys are cheerfull & full of fun, We have considerable sport a hunting bushwhackers & garrillas, They are trying to do all they can in the line of shooting yankees, but they dont make out much. They have got to learn to shoot first. They made an attact on a little party (Co. K.) but done no hurt, shot at Capt. Duffee, the ball passing by his left ear while he was sitting on a log. This company was rebuilding a railroad bridg one & a half miles from town About 70 garrillas, some 5 or 6 companies went down but did not fight much, We persued them, gone all night but did not get any. & its well for them that we did not. for we would not take any prisoners, they would have swoung on the nearest tree. That is our order & I would like to see it exicuted. Night before last a union soldier was shot by them, put 7 balls through him. Evry union man is scared to death when they here of the garrillas comeing. Lives & property is all the time in danger, They are to be pittyed, They dare not go to their homes, nor to their families, but stay within our lines It is not often that they will moles the women & children. Evening, Just eat my supper & had a good smoke from my little Dutch pipe, made of wood & horn. We dont get any clay pipes in this country, You asked me if I dident wish I was there to enjoy the snowstorm or the sleighing. I certainly dont think that I could enjoy such a storm as has been represented to me, I would like the sleighing part first rate, but deliver me from such a storm, I dont wish to be understood that I dont want to go home but I dont want to see such a storm. That cold snap must have frozen your sweet potatoes, did it not? And you say that the roads have not been broken yet Why dont you set some of those copperheaded serpents to crawling about & break your roads. What better use can you put them to, I will send you some verses to read to them in a few days which will make them crawl in their holes & keep out of sight. Well, you will give my best wishes to your company when they come to make that visit & eat the chicken pie, You must have that head of yours pulled if it aches to hard, You are not obliged to write when you dont feel like if, or when you are not in good eumor(tion) spell it You must do the correcting, I cant afford to do both, How did I spend New Years, I can tell you. I set hovered over a little pile of green black Oak wood, piled up in the fireplace, with a smoke under it, & tryed to keep it warm. I could not. I tell you it was a cold day. I had a good dinner & dined with the Gen. Now about Old santyfoot. The old hog did not think enough of me to give me a pipe full of tobaco. Here I will take that back. I did not know as you called Father Old Santy Claw, he is a nice old fellow. Why dident bring me something. I think that he brought you & Laura some nice dresses. All that I had for New Years preasent was half a pound of candy that I bought with my own money & eat it all, I think I had a sweet time, So you think such fat letters is just the thing, What do they amount to when I have no news to write, I have to write something if it not so nice when I write so much, Now I will take a chaw of tobaco--When you churn again save me some butter milk, I am fond of it, And I wish you would mail me 6 or 8 mince pies, I will pay the Postage, Dont be so selfish with them & keep them & brag over them. We can beat you all to pieces on pies, We have them made out of potatoes, made about the size of my hand & sell them for 10c each. If I should hit a man in the face with one of them, he would think an earthquake hit him. I got my boots taped with some of them a short time ago, they ware well. I am not speeking of Mrs. Rodgers pies, but those made & sold by peddlers. They also make what they call ginger bread, We are short on it for shovels, just put a handle on a slab of ginger bread then we are ready to go to work on the forts, We take some of our fancy bacon to greece them then how they will slide into the red clay, We have to do up our feet in bacon to keep from getting stuck in the clay & mud--I have answered your question in reguard to the lumber to Geo. I wrote him a letter & I want it drawed. I will pay the cash I have it in my britches, You tell the clock to be travleing Tell him I said so, give it a swing & it will go, he has just so many seconds to measure off before I come. I have not hurd from Nashville yet & dont know whether I shall go or no, You must be patiant time will tell how it will come out. You tell those that pretend to know, that they dont know anything about it. Now I will tell you what I know about it. I think I have a chance to know, If I receive a higher commission from a private I am mustered out & mustered in at the same time, being mustered out does not discharge a man, I can get heigher wages while a private to by takeing a proper corse. I can get 25c a day extry pay by makeing out a requisition & send it to Washington & signed by the Sec. I shall get all I can I will asure you. One word more about that box, The little bag of crullers you sent me I did not find untill last Sunday, they were broken up so I thought they were dryed fruit so I did not open them untill last sunday. They are as good as ever, You can get that record fraimed if you cant wait for me I dont want it soiled for mine cost me $1.40 If you keep it in the case & lay it away it wont soil, Well I think I have abused you long enough for one evening & now I will stop right here

Head Quarters of the
19th Mich. Vol. Infty. 1864
McMinnville 10-a-c
Jan 24th

My Dear Wife

   As i have a little leasure time this evening i thought it would be a
good chance to sit down to my desk & have a chat with my old chum. But
wheather my chat will be interesting or not i dont know, I dont get much
news to tell u, I am well, Fat as a buck, Never felt better in my life, I have
lots to eat & that is good. Now if i could get read of my ich i would be
all right. The ointment that you sent me does no good, I have got to take
something to 2 clense my blood. The ointment will cure what comes to
the surface, but wont stop the prickling & itching. u sent me the meadicen
not telling me what the name of it is, or how often to use it, & how much,
is it what the Doct. calls his Brown Ointment, I have sold just 15c worth.
Tim Dagget came back to the regiment yesterday, He brings no news from
u, Why dident u go & have a chat with him, Mr. Baker has come back
to the regiment again, He was in the Ohio 9th Battery. He did not want
to come to the regiment. His face is as long as your arm & he begins to
grunt & complain of being sick just as he used to when he was here with
us before, He is not much of a soldier, no more that i be, I think my will
is good enough but my health has not let me do my duty, The boys & all
hands talk funny stories about Dave a playing off. Dont seem to like it
much. Capt. thinks that he had better come to the regiment & go to work,
& so do i i. They all think that he is afraid of the little whistleing minnes
& the shreeking shell. I dont blame him for that, Who wouldent when they
will almost knock a man down when they come within 10 feet of him &
the skreeching of one is enough to scare a man to death. We have lots of
fun here a hunting rebs, bushwackers & garrillas. A party wennt out this
evening after some bushwackers, We scout nights & watch daytimes.
Each one of the scouts has 2 navy revolvers that shoots 6 times each & a
rifle that will shoot half a mile with accuracy, makeing 13 shots with out
haveing to stop to load. Some carry carbine & some the spencer rifle they
shoot 8 times with out stopinng to load, Now i must give you a discription
of this Sabeth day & how I spent it. The sun rose 2 minutes earlyer than
yesterday. Evry cloud was brushed away. the air mild & fresh & all was
pleasent As the sun clime the mountains it grew warm & at mid day the

weather uncomefortable warm with a coat on. Wouldent this make you think of home, What els, I hurd the little spring birds sing, indicating that they were happy too, The roads are dry & dusty, As soon as i got my breakfast I had to take a pleasent walk to the river & I have been traveling about most all day a looking at the surrounding country, visiting the woods, rockey clifts, caves &c. My good friend Charlie Freeman went with me. he helps me survy, I saw one of the handsomest orcherds in the country, About 1500 trees, handsom land, But, no fences, many of the trees turned up by the roots, many with the bark all peeled off & some choped down. Large & handsom brick houses are torn down to help build our forts & quite a nomber of wood building are used for the same perpus, If a building is in the way or obstruct the range from the fort it comes down or burned up, If it be a Union mans property, he is payed for it & if it be a rebels property I'l laugh to see him get pay for it, Our company has cut down a splended hickery grove & used the timber in our fort, The owner is a rebel Capt, we have burned up most evry rail on his plantation, But dont you believe the old lady curses the blue bellyed Yankees? she does that & that is not all. I milk her cows sometimes, & occasionally make a pig squeal, & that is not all. I some times hear rooster crow in our camp. We have lots of domestic about our camps, namely, Rats & mice hens, roosters (have eggs too) wine, cows & horses, & cats & dogs Why not live while you can when Jeff pays for it, I shouuld hate to have to march while we are so comefortable situated unless we were going to march home. I think that we shall keep in command of this post this winter, We have been here just three month to day, I have found some very nice folks to visit with these long evenings. I think that Dave misses it if he dont come here, There is lots of pretty girls in this town especially where I board, the Gen. Daughter, Mrs. Rodgers is as kind as a mother to me. When she wants any earends done, I do them for her O, what a beautiful evening this is, very warm, The moon with its large bright face, silently creeping through the broat sky all speckeled with brigh stars, objects that we both can see at the same time although we are many miles apart, You must excuse me for to night, for it is now 11 oclock, & Joney is crawling in bed, Goodnight. Jan 25th 24 hours has past & nothing has been done to this sheet, I have a little good news that came in about 4 hours ago four rebel deserters came in right from the front. They say one regiment infantry & one of Cavelry (of the rebs) marched in Chattanooga with their arms & gave themselves up as prisoners of war, What does that look like, I tell you the confederate army is hard up, They begin to think that one fourth rations is not the thing. You must keep quiet a little while longer & you will see us again, marching in Otsego with the song of Dixey They must have one orr two good frogings then I think they will give up. We have one plague to contend with & that is the small pox. There is about 1000 cases in Murfreesboro including the negroes, The everage of the deaths is 16 per day, There wwas one or two cases here but they were disposed of & the building burned. The regiment has been vaxinated, & evry colored person included. To night is another of those beautiful warm evenings, I have a good notion to be homesick when we have such nice weather. But that wont do, This homesick & playing out buisness is not so nice in a long run, such a name will wair like iron, & I know of some that has that name, And another name is looked upon as a small sum, The Conscrips, You better believe they get hooted from evry direction. Well, my noddle is about emty, the news has all run out on this peice of paper. I calculate this letter is rather a dry one, but I do the best I know how. If we could march a few days I might something new The mail leaves here in the morning, so I will seal this & let you have it. I am well to day/night I am all right now in to health, My love to you all, Your Husband Buckshot Millie Prentiss Esq

Sabeth, McMinnville, Tenn.
Head Quarters of the 19th Mich Infty
January 31st 1864

My Dear Wife.

Your good letter of the 19th came to hand last evening & it brought me the best news that I have heard scince I came into the army. It is news that I did not expect to hear, How happy it makes me feel to know that my Dear companion is on the road to that happy land where we all shall meet our Saviour, Never to be parted again. Dear Wife, how I wish that I could have been there to assist you, It would have been a happy day to me. But how differant, I will send you a coppy of what transpired here that day from my Diary, & you can see that the sabath day is hardly known. Sun. 17 McMinnville Jan. 1864. I went to drafting this morning not knowing it was the Sabeth day I spent the remainder of the day in reading & writing Nice warm day, some prospects of rain. Our scouts came in & brought 8 horses that they captured, They had a fight at Rock island 13 miles from here. Killed 4 rebs & 3 horses & wonded a number, All right on our side except one horse killed, that was shot while crossing the river, You can see that I know but little about the sabeth day & religeous privalidges, How I want to get out of this army & come home, Last night was a sleepless night for me after reading your good letter, I cant express my joy /when I read your {crossed out} but I will say that I am glad to know that it it is so, also glad to here that Laura has taken a part in the good work of the lord & I pray that their may be more, I am affraid that I am not a doing my duty. I am not quallified to do any good here in the army on the subject of religion, any more than to know that I do no rong. The men are so hardened in sin that it is almost impossable to move them. I am still trying to do my duty as a Christian & as a soldier. Now Dear Wife I hope you will live true to your maker & do better than I have, I have been very wicked, so many temtations are continually before me to lead me astray, I dont consider that you have neglected writing to in the least, I would be willing to go without letters all the time than to know that you were not a christian. I hope you will pray for Your Dear Husband in the army a battleing /the {crossed out} for the freedom of your country & which I am willing to lay down my life to save our homes. I hope the time is near when I shall return to my Dear Lonely Companion & to live a happy & a christian life. O, how pleasent, May God have mercy on us & be with us through our trials & troubels & if we should not meet again here upon earth may meet each other at the throne of our dear savior, I feel that it is very necessary to be prepared for death, I know not what moment I may be cut down, Evry few days some of our number is killed by our enemies. One Union sodier shot last night (not our regiment) he was marched from his dweling into his lane & shot 4 times in the head & a number times in the body, striped naked & left laying on the ground most all day, This happened about 10 miles from here, You will Pleas excuse my short letter, My eyes trouble me very much by candle light & the mail goes out early in the morning. I am well. I shall go to Chattanooga I think next wednesday From your unworthy husband Charlie Millie

Dear Wife

Here you find me at Chattanooga, I arrived here yesterday morning at 9 A.M. I had a pleast trip. I found the country compleatly filled with troops & business lively. I have finally got the position that I have long looked for & am well pleased so far. Have not commenced worked yet. But I shall tomorrow I think I have found a place to learn something There is some 15 or 16 to work in the office plainty of paper & tools &c. Have a middleing good boarding place. But not as good as I had at McMinnville. I think that I shall like Capt E.W. Merrill first rate & the boys that are in the office I like first rate. You must not expect a very long letter from me this time. I have not got settled yet, all are strangers to me. The 13 Mich. is out here some where so I have been told. I shall look around after a while & see if I cant find some acquaintances. I have got my picture taken while at McMinnville. Mr. Mabbs wanted me to sit with him. I did so, when I saw his picture I thought that you may want one so I got him to sit with me. Cost $1.25. The 4th of this month I sent $20. to you by Capt. Duffee to Kall. I told him to keep it untill you sent an order for it so you go & get it. I thought that I would keep $20. for my own use. There is no telling when I shall get pay again, Also in case that I should be sick, I have sold envelops & pictures enough to buy me a watch. Paid $15. for it, I cant tell you much about my extry pay. But I think my wages will amount to about $25.00 per month. that iwill be better than a slap a crost the mouth, I am glad that I dont have to go to Nashville. The small pox is rageing there very bad. About 50 new cases evry day. soon as I get regulated & a little time to sketch the Lookout mountain. It is a very prominent bump & a very sightly place I expect that Lieut. T.W. Clark will sent you his picture for me. I made him a draft of a fort that he built. I hope you will write as soon as you get this, I dont expect to get any mail untill I get answer from this. It will all go to the regiment, I want to write a letter to Capt. Hubbard to day to let him know where to send my mail, Direct your mail to me

Mr. Charles H. Prentiss
Draughtsman
Head Quarters Topl. Engr. Office
Army of the Cumb, Chattanooga Tenn
Care of Capt Merrill

If you direct my mail in this stile I will get. I am well, I dont know as I ever felt any better. I hope this will find you all well & enjoying yourselves. And I also hop you will stick to the good cause that you have undertaken. Do your duty if others do not. let your light shine & you shall liberally rewarded, I still remain your ever Dear Husband   Charlie Millie

Topographic Engineer Office Head
Quarters, Chattanooga Feb 11th 1864

Dear Wife

I suppose it about time for me to write another letter at least you will expect one. News is rather dull here at preasent. I am very much pleased with my new place. Cant tell how long I shall stay. I hope that I can stay as long as the war will last. The only trouble that I have is, my eyes are very week for this kind of business, I may have to quit work on that acct. I can hardly see the rules on this paper this evening, I dont get any chance to work day time. We have to work 7 hours a day & I have sundays to my self. I would like if I could send you a specimen of my work such as maping & lettering. *{The following is printed in a very small hand}* This is the kind of lettering that I have to do. which requires a very stead hand. It is also very tiresome. I have got a very good set of tools & have a good chance to learn. I find that I dont know much about drawing when I come to see others work. We have some splended workman & penman, Well Dear Wife I hardly know what to make a letter out of. But I must cunger up something, I went up to head quarters last evening & hurd one of the best brass band play that I ever hurd, It almost made me cry. I found the Mich. first Engineer & Machanic, but found no acquaintainces. I hurd that the 13th Mich had gone home on a furlough so I could not see any of them. When I get a little chance to go about, I will have something to tell you. If It is pleasent next sunday I intend to go upon Look Out mountain & see Virginia & 6 other states at one sight, We have a good glass, We have evrything in the surveying line, There is a number of caves that I intend to explore. There is one thing that I am badly afflicted with. That is boils. I have 6 to sit on, some will soon hatch I hope. Also some on my hands, on the back of my right hand & two on my rong rist. Here is a lage white page before me. Now what shall I put on it. I cant half write when there is so my around me, some singing, some telling stories. Henry Bush is singing the Soard of Bunker Hill & playing the guitarh & makeing all the nois they can, & some riting my table &c. put it all togeather I think I wount write more to night. Good night. Sunday Morning Feb. 13th, Now I will make an effort to finnish my letter. For the past week it has been very dry & dusty, This morning we are a haveing a very pleasent rain & the weather is very warm. I have been confined to the office very close this week & have not been able to see much of the country about here yet. We have to work 7 hours a day & after hours are not long enough to go about & see much. However I took a short walk yesterday noon to a rebel fort situated on a heigh knobb, commanding the 10-a-c river & ferry. The cenery is handsome & pleasent. Can see many miles away, Can see a large number of forts as far off as the eye can reach, tents without number & soldiers the same, It beats all how many soldiers there is hear & it is a small part of the army. Thousands are moveing to Knoxville where the rebs are consentrating & intend to make a brake into East 10-a-c. We are ready for them. From this same bluff or knobb I could see I should think a thousand dead horses & mules; all exposed to the sun, laying on the river flat, If it stops raining to day I intend to take a walk on another heigh point which will be much more sightly than the one yesterday, There is one hundred cars of subsistance comes into Chattanooga evry day, It is surprising to see what it takes to supply 150 to 200 thousand men, all the supplies of the Knoxville army comes through this place. There is a number of caves that I intend to visit as soon as I get an oppertunity, Also coal mines & copper mines, The worst undertaking is to climb Look Out Mountain. I want to start early in the morning of some day when the atmusphere is clear. Then I will take a glass that belongs to the office. Then I will tell you what they are doing in Richmond Va. &c. The heighth of this just 1460 ft above the Tenn. River. Apples sells for 8c cents a peace, Butter 50c lb. Eggs 35c doz / Paper 75c quior, Common Wool hats $6 to $9. Boots $15 a pr. Honey $2 lb. & evry thing els the same propotion. I have an idea that it cost something to live hear. News papers 15c apeice. I can get all the paper I want to use while I stay here. I like my new place first rate except the liveing. That is tuff. Ill not mind that if I can keep well as I am now. My time is half out the 5th of March. But I have no idea that

I shall have to stay my three years out. I am makeing about $30 a month now. I think that will do very well for a privite soldier. I get $13 per month as a private $12 per month as a Draughsman & $12 per month for rations. It cost $7 per month to eat. I am also allowed $3.50 per month for clothing. on the whole I get $40.50 & board & cloth myself. I have told all the news that I can think of. I have not so good place to write as had In McMinnville. I want to be alone when I write. So you will excuse this white paper. For fear you have not my last letter I will give you my address again, Charles H. Prentiss Draughsman Topl. Engineer office Head Quarters of the Cumb. Chattanooga Tenn. I would be pleased to have you all write often, I sent you $20 by Capt. Duffee, you will have to send an order for it or go & get it. I told him to be careful who he let have it. I have not hurd from you in most 3 weeks. I will close, My Love to you, Yours as ever

 Charley Draughsman Millie P

Head Quarters Top'l Eng.
Office Army of the Cumberland
Chattanooga, 10 A.C. Feb 21st 1864

My Dear Wife

 Hear I am again, yet alive & well, My health has been extreordinary good for the last fore weeks. Never was better. I would enjoy myself first rate if eyes would not trouble me so & the itch. I dont get any better, I am sorry to have to put you off with one letter a week. I have to for this reason. The boys in the office are very wild & full of fun & it makes out to be avry poor place to write. I have also been confined in the office & have not see much that would be very interesting to write, Last Wed. noon I took a walk up on Camron hill. This is a hill is 800 ft heigh & is a very pleasent sight to look in all directions. On the point of this hill is breastworks & forts through'n up by the rebels. Commanding Tenn. River & flats & a large extent of country Whare our army had to approch & cross the River. It so happened that the rebs were easily scared & was driven out out of this city by a single brigade & battery. Commanded by Wilder, You have hurd of Wilder brigade I presume. At the that Wilder approched & exchanged a few shots the rebs though our whole army was comeing & they vacated the City. This hill stands near the city, about one hour's walk to go & come. I will try & tell you what I saw at one sight. At the foot of the hill on east side on the bank of the river is the boneyard, Perhapse 3,000 dead horses & mules all exposed to the suns rays. Some 10 miles of the Tenn. river in sight. Acrost that that one pontoon bridg 2 currant ferrys, 2 steem boats, on the bank of the river 4 government sawmills, At the foot of the hill (south side) building a croten water works to carry water to the forts on the top of this hill to supply the camps & other camps about the city. About 5 miles North West can see Hooker's Corps in camp. In another direction a large camp of regulars & to say all the ground is covered with troops camps, waggons, mules both dead & alive. I should guess that there was about 50,000 here now. Look Out Mountain sticks up like a bump on a log hiding evry thing behind it. Looking past the Lookout mt. I can see a range of mountains in Georgia with the naked eye. From this point I can see 150 miles with the naked eye in a clear day. A splended view of this city & many other places not worthy of note. This morning Nate Finigan & myself took a walk. Now I will try & discribe what I saw this fournoon, or a part of it. We first started for the new soldiers barrying ground, pass the Depot. Here is a larg amount of machinery brought in on the cars to be put in opperation in this City. I also saw a number of piles of provision (some 8 or 10) larger than your house. I took the track that leads by the New National Cemitary. No track on the road as far as I went. The Cemitary hill is shaped like a half globe, a true round. Commenced building a stone wall around it. The length of the wall fence about 2 miles to enclose it. On the summit of the nole is to be a National Monument built of stone 80 ft. square & 80 ft. high the shape of this {a small drawing of a pyramid} a pirimid There is a number of thousands of poor soldiers now sleeping in this mound. the most of them w ith their names on a pine plank discribing there State & regiment & Co. as far as they can find out. From the sumit of this hill I picked up a pebble which I intend to always keep. I also picked it up from the very spot where Gen. Grant stood when he was viewing his and the enemy's armys while the battle of Chattanooga was fought. From this point the whole work could be see. After tooking look about here a while I went over to Fort Wood & another fort & see the works Tese 2 forts done the most of the work was done in the battle of Chattanooga, Then went to a Cave. This Cave is in a clift of rocks on the river. I found that it was a hazardous place to get too. I had to climb on the shelve of rocks over the river. some places was some like climbing up the side of a log house, Foot holt rather limited, & some ice on the rocks. At last I reached the hole & an awful hole it is. I went in & found it very warm. I dare not go in a great ways for dead air. This cave is not ventelated like other caves that I went. This cave goes all about under this city. The interior is not hardly worth discribing. Most all of the wemen of the City for refuge went in this cace when the was rageing. the shells flew all about the city & in the cave they were safe. From here I went to my quarters & eat dinner, came to the office & commenced this letter. so you have the details of my fournoon's walk.-- I feel well satesfied with my new place. This is just such buisness as suits me. But my eyes dont like the traid. I have where I know all the movements of the army. but I have to keep my mouth shut. You may look for one deep into the heart of seceh before long. The reason it takes so long for the army to move is because they have to get maps & reports from spyes. The whole army has to wait the Engineer Corps. A map of the whole country has to made & evry road & path, house, mill spring, stream, river, hill, mountain, swamp &c. has to be very acurate then handed over to the Generals. Then when they get these maps & supplies a move is made. The largest part of our troops are gone to make Long street a visit. Woe bu unto him &c.-- I begin to want a letter from home. I have not had a letter in most 4 weeks. This shifting makes bad work with mail. I am expecting another such a good letter as I got the last time. Dear Wife I hope you will continue the good work that you have undertaken. I often think of that letter. I feel as though I wanted to go home. I am tired of liveing this kind of life. It is not pleasent. I know not what minute that I may be shot by the enemy. We are exposed daily. I dont make any calculation on comeing home untill my time expires. but if the war ends before that time, all is right. But mind you one thing the story is most told. Mobeal is a easy place to take. If I dare I would tell you the plans--Well, I will pull for a close, my story is all told (on paper) for this time You may Direct your mail as I told you Head Quarters, Top'l. Eng. Office, Army of the Cumb. Chattanooga 10-A-C Care of W.E. Merrill. Charles H. Prentiss Draughsman. Well Good bye. My love to you all. Charlie

                    Head Quarters Top'l Eng.
                    Office Army of the Cumb.
                    Chattanooga Tenn Feb 28th 1864

My Dear Wife,

    The time has come again for me to write another letter to a lone companion who's heart is hourly beeting for a loved one who is far away a fighting the battles of our Country & enduring the hardships of a soldiers life, that is not at all pleasent for me, All though I make the best I can of it, I would give all that I possesed if I could be permited to return Loved home. You may judg from the countainance of my letter that I am fairing hard or getting homesick. This morning I took a walk out of the city where it was all quiet & still, & the first thing met my ears was the sweet music of the spring birds. What will tuch my feelings quicker & bring back my younger days of my childhood, then to think that I am bound to stay. Cant go to my home & family & cant even pass the street without being haulted & to show a pass from a General saying that I may pass within the lines, This military & it cant be helped. While out a listening to music of the birds, what do you suppose I could hear. It was the booming of cannon some 20 miles distant near Daulton where we are fighting & have been the last 4 or 5 days We whip the rebels evry time & are gaining ground. We have a good man at the wheel here. That is Gen. Thomas. Gen. Grant makes it his home at Nashville. He is not liked very well here. I like my place first rate, & I think that Capt. Merrell likes my work. I think I shall stay here as long as my work is accurate. I find that compileing work on map is the most difficult work I ever found, Time is no account here. they want want the work done acurate & good, I work on a space not larger than my thumb nail a half a day sometimes, that is very slow work, & that is not all. I am getting a good education at Uncle Sams expence. But he dont feed me well enough to suit me. My liveing is not first rate. I cant go stinking sowbelly, we have fresh beef about once in 4 days, this is quite a treat. I will stand it if I only have good health. My health never was better. I suffer a good deal with the itch. Cant get rid of that, It is not the regular ich, It is what we call the camp ich. If I could have some thing to clens my blood it would stop it. My eyes trouble me very much. I have to avoid reading entirely to save my eyes for my work. I do steel a little time to draw for myself. We have some good artists here & they take good deal of pains to show me. The worst of it is, some of them will drink & carry on. This dont suit me. There is 4 in the room with me. We all sleep in the same room, each one has his own bunk, they are fixed like this {here is a small drawing of double-decked bunks with men sleeping foot to foot} about 2 ft wide this Diagram represents us all at bed in a warm night with nothing but my overcoat to sleep on & my knapsack for a pillow Have a fireplace in the room & a nigger to tend that, bring water, sweep out & brush our cloths, black our boots. We have a guitarh & a man that plays it well. On the walls hang some pistols & swords, showing defiance to a traitor if he should make his appearance Also some maps paisted on the walls, a looking glass & towels, evry one has his own towel. Some factory cloth for window curtains. Some candle boxes for chairs, 2 long tables, one against the wall & one in the senter of the room. A water pail, wash dish & soap, a large book called Websters Dictionary, indian rubber inkstand, paper, Draughting implements, Water culler paints &c &c &c... Their I guess you have got all except my big spittoon, a drygoods box filled with sawdust. O, yes I forgot & sorry to say in bunk No. 2 lays Will Waggoner with his eye bunged. Out on a spree night before last, & I think he will be discharged for it. Your letter Dated Feb. 21st Came to hand a few minutes ago also one from Sister Laura. Glad to here from home once more. I think it came through in good time, it lay in the other office 2 days, the 2 offices are connected. The office I stay in is the largest has 3 rooms full. I am glad you got my Diary, they stuck on a good price for Postage. And so you think the picture is not a good one, You did not think to make allowance for my good health & fleshing up, I am flesher than you ever saw me. I weight about 183 lbs. I am too large for my clothing, There is 2 ts in Chattanooga. I wish you would number your letters then I can tell if I get all of them. According to my Diary the letter I just received is No. 29 namely. (Feb, 21st No. 29) When you write just make a memmarandon then you wont forget I have a list of evry letter I mailed & received. I you dont know how to do it just look in my Diary. It seems that Elder Wolfe is a doing the big thing in Otsego. I owe him a letter & shall try to answer it soon. I am very buisey now & have something to do all the time. Time seems short. Now about the bed cord. sorry to hear of such a axident Any bones broken, I think it is to bad to be drawn out of a nice slumber into the cold, just lay still & I will some & mend the cord or bring you a new one. I would be glad to see the change in my old friends. I am happy to hear that something is done in Otsego. I hope Elder Wolfe will persevier. You spoke of what a nice chance it would be for you to come & see me. The comeing part would be all right. But the accomidations is scarse. No hotels, no place to sleep nor stay. Nothing but men & wenches to be seen this is all the objections I have to your comeing. It is not safe for a respectable women to be seen here. I saw this morning the Hon. P. Brownlow & Daughter on their way to Nashville. Fine looking man he. I wish you would tell Majer Eaton to call & see me when he comes back, Call at the Topl. Eng. Office first brick building north of market st. on Main st. Sign on the door Topograic Engineer Office Dept. of the Cumberland. Come to the door at the head of the stairs where he will another sign Positively no Admittannce in the drawing room, push & he will find me. My expences were paid by the government. I understand that you received the money from Capt. Duffee, that is all straight. I have sent for a magnifying glass to use in small work. If I had a good pare of specks I would use them. But cant get them here, There is times that I cant recognise a person acrost the room. I dont think of anything that I want from home. You may send anything you like. O yes! Just poped into my head. I want a military vest. Not a very poor one & not a very costly one. A black or a dark blue. Not to cost more than $5.00 He can get it on his way out here, I would like to have him pay for it & I will pay him when he brings it. A vest hear will cost $11 to $12. such as I can get in Kallz for $4. I thank Laura very much for her letter & will annwer it. I think I owe Mary a letter. I saw day before yesterday 250 rebels all walking with cruches the most had but one leg. What a sight. They came in from Knoxville, Pleas all write as often as you can. I suppose you know now where to Direct now. Be a good girl & keep a stiff upper lip. Yours in Love Charlie Millie I send you a leaf from the Ivy vine grom a garden in this city. Keep it

{Undated letter page from this time period.}

When we are out of the service you will find that officers ill rate lower than privates with a few exceptions. There is a few human beings & they are highly respected & are really distinguished. When you see an officer looking rough & not afraid to go into the tent to see his boys & visit the hospital & cheer up his sick men, roll up his britches & wade in with the rest & say Come on boys, (not go on boys & he step behind some large tree, stump or rock) Then we can make up our mind that we have a man. Now I will compare two captains that I am acquainted with. Capt Hubbard for instance, When he has no business to tend to, will go in the tents & sing & chat with the boys. It makes no difference who it is. He go lookking like the soldiers, not all starched so stiff as to brake when he bends a little & every day alike. Now take the Capt that has command of this office. Cant speak to him for fear he will snap your head off. An ugly scowl is allways on his face, & so disliked by all of the department, All because he is a Capt & has a little authority over a few men. You have no idea what a change it makes in a man to pumpkins rises on their sholdurs. – I am getting along first rate at my new business. I like it well. Not very badly drove with now. I learned last night that the rebs had blown up Tunnell Hill some time last week & ordered all of the inhabitance to leave Dalton & their army is in retreat for Atlanta. Tunnell Hill is where the R.R. runs through a tunnel ½ mle. You may look for some good news from the army befoe long. If Shermans retreat had not happened you would have hurd it sooner. There will be a general movement soon. Gen. Grant is agoing to do the large thing. – A sad accident happened on Look Out mountain last Thursday. A photographer while placing a Gentleman & Lady to have there picture taken stept on a sock that gave a way & he went hurling through the air in the rocks below, he fell about 100 ft. was killed instantly. There is one particular dangerous rock where many go to get their pictures taken

Head Quarters Topl. Eng. Office
Army of the Cumb. Chatt. Tenn.
March 6th 1864

My Dear Wife

After a hard & tiresome walk of about 10 miles upon LookOut Mountain, I will try & write you a sort of a letter. I will make it as interesting as I can. I am well. I enjoy good health now days. I feel rather gant at preasent for I have no dinner & it is now about 5 oclock, have supper at 6. Perhaps you will be interested with the details of my walk to day. After breakfast I first procured a pass to pass the pickets, then off I started. In the first place the heighest & nearest point of the mountain, is 2 1/2 miles from the center of the city & 5 miles to get there by the way of Summerville. I started out alone, it being a very pleasent & warm day. I could help but stop & listen to the sweet music of the birds & to the peepers & larg frogs in the water holes on the side. A thousand thoughts passed through my brain of the gone by days, & here I am in a desolate country far from home & deprived of the comforts of a christian life. Then look about me. Here I stand upon a battle field surrounded with rifle pits & forts where many human lives has been sacrifised for the freedom of our country. I passed on. Come to the ruins of a large Tannery which has been demollished by our forces, then to the pickets. Hault, Your pass, I pulled it out & stuck it under his nose, he read it, all right, go on. After crossing Chattanooga Creek I came to the foot of the great pile of rocks called Look Out Mountain. I commenced to climb. In 2 miles I had to rais 1680 ft. By the way were large rocks in squair form, many of them larger than your house, that have broke off the ledges & rolled down the mountain. I saw 3 rocks that were about 100 ft. long &

from 50 to 75 ft. squaer that had come from the ledg, such is the sean that I have discribed, I finally reached the top & on the top is a cluster of fine dwellings built for summer use for the large bugs. This is a very pleasant & cool in summer. That is why is is called Summerville. After I reached the top I came towards the village (Chattanooga) to the point the most sightly place I ever saw. I cant discribe the senery that I saw at a glance, but will do the best I can. Here I am nearly 1700 ft up in the air. The 10-a-c river at foot of the mountain look like a large snake, could see it at the distance of 20 miles with my glass in an easterly direction, crawling through the valleys. Away to the northeast could see the Cumberland mountains. South of them the smoky range in North Carolina, & a number of other ranges that I dont know the names of. Ringold, Tunnel hill, Mishion ridg, Chattanooga & all of its fortifications are all in my sight. Here I am looking into 7 different states & not move from my tracks. I saw six trains of cars in different directions all on the move at the same time. What a sight. I stood on a ledg of rocks & picked branches from the tops of tall trees. Can stand at the foot of same tree & pick branches from the tips of other trees below this. On the point of this mountain is a liberty pole & on it is the stars & stripes the good old flag that we are fighting for, also forts built by the rebels. The track was not visible to the naked eye & could not distinguish the number of the cars in a train from where I stood although the air was very clear. A large size house did not look larger than my fist. Now the next thing is to get off the mountain without going away back, to far & too much work. So I made up my mind to come down the front of the rocks {crossed out} mountain. I have 125 feet of perpendicular rocks to clime down on ladder & shelves of rocks. Dangerous to think of but I did it & come out safe & started back to the city very tired. Here you have a out line of my walk, I dont know as it will be very interesting but it is the best I can do this time. My work is the same thing evry day. No news to tell you about the war, all is quiet at preasent. I got a letter from you last sunday but none since. I dont hear from the regiment yet. I forgot to number your last letter which should be 49. I like my place very well except the Capt. Capt. Merrill is rather a small pattern Dont mean to give us any privilages. But as far as that is conserned we dont care. I would like to see him stop me from makeing pictures. Ther seems to be some trouble in getting our extra pay. But I think we shall get it. About $32 due me now. My eyes get no better, My itch gets no better, One thing more about Uncle Sams work. He is a building a large bridg acrost the 10-a-c river. The river is about 1/2 mile wide, Also building a depot &

a number of ware houses some of them 1000 ft long. You have no idea the amount of buisness done hear. I can count at any time from 500 to a 1,000 army waggons in motion, some hauling wood, some commissaries, & evry thing els pertaining to war. I will send you a Holly leaf that I picked from a bush from Look Out. It is an ever green. I had to do some tall climbing to get it. I would like to get more letters than I do. It seems to me that my friends are forsakeing me, I get about one letter a month & some get 2 evvry day. I hope this letter will find you well & enjoying yourself also the rest. Pleas all write often wont you. These verses are for George. give him my best reguards. Also Father & Mother & all. My sheet is most full & I will close for this time Yours in Love Millie Charlie

Head Quarters Topl Eng Office
Army of the Cumberland Chatt
Tenn. March 8th 1864

My Dear Wife Millie

Yours of the 28th came to hand yesterday & I will acknolege that I was glad to hear from home again. You say that you are tired of conversing by writing. I take the most comefort when I am studying up something to say to my own true companion. One I know that loves me, one that lives for me & prays for me. O how thankful I feel that my dear companion has taken a new course in the world. It may be the means of others following. Watch & pray & you will be rewarded. I will try & do my duty & try to meet you in that place of rest where parting is no more. I dont feel much like writeing tonight but I take this method of passing away time. It is a very warm rainy night. My eyes is hurting light is to dim & I will have to limit this job untill daylight. Daylight has come and I will try & write a few lines more. I dont know but you will have to put on your specks to read this small letter. I am well & fat as a bear. You dont know how much better I enjoy myself when I am well. I have come to the conclusion that this is the kind of work for me to enjoy good health. Tuesday evening March 12th Well here I am again sick this morning & last night with the Diarrea. I dont feel much like writeing a letter today but you will look for one & I dont want to disappoint you. Henry Bush is right under my nose singing and playing the band work & if I make any mistakes you must overlook them. Tell Geo to send me his worms pictures. I think we have some that will match him. We have everything that will make fun. I will mention one. It is what we call a bunkroom bug or a Libby Prison bug. Take a piece of wood about 1 1/2 inch long then cut it in the shape of a spider head & body get some strips of indianrubber about 2 1/2 inches long put a pin through the center then through the center of the body. Paint it black then fasten a long horsehair to the center of the back then tie the other end to a stick 3 or 4 feet long. then step gently behind some person you wish to play the joke on & let it come down over his face. I have had lots of fun and other trick. The Tennesseans think the devel is in the yankees. We also have some a makeing comic pictures. We try to pass off the time as well as we can but it seems very long. I dont see as the war has closed yet but everything looks bright on our side. If I can remain here untill the war closes I shall not mind it much. I have enjoyed better health since I came into this kind of business than I have since I enlisted & a good chance to learn to be an artist. I would like to have you come here first rate. But they have no hotels nor no place for a woman to stay. It is no place for a respectable woman to be. You could not pass the streets without being insulted more than a dozen times. Therefore I should advise you not to come nor Mrs. Baker. All respectable ladies have left the city but the other things both black & white & many of our soldiers suffer by the means. (This is a better pen) I thand the lord that I am out of the scrape. I know of some Col & Generals that have their wives here. Their quarter in dwelling houses, they cant ride through the streets with out all kinds of remarks being made. A soldier was married here not long ago & he is not aloud to stay with his wife. So it would be with us if you were here. No mercy. No kindness nor anything it is shown to a private but poor bread & stinking meat. He is treated wors than the mules by his Superiors. Mr. Baker was sent back to the regiment from the 18th Ohio Battery just before I lift the regiment & he got rightaway sick again & went to the hospital at McMinnville & I think he is thru now. He dont amount to any great sum in the army. I received a letter from Dave from Kallamasoo last evening. I suppose that he will manage not so as to come back again. [So would I] For this is a hard country to live in. Cant buy a thing without paying 10 times as much as it is worth. [Lots of apples here & sold at one dollar per dozzen While the suttlers get them for $2 a barrel north. & butter that will out rank Lieut. General Grant for 75 c per. lb. Boots $10. a pr. & evry thing its in the same propotion. I have to pay 15 c a peice for washing. It costs me 45 c a week for washing. Shirt; Drawers & socks. 25 c for pants. $.50 for washing Blanket. 75 c quire for letter paper. So you can see how I come to write such small letters] But I will add, if this is not fine enough I will make it smaller. I have a good deal of very fine lettering on maps to do. just like This Beever Creek Mounain. Vixburg. You just try it and see if will try your eyes a little. I have sent for a magnifier to work with I know the whole art of map makeing now and will tell you all about it when I go home. If it will agree with my health, I will make it my business hereafter. It demands big wages, from $2. to $5. a day. We are haveing beautiful warm weather & flyes are very thick in the rooms The wild floures are in blossom &, &,, &,,, O how I wish that I was at home. But no Uncle sam has got some stinking sowbelly for me to eat first. & he wants a few more rebels killed. The commandment reads. Thou shall not Kill. We head it not. What will Brother Lighton say to this. The penelty is great. If I dont do my duty Death is my portion. So you see if I see a Reb. behind it a tree a pointing a musket at me I shall pull the trigar---------------my story is changed. I have just witnessed a funeral peroscion passing by of the Col. of the 24th Ill. who was wounded at Tunnell Hill some 16 miles south of this place & died last Friday. The tears would come when I saw the solme movement of military funeral. I will discribe it to you if I can. In advance of the whole column was the brass band belong to the regiment. All instruments were carried under the right arm While anothar brass band was was a playing a very solumn durge. The field officers of some other regiment followed behind the band then the regiment with arms reversed. The gun and sward is carried under the left arm with buts up & supported by the left hand behind. The battle flag was raped up close to the staff, also the banner. Next came the corps on a larg gun carrage with the gun taken off & covered with a larg flag. The coffen placed on the hind exal. The wheels all enter woven with pine bows and drawn with by 8 larg cream horses. The pall barrers was 6 Col. from other regiments his scared scabern lay on his coffen, his horse was lead behind clost to the coffen. You could help but to shed tears to see this. The horse being led clost behind his rider & the saddle emty. The the ambulance with the mourner, his wife, then about 50 horses with Generals & Col. & 6 emty saddles for the pall bearers. Then a load of hard bread to finnish up with that hapened to fall in behind. It was the choice of the widow to have him buried in the national cemitary. That is a splendid place. Yes, Dave and I parted in good friendship. I never have had any words with him yet, only he seemed to blame me some in regard to the things in the box. I did not feel disposed to be blamed so I fired back. I did not know Jim Steels father that you speak of. I am glad to here that Jim has mended his ways. Now the next thing is to stick to it. The church must have improved a good deal this winter. I. George Otto has done staining business he had better enlist & come down here & place himself in front of a 24 pounder & blow himself out of existance. Then he would not miss himself & she too. They are furloughing a few at a time untill they all get sent home out of the 19th I dont know as I can be one of their number any more so I will content myself to stay. When I go home again I want to stay. My parting with you this last time was worst than the first. The third will be wors than the second time I have some of the things you sent me in my knapsack yet. The T I mean to hang to untill I want to use it, also the nutmeg. I dont know what may turn up yet. The crust I eat up & the cakes. I sold the fruit I sold to Mrs. Rodgers. I told you about the butter. How did the flax raising turn out also the sweet potatos. Why dont you tell me about the potatoes. If you want to spin flax I will make you a wheel when I get home. I would like to have a good toe towel the one you gave me is most worn out. then I will have to use a better rag. Do you know anything about an Allmainack of 1864 that you sent me. I have not seen it yet. I want one or a calendar for 1864. I will send George a pattern for a wooden man I want to see him try his skill on wooden things. Well how much lumber has Geo drawn for me. Do you have sleighing now. What is the weather up north. We have peach trees in blossom here now. If you want to know what I am doing now days I will tell you. I am makeing a map of northern Georgia You look on the map & you will have an idea of what I am a doing. You may tell Doct. Hopkins that his ointment has done no good, or that I did not use it right. I have had no instruction how to use it, how often & how much. I am very much afflicted with the itch. I think your best way to write or to answer my letters would be to to refer to the last letter then it will refresh your memmery as to the questions that I ask. I have sold all but one bunch of envelopes you sent me. Now Millie I want to see you beat this letter if you, if you will I will give you a prise of a ring that I made of clam shot with your name engraved on the back. It is a rellick of the battle field of Stone River (I picked the shell up there) You will find as much writing on this little sheet as there is on a fools cap sheet. The funeral procesion has just returned. I feel very bad this afternoon. I am a going to take a good dose of Phthisic to night & I think that will fix me out all right. Love to all a soldier Charlie Millie

{The above letter of approximately 2000 words was written on both sides of a sheet of paper which measures six inches wide and five and one-quarter inches long. There was very little margin except at the top. It was transcribed by Nancy Jordan from a photocopy which had darkened. The writing is clear but very, very small.}

Topl. Eng. Office Head
Quarters Army of the Cumb
Chattanoog March 22nd 1864

My Dear Wife

I just received your letter of the 12. You did not say a word about the sweet potatoes. Nor you dident number your letter as I requested you Your letter of the 12 is No. 31 according to my reconing If you will be so good as to number them you will pleas me very much, No matter if you call it N.100,000,000000. In reguard to the vest I want Eaton to select it for me, because he knows just what I want & I want to pay him here & not risk money on the road by mail. All well.

Yours in haist

Charlie

Head Quarters, Topl. Engr.
Office, Army of the Cumb.
Chatt. Tenn. April 15, 1864

My Dear Wife,

Seeing that I have a few leasure moments I thought I would improve them by scribleing to you a few lines to let you know how Old charlie is getting along. I see him evry day & he says that he is well & feels pretty

Finegan takeing information.

well Now days. I feel somewhat tired & sleepy this evening owing to my being up late last night. Finnegan & I worked last night night untill one oclock a make a map for General Sherman also hunting up information, of the Vicinity of Rome I expect there is something up, there seems to be a great deal of stir a mongts the troops. We are considerabley crouded with work at preasent for a certain map then General Thomas very much. He was in here last Thesday & made quite avisit. I have got 104 pages of information that I have taken on fools cap & have not got half done yet then I have to regester it, then have to make duplicates to hand in to the clurk for distrubution. I have plenty to do just now. Let me say to you hear as Baker says, while I think of it, have you received a five dollar greenback from me. Pleas make mention of what I send to you so that I that you have it, oh! yes did you get my likeness I sent you in Mothers letter. good thing aint it. Well if that dont suit you I will try it again & keep trying untill you are suited, But if I remember right you are easly suited. Dave asked me for one & I sent him one just like it. You may think that I am hard hearted to surve you so but it the best I can do at preasent. I wish you would send me another of your photographs if you have one to spare. I have not received a letter from you since last Wed. week, & I am getting impatiant to here from home again. I am troubled a good deal with my eyes I can hardly see the rules on this paper I cant hardly read my testiment the print but I so manage to read a few verses. Candle light is the mischief. I want you send me a gob of your good warm sugar if you make it this spring. I suppose you are hard at it now days. & down here the nature looks green, fruit trees are in blossom, birds do sing so sweet & & & & & I I I am am not at home yet. But this I cannot help. I shall make the best I can. God ruleth all things & doeth all things well. I will find no fault but look a head & squint for the bright side of the picture if there be any & I trust that you will. one of the boys time is up today that is here in the Office & I wish it was mine also. Time seems to pass very fast here in this buisness haveing my time occupied but my mind will wander home when I am takeing information in spite of my buisness. To here me ask questions you would think that I was quite a lawyer. I have got one of the shortest candles you ever saw {a drawing of it} this is a correct likeness of it I believe I will turn out for to night & wait untill day light so good night. Sat. evening Apr. 16, another 24 hours has passed & now I will resume my letter. I received a good letter from you & Mary & I enjoyed it first rate too. Now while I think of it I will tell a little news which happened here today. This morning at 8 oclock a fire broke out in the military prison & consumed {At this point the letter is cross-written in red ink} the large brick block they were totally distroyed, there was about 500 prisoners in their None of them escaped. Yesterday a rebel capt & sargent was brought in & took lodgings there & is supposed they set them on fire. This capt. was an Engineer & we got some valuible notes & surveys to add to our maps. I wished we had more he tryed hard to get away last night but did not make it out. Now to your letter, you speek as though you was sorry you got the vest. I guess it is all right. I think it fits first rate, only I have not seen it yet. If it will fit Father it will me. Who will care for Mother now, can you sing it. Did you get the letter with the of the Virgin & christ, you did not say. I think a good deal of that You may let the shirts go. I can get along without them. Wollen shirts are bad for me when I am within so, & the gray backs will not trouble me so much, wool is just what suits them. I am sorry to here that Elmirra is sick, if you see her remember me to her. also to the Hunt girls. I believe I will drop them a few lines. Do I understand you that they have joined the baptist church, I hope it is so, I am glad to know that their are so many united the ch. Tell Charlie Franklin Ill court marshal him when I get home, for disobeying my order. I suppose that you know that there are 36 hundred seconds passes off each hour & 4,400 each day & if they are to long, bite them in too. Well I cant tell you just what I think about reinlisting. I think that I will do it when I am payed to & not before. I think I have lived on sow belly long enough all ready. That is right I am glad that you are a going to number your letters. You should have numbered 2 higher, it should have been 36 instead 34 but never mind that. you know I received 2 old letters a few days ago that I did not know was existing. Sunday morning April 17. this is one of the prettyest morning you ever saw & O how I wish I could spend the Sabeth with you & go to church. But the great space between us prevents. Tell Father if he dont the ague to me down here where it is healthy. I have not had the real ague scince I was a soldier. Yes, I received the letters that you sent to Murfreesboro last Friday week. What does george think of the letter or April fool that I sent him. You can use all the varnish you want but I dont think it is very good, to prepare it for use is to thin it with spirits turpentine. Geo will tell you how, use a clean brush. I think there is one there that I have used for varnish, to make it look nice put on not less than 2 coats, 4 will do. make the varnish middleing thin. I think of nothing more at this time Love to all I still remain your Husband Charlie to Millie

Yours of the 15ᵗʰ (No 35) came to hand yesterday & was overhauoled in short in short order, & now I will try and answer it although I dont feel much like writeing. It is nearly night. I have been hard at work all day makeing a map for Gen. Thomas. The details were brought in this morning & he wanted tomorrow morning so I have it done & delivered News is rather a scarce artical & I hardly know to fill up my sheet. I can fill it with pictures wasyer than with words & I am geting tired of writing at best. I have about 200 pages of information & have to write it all again in a book then make extracts for the capt. I have to write all and most of the evenings. But say nothing I had rather do this than to go back to the regiment. they have the small pox. What does Geo. say about say about his picture. I am sorry I sent it. I did not think that I had it addressed to Laura. I sent it for sport not for an insult. You will tell Laura wont you. I will send you my picture this time. I have no rest to get my phortograph taken so I went to the looking glass & took it my self. I try to look good natured so you would not think that I was down hearted or got the blues. I have not got the blues very bad but I would like to go home first rate I have got trired of drums & fifes which I am hearing now. O! what a nice day. nature seems to smile, the river flats look green & covered with convilesant horses & muels. Also the forrest is green as mid summer & spotted with with white blossoms & who can help but think of by gone days. I dont here you say any thing about makeing sugar. If you can I wish you would tell me if Charlie Stratton is at home with his regiment or where he is. A part of his regiment is here & the rest will be here in a few weeks. -- Well I have had to go & pack a lot of maps to send to the Gen. & Col. &c. so I have had but little time to myself to day. but never mind its all for the Union I wonder if Chandler Eaton has got over his & ill feelings towards me if not he can shut. I am sorry that Mrs. Eaton is sick. But poor Edd he must be an object of pitty if he cant get a wife. Do you know what Reg. he is in. He may be about hear some whare. I dont get any letter Charley Franklin yet, if he has been lucky enough to escape comeing in the army he aught to do as much as to write to his friends in the army. I would like to send you a Piny toe from our door yard, but it is to late in the seson to take one up. the stalk is about 10 inches tall. We have had a cold wet backward spring for this climate. -- I would write to you oftener if I had any news to tell you & more time, but if you cant get along with one a week I will send two a week and say I am well then fill the ballance with pictures {hear is a small drawing of an ass and a question, written in red ink dont you hear my ass bray} such as this &c I can reenlist if I want to & get $70.00 bounty. But I dont take any on my plate I have all the enlisting I want. let those go that have not gone to take a good snuff of gunpowder, & wallow through mud day after day & sleep in it at night. No worst for them to than it is for me I refer to those that has good health & loves whiskey not Father nor Geo. Yes I know I can /come {crossed out} go home 30 days renlisting but I dont bend myself 3 years long & lose my place here to go home 30 days. I am en to one firlough a year any how & perhapse I can get one some time between this & fall. You speek of airing my clothing & think of me. I suppose you dont know that I have your face in a nice gold locket & carrys it where I can pull it out as I do my watch & see you smile at me. How many differant thoughts pass through my noddle, the locket price $6. The rest of my photographs I have arranged in my record, first Father & Mother & Marys on one page, then Geo & Laura & Elsie, Elsies in the middle, And Sophie Elsie on another page. Now I want Daves to put

with S. picture then on another Gen. Thomas & Will Waggeners, So you
see that I have it arranged so that I can see the whole family evry time that
I open the book. There has been some improvements in our ration dicker.
We live good deal better we have Now days bakon & bread, Before we had
nothing but bread & baken, & some times we get saur krought, Pleas write
often, I will close. Your in love Millie Union Charlie

HEAD QUARTER TOPL.ENGR.OFFICE.
ARMY OF THE   CUMBERLAND
OFFICIAL BUSINESS

Chattanooga April 27. 1864

My Dear Wife,

Again with pleasure I make some more turkeys tracks for you to trace
& retrace in reply to yours of the 23rd ult. No. (O, the number has sliped off,
or els she forgot to put it on.) accompied with your face, & I must say that I
have enjoyed myself hugely a looking at it & showing it to my friends. I call
it a good picture, but one thing, that is, the say that there is some fly specks
on your cheek, but I know what they are & I would just like to be where I
could pick them off, I am feeling very well now days, & have lots of work
to do. Nate Finnegan & myself has beat the crowd on makeing a map which
was call for this week & is to be published this week 150 coppies of them.
We commenced yesterday morning & got done this afternoon. I can tell
you just how many guns or peices of cannon thas at Dalton & evry foot of
brest works, & how they calculate to defend themselves, but I dare not, So
you found Edd. Tiffany did you. I would be glad to se him, does he look like
the same old chap, did you tell him to write to me, why didnt you. I wish I
could chat with him about Dansville. When you write to me again tell me
all about Dansville. I am very much interested with what you have told me.
But I want to here more, How has Rob Lippy turned out. They must have a
starveing old band by this time. We have one of the best brass bands in in
the U.S. belong to the 15th regulars. They will bring the tears to your eyes to
have them play some of their music. Perhaps I am not quite so bad looking
as you think I am. I have improved some & you may think so if you have
my last letter. I will try & do better still & not look so ugly & the swelling

is out of my face. I will send you a little keep sake on a bible mark in this letter. I did not do the lettering on it, Only one shilling for your picture, suche at chatt. would cost $1.50 & $6.00 a doz. for Photographs, I hate to pay it & I want the pictures. We are haveing very hot weather Now days What kind of a frame have you for the record, have you a glass over it? if not you had better get one, it will soon spoil without it. My eyes are not so bad as they were. Dont get any news yet only my liveing is getting better: had some butter for supper, one half made of lard the other half of tallow & old enough to walk alone at least it smells so. Snowballs are in blossom out here, how is it with you. I guess you are not makeing maple sugar this spring are you, you dont say anything about it. Well you say that Old Mr. Drew has gone up the spout. I cant say that I am sorry for you I am death on Northan rebels as well as Southern, & his sins we are not accountable for. You must excuse me tonight for my sheet is nearly full. Yours in Love Charlie Millie

Head Quarters, Topl. Engr Office
Army of the Cumberland Tennessee Apr 29 1864

My Wife

Spring is around with its opening flowers,
Its balmy airs its golden tinted skies,
Its thousand charms with sweet enjoyment rife
Its songs of birds, which from each vale arise,
The world is full of life how could it now fade
Fall like a rose in its sweet bloom decayed.
Once more this eve thou'rt in thine home with me,
Thy gentle voice falls on the listening ear;
Again thy soft glance comes all dreamingly
A dear illusion as thyself went there,
Blest be kind memory for these visions sweet,
Blest, that e'en thus, earth's love & last we meet.

Millie   Charlie

I mail with this letter a roll contain some pictures. the 3 smallest, a view of Chattanooga they belong togeather the left hand one, a view of Lookout in the distant. Cameron hill on the right of the middle one & left of the 3rd one Rackoon mts to the rear of Camron hill & Walden ridge to the rackoon mt. the other Photograph a view of my head quarters, see if you can find me out. Pleas take good care of them, the other the one I told you to work a fraim for. Take notis N.B. keep this coulered picture out of the way of the flies for they will dobb the ink on coulers, you will see a little of their work on one corner now If I was to make this over I could do better but this is the first brush painting I have undertaken & your portrate I took from your last picture you sent me I left off the headdress. If you have an opportunity to send to Kal. pleas enquire if the vest was sent from Geo. Anderson, if it is there get it & have it sent by mail. do it up stout & leave one end open so the P.M. can see what it is. Ill risk it by mail yours in haist Charlie

Chattanooga, May 1st 1864

My Dear Mille

Now a few moments with you. The Lord has spared my life & health to see another beautiful May day, & I am very thankfull for the kindness bestowed upon me. -- I am well & enjoy very good health. I have been out this A.M. to dig up some old acquaintances. I went to the first Mich Engr. & found Bill Estriss, you have hurd of him, he is the one that use to go to Fathers singing S. in Martin -- had a good old chat with him. He says that Charles Stratton was here a few days ago & now has gone back to his company I have also have found out that our Regiment is down in Look Valley about 3 miles from Chatt. & while I was gone out Capt. Bigelow came here to see me & waited about 2 hours sorry I did not see him. -- it is to him I am indebted for my preasent position & is my particular friend --When I sum up my friends I find that I have a good many amongst the officers.-- Have you ever received any money of Capt. Hubbard from me, He agreed to send to you my commutation money that is due me while a prisoner when he drew it, the amount is between 4 & 6 dollars. If you see him when he is at Otsego you may mention it to him. If he has draw the money he will pay it to you. I have hurd the 13th Mich is up on Lookout mt. I have had no time to go to see them. I dont get my vest yet. I want to tell you some good news but I dare not but look for a big strike this ... I have not got my Photographs taken yet. I cant get a good one taken here & they charge only $6.00 for a poor picture. I admire your picure very much -- I have to look at it 3 or 4 times a day then I look out the window & see

such beautiful foliage on the hills & mountains & what do I think of. O!
give me back my homestead roof I ask no palace doam &c. -- Pleas sing
it & think of old times. We are full of buiseness now days but I do steel a
little time to make some pictures, -- cant help it. I dont know as I will get
this picture complat before I have to send out my letter. Well what is the
opion of the people North of the war do they think the war will close this
year. I that Grant is a going to do a big job this summer & soon let us all
go home -- That will be nice wont it. I want to get out of this stinking hole.
Hot weather is comeing & plenty of horse flesh above ground -- & Flys
you have no idea what swarms we have hear. I dont know of a better *{The
rest was crossed in red ink, and all I have is a photocopy; the red did not
register. There are three more lines}*

Chattanooga May 5th "64

My Dear Wife,

In answer to your kind letter of Apr. 25. I take the pleasure to scribble
you a few lines to let you know that I am yet alive & well this morning.
We are so badly drove with work that I have to do my coresponding when
I should be asleep. We have to work night & day to supply the army with
what maps they want to use. We have allready isued 100 & have to print
200 more. I do the coulering on them, Some 7 or 8 of our men have gone
to the front, they went yesterday, the army moved last Tuesday, quite an
exciting time with us. I have not heard of the result of the movement but
expect to evry hour. there was about 300 wounded brought in this week
so it seems that the ball has opened. We have a very large force & I expect
they will walk through the rebs like a dose of salts, the 19th has gone to the
front. & I wish I was with them. The 9th has gone also.--But as to the 13th I
could not say. We have plenty men & guns left behind yet. I think there is
about 125 peices at this place now, & some old sockers too, have a number
100 lbs parrits for some of the forts that have just arrived. As I sit here by
the open window this beautiful morning I can hear the booming of cannon
in the distant,--19 engins were about the Depot yesterday evening all in
motion & kept up a continual screatching all night--9 large warehouses
are built & building the smallest 200 ft long by 40 ft wide the most of
them jaimed full of provisions & Quartermasters stores, 5 sawmills in
opperation sawing bridging &c thousands of colard troops are hard at work

on the fortifications & the army on their way to Rome & Atlanta & evry thing flourishing finely. I dont think it will be a great while before you will direct my mail to Atlanta.--If you have so much to say it need not trouble you to compose more letters. I suppose you know if I got one letter evry day I would not be satesfied. You dont know how I enjoy letters from home & also a writing them & fixing them up nice. I shall have to send you a short letter this time. we are drove so & it is time to go to sow belly. Yours in love. From your Husband, Charlie Millie

Head Quarters, Topl, Engr.
Office Army of the Cumb.
Chattanooga, May 11ᵗʰ 1864

Dear Wife,

I suppose it is nearly time for you to expect another letter from the army of the Cumberland, & seeing that I have a little leasure I thought now would be my time to do some yarning. Perhaps you would like to know a little about my health, Well! I am sorry to have to say, -- you know that I agreed to tell you just how I was & to tell you the worst, but I am sorry to tell you that this is a very cold night & a good warm fire feels comfortable this evening there was 5 Car loads of wounded came in yesterday evening, & we had a very hard thunder storm last night & the wind blows hard all day from the North. it must be that some of your northan people want to freeze us out, but you cant do it as long as we have green red & black oak wood to burn & let me say to you that we are just a waxing the rebs & they will soon have to flee to the mountains & the rest of their hiding places & I am a fumbleing over some of your letters to see if there was something that you wanted me to say to you but I forgot how much maple sugar you sayed you made this spring & if you have a long story to tell me I want you commence at the beginning of coarse & you speak of your gratitude to me for my long kind letters. O! if you could be a mouse in the wall & see me overhawl one of your kind letters, you would write letters all the time for the sake of seeing the of of me reading, but I dont consider you endebted to me at all, but Dave is in Detroit is he, do you hear from him I dont nor from Sister Soph, neather. She owes me a letter or els I have not got her last & you know I hardly ever fail to give satesfaction where ever I go & at whatever I do, they all seem to be very well satesfied with me thus far & I may remain here untill go away if I have good luck & as luck will have it I have all that I want to eat & of the richest kind. I suppose you have hurd people say befor now the older whiskey is the better it is & that is the case with sowbelly & the next litter you mit gist put in a pan ov milk & a peck of nut cakes if you pleez. u nead not mind about sending a bol & spune but excuse mi good spiling for I have my ears pierced to improve the health of my eyes & I hav ben kullerin maps all day & I am tired & / you are corresponding with Luut Clank {this line is written waveringly on the paper} tite again, kant help it dont tell any buddy & the $1.00 you may take it out to the P.O. & get stamps &c. I thought it want good but the 5 was good. No you dident me evry thing I sent you, you did not say a word about the Bumerang 6 in the paper I sent you & I am much obliged for what you sent me. I would send you one once in a while if I was not to lazy to get them. I had rather make them on paper, & what do u think of my 2 last letters & when you get the room all fixed up nice I will make you a visit when the war is over & tell you some good long stories &c. my candle is most burned out & I have got hurry up or I will get caught in the dark & if you should hapen to come in here about now you would find me well, well,,-- It is now 15 minutes to nine & I guess you are sitting by the stove in the kitchen write & tell me. Love to you all, remember the soldiers. Charlie Millie Camp Butternut grove Otsego I expect our mail is to be retained here about 10 days This letter is written in black ink, crossed in red ink, and then a small part at the end is written diagonally in green.

Head Quarters, Topl. Engr.
Office, Army of the Cumb.
Chattanooga Tenn. May 15/64

My Dear Wife

Seeing that I dont get any mail from you or any body els, I will write the more & see if I cant make a rase of some after a while I have receive none since your 39 letter but I suppose there letters on the way some where & I still beleive that you would do your duty in writing to your other half, I must owne up that I am lonesome now days. A number of the hands have gone to the front & it leaves me in a large room alone to do as I am a mind to. I have been buisy this week a trimming & colering maps all last week & have 88 maps a head, I have the map of N.W. corner of georgia including Chattanooga printed on my nose wiper & send it to you. I thought perhaps it would be of some use to you when you read the news from Gen. Sherman army. The most of the work on the map is mine. You can wash it when it gets dirty but not in hot water. The 300 maps that we are printing is about 4 ft. squair & that on the rag is a little of the N.W. corner of it. I would like to have you send me another hankercheif, roll it in a news paper the same as I do, I think it will come through safe, but the vest I have not seen yet. Do you know anything about where it is or has it been sent to me yet. the meadicen that you put with the vest hase cured me allthough I have not seen it yet, & my eyes are better than they have been since I was first taken with soer eyes. I dont suppose there is any use of my saying anything about the war news, I suppose you here of it as fast as I do. But I will say that Gen. Shermans army is advanceing rapidly. they are as far as Resacca & have gone through some of the worst places such as gaps in mountains & have saved the tunnell at Tunnell Hill. A dummy came in last Thur. from Dalton. (A dummy is a single Car about 20 ft longer than a common passenger car with a small engine enclosed at the front end)--I have not hurd from my regiment yet & dont know where they are. I am ansious to here from them. you will be more likely to here from them than I will. & If so pleas tell me all about them. It is now dinner time & I must go.-- 2 oclock P.M. Now I will continue my letter. On my way to dinner I here some very good news, that is that Richmond is on the point of surrendering & the rebels are giveing themselves up by the thousands & Gen. Butler is at work of Fort Darling a fort about 5 m. S.E. of Richmond & haveing very good success. The best of the news from the army of the Cumb is kept back-- Here comes a letter from my wife, glad to see you--bearing date May 5th 1865 No 40 Now seeing that you have had a chat with me I will reply by saying that I am glad to here from you again & to know that you are live & well--As for the pictures you speak of are of no account only sometimes they afford a little fun--do you know who was a going to bring the vest out here, some one spoke of sending it by Whit, if it was sent by him & he is with his Reg. it may be up there for all what I know. the last I hurd of the regiment, they were about 10 miles from here on Lookout running a sawmill. I cant go any other day but sunday & go foot & carry a rail & that I know to be a tuff job for this warm climate & climb the mountain besides, however I shall try to go soon. You are sweet enough this spring are you--I was in hopes that you would have some maple syrph when I went home, when the war is over--Charlie Stratton was here a few weeks ago but I did not see him. He did not know that I was here. He stays at Bridgeport. Bill Estress was here & made me a visit yesterday evening. He told me about Charlie. It seems good to dig up some old acquaintances while I am out here amongst strangers.--Dont forget to speek to Capt. Hubbard about that money if you get it I will make you a preasent of it--As for my getting a furlough I think it will be out of the question because there is 5 of the boys time all most out & men are scarse to fill their places & I will have so much to do but never mind there is good news from the front & it will cost me nearly 100 dollars to go & come & that I have not got. I have to pay my own transportation furloughs--while you are getting supper pleas get some for me I think I would enjoy one good meal once more. I am very much pleased with your picture. the boys all say that I have got a good looking wife (Dont wish to flatter you) that just what I think so they are not mistaken. So you think you will get my locket do you but the greatest mystery is how did I get the picture for the locket. You dident know that I was an artist did you. It is hard telling what I can do I hardly know myself. what I can do with the pencil & Brush untill I go at it. You may make one of your pine cones fraims to take a glass 13 by 16 & I will send you a picture to put in it when I get it done. shant tell what it is but it is a kind that you fancy -- the size of the glass in locket 1 3/8 in. very good sixe for me to carry. This peice of cloth will make a pretty lounge, when you get it done I will come & sit with you on it when the war is over. -- I would rather you would send me a pan of good sweet milk than sassafras bough--for we have lots of it here & as I have sayed before my eyes are better. I am very much obliged to Mrs Phelps & hope she will write, I notice that you complain of your sheet getting full, some how I cant fill mine. What kind of a harp is that you speek of that you have received from me. You want to know if your letters are numbered right, you either left out 2 numbers or I did not get the letters but this neednt make any difference now your best way is to make a list & keep in your portfolio tell Elsie that Uncle Charlie would like to see her. I send you a picture of my dasy what do you think of them. What do you thinke or how do you like the peice of music I sent you, I call it good. I have a song to sing to you when I go home, if you were here when I go to bed you might hear me sing it. Geo must be clearing off my farm, that is all right I wish he would clear off the whole of it then I would have the less to do. There I might as well stop & finnish my letter next wednesday

Love to all Your Husband O I am call Charlie Millie

Head Quarters Topl. Engr.
Office. Army of the Cumb.
Chattanooga, Tenn. Wed.
Evening, May 18th 1864, &c

Dear Millie,

I just happen to write you another letter seeing that it has been so long scince you have hurd from me. I must say to you that I do not feel very well this evening, & to tell the truth I have been rather pigish at the supper table & eat a little to much Sow belly & bread, potatoes, beans, onions, molasses & the rest Ill keep to myself. then took a good long walk with Friend Day for exersize & what do you suppose I see in my travels If I thought it would be interesting to you I would tell you & I will anyhow. On our way from our boarding house to the ferry, lying by the side of the R.R. track 6 enormous guns & iron bed fraims, guns about 16 ft long & muzzle larg enough to stick your arm in (& body to if you want to) These are to be placed in fort Cameron on Cammeron Hill which commands the country 100 miles evry way nearly O, I did not think of Look Out (we will have to move that) then still farther on to the Ordinance department were hundreds of teams loading up with amunition (stuff they kill rebs with) then still farther to the large bridge over the 10-a-c river. they have it nearly a crost the river, it is about 2,200 ft long (would make a feller grunt to carry it in his pocket or the buttons would fly) here lay 3 steemers, pontoons & lots of Soldiers a fishing & they ketch plenty of them & very large ones. then we sauntered up main st. where we found the streets jamed full of teems after rations & (sow belly) & could see teams as far as the eye could reach out in the country I the other end of the train must have been at Resacca, so on up the streat I saw a brother soldier so weak in the knees that two others had to draw him along & he was just a heaving up the beer &c. Dident he have a good time, hey? We took one good harty laugh & came on to our quarters, but I forgot a small pile of corn that we passed, it is put up in 2 1/2 bushels sacks the pile was about 300 ft long, 40 ft wide & 35 ft high what do you think of that, I think that is more than george can lift & try 2 times, what has become of him, he dont write any more. I dont know but he is a waiting for another picture, but I have sold the last one, any of you must not wait for me to write for I think I do my shair. I write to you all twice a week & direct to u & I suppose you read it to them ((seeing that they dont know how to read writing &c)) {here is a drawing of a smiling man's face} Well, I guess you have got enough of me for the time & will change the object My dreams are of thee in the hush of night, My visions of thee in the noon of day, Time is forgoten in his ceaseless flight, Whilst I am thinking of the -- far away, since first I gazed upon thy faultless brow, Swiftly have sped the moments untill now, O if I could just happen in upon you just a little while wouldent we have a good time. I will close for this time by saying good night to you all. (Lots of prisoners came in to day) Charlie

Head Quarters Topl. Engr.
Office, army of the Cumb.
Chattanooga, 10-a-c. Monday
morning 5 oclock. May 23/64

My Dear Wife,

Well here I am again a penning a few lines to you. I should have writen yesterday evening so as to mail my letter this morning but on my return from Look Out I found that I was so tired that I thought it would be a good plan to wait untill morning. My journey was a fruitless one, The vest that I went after was not there & whit new nothing about it, Nor any one els. Now the next thing is where is the vest, I dont think i t was ever sent & if it was it is a goner. I would not go up there again this hot weather for a half doz. vests, it is a hard job to climb that mountain, it is very steep & hard to go up on the sunny side & no breeze & I thought that I should melt before I reached the top I cannot discribe to you anything new about the mountain only the trees are covered with green foliage & the ground with wild flowers & it is a very pleasent place on the top. I found the 13th about 1 1/2 m. south of the point, a little beyond summertown. I saw whit, Henry Newton, Boot, Dutch Peat & others that I was not much acquainted with. The 22nd Mich. is camped near them on the mt. We are getting very good news from the front, Johnson has only about 40 thousand & we have nearly 3 that number. We have got beyond the Etowah river, The rebs do not fight but little while at a time then run. There holt is at Allatoona when they get beyond there then we have a very level Country & can use our artillery to a good advantage but not untill we get them out of the mountains. When when we get them out of Allatoona then the chace will commence to Atlanta. their horses & mules are in very poor condition & ours in good. I never saw them look any better. The battle opens again this morning & the baggage has been reduced & have 20 days rations on hand we have been out of rations or short of rations the last few days the reason that of the delay, but now we have the R.R. in good order up tite to the rebel lines the reason of their getting commissarys to them was because of the transportation of troops & prisoners & the waggon roads are so rough & mountainous that it is very slow getting it there by mule power. We think Gen. Sherman will give a good account of him self in a few days. -- I received a good new towell from some body last week done up in a Michigan Hereld & I tell you I had one good wipe on it. You dont know how much a soldier prises any thing sent from home, it seems that money would not buy them -- I will close by saying that I am well but feel rather old on account of my tramp yesterday. Yours in love, Charlie Millie

Head Quarters Topl. Engr Office
Army of the Cumberland Chattanooga Tenn.
May the 27th 1864

My Dear Lonely Wife

Yours of the 14th No. 41, came to hand the 25th & was much wellcomed & it brings me the good news that you are all well & this letter will tell you that I am well. But as for my takeing a peek in to your quarters is out of the question this afternoon, some time when the war is over I will try & give you another surprise as one year ago. You do not keep me very well posted in reguard to farm affairs. It would be very interesting to me to know where you are sowing Oats & how many acres & where you plant corn & how much & all of such little things all though it will do me no good way down in 10ac, but I like to know what is going on at home. Tell Father & George to do that well, dig out all of the stumps & pick up all the stones & be sure to destroy all the thistles. I scarcely know what a thistle is any more. I saw one on Look Out the other day & the only one I saw in Tenn. Well, when shall I look for you home. That is a pirty question to ask. If you will tell me what day the war will close, then I can tell you very near what day I will start for home. As for geting a furlough from Gen. Sherman way down to Nashville & pay out $100. dollars to show my hombly face in Otsego wont hardly pay will it, but I tell you I want to go home as bad as you want to have me. You wanted me to guess what kind of a bee you was going to have in July. I cant think of any other kind of a bee but one of Company bee (B) & that must mean me If that is your expectation I shall be very sorry to disappoint you but I shall have to. I am sorry that I said aword about a furlough. Now if I do not guess right on the bee question pleas tell me -- Now about that hard battle in Look Out Mountain. I will tell you all about it. I had a terrible dream a few nights ago of being in a battle in that neighborhood & I hapened up that way the next day & I saw a dead mule, & a dead snake & grasshopper I did not find out how many was wonded but I suppose there was some. This is all the battle that I know any thing about. I would like to have you tell me where you heard such news. I dont know why you should say that you are sorry to have me say that I wish I were there a fighting. I suppose you know that some will say most any thing when there out of danger, but when they are at it, it is another thing & that is the case with me. If I am not brave I want to make people think so. O! what a sight it is to see the wonded, I cant disscribe it to you, if you could see them you would say that it is the most horrible sight you ever saw. I was told that Col. Gilbert was brought in mortally wounded so I started for the hospital to find him, but could not get to see him but I saw thousands of soldiers that were all cut to peices & yet live. They have all the care that this country will afford them, They have good matrus bed & a fraim built to the bead stead & covered with netting to keep the flyes off, they are very trouble some here. I suppose that you have heard of the death of Col. Gilbert, you will an account of it in the gazett that I sent to George. I have found 2 of our Co. that were sent back sick & they say that 61 were killed out of my regiment, but none out Co. B. 4 were wounded. Vernon Rose had one finger off his left hand (3rd finger) Robert Patterson shot through one of his thies (flesh wound) John Rutgers of Allegan a spent ball struck him in the ribs Let Baird wounded in both arms. This fight took place at Resacca, this is as I have it from the boys that I saw from the front. I have hurd that Let Baird is here in town but I have not found him yet. I am looking about evry day for the boys of the 19th, & I find some poor suffering Brother soldiers out of many & in want of some luxerys & its hard for me to leave them untill I get them something or give them a dollar or two. I remember the old mottoe, A freind in need is a friend indeed. I feel very thankfull that I am yet spaired but when I have to go into battle I go without a murmur. If my health would permit I would go cheerfully & meet my fait & shair with the rest.-- It seems by the way that you read off the numbers that you get lots of mail, if that is so you do better than I do. I get one letter once a week some times one in 10 days. I believe that I have writen to all that I promised & the same ones do not return the answer as they agreed to. Charlie Franklin for instance Saturday morning, May 25th. I saw Wm. Estris last evening & he tells me that Charlie Owen & Duffee son was there yesterday & they say that there is none of Co. B wounded but dont know who, they may be here today & I will find out, -- I have received the towel that you sent, one like that would cost me $1.50 here, if the postage was 25c & the towel 25c then I have saved 1 dollar. You wish me to go to the 10th & get my vest. I have been but No one there knows any thing about it. So I guess the vest has gone up. if Major Eaton had it, it would have come through safe I think. Whit Mansfield says that he did not see him or any of George Anderson folks so as to get the vest. I cant get an hour much less than $10. & I will go with out before I will pay that price. I wrote to Capt. Hubberd about that money but he pays no attention to it, he has used me a little mean about that pistole & I cant say that I like him any to well as a friend, he is all right when he wants a favor & I have done many for him & you see what I get in return.-- I wish that I might surprise you again as I did one year ago, that year has been a long dreary year to me as to you, & I hope that I may be with you discharged from the service before another year rolls around & this war to a close, what a releif it will be to many a soldier-- If the music that I sent you makes you feel sad I will not send you any more. I did not know that you was so easily offended with music, it is the first time that I ever knew that music would make you feel bad, but it is time that it has a tendency to put you in mind of a good many things but never mind I will be with you some of these days then we can laugh over some things that we have cryed about -- I am a going to send you commence sending you a map that have published of Northan Georgia, they are some old proof sheets that I picked up in the office & were given to me, their will be 24 peices the sise of these. I want you to take good care of them & not loose any of them & as fast as you receive them unfold them & press them in a large book & when I get home I will mount them on cloth, there is a great deal of my labor on them & I want to keep them to look at & to see what I done when in the army. We do not have much to do now while the army is on the move & wont have untill we have some new territory I dont think unless it is some small jobs. Have you ever received a handkerchief in a paper from me, I dont think of anything more now & I guess you will be glad to have me stop, My love to all, you will hear from me soon again From Charlie To Millie One thing more this blue star on the envelop is worn by all of the 20 Army Corps I am in the 20ᵗʰ A.C.

Head Quarters Department of the
Cumberland Topl, Engr Office
Chattanooga, Tenn, May 31ˢᵗ /64
Mistake. June 1ˢᵗ

My Dear Wife

Your kind letter of the 22. (No 42) Came to hand yesterday evening so I thought it would be a good idea rise early this morning while it is cool & answer it allthough I have no news to write you, for I think you get it faster than I do. but if I were with you I could find enough to talk about, I feel a little old this morning on account of my haveing so much running to do at drawing ration for our mess & the servents & packing & shiping maps to the front &c, you should like to know if I have a dog. Yes! we have one out hear in the battery that threatens to bite me sometimes & you know if he does, he is a dead dog. but the picture I sent you is not the one. It is one that I coppied off hand from a smaller picture that I had, I called it a rather rough one but I thought you wanted a dog so I sent it to you. I have a cat here & sometime when I have an opportunity I will sketch him & send it so that you may have a cat & dog of the southern breed. You complain of not haveing ambition enough to to write a letter, I would say just for the fun of it I would not write untill I did then write a good long letter, cross line it & so on. fill it up if it is not so nice I like to read them, Tell Father & George not to work so hard for they will not live so long & I dont think it will pay to kill themselves with hard work for I want to see them once more. Tell Mother that I just received a half a letter from her & am a going to answer it soon. I would like a small chunck of that cheese speek of. If it wont greece the letter you might slip in a little peice. It is worth only 75c per lb. here. It costs us like evry thing to live here. We get the first quality of rotten potatoes for one dollar per bush. from the commissary, 12c per lb. for fresh beef, so I am not makeing any thing on my commutation money. This is government price that I speek of. We are not in want of small change for one dollars are small enough some times we can use half dollar. I would not care if I had a pair of pants made out of your toe to ware this summer, for we are haveing some of that old fashion hot weather now. Can you tell me how many Sheep & lambs there are I have forgotten. Wool will be high this summer I think, I see it is quoted at from 60 to 65c this spring -- You say that Susia is a handsome cow, how is it with Nelly, have you soled her yet or what has become of her, Are you rasing any calves from your cows. O, how I would like to just happen in when you get nicely at wrke in the meeting house, wouldent there be some tall squeezing of mops, &c. Well, about that loom. Do you think of weeving for a liveing, if so, it would be a good plan to get that kind of a loom, $100. is a big price to pay for a loom when I can make one of the old kind for about $10. & you know that there is a house to be built some where for us then we will a loom if you want {here there is a sketch of a man's head and a caption Don't feel affended at what I say}--O, yes I do say a good deal about comeing home, I want to very much but I dont see yet how I can you must be patiant. the war will soon be over I hope, then you will see old long ears happen up behind you some where when you dont know it. But the fact of the buisiness is. I am affraid that I will loose my posish hear & that you dont want to do & go into the battle feelds, they want men of a very steady habets & allways ready to do what there is to be done. What we have to do, has to be done in a hurry. I am sorry that I opened my head about a fourlough. I fear that you will be disappointed. So I hope you will excuse me this time & the nest time I will come & tell you when I can have a furlough ({a drawing of a gray back})--Capt. Bour has given me some old proof sheets of maps & some old sections that I am a sending to you. Take good care & not loose any of them. There will be 24 peices for one map. Have you received a map on a hankerchief rolled up in a paper. Pleas let me know. My sheet you see is nearly full one way & will close for this time. I am out of stamps & I may have to frank this letter & that I dont to do. I am useally well. My Love to you & all. From Charlie to Millie

Head Quarters, Topl. Engr Office

Army of the Cumb. Tenn. (Concluded)

Chattanooga June 7th 1864 I dont want to go home by my writing so discourageing about a furlough, but I have explained to you the reson why. I have had nor seen anything to make me want to stay away from my friends.

I have no news to tell you this morning. I suppose that you hear all that I do from the wars except Official business. That I do not tell. I am not very well now days. I have the Tennessee trott, & have had the last 3 weeks, I know just what will cure me, but I cant get it here, The meadicen I want is what you have on your Dinner table to eat, thats what the matter. But I think I am good for it 15 months longer & time will soon carry that amount if we will only make up our minds & be reconciled to it. "Then, weeping sad & lonely, Hopes & fears how vain, yet praying, When this cruel war is over, Then Charlie comes marching home,"--I have three new peices of music that I will send you when I get some stamps, one I have coppied & sent you. The names of the others are. Come listen Ill tell thee my dream love, the other Im Dying far from those I love. They were given to me by Kelly a man in this department whos time is out & goes home to day. Dont I wish it was me! But no, 15 months longer unless sooner discharged & I think that will be. I understand that our troops are crossing the Chattahoochee river. The nearist point of that river is 8 miles from Atlanta. Then when we are there we have the old rat in his hole. People are all looking for this war to close this summer, but I am done provicising for I have been mistaken so many times, How are you for money now I have some but I am affraid to trust it by mail I have 2 bills that draw intrest from the first of march at 5 per. cent one fifty dollars bill & one 20. dollar. I drew my pay a few days ago I understand that I or we soldiers are getting $16. per month instead of $13. but I am of the opinion that I will not get all of my Extry duty pay. We get it sometimes & sometimes we dont. If you can get stamps at the office I wish you would & send me one half dollars worth in a letter & I will send them back to you, stuck on the out side of letters one at a time. Sometimes I can get them at the office here but they are out now & have been some time I want some 2 cent stamps also to send some music & papers & pictures. Have you received a pine stick with some pictures rolled around it yet. It will be mailed at Cincinnatti also a letter. Our Clerk went home & he said would mail them there. You have said nothing of a hankercheif I sent you in a paper. Pleas tell me if you receive them. If you get this you ought to have 7 peices of maps, I will write small letters this time so as to send you 2 peices of maps, If there is any peices missing let me know what No. is gone. I commence at the N.W. corner to number & count towards the East then commence back to the west again, or you can give me the names of some point that /will {crossed out} bounds the missing peice if there be one. You want a compleat map while you are about it & the most of it is my work & I would like to keep them It is some of my first work in that line of buis-- I will send you a butterfly that I made the other day I must close, my breakfast is ready & i want to mail this morning Yours in haist, from your Husband Charlie to Millie

Head Quarters Topl. Engr
Office, Army of the Cumb.
Chattanooga, June 9th 1864.

My Dear Wife,

Antonon Leef.

Yours of the 29th of May Came to hand (No 43) yesterday, & a good fat one it was to. It put me in mind of a snake that swallowed at toad, It contained a hankercheif & a good letter, but it talks as though you had some bad dreams the night before it was writen. Isent that so? Or you must have been provecying something bad about me, or els you have the blues. I think you aught to keep in good spirits for I do evry thing /cherry {crossed out} that I can to make you feel happy, I write long letters (you may leave out the good) & make pictures & do every thing I can but it seems that I dont succeed. I shall have to try something els. I will send you $5. & see if that wont dry up the tears in your eyes. Perhape you think that I am sick because I said in my last that I was not very well. I feel some better to night (Now 9 oclock) but I am not well yet, except the ich, that has left, I have cured that with a sponge, towel wash basin & cold water I bathe myself evry morning at 5 oclock, but the flying axhandles will stick to me & will as long as I live in the army I guess. I shall be thankfull if I dont have anything worse. About that snake & toad letter, I have let Finkbine take that hanckerchief to print a map on it. Will you send me another if I will send this home with a map on it? This is much nicer to carry to meeting & visiting &c. than the one I sent you That hankerchief belongs to a young lady in Shelbyville & I dont want to loose it. She gave it to me when I went through there, Dont know her name, but she is good looking I am affraid that Byron will dirty it so you will have to wash it to much. I will not stand much washing. I have the Towel. I think I have mentioned it in 2 letters. I have hurd from the 19th. I saw a list of the killed, & Fred Campbell of my company was killed. I guess the only one,

& he was of no account to this world. Capt. Merrill feels very bad over the death of Col. Gilbert. He came in yesterday from the front & he enquiered all about him. I dont here a word from Dave yet. Neather have I his address & he owes me a letter. Well what did Soph say of her letter I suppose she let you read it she aught to if she dident I hope you wount feel hurt because I correspond with the Ladys. I do it so as to get letters to read, but that of Charlies is not answered yet. Some times I have a notion to write one & give him a side winder. Then I guess he will write. I never have been informed of Major Eatons haveing the vest. But it came to me this A.M. & I have it on It fits good, I will send you a picture of it in a few days. It suits me right up to the handle. I could not have done better myself. O, give me you yet, for a bargain, this kind cost here just $8. But the meadicen I do not here a word of yet, Nor Whit has not had it. Good night. I will finnish in the morning Good night! Morning has come & I find myself feeling prety well. We had a hard thunder shower duering the night,--I have made the picture & sent it to you & some others, the picture I call the Pet is the one I designed for you to fraim. I am sorry that I cant come & visit with you in your clean fixed up house but so it is. I remarked in my last about my pay. I drew 6 months pay ($78.) am afraid to send it by express or mail because there is so many garrillas through the country watching their chance to destroy the R.R. & capture trains. I will send you a little at a time to make you comfortable & if you are in need of more than I send, you will pleas let me know I do not get my full amount of extry duty money as I expected. Their seems to be a screw loose some where. There is about 48 dollars due me now & I cant get boarded as cheep as I used to. It costs us about $11. a month. The boots that I wore from home are good for 6 months longer. On the first page I tryed to imitate a Autumn maple leif & did not have very good success. I will try it again some time. I suppose you have received you potrate that I coppied from you picture what do you think of it. I inclose 2 sections of map & some poetry. No news from the front of any intrest that I can tell you. Yours with much Love Charlie   to Millie This letter is written in a very fine hand (about 30 letters per 2 inches horizontally and 10 lines to the inch vertically and is perfectly legible)

Head Quarters Topl. Engr. Office
Army of the Cumberland Chattanooga
Saturday evening, June 11ᵗʰ 1864.

My Dear Wife.

Seeing that I have nothing to do this evening to do, I thought I would have a little chat with youns way up north. I dont know as I owe you a letter, but I must do something to kill time. Capt. Bower just came in to light his candle by mine & tells me I will spoil my eyes, doing such fine work. I hope you dont call this fine work. It is only 3 lines in one rule. I can write 6 lines in one rule & have it plane to read. {Here the lettering gets smaller for a short space} I do this fine work to show you how to fill a sheet to your old man when he goes to the army.--Roenna? I feel lonesome this evening & Ill tell you why {here the lettering returns to original size} The last ten days has been very wet & cloudy & some little mud, not exacly mud but worst than mud something like whightwash. It cost me about 10c evry time I go to my meals to get ferryed across the road & streets & 5c worth of blacking to put my boots in good passable order, say nothing about the ware & tare of a brush & the hard labour of a collared black servent about 1/2 hour &c.&c. & that is not all that makes me lonesome. Two more of the boys of this office left for home today, Dont you spose I would like to go too? No. 15 months more hard labour in Uncle Sams servis unless sooner discharged, but that sooner discharged is a great while comeing around but I Can Wate, can you? Wall what about the War. I hurd some good news today but dont know how true it is. I hear that Gen. Sherman is within 4 miles of Atlanta & intended to go in to day.--25 minutes to 10 So good night.--Sabeth morning, June 12ᵗʰ. This is a very chilly disagreeable morning. The wind blowing very cold from the N.E. I am sitting by my desk with my coat buttoned up & fingers quite numb with cold. I have a notion to build a fire. I believe this is what people call the sunny south but it seems to me that we have as much cold weather here as you do at the north.--we do not here much direct from the front now. It seems to be very still except the prisoners that are brought in. Last night there was a pile of them came in, so they must be doing something. Gen. Sherman does not allow anything to be published from the front if he can help it. Evry thing is a moveing right & I expect that we shall move our head Quarters to Atlanta before many weeks. That is what I mean by your haveing to direct your mail to that place.--As luck will have it & it is just as I expected when

I ordered some stamps I can get all I want I got one dollars worth yesterday, so if you want some I can lend you some. If you have not sent any its all right; but you can stick them on the out side about 2 in a week & only one on each letter. That will satesfy me--Roenna I want want to see you very much. I think of you often. The memory of thee, some wondrous spell, hath cloth with joy & hope, each lonely hour, And thy soft tones seems still with me to dwell, like fairy music in their magic power & as I note thine absence with regret, I see thy dark eyes beaming on me yet, I have been with the in the land of dreams, & oft with thee have wandered far & wide by moonlight lake by summer woods & streams, I've gazed on thee in gladness by my side, whilest with thee was one long summers day which blithely fled in blissful hours away. Though only dreams they were of thee-of thee, with whom my spirit revels even alone, then let me meet once more in ecstasy evenin the land of dreams, thou art the world to me when thou art nigh, & thy sweet smiles will be with me untill I die. Then let me look upon thee, meet thee still heedless of dark hours of war with dim shadows in thy absence still defy each ill, which may joyous hope still crown thee with her light and the bright future know for thee some unexpected time,--(Gone to breakfast) Again I will resume my letter after takeing a long walk up to the depot & down to the steemboat landing. I should judg that I saw as much as 2 miles of track covered with cars, & the most of them loaded down with most evry thing needed in the army & passing the waggon yard where there is I should think about 1,000 new waggons ready for use & as many more at the shops to be repared. It would be a great sight to you to come down here & see what we have I care nothing about it. It is an old story with me & the rest of the soldiers here. I think it is very amuseing to me to stand on the streat morning about 1 hour between 6 & 8 oclock to see the men go to their labour. The streats will be filled from one end to the other with 6 mule & horse teams hawling timber, lumber, logs, wood, Commissary, machinery &c. (we have 7 sawmills in sight of this building) & the sidewalks will be lined with men both black & white, some with picks & shovels on their shoulders enstead of a gun, some with hamers & drills to the stone quarry. A long string of darkeys each one a wheelbarrow. At 5 P.M. the same on their return from work. then from that time untill dark the streats are full of mules & horses a going to & from the river a watering them. Such is the current of business in Chattanooga but I have not told you of 1/6 part of what is being done here to make this a strong place. We have a number of miles of brest works & forts. We have 99 banquets &

each one containing a scege gun. This will be heled as a military post for many years also Murfreesboro & many other places in the south,-- On going to breakfast I come across a Lieut. of Co. G. of my regiment this morning. He will be here soon to have a visit. He is a particular friend of mine. I would tell you his name but I cannot spell it so you will have to guess at it. He came from the front about 3 weeks ago. I will wate & fill up my sheet untill I see him I may get some news to tell you.--Evening 8 oclock. Now I will endever to finnish my scribling. I received your No. 44 today bearing date June 5th & I will answer it in this. I am glad again to hear that you are all well & as you say thankfull that your lives are still spaired & enjoying the blessings of a home fireside. You tell about your tiny little songsters I have them come to visit me, frequently a little favorate of mine comes & sits on the wood pile & gives me a song or two then off it goes laughing how it has cheered me in my lonely moments. You speek of receiving a roll of pictures from me, but you did not say wheather it was worth fraiming or not--Yes I sent Geo. 2 pick nicks, & I shall mail my knapsack to him with this letter. Well Sophie seems to be willing to let you read her letter, that is all right, they are nothing, Mearly a repetition of what you get first only in a little different form. But I should judg that you had rather I would not corespond with her. I must say that I would like to get more mail than one letter per week & If I get then I must write them or write about 4 & receive one, that is the way that my corespondents turn out you & family excepted. I try to set a good example on writing but few heed it. But now I am in a bad fix. I promised Sophie my picture & you dont want her to have it. Now I have to tell a right out lie & lose friends perhape or send her the picture & mar your feelings. What shall I do, I am sure that you can not have any objections. I am a going to have a dozen taken tomorrow & pleas send me a list of those that you want to have one, Now then /shall {crossed out} be honest, shall I tell a lie or give her a picture. I think a great deal of my word & caricter, More of that I do of her or the picture, I would not be caught in a lie for nothing. Hear I have come to the bottom of the page & what shall I do. I will turn it up side down & go on with my story. You speek as though you wanted a large Portrite I cant afford to pay 7 dollars for a poor one so you will make you one to hang on the wall out of sight somewhere say under the bed. O my trip to Look out I care nothing about now after all is all over with nor my journey through Dixey but I dont want to travel it again. I will say again & again I have the vest, I have the vest, I have the vest but No meadicen, No meadicen I never had it explained to me before nor behind. You done your business correct only you could have let him get it for me & save you a trip to Kal.-- Shit on such a B as you tell of. Yes, I understand more than I wish I did. Cant you charter a knot hole somewhere to crawl in about that time. Keep mum these last two lines. Yes I remember well one year ago & you will find that I have mentioned it in some of my last my eyes pain me & I will close. I have not said half I want to & my sheet is only half full yet, If you cant read this get Mothers specks. Yours with 14 yards of Love. Charlie

Head Quarters, Department of the
Cumberland, Topl. Engr. Office
Chattanooga, June 18th 1864

My Dear Millie

Your long kind letter of the 12th inst. (No. 45) Came to hand this afternoon. & you speak as though you had no letters to answer or you do not get any I think I have mailed to you two letters most evry week for the last 5 or 6 weeks & I think you aught to have some to answer except this week I have writen but one, I thought it would take you what leasure time you had in one week to read that. & I have been very buisey amakeing a map of Chattanooga to send to washington & what leasure time I had, I was glad to rest because I have been very ill the past week but I feel some better this evening. Also my eyes trouble me some. I try very hard to keep you all interested as much as I can but dont suppose I make out much but one letter has to do me for one week & some of them are short at one end. It seems to me that you put off writing untill you get in a hurry then you cant think of any thing to say. If you want to write a long letter you must do as I do Lay awake nights thinking what would be interesting to me--I will acknoladge that I send you a stingy peice of paper but it is most all coulared with the point of my pen. & a full 3 cents worth is scealed within the envelope & I dont know but more sometimes, Dont I. I am glad to hear that you are all well & enjoying the blessings & comforts of life, the same that many of us are deprived of, expectially hull corn & milk & such little things. I see you speek of the vest again, I have it on, & I got it with climbing the mountain, & I would not go up there if I never got it. You have no idea what a task it is to get up there,--Major Eaton & Capt Hubbard has been here to make me a visit. In reguard to the money, the regiment has not drawn their pay, there is 7 months due them. I have my 6 months pay in my pocket. Capt. Hubbard is better of his wound & is getting well, it will be some time yet before he will be able for duty. I also saw Capt. Duffee this week & quite a number of officers from the regiment. I have learned that my friend Capt. Bigelow is dead. He was shot through the bowels & died on his way here. Also a number of my friends are gone & yet I am spaired, but I feel guilty that I am not with them to shair the hardships with them. If my health would have been good I should have been with them. I dont think it is anything to brag of because I have got rid of fighting. & when I think of the hard ships while a prisoner, I feel as though I must be there, I owe them an old grudge for their treatment, None of you Northan can realise what we suffered there. I will close for to night. Love to you & pleasent dreams to you Charlie {The above was written on a piece of paper 9 1/2 x 5 1/4 inches; the reverse is slightly more full because he did not have to put any heading on it.} Sabeth morning June 19th /64 I am not very well this morning, but nothing very dangerous Ill live through it I guess. I saw last evening Doct. Bently right from the front & he says that Sherman is takeing prisoners by the thousands. Last Thursday they took 1500 at one hawl & our millitary prisons are all running over full & large squads all about town. Evry thing is progresing finely. It seems to me that the present war is a king of a railroad war. The car, the track, the bridge the trestle work, the tunnell are subjects for important military considerations. Military strategy is great on railroads. The military railroad depots & establishments at Nashville and Chattanooga goes a head of anything I ever hurd of of the kind to be seen elswhere in the U.S. The New York Centeral & Erie roads can make no such a showing of multitudes of locomotives in round houses & upon side tracks in the various processes of repair, being whiped, ready to get off, with steam hissing from there valves or just come in, with running gears all spattered with mud or grimmed with dust &c. One may see as many as 40 engines thus collected in the yard at Nashville, & I have seen 24 at this place at one time all in motion. The machines never get cold while in order to run, are constantly upon the roads, with change of engineers. The large number of freight cars are also in constant use & opperation--then long trains come in unloaded by a large fupply of good stout fat buck negroes, the axles are greeced & reloaded & away they go again ladened with hard bread, sow belly, pickeled pork, hams, Cattle, Clothing, Amunition guns & big bull dogs for the army & as I have remarked before, It is surprising to see the amount of buisness done on these rail roads & to see the large buildings 40 ft by 200 ft all jamed full & about 16 of them new. The quarter masters calculate that they have about 6 months provisions clothing on hand for 150,000 men & feed for mules & horses the same length of time. So if our communication is cut off between here & Louisville you need not be affraid that we will starve. I dare say with safety that we are feeding in this vicinity about 15,000 prisoners, this is mearly guesswork with me but I am sure that there is 500 for I saw them yesterday evening. I tell you what it is I dont think much of the Soldiers Aid Society, for the availes goes to support the officers & to make themselves comfortable & the poor sick & wounded may lay and grone for their shair. I would not say this if I had not seen it, If there is any left some choice freind may get some of it, It makes no differance what it is, clothing or eatables or what, the officers and clurks will fether their nest first, I dont know how it is with you but an officer is looked upon as one of the lowest grade in these parts with some exceptions. There is some human beings amongst them. Well, as you say I think you have hurd enough of my complaints, and the Society is a good thing if the sufferers could get the availes of them.--I hope you will have a good time at Paw Paw. I had a map printed on my new handercheif & sold *{This is the end of the sheet, and the rest of the letter is missing.}*

Head Quarters, Department of the
Cumberland, Topl. Engr. Office
Chattanooga, June 18th 1864

My Dear Millie

Your long kind letter of the 12th inst. (No. 45) Came to hand this afternoon. & you speak as though you had no letters to answer or you do not get any I think I have mailed to you two letters most evry week for the last 5 or 6 weeks & I think you aught to have some to answer except this week I have writen but one, I thought it would take you what leasure time you had in one week to read that. & I have been very buisey amakeing a map of Chattanooga to send to washington & what leasure time I had, I was glad to rest because I have been very ill the past week but I feel some better this evening. Also my eyes trouble me some. I try very hard to keep you all interested as much as I can but dont suppose I make out much but one letter has to do me for one week & some of them are short at one end. It seems to me that you put off writing untill you get in a hurry then you cant think of any thing to say. If you want to write a long letter you must do as I do Lay awake nights thinking what would be interesting to me--I will acknoladge that I send you a stingy peice of paper but it is most all coulared with the point of my pen. & a full 3 cents worth is scealed within the envelope & I dont know but more sometimes, Dont I. I am glad to hear that you are all well & enjoying the blessings & comforts of life, the same that many of us are deprived of, expectially hull corn & milk & such little things. I see you speek of the vest again, I have it on, & I got it with climbing the mountain, & I would not go up there if I never got it. You have no idea what a task it is to get up there,--Major Eaton & Capt Hubbard has been here to make me a visit. In reguard to the money, the regiment has not drawn their pay, there is 7 months due them. I have my 6 months pay in my pocket. Capt. Hubbard is better of his wound & is getting well, it will be some time yet before he will be able for duty. I also saw Capt. Duffee this week & quite a number of officers from the regiment. I have learned that my friend Capt. Bigelow is dead. He was shot through the bowels & died on his way here. Also a number of my friends are gone & yet I am spaired, but I feel guilty that I am not with them to shair the hardships with them. If my health would have been good I should have been with them. I dont think it is anything to brag of because I have got rid of fighting. & when I think of the hard ships while a prisoner, I feel as though I must be there, I owe them an old grudge for their treatment, None of you Northan can realise what we suffered there. I will close for to night. Love to you & pleasent dreams to you Charlie {The above was written on a piece of paper 9 1/2 x 5 1/4 inches; the reverse is slightly more full because he did not have to put any heading on it.} Sabeth morning June 19th /64 I am not very well this morning, but nothing very dangerous Ill live through it I guess. I saw last evening Doct. Bently right from the front & he says that Sherman is takeing prisoners by the thousands. Last Thursday they took 1500 at one hawl & our millitary prisons are all running over full & large squads all about town. Evry thing is progresing finely. It seems to me that the present war is a king of a railroad war. The car, the track, the bridge the trestle work, the tunnell are subjects for important military considerations. Military strategy is great on railroads. The military railroad depots & establishments at Nashville and Chattanooga goes a head of anything I ever hurd of of the kind to be seen elswhere in the U.S. The New York Centeral & Erie roads can make no such a showing of multitudes of locomotives in round houses & upon side tracks in the various processes of repair, being whiped, ready to get off, with steam hissing from there valves or just come in, with running gears all spattered with mud or grimmed with dust &c. One may see as many as 40 engines thus collected in the yard at Nashville, & I have seen 24 at this place at one time all in motion. The machines never get cold while in order to run, are constantly upon the roads, with change of engineers. The large number of freight cars are also in constant use & opperation--then long trains come in unloaded by a large fupply of good stout fat buck negroes, the axles are greeced & reloaded & away they go again ladened with hard bread, sow belly, pickeled pork, hams, Cattle, Clothing, Amunition guns & big bull dogs for the army & as I have remarked before, It is surprising to see the amount of buisness done on these rail roads & to see the large buildings 40 ft by 200 ft all jamed full & about 16 of them new. The quarter masters calculate that they have about 6 months provisions clothing on hand for 150,000 men & feed for mules & horses the same length of time. So if our communication is cut off between here & Louisville you need not be affraid that we will starve. I dare say with safety that we are feeding in this vicinity about 15,000 prisoners, this is mearly guesswork with me but I am sure that there is 500 for I saw them yesterday evening. I tell you what it is I dont think much of the Soldiers Aid Society, for the availes goes to support the officers & to make themselves comfortable & the poor sick & wounded may lay and grone for their shair. I would not say this if I had not seen it, If there is any left some choice freind may get some of it, It makes no differance what it is, clothing or eatables or what, the officers and clurks will fether their nest first, I dont know how it is with you but an officer is looked upon as one of the lowest grade in these parts with some exceptions. There is some human beings amongst them. Well, as you say I think you have hurd enough of my complaints, and the Society is a good thing if the sufferers could get the availes of them.--I hope you will have a good time at Paw Paw. I had a map printed on my new handercheif & sold {this is the end of the sheet, and the rest of the letter is not with it.}

Head Quarters, Topl. Engr. Office
Department of the Cumberland.
Chattanooga X-a-c. June 24ᵗʰ 1864

Dear Wife,

   Time has come for me to commence my scribbling agin to a companion
far away. This letter will tell you that I am some better than I was when
I wrote to you last, but I am not right yet, but I shall come out straight
after a little. I have not received a letter from you scince last Satterday,
conciquently I have no letter to answer (as you say) I think you are indebted
to for about 28 letters & if you intend to pay yor honest debts you will
have to scratch very fast to have the debt paid before I go home. I was
talking with one of the members of my regiment last Wednesday & he
tell a sad story about it. The regiment came here from McMinnville with
about 800 men. Now they must number not more than 200 for duty. Had
35 officers (commissioned) & Now 8, with the regiment. Capt. Baker of
Co. E in command of the Reg. All of the staff officers are killed. The Col.
& Major Griffin both shot precicely the spot by sharpshooters in the left
brest just above the heart. Capt. Bigelow through the bowels on the right
side, Many of my friends of the Reg. are gone, & it makes me feel sad to
think of the boys that I tented & messed with, & the hours that we have
spent togeather a telling over what good times we would have a going home
from war & what luxeries we would have when we get our liberty, then
think of the change, Number of these comrades are cold in death & others
are sick & wounded in hospitals, scattered all over the country, far from
their friends, Companions, Mothers & sisters. O, the horrers of war. When
I think it over I make up my mind that there is but one thing to be done.
That is to prepare ourselves die happy & meet our friends in heaven where
our sorrows will be at an end, where we will be marching with angels &
mingle our chorus & forever be happy. O for that place we must all go, I
hope you will strive to do right & when you leave this world, die happy. It
builds me there a house of air, A castle wide & tall, with terrets gleaming
tall & fair, against the cloudless sky, within gods holy book the sweetest
words, that ever a poet wrote, Like troops of heaven's melodious birds, in
sunshine sing & float, May the Country soon see the time when peace will
again spread her wings over the land & we all can return to our homes &
firesids except those who have fallen for there country & there bones lay
bleaching in the sun's hot rays, Many are thus situated, where they have

fallen a few shovels of dirt was through over them & the rain has washed it off, & our heavy army waggons are passing over them, crumbling there bones fine. This I know to be a fact.

June 26th Sunday morning. Now I will continue my letter, I cannot boast of feeling very well. I have a very hard cold, the first I have had in a long time. I was carles when I got it, I with with 3 others set out on the magazene back of our building a few nights ago a cerinadeing the brest works & caught a hard cold & we have had extream hot weather since, The sun shines so hot that I preffer to go without my dinner than to go out. I hear last night that our regiment had but one line officer that is capt. Baker of Company E. who has command of what is left.-- The poor in this vicinity are makeing what hay that they can find. They are also bringing some butter, eggs, Onions, Lettis &c. Onions sell readally at $1.00 a dozen, butter 80c & 90c per lb. & gold at 230. I think that our green backs are getting to be as worthless as the confederate money,-- It is getting to be very sickly here now, & I hope that I will not stay here long. some of us has to go to the front in a few days, but you may direct your mail the same untill I tell you to change it,-- I saw them drawing away some large 100 pound guns to mount on the forts, they are of such enormous weight that It takes 16 horses to draw them through the streets & have about 150 niggers to help, up a little rise, They are as large as a good size sawlog, will do good service at 5 miles distant.-- I have not received a letter from you this week. What has become of you, It is near breakfast time & we are a going to have a corcher today. Love to all, From To Millie   Charlie

Head Quarters Topl. Engr.
Office Army of the Cumb.
Chattanooga, June 29th 1864

My Dear Companion,

After a long silence of nearly 2 weeks I made out to get a good letter from you. I have just finnished & mailed a letter to Father eat my dinner then put a press togeather. The Capt. said I had done it well then handed me a letter from you (No 46) After haveing a good feast over your letter, I hasten to reply I am glad that you feel well paid, If I am not mistakened I think that I send you some money in 70 or 71, you did not make mention of any so it must be in 71. I am sorry to here of its being so dry up North,

It has been very dry down here. These showers that I spoke of in Mothers letter just mearly layed the dust. Sorry to hear that crops are injured for we soldiers will want all that you have to spare, I am affraid that will have a long seige of it before it is over with.-- I have no convieneant way of sending money to you & I dare not risk large bills by mail, there is a good deal of trouble on the R.R. between here & Louisville. I will try to explain those bills to you. I have 2 bills (greenbacks) (uncle sams) they draw intrest. It reads like this, The United States, Two years after date, will pay to Bearer, Fifty Dollars with intrest at Five per cent per annum Payable at maturity

Washington April 4 1864 Uncle Sam you understand these bills are our U.S. money. All bills from 20 dollars up, draw intrest I have 2 of them one 20 dollars & one 50 dollars Now do you understand? I guess you do. I should think you might see that you have made something by my staying here. I think that I have made out to save my life by staying hear, even if I do pay out largely for my board & whiskey &c. & besides that it is a good school for me. I had rather stay here for $13. per month & work day & night than to stay in camp & suffer with ill health as I have done. I think I can get along without a handkerchief, you need not mind about sending one. I can use my shirt tail if I am badly crowded but if you do, send a thicker & heavyer one. I dont want any stamps now I can send you some if you want somed. I can get all I want at the Christian Comission office a place that I dident know of before I wrote for them. Tell George that I gave him credit for this vest. I will send him a picture for it. It is getting dark, & I have to stop. I have got another washington job & have to do my writing when I can ketch it, I cant do much by candle light, good night, on account of my eyes-- July 1st Now I will try & finnish my scribbling. I should like to know what you do at your Society, what do you do. I am ignorant of what is done. Capt. Bigelow is killed, the one that you have the picture of. I am sorry to hear of the death of so many of my friends. You asked me the question, if we would live togeather 30 years, I think that we shall if we can only behave ourselves & if we dont have to be off to the wars all the time. I calculate to live a hundred & 30 years yet, if nothing hapens-- You will find me on that view sitting on the railing in front of my room. I think that I may get some more views if I can get some worke to do to pay pay for them. Mr. Cressy offers me 45 views of that same size for $25. they are splended, some are of the bridges at this place, of lookout, of differant battle grounds, Tunnel hill & others. I have the promise of some over work such as puting on borders & printing on the titles & let me have some pictures for it. I will send you a harper with this letter. & this picture is for George & Laura, I dont hear a word about Elsie, I should think that you had better have a settlement on the Contract not let it run to long. Remember me to all of my friends. Love to you, yours as ever Charlie to Millie

CHAPTER 5

JULY – DECEMBER 1864

Head Quarters Topl. Eng.
Office D. C. Chattanooga
July 3rd 1864

My Dear Wife,

I suppose you would like to read another letter from the Army of the Cumberland from you know who. I have no news of intrest to tell you, but I must tell you something. I recoollect very well where I was one year ago to day. I was at Guys Gap a suffering with a broken rist & eating blackburries, & the same time we had avery wet time. How things have changed since that time. When I was there I expected to be at home before this time. I begin to think that I am not very good proffit & will not provicy any more, but will come home when Uncle Sam will let me. Dont know when that will be, I hope soon. It seems to me that I got a peice of cheese last evening from the Michigan Christian Herald Society, a peice about 2 by 4 inches & 1 inch thick. That must be some Roenna's work. Dont care who done it I had a good laugh over it, all alone, I had to waken up in the night and laugh about it. Quite a joke on charlie, If you reccollect how much cheese there was you can tell how much I can get here for 15c. I dident expect when wrote to you to send me a bowl of bread & milck that you would send it, but I see that you have commenced by sending the cheese first. When I am at home I am in the habit of eating cheese with such a dish. Give me you yet, for a wife. I believe you do think of charlie once in a while. How I wish I could be with you tomorrow & spend the 1/4 with you & friends. Just think of 5 years ago what a change in the climate, I tell you it seemed good to get holt of a home paper once more. I have been reading in the herald all day. I have asked to have papers sent to me but they dont come, I get nothing but Southern papers. Pleas send me the Herald & Tribune once in a while. I will send you all you want, I have one here now that I will mail with this letter to some body, I guess Father. If you will just listne in the morning you will here one of our 100 pounders bark-- The gun is 300 feet above the city & will be fired 35 times for the national salute. The gun is in for Camoren on Camoren hill, to commence at sunup. I am to work on a map of Chickamauga battle ground & Mission Ridge to send to Washington. The map is about 24 inches squair & the surveys has cost the government about 3,000 dollars allready. Only think what an expence for one little peice of paper, but that is nothing. Uncle Sam is rich & has deep pockets, but I am affraid his shinplasters will be worthless when gold is worth 2.40. It is getting to be as bad as Southern money. I dont expect avery good time tomorrow, not anything more that to work. I understand there is to be a celebration on Lookout mt.-- Our men continue to lay in line of battle about this place but no rebs have made their appearance yet, Dont hear much from the front lately. I expect that Sherman will have a celibration down there. Also Grant, I understand he has them cornered. I am middleing well except a hard cold & head ache. Monday morning, 4th of July, 5 oclock The National salute has fired from the 100 pounder, the peice was pointed over the city towards this building & the Noise & pressure was so greate that glass fell from the windows of a meeting house. Dont sound much like the guns that you have in Otsego. The brass bands are playing the old Star spangled banner & other peices a being fired at this place. I am well this morning. I hope to hear from you soon. Love to all. From Charlie You will hear from me again soon. C---

Head Quarters, Topl. Engr.
Office. D.C. Chattanooga, X-a-c
July 7th 1864 1864 1864

Dear Millie

Your kind letter dated June 27th (No 47) Came to hand yesterday & I found in it a little missage from Mother. Glad to hear from you again, & the only mail that I received since a week ago yesterday except a peice of cheese, & I think it would be better for me if you would not send me any more. I eat about one half of that & made me very sick one day & night. I taisted so good that I made a hog of myself eating it without anything els. I think it is the first that I have eaten since that you sent me last fall. I blame no one but myself, I feel well now,-- Now is reply to your letter. You ask me how do I do this morning that is the morning of the 27th. If I remember

I was sick all that day. I commenced vomiting in good season that morning right away after breakfast, on my way from to the office, & kept it up at intervals through the day, but the worst of it is, I spattered it over my boots that I had just pollished up so nicely. I feel middling well now. I have taken any meadicen since I came to Chattanooga, I wish you would send me a box of the Frost pills if you have any, if not, send some other kind. I cant get any here. I must go to Breakfast, will you come & dine with me?-- Now after haveing a good breakfast for Soldier I will continue. I am glad to hear that you are all well & enjoying yourselves. (but hark! what about that B,) have the bees swarmed yet. I mean the honey bees. Evening 9.15. After a buisey day labor & a hot one too I continue my letter. I have just had a littlesing or rather some howling untill I am so hoarse that I can hardly wright write. We are haveing steady hot weather at 98 degrees & the ground very dry,-- I suppose you feel as though you was lucky in getting good help to your summer work,-- The bugs, flys, millers, large pinch bugs (weight about a lb.) large grasshoppers, & evry thing els are buzzing around my candle & torment me much,--wish you would come & keep them off while I write your letter,-- It seems to me that Father & Geo. is doing a staveing business to handle over 6 ton of hay after tea. Yes here comes a drove of young spiders on my drawing table.--but no musketters yet dont get them untill late in the summer. Tell Geo. to build me a good barn & fill it with hay, he knows where I want to set it.-- In exchange for his trouble I will give him some valuable hints on farming in the Southern style when I go home, which will be of no use to him whatsoever,-- Well, I declare you have got me on the letter dicker. I dont wish to have you have you flatter me on writing fine letters, but when you get this you will find that you have a very corse one for the office was locked & I could not get any note paper, but as for composition, spelling & writting, I think that I am some ways to the rear. I should think that any person might scrible over a large sheet of fools cap & fill it with lies & nonsense as you do find mine. There goes a light of glass, another one of those large two horned bugs has come through the window & knocked his brains out, but what is worse than all the flies make me a good deal of work. When my paper is uncovered they will drop a speck on the paper & stain it, the only way to get rid of it is to make some roads to it & call it a town & name it, but sometimes they dont drop it in the right place, then I call a post office or corthouse, you may think that I am yarning it some, but that is the way the map looks made by a careless draftsman, covered with Tobaco juice & flie specks &c. but not a spatter or a drop of ink has been carelessly placed on any of my papers. The Capt. gives me credit of haveing very clean work,-- Well about that that picture or profile of my countainance including the babboon feitures, (you spell feetures, I cant) of a black sun burnt soldier, his cranium enclosing a volumn of nonsence intermixed with with a few soft brains. Does it look like any one that you that you have seen before or elswhere be quick & pass your opinion & if it does not suit you may paist it upon the wals of some delaberated hogpen or in a hog hole under the fence where you wish to keep them out & I will garrentee that they will not come nigh nor trouble you again for one week, then I will send you another, but I do not like to run the risk of brakeing another Camory, going through another surgeocal opperation of the kind. It will ampitate $6.00 out of my purse & I will not feel it. Thats whats the matter, Well, supposen I change the subject. What is the matter with Soph. Is it possable that she does not come to see you any more, So the world goes. If any of you have anything crossways, let it out & begin anew, live happily with all of your friends, overlook att these little squibbs & take a new start in the journey of friendship. I know we all have our ups & downs but mind you that there is a better time comeing if we are only prepared to meet it,-- A friend in need is a friend indeed. I have found this to be true while a soldier.-- There must be some mistake some where. Silence Do I understand that you have been through two knot holes, must have been large ones,-- I do not think you have forgoten me, that is not what I mean, what I mean is I want letters, want letters, more letters, let them come, I am not harboring any such idea, I am not finding any fault but you know I must fill my sheet with something or els you would pitch into me. What about the war news have you any thing new up in your climate, I have nothing but what I suppose you have hurd 3 or 4 times. I have not hurd from our Regiment in a long time. I here that Gen. Sherman is down in Georgia pecking away at the rebs & Grant in Virginia some where, I will finnish in the morning. Good night, Friday morning 5.35 After a good night rest I continue my letter again this pleasant morning. can here the birds sining sweetly through the inumerable revellee drums & bugles in most evry direction. How glad I would be if I could out of hearing of them again & get where I can hear the little songsters sweet notes mingled with pleasent tones of the Cowbells again, Time will tell when that will be, You have no idea what a large number of prisoners (Union men) are brought in from all parts of the North for deserting, some of these have enlisted the fourth time. They would enlist, get their bounty, go home on a furlough, go to some other place & enlist again & so on untill they get caught at it & brought in here & lodged in the military prison. Such a place as the prison is is beyond the discription of my pen, The filth & stench is enough to make a person sick of life & wish himself in his grave to stay there the prisoners do not look like human beings. Why! Who has controll of the prison gates, O! the kid glove officers that can lay in there tents from morning till night & day after day & live on the nice Sanitary goods that are prepared by our liberal harted ladys of the North, many of them has been imprisoned 18 months, many are nearly naked haveing nothing but a pair of drawers to ware, & live on the scanty army rations, our own men, think of it, our own Soldiers are treated worst than the rebel prisoners, Many of these prisoners crimes are near nothing. I wish that I could see the day when the most of the under officers could be placed in the same predicament. It seems that a man feels as though he was lord of the great universe when he gets a couple punkin rines on his sholders, What I have writen I have seen. If the officers would have done their duty this rebelion would have been put down long ago & thousands of lives saved, but if a private does not their duty they are bucked & gaged & a guard of their own comrads placed over them to watch them. If a private is sent by his officers to another of same command on buiseness, we can hardly get them to grind a word out, then if the work is not done right, then ketch hail columbia. I hurd some officers & clurks makeing there braggs how well they lived. & where they got their good liveing, but I never have hured any of the boys brag of there nice liveing that have layed in the hospital for months & had a leg or arm sawed off by the army butchers. The Doct. thinks it is not good for them but it is good for their pouch but for a private one that does all of the hard marching on foot fighting then dig entrenchments all night, & stand picket the balance of the time. This the way that soldiering goes. I speek of the general run of officers & docters. There are exceptions to be made. I do not allude to them. I am well this morning except the back door trot. It is near breakfast time & will close. I dont know as this the kind of letter you want but it is the best I can do this time I will close by saying that we are a going to have another hot day & My love to you all, get your shair. Charlie To Millie

Head Quarters Topl. Engr.
Office. D.C. Chattanooga Tenn.
July 11th, 1864

Dear Wife

Yours of June 27, 28, 29, 30, 31, & July 1 & 2nd just came to hand also
an envelop enclosed in a hankercheif, which makes me all right again on
the hankerchief question. I an a thousand times obliged to you. Now the
question arises where am I going to get it washed so clean & white as it is
now, I expect I shall have to do as I did this morning with my towel &
socks. Take the wash dish, some cold water & some soap & go at it. The
women down hear dont know much. They certainly dont know how to do
agood job of washing & cooking, I can tell you what they do do. The first
class ladys chew tocaco & snuff, rather eat snuff, they carry a small brush
in their snuffbox, when they want to take a little snuff, wet the brush, stab
it into the snuff then dobb it all over their teeth, if they cant get a brush
they get a soft peice of wood, most of the women smoke also. How do you
like the style, Well I will go back to my letter. You dont know how I enjoy
such good long letters, O, yes I came near forgeting to mention Laura's
letter, glad to hear from her again, It will be my next job to answer hers,
Your letter seems to be a kind of a Diara, not a Diarrear or what you call
it, but a memmorandem. I scarsely know how to take my text from it, but
it is just what I like to read & hope you continue to do so. I did not dream
of hearing of the death of my dear friend Vernon, My old tent mate & mess
mate. It makes me feel sad, Vernon was one of the best friends I had in the
company & we have set for hours a chatting & make plans of our arrival
home & what a good time we would have. But the story is told with for
Vernon. He was a good boy, allways ready & willing to do his duty as a
soldier. I have not seen him since I left Murfreesboro except when I pass
him on the road from McMinnville to Murfreesboro when on my way out
hear, did not have a chance to speek with him. Who will go next, as you
say. I feel sometimes as though it would be my turn soon, but I am yet
spared, allthough I have been made a mark of a number of times by the
enemy. but God has seen fit to the shots harmlessly by & to spare me a little
longer & I am truly thankfull for his kind & tender mercy. It seems as
though most all my friends were gone, I hurd from my regiment to day, by
Lieut. Shafer, They are guarding the R.R. Bridge over the Chattahoochee
river, He had but little time to talk & conciquently did not learn much. You

may not look for a very interesting letter to night for I feel very tired. I have worked very busey today & to finnish my map of Chickamauga battle ground. The worke suited them so well that they made me put my name to it, & I did so. Now you can judg whether my work suits or not. The Capt. says it is no more than right that I should have credit for my work. & I think just as he does. We are haveing extream hot weather now, at noon we had a powerfoul hard shower then came off very hot, I can hear the thunder in the distant now (10 P.M.) & we may get more before morning. I will close for to night. My eyes will not allow me to write longer, good night! Another night has gone & here you find me again, It seems to me that you are behind the times or to late to set the cabbage plants, I see that some people have raised cabbages hear & they nearly got their growth. We have a few good gardens about hear, but they do me no good. The country people are bringing in Due burries, black burries, & huckel burries, & & sell them readily at 25c quart. Cherry time is past about 6 weeks ago. I did not get a taist of one. Harvest apples are comeing in now which sells at 5c each. I go hungry before I pay 5c for an apple that is not more than 1 1/4 inches in Diamiter. I will tell my 2 last days Diary. Sun. 10 I arose early, washed, changed clothing, &c. Done some writting, went to breakfast at 7, thence took a walk with Charlie Murray at 9 returned to the office & remained untill dinner. after dinner Charlie & I took a walk to the big bridge at the ferry, seeing that they have the bridge nearly completed, went up main st to the depot there we found a large number of rebels prisoners just a starting for the North, buisness very lively about the depot engins all in motion, prepareing trains to go, some just come in loaded with evrything except gold, Also saw a torpeedo that our men caught a bushwhacker putting under the truck, near Dalton he will have to pull hemp or made a target of, Alarge number of engines stand at the Docters office for repares, started for the office by the way of the stone fort & saw one of our boys of company F. He tells me that 2 more of my company came in wounded, E. Pratt & Will Anderson. (Anderson lives up by Russell Fenners) The weather hot & some prospects of showers-- Mon. 11th After breakfast went to the Commissary for rations, gave them to Ned. to carry to our boarding place thence to Capt Wickershams after a load of wood for the mess, thence to the office, after cooling off a little while went to work putting the title on my map. I completed the map to day, went to main street, where I saw about 1500 rebel prisoners going towards the depot. At 7 P.M. received 2 letters from wife (No. 48 & 49) 49 containing a hankercheif. Evening commenced to write a letter to wife. Weather hot, shower at noon. There you have 2 of my days adventure in the southern confedercy,-- I think enjoy myself eating currants & some other little notions that you have, I suppose your strawburrys are all gone by this time,-- I will send you that music I spoke to you about in a day or two. I will not complain of short letters any more. You must make some allowance for me, for you know that I am a great hand to complain. I have just fixed up the music to send to you & put in 6 peices of maps, a sign table that I want you to save for me. A picture of the orphan chicken, I did not finnish that yet but concluded to send it to you, And a view of Chattanooga & Look out in the distant. This view was taken from the upper piazza of this building looking nearly South You can see in the fore ground the inside of the brest works which enclose us. A dwelling house on the left is where we do our eating & you can imagine you see me going there at 7 in the morning, 12 at noon & 6 evening, the Lady that lives there is a fine woman, her name Mrs Conner, that long string of guns you see in the center in the distant is captured Atilery from the Mission ridg fight & the liberty pole stands in front of Gen. Steadmans Head Quarters. I will explain the rest when I see you, Such views is sold for $2.00 each. A friend of mine made me a preasent of that this morning. I think I have sent you the whole map now. I dont know how much it will cost to send this roll I put on 12c & if that is not enough you may pay the ballance. I wish you would tell me how much the other roll cost & this too then I will know what calculations to make. 8 P.M. Capt. Bower broke me off this morning and gave me another job of makeing a map of Chattanooga that will last me about 2 weeks. I am happy to hear that you have such good neighbors, but I think you have me tight now, & also think you have sent to a poor place to get a preasent for your prety baby you speek of. What shall I do, Shall I ma a picture & bend to it, That is all that I can do hear. I have an old shirt that you might make a new dress for winter. & 2 pair of socks without any feet to them & an old pair of pants with a pair of eyes in the seat which might be a curiosity to some of you, but my boots I cannot spare yet. I might pick up a pair of government shoes some where. As I am writing I have a tamed martin bird sitting about 18 inches from my pen & it is asleep. I wish I could send it to you. It would sit on my head & sleep if I would put it there. -- Your request is to me to be a good boy I dont know how to better myself any, but I will try & kill all the rebs I can conveineantly for that seems to be the game down here, to kill each other. You see that I am comeing to the last corner of my fools cap & will wind up for this time.

I will send you couple more pictures to look at it but you must not afraid of the snake in the sleave, it will not bite. You can give Charlie Franklin a profile if you want to I have about a dozen left but I dont like them. I will have some better ones before long, One thing more if I have not mentioned it before, that is my old wedding suspenders are worn out & I want to make out their discharge papers. I cant do it unless you send me some new ones, cost $2.00 a pair here. I think you can get them for about five bits, If I remember right I did not Number my last letter, it went off in a hurry & I forgot it. I tell you what I think about it, that is, I think that I am elected to stay in this department the rest of my time, what do you think. I am well tonight. Dont let the Maryland raid scare you any, You will find those raiders in a trap before long I think. I am at another corner will close again. I still remain your Soldier Husband. Charlie Millie jr.

Head Quarters Topl. Engr.
Office D.C. Chattanooga, Tenn.
July 17th, 1864

Dear Wife,

Another Sabeth has dawned upon us, & yet I find my life is spaired. The weather is very hot in this climate & is what I call uncomfortable warm. I have not received any letter from you since I last wrote conciquently I have no letter to answer. I have the honor of telling you that General Prentiss is my own Cousine. I found out all about the Prentiss family. You have hurd me speek of my Uncle Edward who lived at Quincy Ill. Shortly after he went their his brother Harry Prentiss went there, They had a large family of boys and are now all officers of high rank in the army. How I should like to be with you to day & excort you to the meeting. I think I should enjoy my self much better than to /better {crossed out} be here a scribbleing, a slow way of talking I calls it. but so it is. & I must be content with the privilage that I have. O, if this war would end so that we might all return to our homes again. Through ranks of fire & seas of blood, many poor Soldier have forced their way to meet the enemy to serve our country, our homes & our friends. It is awful to think of the large numbers that have fallen & left on the blood stained battle plain to answer to their calls & crys. Who will answer for this great sin. As I set at my table, a looking out the window towards home (my window faces to the North) thinking what would interest you, my mind runs along the great space between you and me, and to think of the blue sky which is only your head is visible to me. I cannot discribe my wandering thoughts of the by gone days. and it makes me feel bad to think of the obstructions which are placed between us to prevent me from my home. Nothing but time, patiant, persevearance & courade will remove them. I guess you will think by this letter that I am homesick or have the blues. Not so. You expect a letter from the Engineer Office & it must be filled.--I hear that the rebs are stiring up a bad smell about Washinon. You all may be very much excited about it, but when I see all the Generals so cool about it I shall not trouble myself. Washington is safe enough. Maryland is a secesh hole at best, & it will do them good to stir them up a little, so let them wiggle. They will never leave their with all of their plunder if what I hear is true. So keep cool and keep your shirts on. Evry thing is working kind throughout the whole establishment. I told you in my last that Laura's letter would be my next job but I have been very buisey the past week makeing a map of Chattanooga and fortifications for the commander of this post. I will try and do it this week. This letter will tell you that I am well.--Not much excite ment about hear at preasent only the large numbers of rebels prisoners are passing through hear constantly from the front. Daily labour is going on kindly & we do not meet with any opposition at this place yet as we expected. Rather too many blue bellys (so the rebs call us) & bull dogs that wont bark only as we pull their tails {small drawing of a cannon firing} There are large numbers of machanic's building ware houses, fraiming bridges &c. We have from one to two bridges fraimed & ready to rase for most all the crossings between here & Atlanta. Large numbers of teems are drawing in logs to the mills for timber for bridges and magazenes & evry thing els for the use of the army. I had forgoten. There is some excitement hear among the women. All of the secesh Ladys have to leave & go north of the Ohio river. Good for them. I hope it will larn them a lesson, & make them keep their mouth shut. News is rather scarce with us at preasent. I have just been up to the Tellegraph office with a dispatch & I find the sun just pores out its heated rays hot enough to melt a nigger. The poor boys in the field must suffer with the heat & some of the prisoners suffer still worst, these that are in the hands of the rebels. O, earth, thou dark place, thou haunt of sin, of misery and sorrow, pains and death, where no enjoyment is, but soon its clothed with gloom & desolatiton, where poisnous weeds are & serpents (rebs) lie wating in silent for the foot that treads the dreary midnight beat,

CHAPTER 5   JULY – DECEMBER 1864

where the chilly winds blow drom the caverns & over tall rocky clifts and
with a dreadful sweep, touch all things with their might power & blight the
brightest sweetest flowers that strew lifes path where lightning's flash and
thunder roar and death goes walking through our midst mowing down his
thousands with his dreadful scythe and filling all the air with schreiks and
groans. Oh earth what art thou. Who would cling to thee. Who can look
upon the sun, the moon, the stares, and the buds & flowers and mountains,
and valleys & feel not in his heart that death is there impressed on all he
sees. O what but sin could make this world so desolate. O, what but guilt
could write such gloom upon the things we see. The work of God's kind
hand which he created at his will and called them good. It is his will that
so many of my comrads should feel in the crimson battle field. Friends!
pray for the poor soldiers that they might be prepared to meet their creator
at the judgment seat. If we were pure & sinless we should look with other
eyes upon this beautiful earth which he calls good. It would not be a waist
of misery and death for this glorious country, we should not feel a weight
of gloom upon our trembleing soul's when seeking for a smile to cheer
our way. Alas, how many thousands bear the awful weight guilt upon
there souls. How many sink into the pit of hell to feel through all eternity
the wrath of heaven. Distressing thought and is this dreadful thing woven
with our very nature. God hates sin and he has set against it the dreadful
contance of eternal wo. I hope that we may all be prepared and meet each
other in heaven if we should not meet on earth again. I believe you have
not forgotten me in your family prayers.--I wish you would send me the
chorus Glee book, just do it up strong, leaveing one edge open, we have
some singers here & no music. It will be a good passtime for us. My eyes
are about the same, my health is very good. I have some better board than
I use to, but it cost is very heigh. Cant help it, must have something to eat,
our green backs is not worth much now. Perhaps about 35 per cent.--I will
have another pirty little song for you before long, but I am thinking that you
will not sing it more than once through then you will stop and cry about it.
I think that I have writen enough for this time & if this letter does not suit
you, you may send it back. What do you think of my envelopes, these are
some of my own manufacture. Write soon. Love to all, Yours Truly Charlie
Dra. Needle Picket These pictures are my friends in the office. Take good
care of them Charlie No. 77

- 251 -

Head Quarters Topl. Engr.
Office D.C. Marietta, Thur.
Evening, July 21ˢᵗ 1864

My Dear Wife

Again I pen you a few lines to let you know where I am now. The heading says that it is Marietta, 118 miles farther from home. Last Monday evening a dispatch came for me & 2 others to report at Marietta soon as possable, so we started at 3 oclock Tuesday with a small stock of stationerys, had a very pleasent trip but we road in great fear, It is very dangerous traveling through this part of the world, I arrived hear yesterday at 5 P.M. I am well, I started in persuit of the office at this place, after traveling a while I found it, got a teem went after the goods & baggage & delivered it all safe at the office. we have a very nice place in a large dwelling in a nice shady grove, Marietta is a very perty place the place is full of shade trees so much so that you can hardly see any buildings, We are now allmost right under the enemys nose, we all keep our good old trusty peices loaded & primed & sleep by them at night. I dont want you clame any uneasyness about me if I am under the rebs sount, if they should come in reach, they might get snubed, I dont think I shall boast much what I am a going to do but when it is done then I will tell you all about it we are expecting Wheeler to make a raid in here to night If he comes I will tell what he has done & if he does not come I will not say any thing about it. I am afraid that I will not get my mail very regular our head quarters is so diveded, apart in Chattanooga some here & some at the front I have heard for certain that we have entered Atlanta. I hope there may be no mistake about it. I have been out with Charlie Day this fournoon a surveying the railroad, battle ground, brest works, rifle pits &c near Kinesaw mountain I tell you I kept half an eye on my work & the other eye & a half on a watch for rebs. The ground looks as though a drove of wild hogs had been through the woods a rooting up the ground, whe the shells have lodged & exploded, The trees are all cut to peices, for instance, I saw one tree about 1 foot through that had 44 ball holes in it, I saw some stumps that was so cut up that I could not see the mark of the ax that choped the tree down, what do you think of that, This battle field is a little North of the Kinesaw mountain, The balls can be picked up by the bushel, & peices of shells. A very strong smell of human flesh is easly distinguished, I cant begin to tell or discribe it to you I will close for it is late & I am very tired, the weather is extreamly hot, You may change your direction a little, Mr. Charles H. Prentiss Draughtsman Head Quarters Topl. Engr. Office Marietta Ga. Care of the Office. Remember dont borrow any trouble about me I will turn out all right

   Charlie Millie

                                              Topl. Engr. Office, D.C. Marietta
                                                          August 2, 1864

My Dear Wife,

   Hear I am again, You see by the heading of this letter that I am in Marietta. & so I am, arent you glad that I am a way from the front, But hold on, I am going back in the morning at sun up to resume my dutys on the field. I was sent back after some stationarys for the office, such as drawing paper, pencils, Compasses, traceing paper & linnin &c. &c. I like it first rait in the field, much better than at the office away behind all the rest. I hear lots of good music such as the naying of mules & brass bands, the thundering of artilery & screeming of shells, rattleing of musketry & to enjoy hard pilot bread & salt pork & the flying axhandles & to breath the pure stench air so nicely perfumed with the decaying horses & muels & human flesh on the whole I think it is very pleasent, who wouldent like to be a soldier, hay? Its not me. There is one thing about it we have got rid of the little troublesome varmin, There is nothing to molest us but lice, bedbugs, flees, scorpeon, mosquetoes &c. &c. But in spite of all the plagues & the constant roar of cannon I take my blankets, roll myself up tight, seel the corners, lay down on the ground & sleep like a charm sometimes I try a new way to sleep. Take my blanket, geather both ends, tie a roap around both ends & tie the roap to two treas, thus {a small drawing} do you understand, same as the natives do where there is reptiles & such like. (I feel perty well tonight so I do. My has improved since I took that nice little dose of castor oil. I took little less than a gallon) I dont this would be any place for George on account of the flies. there is about 40 on me now. I thought it would be well enough to commence a letter here this evening to pass time as to sleep so much. Thursday morning August 4th Hear I am in camp near Atlanta enjoying myself as well as I can under the circumstances. I am well this evening & feel better because Lieut. Wharton is now deal out our Commutation money $12.40 each for one month, that will hardly carry me through a month. I have a very good stock of money on hand & I wish it was at home. There is $122.00 of it & I dare not risk it by mail nor express & If I should get capured again I might loose it. But there is no danger of that, my way thinking. Any how I do not feel much alarmed about it.-- Now a word about war for I expect you will expect to hear some being that I am at the front. Evry thing stands firm yet. The rebels on our right drove in our picket line but they were soon drove back without any loss on our side. About 2 this P.M. they undertook brake our line on the right & flee into Alabama. They were driven back into there holes again. There is alittle to much power in sow belly & hard bread for them to brake through. I did not near what their loss was nor ours. There was also heavy cannonadeing on our left this afternoon. There has no report came in yet this evening. It is so quiet here that I have but little to tell you about the war. The officers all feel confident of going into Atlanta within a few days. But I cannot tell, The rebels are very strongly fortified. They have some very strong works & some heavy guns. I am expecting to hear a terrible noise evry day but cant say what day. I believe that Gen. Sherman has his big guns all in position or nearly so to shell the city. 100 /in all {crossed out} besids some fling artillery in case their should be some running to do. I hear by rebel prisoners that Gen. Johnson has 30,000 troops in Atlanta, but we think that 25,000 will cover all his force. A little snarl of gray backs were broght in at head quarters this afternoon. You have undoubly hurd of the capture of Gen. Cook and all of his forces about 1,500 strong, /It is true {crossed out} that made a raid below Atlanta. It is true that he was badly routed but most all have come in safe but lost there guns, They had a large waggon train that they had captured & on there way home lost it, but the rebs did not get it. Our boys burned the train, then scatered. We all felt rather down when we first got the news & perhaps you got the same that we did, that was Cooks whole command was captured, I started from Marietta yesterday at 2 & got to camp at 7 & when I started away they were makeing preparations for a rade in the town on the government supplies, for there is a large amount of them there. There is from 4 to 6 trains comeing in daily. They have a barracade a cross each street at the out skirts of the town & a heavy tree fence all around the town. So let them come, I delight to see them come. You may ask yourself if it is safe to travle through the country. I feer no danger. I have a good 7 shooting carbine & keep one eye to the front, one to the rear & one on each side of the road in the bushes. Dont you feel alarmed about me. I feel safe & dont think there is any danger, just let your head rest easy. I received your No 52 yesterday while at Marietta also a note from Mother. But dont hear a word from George. Why dont he write or is he mad, I would like to hear all about the farm &c. It is all interesting. He dont have to work sundays & I do. I will steel time enough to write my letter in spite of in spite of Uncle Sam. I have been at work hard all day & now I am useing my sleeping hours to write to you all to tell you what news I know of & what I am at liberty to tell, then when I get done I shall spread out my blanket on the damp ground & take a good snose. Something is the rip at the front now (10 P.M.) heavy firing has just broke out on the /left {crossed out} right. I think the rebs are trying to brake out. We have one kind of varmin that I feel somewhat afraid of, that Is the scorpion. There sting is bad. The swift is very abondant hear. I see very few snakes. I dont think I will tell any snakes stories this evening. I feel some tired & will draw to a close. You may direct your mail Topl. Engr. Office D.C. Maj Gen Thomas Head Quarters near Atlanta Ga.-- My love to all & the little one Millie Yours in Love Charlie

Head Quarters Topl. Engr. Office in
the field near Atlanta, Aug 7th 1864

Dear Wife,

It is with much pleasure that I write you one or two more times to give you a little history of Millitary affairs & local. I must acknoledge that if it was not for you & my friends that I would like to be here. I have been out to day where yould consider it very dangerous, yet I felt very safe while the bullets were flinig very thick. This morning I eat my nice little ration of hard bread & pickeled pork then went went to the office & spent about 2 hours at reading over my old letters then I took a notion to hunt up the regiment. at 9.30 A.M. I started for the 3rd Division hospital of the 20th A.C. There I found Capt. Hubbard quite sick with the Chronic Diarrear & a Callomel soer mouth, he looks hard up. I feel sorry for him. I should judg there was about 300 sick at that hospital. He is liked well. While I was there the brass band played a nice sacred peice then the people or soldiers began to geather for sereces. I stayed apart of the discorce. The text Hebrew 2 C. 3 V. There I learned where the regiment was. About 2 1/2 miles to the right Thince I started, The sun poring down its heated rays, hot enough to wilt a person, but I am use to it. After travleing a long time enquireing where the 20th A.C. is, yes its way over there, I found it. Now can you tell me where the 3 division of the 20th A.C. is Yes, way over on that hill there. I traveled on almosted & very thursty, finally I found that place. Can you tell me where the 2nd. Brig. 3rd Div. of the 20th A.C. is? Yes, follow that ravine down & wil take you to Brig head quarters, I started & found that, What regiment boys? 85th Ind. Where is the 19th. Right there on the right, Wherever you find the 85th, you will find the 19th closs by. I found them at last. After traveling about 3 miles under the scalding sun the first man I met was Sarg. Dugan a man that use to work for Horice Sornsburry, the next Orderly Hager, then one after another untill I saw about 20 of my old comrads all of whome seem to be like brothers & apperantly as glad to see me as they would be to see their own folks. It is strange how people will become attached to each other in the army. Nearly 6 months has passed since I saw the regiment. I thought the boys would shake me in peices. They could not tell me enough of their adventures. I of course had to tell them of my little adventure with the bushwhacker, they thought I done it up bully, & that is what I thought but I was affraid that something might be wrong is why I chose to keep it still for a while, I am getting away from my story. I found the boys well except John Hogle & Ed Baird who was some sick. They were enjoying their good dinner of hard tack, coffee, salt meat & desicrated vegitables, a meal that any body els than a soldier would starve on. I sat down & dined with Mr. Hager, then after eating went with Auga Brown down to the skirmish line & payed a visit to John Duel. I found him well. The pickets & skirmishers keep up a continual firing all the time, The mineys are flying fast & thick so near that I could smell their breath some time Tuesday the 9th I have just picked up my portfolio & pen to see if I can jirk off a few more lines to compleat my story. While I was there I hurd a tremendious cannonadeing on the extream right, about 6 miles distant. The 14th Corps was engaged & I understand yesterday that the rebs have turned our right some but dont know how bad, then yesterday evening we had regained our former position. I stayed with the regiment untill 4 P.M. when I started back & John Young & Auga Brown went with me to a fort of 4 20 lb. guns, here I had a fine view of the City & rebel forts, saw 3 rebel flags, we got upon the paripet of the fort but we did not stay there long on account of their sharpshooters in buildings in the city, about one mile distant, but no one got hurt that time. I stayed there as long as I wanted to then started on for head quarters. when I got there I found out that we had to move our quarters about one mile to the west of our head quarters in a small white house about the same distance from the front & clost to the

R.R. The cars run within 1/2 miles of Atlanta, The first train arrived here last Friday P.M, & such a whistle they gave you or I never hurd before. One single blast about 5 minutes, that I call one long breath. What their object was I do not know but I suppose to let the rebs know that the old iron chief had arrived with 3 onehundred pound guns which he had brought to give them a welcom cerinade some of these times when they least expect to hear them. I tell you what it is we have got a tuff job before us, but I do not anticipate any doubt but what we shall go in some time /this {crossed out} in a month but not much sooner. Our troops are in good spirits, have plenty to eat & good water & lots of fun shooting at the rebs at a great distance. According to information that we receive from deserters & refugees they acknowledge they have lost 23 thousand killed. They have in our immediate front 4 sixty four lb. guns & when they speak the earth fairly trembles, but it will tremble worst when the 100 lbder speaks to them. I wish you all could be here a little while and hear the roar of cannon, you would say you never hurd much thunder yet. That noise they make in Otsego sometimes sound like a report of a pistole in comparison to these guns. Yesterday morning we moved to our new quarters where we found a great plenty of bed bugs, flies, lice & mosqueetoes & occationaly something els, what goes through the air & makes a terrible noise as it flyes, but they light harmlessly on the ground. You may think by reading some portions of this letter that I was in great danger, but I am as safe here as you are in Otsego. Borrow no trouble & make up your minds that I am trying to my part of the fighting if I am not in the ranks. If evry soldier that has enlisted into this army would make shure of 8 rebels there would not be many left now. I never have shot but 4 shots at them yet 3 of which I am shure took affect. The fort that I mentioned a few minutes ago are poreing into the rebs a deadly fire also a number of other & it is raining very fast. I can scarcely hear any noise about the building. I have been promoted from a draughf tsman to a photographer (but you may direct your mail the same.) When we are in the field we have to photograph our maps because it is not conveniant to carry the press & we cannot suply the demands of maps by hand traceing. I will try & send you a spicimin some of these days. It is very pirty work & a good photograph printer gets $30. per. week. I am glad to get the chance to learn & will cost me nothing here, but in Citys would me $100. & find myself. The remark that the Capt. made to me yesterday was that I had a year to stay & I could learn to be a one of the first class Photographer. I think that is a very good indication of my remaining in this office my time out. The main secret is to learn to prepare the cemicals. We have the very best of cemicals & materials. We have a large Camory that cost $150. in New York. Those large views I sent you is a specimen of pictures that is done by a good artist. A good artist is makeing $5 to 800 per month & pay a good printer $120 per month You have no idea what a citizen can make down here out of the soldiers. It is near dinnertime & will stop for the preasent. Tues. evening the 9th. Dear Millie. I have some sad news to tell you. The death of Sargent Hager. After I had got through with my days work, four of us concluded to go to the front to see how they got a long. And on my way over I met one of the boys of my regiment & he tells me that Sargent Hager was shot while in his tent. I understood him that he was shot day before yesterday It must have been soon after I left him, Sabeth evening. The ball entering the right side of his back bone, just above the hip bone & comeing out in front. He lived through the night & died some time yesterday. Dont know what time. I am glad that I made him a visit when I did. I had a good visit & eat a soldiers dinner a few minutes before he was shot. I dont see how he came to get shot when he was behind the brest works unless the ball passed through one of the port holes where a cannon stood. O how sudden the change. Little did he expect to die so soon. Although we are in the midst of dangers, where we should be prepared at any moments call. When will be my turn to fall. God only knows. I heard of this where I stoped at the cars to see them unload some very heavy guns. I went on to the head quarters fort where they were throwing shells very briskly into the city also from evry other battery. The rebels had not hardly made a reply all day untill I had been there about 15 minutes when they (rebels) commenced to let the shells very rappid. One exploded about 5 rods from me. I hurd it comeing & I think I layed down flat to the ground uncommonly quick to avoid the fragments. Another followed, & another, & a good many. So I made up my mind to get out of there as soon as possable. I went backwards & sidewards & evry other kind of wards & kept my ear up in the air to see when they were comeing so as to dodge them, as they come & so we did dodge them, so we had to go about one & a half miles. If a man will keep his thoughts about himself & dont get scared he can keep out of the way in an open field without any trouble, for they make a terrible racket when they come or go. I have got so use to the differant sounds that I can tell what kind of ball or shell is comeing also of the small kind. A ball from a sharp shooter is a very fine keen hum, those I dread wors than the shell. After a thing has happened, It will do no hurt

JULY – DECEMBER 1864

to tell about it, but I do not mean to expose myself, & now I will tell how expert the rebel sharpshooters are. I stood in the fort mentioned with a man on each side of me, (those that went out with me) & was explaining the location of the rebel forts, we only had our heads exposed a sharpshooter spied us from the top of a large white house in the city one & one fourth mile distant, sent a ball at us & passing between our heads. Our heads was not more than 14 inches apart. That I call pretty tall shooting if you dont believe it, ask George if it taint, for it use to bother him & me to shoot a squirrel out of the butternut trees not more than 2 rods off. But what pleased me the most while there in the fort, the artillery man lay there flat on their bellys busey writing letters & laughing at us to see us didge when the shells fell & exploded so near. I dont deny that I was not scared for I was & my knees began to tremble & get week, but I had strength enough to get away. Those rebs you know are very careless & dont see wher they what they aim at. Some shells from the same fort passed over our heads I should think about 150 ft above me. So I dont think they are so expert with artillery shooting as our men are. On my way back I saw about 600 rebel prisoners that had just been taken in out of the wet. I hope you will not feel anyways concerned about me for I wanted to go & see what news I could pick up for you. You like to here news as well as anybody. It is now 15 minutes to 10 & the big guns are roaring very briskly. You will excuse me for the night & this little letter. I am well & enjoy hardtack first rate. Pleas write often & tell the rest that I should like to hear from them as well as they do from me. Direct your mail Head Quarters, Topl. Engr. Office, Army of the Cumberland, Near Atlanta, Ga. Yours with much Love Charlie Prentiss to Millie Prentiss

> Head Quarters, Topl. Engr. Office
> Department of the Cumberland, Near
> Atlanta, August. Wednesday evening
> the 10th 1864,

My Dear Millie

It has been such a long time since I have writen to you, I felt it my duty to write some this evening. I have not mailed a letter to since this morning & that Is a small one & wont last you but a little while to read but the effect may last longer if you have not hurd of the death of Sargent Hager, I have been fumbleing over some of my old letters & I find there is a few questions to answer you, & something that I want to say to you. I asked you to send me a pair of suspenders. My old ones gave out & I was obliged to get me a new pair which cost me only $1.25 In Marietta. Cheap. I could not hold my pants up & it wouldent look well to have them clear down below my middle jointts, my knees for instance,--I will change my subject just 1/2 a minute, for fear I may forget it. It is now 15 minutes to 9 & those big guns I told about are makeing too much noise. The report jars this house so that I can hardly write & they are about one mile distant from me. I can give you no idea what a noise they make but it is louder than any thunder you ever hurd. We are shelling the city with 5 minute guns on one shot evry 5 minutes.-- Now back on my little cattalague of notes, I dont want you to tell me so much about your makeing so many good cakes & pies, it takes away my appatite for sowbelly & hard tack which is much better than a few days ago & I wont eat any thing els. I have all that I want to eat of it. O, how I enjoy them, wouldent you? but those good luxurys you tell about makes me want to go home & help you eat them & it makes me homesick to think about it. I think a pare of shirts would suit me first rate off of that peice of linnin you made. I would make the shirts do the scratching, & tickle the lice to death & run the shives down the flees throat so they couldent bite, & the cloth would be so stout the bedbugs could not naw through. Now what will I do with the long bill insect. O, I would have nothing to do only to fight them, I have more pictures to send home of my friends when I get a good ready & have room in the envelop.--In reguard to those old blue cloths you spoke of. If you want any you may come & get them, but as soon as you see the families that occupy them I think you would drop them quicker than you picked them up (I dont speek of mine but those that are scattered along the road & other places.) The best that I can do for you. Is to ware home a pair if I ever go home.--I wish you might be with me to sing, I would give most any thing to hear a femail voice again. We try to sing some but it is only murdering music the way that we sing & sometimes worst that that, but we must do something to pass away evenings. The only comefort that I can take is to chat with you with my pen instead of my tongue. The one that has told all to you that you have been reading, you have not seen. I have only one fault to find with him is, that he cant spell worth a cent. That fellow is gold pen, when I go home I will give it to you for a keep sake, & when you see it in your box or drawer you may think what comfort Mr Gold Pen has been to you to tell you all about your Charlie in the army. You wish to know how I found out that Gen. Prentiss is my cousin. Peter DeKriger (that fellow I sent home to you) told me all about it. He (Gen.) useto be Col. of his (Peters) regiment & his Father is a brother to my father, conciquently his father is my uncle & his children would be cousin to my fathers children. I must be a son of my father & a cousin to Gen. Prentiss. You fishstay dont you? if you dont let me know & I will tell you another lingo about my grandfathers childrens children.--I have no doubt but that my letters suit, but do you read to the public all that I write? espetially about the bee How many have you had published in the papers. If you have not any yet I will send you one to publish some of these days, tutching sanitary goods & how they are disposed of. I suppose you are not aware that the hospital clerks & Docters make parties & spread the tables with the good luxuries that are sent to the sick & wounded & ask hundreds of officers to come & dine with the, are you? Ask a soldier that has layed in the hospital 3 months or longer & see if he will tell you that he had any nice jams or sweet cakes or any thing of the kind & see what his answer will be I will garrentee that he will say that he had nothing of the kind. It is 10.30 & the big guns still roar tremendiously & I will go to bed or to blanket on the floor, Good night.--Thursday evening the 11th Again I continue my duties of the evening. The weather has been warm & stormy & the mosquetoes are very good natured & very fond of kissing me,-- Atlanta is not taken yet. Our lines are coiling about the rebels works & I think they will say that you are squeezeing us a little to tight.--Our lines advanced last night within 1/2 miles of the city. I do not mean the whole lines the right wing only. It seems to be very quiet this evening I suppose the boys are diging & throughing up brest works the best they know how. We have one battery placed now where we can rake some of the streets. I expect to here a tremendious racket here in a few days, (I will mark thus o to evry cannon shot while I am writing) I have been told to day that 3 more of our o regiment was wounded yesterday, none of my o company, ooo our regiment is in the oline that advanced last night. I received 2 papers from you yesterday & I saw a peice o stating that Hooker was killed or mortally wounded I forget which. It is not so. oo Gen. Crook fell mortally o wounded o a short time a go. Gen. Hooker has o left us & gone to Washington. I saw him at Marietta o on his way there. The boys feel very bad about it. General Williams o takes his place ooooo Gen. Parmer has resined & o gone home. I would like to know what you feel gloomy about. I am sure that I have hurd nothing bad yet. o It is o reported here this evening that Mobile has o fallen. o that dont look gloomy o does it. O old socker If I keep o up courage you ought too. o George could play off if he knew how but I dont think that he nead o to be ashamed. o if he will follow my directions he will get out of it, that is o to o get a box of hard tack & sowbelly & coffee without milk oo sleep on the ground & get the rhumitism, put a little o snuff in his eyes o get the diarrear & piles & consumption &c. he will not pass examination & will get clear. o he must pretend to be very o near sighted & cant read a sign across the street when o the letters are 18 inch tall, o Tell him to follow my directions o & I risk him, o When you get tired of looking at that snake on that picture you can wet it & rub it off. My tame bird I left at Chattanooga. ooo O All soldiers get $16. per oo month. I dont know how I can explane to you my position or the view any plainer o than I did. Wait untill I go home then I will tell you o all about the views (O shell near by let them come) o I will try to answer Mothers letter soon. o I think I have writen enough for to night. o Satterday evening August 13th oo I suppose you want to hear how the battle goes to day. There has been none to day, ooo it is oo very quiet o to day o & this evining. o Dont o hear much o from oo the rebels. oo Our o lines have o advanced oo both on the right & left. o the o left has possesion of the ooo rail road on the o east side o of Atlanta oooooo & the 14 o Corps is very o near East Point oo & will soon oo cut that o railroad. I will not imitate any more reports of large guns, you can get an idea how fast they come while I write as fast as I can. this we call very quiet but in the day time I cant keep count because they come so fast. My eyes feel very bad & I will finnish to morrow if I live good night, Sunday afternoon Aug. 14th. I have just finnished 2 large letters & I will try to finnish this sheet. It is very quiet at the front to day. There is scarsely a gun to be hured only by shells when they undertake to crall out of there holes. No news since last night,--If there is any money sent to you from about Allegan someplace send it on to me. I forget the mans name & where he lives. John Rutgers of my company is here & out of money & wants to send it in my care.--That Sargent Pullman you saw last fall is dead, he was shot in the throat. He was promoted to Lieut. one day & the next was killed. I want to go to where the regiment is but, but I am affraid of the mineys. I have to expose myself to get to them. I suppose while I am writing away down in Georgia you are enjoying your self in church if you are well & allive. I had a nice little preasent a few days ago by Peter DeKriger It a pocket looking glass cost $6. in Chattanooga. I hear lots of brass music evry day & am getting tired of it.--You see that I am nearing the bottom of my sheet. I think I have writen enough for this time. You must not think hard of me for that us (U.S.) letter for I dont mean you, I think you do first rate & I have no reason to complain. My Love is always with you Millie?

From Charlie Please excuse my lengthy letter. Write soon. Charlie No. 88

Head Quarters Topl. Eng. Office A. C.
Near Atlanta
August 24th 1864

Dear Millie

seeing that I do not get any letter from you or any body els I will keep writing I have had no letter scince the first of this month & can you tell why I dont see how you folks can expect to receive letters if you dont write some & look for an answer. I think that I do my shair of writing & I will shut down if I dont some in return There is know one in Otsego but what wants to here the news fresh from the front. I am where I can get the most of it & if the friends want to get it they must write to me & I will answer them. Millie? you must excuse me for I feel a little what you may call cross to day but more disappointed than anything els. All the boy get a letter most evry day & I get one perhaps in 2 weeks & I write 2 most evry week & I am looking ansiously evry day for one but none comes. I have writen 4 or 5 to cosine Ira & you have seen what kind of a letter I got & that did not cost him any postage, he sent it out by Maj. Griffen. I would be ashamed to send such a letter, I have written to Uncle Lauren, but no answer, also to Uncle Henry Clark no answer, Elder Wolfe owes me a letter & lots of others not mentioning. But never mind I will be out of the servas in one year & three weeks then perhaps I will have some friends in the army that is drafted. May by I will write to them. I will if I agree to, I am not a shooting my arrows at you Millie! but to those who made me promis to write & who agreed to do the same & dont do it. I tell you it is no very pleasent job to be away down here exposed to shot & shell day & night & not here from my own town once a month. The most that I wish is that the copperhead of the northan states had to come down here & sleep on the floor & ground & frozen ground as I have many atime & nothing but a thin blanket to cover up with & have soldiers liveing, lay in intrenchments day & night in the. (See what the flies have done to my letter, I left it on my desk & went out

- 263 -

a few minutes.) mud & if they stick up their head above the works a miney comes singing along very spiteful as though it would take a mans head off or drill a hole through it. It makes me mad to think of a copperhead I to my opinion that they will have to keep their mouth shut when the soldiers get home or there will be some dead ones, We are getting use to shooting just such men. I feel a little better natured than I did when the mail came & try & finnish my other sheet, Here is two large letters for you to read {This part of the letter is written across the page in the form of capital letters U S}

> Head Quarters Topl. Engr. Office in the field Near
> Atlanta Georgia, Army of the Cumberland
> August 21st 1864

My dear wife

Seeing that I do not get any letterfrom you I thought that I would write another letter to you & see if it wouldent bring one. I have no particular news to tell you to day but I must cunger up something for you to read. I have not been out to the lines the past past week. I have been confined in the office a makeing a map of Atlanta for Gen. Thomas I am doing my best now & as fas as I have gone it looks first rate The officers of this office think I am learning fast & keep my work the cleanist of any one here. I am glad to know that they are satesfied with my work & I work more hours than any other one. All the trouble with me now is my eyes, the most my writing I do by candle light. Our lines of fortifications are about the same as last sunday except on the extream right & left, they are working around the city like a great serpent drawing his coils around his pray & soon the head & tail will meat. We have commenced of the Georgia railroad and are drawing near the Atlanta & west Point road road near the junction at East point 6 mi. below Atlanta. Heavy firing is constantly kept up around the lines. Last thursday morning at 3 oclock I saw a large fire in the city also in the same evening I have been toled that we were throughing greek fire in the city but I doubt it some. The prisoners we take seem to come in very hungry, they complain of not haveing enough to eat & I believe it, Gen. Thomas made a big hole in their haversack. He took & burned 100 waggons of commissaries & shot their mules. Sabeth evening 8 P.M. I have just returned from a walk. This afternoon at 4.30 I took a notion to go to the regiment & see some of the boys. I did so & had a good time but did not see Sar. Hager there. I was mistaken about his being shot while in the tent. He was standing in the alley between the tents with his back towards the brestworks near a port hole through the brest works It was done a few minutes after I left. I found that the balls were flying as thick as ever but none came very near me. Friend Duel is well & Mr Mabbs & so are all that were there. John Duel tells me that Capt. Hubbard has gone back to Chattanooga sick. I have not seen him since I wrote you last. I also learn that Dave has got his discharge at last & I suppose that he has earned it for it is about one yeare since he went to the hospital. I received a letter from him yesterday & I answered it last night I got another one from John Duel today that he wrote about 3 months ago, but I dont get any from you. Something must be the matter with you or the letters but I think they along after a while. The lines have been very still to day it being sunday. I have been a little nearer the city today than I ever was before, our brigade has advanced about 50 yds. & the skirmish line is about 30 yds in advance of the line of work. The boys dig a squair hole about 2 ft deep & spread the tent over it to stay in & build up 2 tears of poles & fill in with earth the highth of their heads to stand behind when in their camp. this makes it very safe against the minneys but for a shell they might as well hang up a peice of paper. we have bursted 4 of our best 20 lb. parrets on account of their being used so much. but we have new ones in the place of them. As news is rather scarce I will fill up united states {this part of the letter is written in red ink forming the letters US, and surrounded by the rest of the letter written in black ink} with a few lines of poetry. Hither turn the restless gale, whither art they going with a sad & sober wail, Yon rift clouds lightly blowing, O pause a while within this dell, Heed I pray thee heed me, List the tale I prove to tell, Then on this message speed thee, Speed thee on the tented field, Neath yon hostile Southern sky, Where our noble heroes yeald Blood & life for liberty When beneath yon scorching sun From home & friends afar Suffer they till victory's won For freedom's glorious star. Fill them with this breath of thine While they guard the Southern gate We beneath the northern pine watching & praying wait Watching for the glorious morn Of peace returning ray Praying toward their safe return From the bloody fray To twine a boquet fair & bright One that will charm the mentle sight And help fond memory to trace Each form of friendship and of grace Each dear fimuliar absent face we sometimes to a far off friend. A message call a letter send A of times the same in return. From abset ones for whom we grieve We read each friendly word and true Love primptings of the friends we knew. And reading thus it doth recall Each friendly word that use to fall In accients sweet as silvery bell From laughing lips we loved so well, When wanderings now we scarce can tell--when turning to earths cares again Its busy paths we tread Those words eer form a sweet refrain Those pleasent words weve read And thus though we our friends may roam They may clasp their hands with those at home And for the joys afforded them Our thanks are due the wonderful pen,-- Well Millie how do you like them 2 large letters. We dont have any interesting news while the army is lying still & shooting at each others pile of dirt this dont amount to much. I hope you will excuse this short letter for I dont feel much like getting up a foolscap tonight. I still remain your affectionate husband Charlie Prentiss Millie I dont see how I can get along without scribbleing a little more for my room is still & I have nothing to do to day. I have to write with red ink because some one has stole my black ink. I should think by your letter that you was learning to milk & do choers. I dont know how many Cows you milk this summer. I think that I should like to enjoy a ride with you as I did five years ago but as you say, how differant. how things have changed om 5 years. Now about 600 miles space lays between you & me. Where will another Anniversary bring us. I hope that we shall be differantly situated that at preasent. Time will tell. Last Friday I went upon Kenesaw mountain a surveying. I cannot give you any idea of the battle ground. From the mountain I could see Atlanta with a glass. Looking to the S.W. could see but mountains. Lost mountain is a round pile of rock up about 1000 ft. above the surface in an open level country & look like a large monument. From the Kenisaw the country looks splended. Yesterday I went to the military college which is another splended viewing place. With a good glass I could see the smoke & dust rise from the battle that was in opporation at Atlanta. The collage buildings are used for hospitals for the fourth A.C. I have not found the 20th A.C. hospital yet. my friend Jim Batchelder is there a hospital nurse. I dont remember of mailing a bundle of papers with No. 72. I dont know what you mean. I send so much that I cannot keep track of it. I mailed a roll of music a few days ago. How many pounds of wool did you have in all. Come. you must tell all & not half tell a story. I think Geo. has hid that missing fleece & some day get it & sell it for whiskey. {a drawing of a jug} Who done the shearing for you.-- I have got the cheese you sent me & it made me sick too.--I dont know but I am thankfull that I am not with the regiment but I felt more thankfuller that that bushwhacker did not kill me. As far as suply is concerned I do not think there is much differance. I want to get a crack at a few more. How is it that I am getting so hardened that I want to kill a human being. It useto be all that I could do to shoot a sheep but now I crave the job of shooting a man Dont you think that I am getting hardened? Wont you be affraid of me? I hope. But I tell you what it is. A man must not abuse the coulers, the emblem of the United States if he does not want to hear from me. I never knew how to prise it untill I was a prisoner. I never thought that I should cry when I came in sight of the stars & stripes. But I did do it & not help. In such a case I would shoot a man as quick as look at him. I guess I will stop for this time Yours in Love I will send you a lief of an old Hebrew bible that I found & a wild rose lief from tunnell Hill. If this rose lief could talk it would tell some hard stories Your Husband Charlie Millie

Camp in the field near Sand Town Aug 27

My Dear Wife

I received 2 letters from you a few days ago & I have no time to answer them as I have been put in as foreman of this squad of the Top Engr. Department while on the march & I dont know but longer. The one that had charge before has gone home, his time is out & I have so much to do that I cant you much for the preasent. The army has to wait the generals

Prentiss makeing a map of the country near Jonesboro, Ga. Sept. 1st. 1864.

motion & the Gen. has to wait my motion & they dont move unless they have their maps. I am well & tuff as a bear I would like to explain to the object of this move but I have no time now. Our supplies will come by the way of Vix Burg after this. You all may think it is a foolish move to let the rebs loose & go north but you will here soon & be satesfied with the move. Gen. Sherman will give a good account of himself dont be alarmed. We are in a crowd of about 75,000 & I feel safe. You may direct as last I told you, the letter will find me. Yours in haist Charlie Millie

The Lord is my shepherd, I shall not want. Thou preparest a table before me, in the presence of mine enemies; thou anointest my head with oil, my cup runneth over; Ps xxiii. 1 & 5. verses

Maj. Gen. Thomas Head Quarters, Dept.
Engr. Office, Army of the Cumberland,
Camp 6 miles South of Jonesboro Sept. 3rd

Wife.

Again I have the pleasure of pening you a

Again I have the pleasure of pening you a few lines to let you know my whereabouts, I am well & have had good health while on this campaign & have enjoyed my self hugely with one exception, that is we had so short a time to get ready after I was notified that I was a going, that it was to late to get a supply of rations, the headquarters commissary had packed up, consiquently I had to go hungry some of the time. A few days after we started, some chickens happened to get into my dish & I partook thereof, but are getting along finely, You have undoubtedly hurd of the rade that Gen. has undertaken to the rear of Atlanta. For fear you have not I will tell you a little about it. On the 24th of Aug. I was chosen as foreman of to go with headquarters to take information & repare the generals maps, on that day we started, at the same time the 20th A.C. was sent back to Chattahoochee river to keep the rebs back while 85,000 of us went around the city to see what we would find. About one hour after we left camp the rebs swarmed out of the city & captured our headquarter eatables, but the most happened to be supplied with 10 days rations except our office. O, the rebs thought they had done a nice job when they came out. They had hurd that a little rade was a going to be made, but had no idea the whole army was a going. So on we went, atraveling through a very dreary country over hills, bad roads, thick undergrowth, few small patches of clearing the dwellings burned & in ruins & on the whole a very desolate country to Sandtown thence south west through a little better country to the Atlanta & West Point R.R. where we camped one day, the troops busey distroying the railroad. They tore up 8 miles at that place & burned the depot at Red Oak. Up to this place we found but little resistance, but as we neared Jonesboro we found lots of them, most all of Hoods forces except a malitia that was left in Atlanta We went on to the Macon R.R. where we had one of the hardest fights in the campaign. Our loss is said to be about 2,000 killed & wounded but I dont think it, but the rebel loss was terrible, dont know their loss but Gen. Thomas says more than 3 times that of ours. Our camp was 2 miles North of this battle ground where we remained that day (last Thursday) Our boys cleaned them out nicely & followed them up, shoveing into them the shot & shell. Friday morning we struck tents & followed, passing through the battle ground. We passed over it at 11 A.M. & haulted to let a portion of the army pass, so I got a chance to look around alittle. The scean was horrible, there were hundreds lay dead piled in heaps & in ditches, some crying for help, some trying, some beging to be shot to put of their misery & so on. No pen nor words can discribe what I saw, The men lay in piles like a pile of wood carlessly thrown out of a waggon, some with their feet up & some wounded under them trying to get out. Thus they lay all that night & that day. We soon went on to Jonesboro where I saw many ruins yet hot & smoking & there last & dear R.R. was torn up. There lay there last hopes, but they lost it. (I should have mentioned that we captured all their artillery except one battery) We marched on 5 miles below Jonesboro (South) & pitched our camp in a large opening (4 P.M.) where I could see about 2 miles. One half mile a head of us were 2 lines of battle were advanceing through a large cornfield & the rebs on the opposit side in a peice of woods. About one hour after wards a tremendious thundering of Artilery & musketry was hurd & I could see the whole about 5 minutes but the smoke soon put them out of my sight. A charge was made & we took their last peice of artilery & cleaned them out nicely. Millie? I am tired. I have been at work hard all day fixing up Gen. Shermans maps & it is now 10.30 P.M. & I have not hardly been away from my table to day. Good Night. Sunday morning Sept. 4th. 2 years tomorrow I was mustered in the united states service to serve for the turm of 3 years. 2 of them years are gone. 2/3 of my time has expired & the remaining third is to be told one year from tomorrow when if we both live we shall see each other & I shall be my own man again. I think we shall remain in camp to day. We some expected to return to Atlanta to day but dont think we shall go untill tomorrow if we do them. The enemy are still in our front & the big guns are whacking away at them to draw their attention while a portion of the army is going around them. Last Friday morning I was wakened out of a sound sleep between 3 & 4 by a very thundering noise did not know what it was at that time but hurd since that it was the magazeen in Atlanta. (I was just 12 1/2 miles air line) The rebels set fire to 85 car loads of amunition mostly shells & powder, they were prepared for a long seige, but old Sherman was to smart for them. They had an emence supply of commissaries, they distroyed what they could /{this page has writing around two blank spaces which form U S in capital letters} of them & destroyed locomotives (we saved one) & sundries other things then lift on suspition. But the nicest joke is that the rebs had whiped the yankees & had retreated across the Chattahoochee river and the citizans came from all parts of the country the distance of 30 miles to Atlanta to celibrate the great victory (while Gen. Shermans army was silently creeping to the rear of them) but when they get there they found nothing but bluebellied yankees in the city, what do you suppose they thought. I am shure I dont know but I supposed they droped their tails & got out as soon as they could. You will find that the rebel army is nearly played out. We have had very hot weather on our march & very dry except yesterday we had some hard showers & hard winds which nearly took our tents up by the roots. I have been very buisey & worked day & night since we started out. As I am the head draughtsman down here, they look to me for correcting maps & Lieut. Wharton takes the information the most of the time Since we have come to a standstill I am not so badly drove I put the surveys on my campaign map yesterday so I have to day to my self This is one of them tremendious hot days you hear me tell tell about so much We have more to eat than we had a few days ago. We happened to get hold of a box of hard tacks & a drove of beef cattle are kept along with the army so we will not starve. As I get deeper in to Georgia I find the country better, We have destroyed thousands of acres of corn, Sugar cain, tobaco, Cotton, sweet potatoes, O, we dig the sweet potatoes & live Last tuesday I had but one hard tack to eat in all day so when I came to a good old garden I made a rade in it & found nothing but but 2 ripe summer squashes. I took them along & had a fine breakfast on to of them. I am not alone in the hungry dicker. There is 6 in the mess. The game is here that each one must look out for him self conciquently /I {crossed out} my hand had a cramp over some chickens heads & for the life of me I could not let go of them, that night night I payed a darkey 50 cents to cook them for us & dident we live? I got 4 fowls cooked the last yesterday, so you can see that we are liveing high just now. When we started out we had not a single thing to cook with but now we have a good supply such as spiders, skillets dutch oven coffee mill, &c. the coffee I took from the chimbley of an old diserted log house, there is no such a thing as starveing a soldier if he is only a mind to look out for him self I sent you a ragged looking note a few days ago, but I had no time to do any better as the rebels was closeing in on our rear & I wanted to let you know where I was a going. I have been healthy & tuff except a very hard cold that I got by exposure, am better now, I have not hurd from you in a long time as our communication has been cut off but is opened now. As my sheet is nearly full I will close, Direct your mail to Major Gen. Thomas head quarters in the field as before. I shall go to Atlanta tomorrow.

Yours in Love Charles H. Prentiss

Millie

Head Quarters Topl. Engr's Office
Department of the Cumberland
Atlanta, Ga.
Sept. 10th, 1864

Absent Wife: Again I address you a few lines to let you know I am still alive & well, & you will notice that my letter is headed from Atlanta. Yes I am in that great city that we have been so long afighting for. I entered the city with General Thomas's headquarters last Thursday (the 8th) from the South as we returned from the raid. As I am very anxious to inform you of my whereabouts & my time is limited I think that I shall be obliged to send you a short letter, & I know that you are anxious to hear from me. I had a very good time on our trip to Jonesboro, & it has proved to be a successful one, & I think it has saved many lives by doing so. Sabbeth Morning the 11th. I will try it again. We are just arunning over with work & I have but little time to myself. We have a full campaign map to make commencing at Chattanooga & going south as far as Jonesboro, & I have to work day & night at preasant. Our campaign has ended for the preasant, the army wants a long rest, they have had a hard time, but I suppose as soon as they get rested & reorganized & the 500,000 gets in the field & drilled that they will make another sweep towards the gulf. You know the new broom sweeps clean & that will be the way when we start to gain. Gen. Sherman is loved by all his men, but when he made this last rade they began to think that he did not know much, but he has had his plans & they worked well. You see, when he started out the 20th A.C. went back to the river, all in one camp & left the country all open northward so the rebs had full swing & the 5 corps went south, making a clean sweep. We had got the Atlanta & West Point railroad cut before the rebs smelt the rat. As soon as they (the Rebs) found it out they took their army down to Jonesboro (all except one division & some militia) & as soon as they left the city the 20th A.C. moved in without much resistance. It was impossible to take this city by assault. You northern people have no idea what a strong city they had here. I think there has been at least 15 or 20,000 lives saved by this move. All of our generals here was against Gen. Sherman in regard to this move except Gen. Thomas. Gen. Sherman's last words to his generals was: Gentlemen! these are my plans. I want you to see that they are well executed. Now what do you think of Gen. Sherman? I think everything of him. He is a good, kind, sociable general. I have had conversation with him in regard to information, and he has asked my judgement in reguard to routes to move on, but I tell you I felt like a small speck when a general comes to me to counsel on war matters, but so it is, and the officers of this office have chosen me to take this part of the business & I feel proud of my position, and I think if my time was out I should hire out in this department. I find that there is nothing like being on hand evry time, tending to my business & always sobr, independent from all intemporate habbits (exceppt eating). I shall stay in this department the remainder of my time, so Capt. Rugar tells me. I will tell you what my business is. To take information, compile & put together surveys, & examine the maps to see if they are correct, & to learn 2 boys in my room to work on maps. I have been in this business nearly 7 months & have very good knowledge of what is to be done. I have the best set of instruments in the office. I think I have braged long enough & now I will tell you a little about the city, that is a general outline. I will give you the details sometime when I have a little more time. The building which I occupy. It is a large brick house similar to the one we had in Chattanooga, halls through above & below. A shell (our shell) entered the back door of the upper hall, passing through & making a large hole through the brick wall & carring off the banister on the porch, crossing the street & entering a Methodist church & so on. Another shell carring off the northeast corner of the building tearing the cornice off each way, a large hole in the roof (6 ft. sq.) & the seeting of the room in that corner of the building. You can make up your mind one shell passing through a building makes things rattle. There are numbers of other holes in the building not worthy of mentioning. The damage of this house is nothing compared to some in the city. 240 women & children were killed here during the bombardment, large numbers of buildings were burned by shells, the large car factory walls was like a sive. As far as I know we got 10 large 64 seige guns, 5 of them spiked & 5 was not. (lots of mosquetoes) 2 locomotives that was not ingured. I have not had much time to look about much. I'll tell you some other time more about these things. The regiment is about 1/2 mile from me. I have been there to see them. Now about that stove. The stove is worth $375.00 & the clock 5 cents. I had rather have the clock than the stove. I shouldnt think you could expect me to set a price on the stove when I . . . in 2 1/2 yrs. & been in use at times. Father & George can tell you better than I can, and their judgement is good enough to send me. It cant be worth much get all you can for it. I think the clock is worth about, a-b-o-u-t, let me see, about $2.50, I guess, get what you can & let it rip. I don't want it. Mon. 12th. Now I will try again & see if I can finish. Just as I got nicely to writing yesterday the Capt. came in with an armfull of surveys & I had to go to work. I received your 56 & 57 letters. The 57 came to hand today. I do not want any suspenders. I was obliged to get them here about a month ago. I have not received the glee-book yet, have you sent it, I should like to enjoyed the raseing at the Junction with you all. You speek of not receiving many letters. I think I have written as often as once a week except while on the rode. Our communication was cut off & I thought it was no use. I hope our work will slack up by and by so that I will get time to write more. (If I make mistakes you must not blame me for 5 or 6 of the boys are singing & playing the piano. We have a good piano that belongs to some rebel women, but it belongs to us now.) There has been 4 weeks at a time that I got no mail from anyone. We are a great ways apart & a letter has a hard road to travel. You speak of my being in danger. I see nothing to be scared at & you know its all in knowing how to dodge a ball, but the ball that hit Sarg. Hager was a stray one from the picket line. He was not exposed to sharp shooters. You need not think they will get a chance at me. Dont you feel alarmed for I know what danger I am in & I dont tell it any worst than it is. I may be as safe here as in the north by what I hear of the copperheads. I have given up the photographing. Capt. cant spare me from my other work. No, I havent found any way to send any money home. I understand that Capt. Hubbard has gone home & I did not see him. I think as George says, if I can get $5.00 a day here in the office at drafting I should stay after makeing a visit home after my time is out, I must see home first. I think that Geo. would make the most money by going into the army at the reat he is paying out to keep out of it. I would advise him to keep out if I could, for there is no fun in soldiering, my way thing, but some body must go. You will excuse me for this time for I have had a hard time a writing this. My eyes are tired & it is very late. Love to my dear Millie. Good Night. Charley to Millie

P.S. Direct your mail H.Q. Top. Engr. Office D.C. Atlanta Ga. the same as you use to

                                        Department Head Quarters, Topl.
                                        Engr. Office, Atlanta Sept. 18.1864

Dear Wife.

Yours of the last of July some time, dont know what date to call it, so many of them, Posted Aug 3 came to hand last tuesday. Some cause it got delayed or lost, or strayed or stolen. All the news I have to tell you is that I am well & have enjoyed good health scince I last wrote you. Our work is so pressing that I cannot get time to write, I have to work day & night & sundays & my eyes are hard up & you must excuse this short letter. In about 2 months the campaign startes again & we have an awful sight of work to do in that time, I have to compile all the surveys as fast as they come in (if I can) one inch to the mile then the rest take from my map & reduce it to one fourth inch to the mile & prepare it for publising, so you see the work goes through my hands first. I have to represent all the locations of houses, fields, trees, hills, lots, (Section lots) streems, springs, rivers, churches, school houses, mills (saw & grist) graveyards, bridges, fords, forts, fortifications, riflepits on both sides waggon roads, rail roads, rocks, &c. &c. & I find it a hard job to get them togeather in such a rough country as this, you have no idea what a rough country this is, I am sure I did not & I would not take the best 1,000 acres & live on it if they would give it to me, & such looking people & huts they live in is enough to make a man tired of life. The white inhabitance all look alike, tall, thin, spair, raw boned, long hair, & they certainly do not look so inteligent as the most of the blacks & seldom come acrost a man that can write his name. & the dommon class of femails are of the same build in statur, long, slim & looks as though they had but one garment on, look like a shirt on a pole than any thing els. Now for an explanitaion of their huts, or log cabins & out houses, I have traveled all day through the state of Georgia & did not pass a single farm house. They first build a fire place & chimbly then build the house to it, & if any differance the former the largest, the house covered with shakes, one or two small sheds, no wood house, nor barn, but the main thing is a smoke house to smoke bacon & sausage. I have not seen a plough or harrow, threshing machine, straw cutter, nor any other kind of farming impliment since I left Mich. I think if I remember it right I have seen one or 2 waggons espetially the army waggon. I think I have told you enough about the Georgia folks. My eyes smart so that I can hardly see, I have hardly left my seet to day, only to go to my meals & my stool is very tired. Pleas write your letters the old way I still remain your true & affectionate Husband Charlie to Millie

Department Head Quarters, Topl. Engr.
Office. Army of the Cumberland
Atlanta, Sept. 29th 1864

Dear Wife,

After amuseing myself a few minutes at the piano I concluded to write to you a few lines. I received yours of the 11. 12. 13. 14. 15. 16. 17. No. 60 a few days ago & it found me well & hard at work on the Campaign map. This campaign map that I speek of if a large. it is about 10 ft long & 7 ft wide & you have no idea what a sight of work there is on it. I can work a week on it & you could hardly tell where I have been to work. A week ago today Gen. Sherman was in here to see it & called it well done, day before yesterday Gen. Thomas was in here & he told me the map was correct & the work was good. Pretty good compliments for Charlie. A great many of our troops have gone to Bridge Port to meet a rebel force that has gone there to distroy the bridges at that place. Gen. Thomas has gone, He went today. If they distroy thoes 2 bridges you will hear of us crying hard tack & sowbelly, but I do not anticipate any danger yet, 200 officers were exchanged at this place yesterday. They are right from Charleston. They are some of those that were placed under our fire. You have undoubtedly hurd of our placeing 1,000 of the rebel officers under their fire at Morris Island That, it seems has been the cause of the exchange of officers, I dont know what you would do if you should hear them tell their stories. A Capt. of the 1st /K {?}t Cavelry is one that I had conversation with, & he tells me that the food they had was poor musty bread & bacon. The bacon was perfectly alive with maggets. This he said was nothing. They had some wounded soldiers. They take no care of them. Let them lay & rot & die in the prison. He told me that he saw wounds just filled with maggets, & their limbs would swell so that the hide would crack open & furthermore & what is worst than all, he saw a wounded man that was so bad that maggets passed his bowels & yet alive, What do you think of such warfair. Who would have thought that this enlightened race of people, the people of these united states, could be so barbarous, They are worst than any tribes of savages I ever hurd of. A Capt. was shot there in the prison for dipping a bucket in a spring they had there by one of their guards & the guard got a leave of abesence for 30 days. This was done to encourage others to do the same. O! how I wish I could have command of a little army if I was capible of handleing them, I would have Andersonville my watch word. Thousands of our poor prisoners have died at that place for the want of a little care. My Dear Friends at home, you know of but little of this war, & I cannot tell you of but little about it, & it is my candid opinion that this war will not cease untill we totally nihilate the whole rebel race, If I live, I calculate to surve my full turm of 3 years in this war, Many thousands more of families will be made desolate before this war will end I dont want you to harbor the idea that I have the blues & that I am home sick, for I am not, I feel proud that I can do so much for our country as I am, I stand number one as workman in this office, so the Cheif Engineer, Col. Wharton says, He comes to me to council about the work & brings the Generals to me. What do you think of that, Dont you think that I am some on a stick, My wages are the same as the rest, $16. per month & 40c extry duty per day. My wages cannot be raised only by promotion, as an officer in /the {crossed out} my company, & if I should be promoted I should have to muster for another 3 years, (The band is playing Home again & it makes me O, I dont know what,) I received a paper from Geo. day before yesterday & I mailed a letter this morning to him & in case that he should not get it, you tell him that the campaign paper does not take very well, The boys seldom get papers they subscribe for, My company are stationed at the soldiers home, clost by & I run over there occationally. I received a good letter from Sophie this evening & a few words from Dave, Pleas tell dave I sent a letter to Detroit with a picture enclosed for him. Pleas tell Sophie I will answer her letter as soon as I get time, also Mothers & I think there is one due to Father & Mary, but when I write, I write for the benefit of all the family, only the name to change. According to your letters you have had a treshingout, you said the threshers had come just in time to get dinner. Sept 30th evening. Now I will make another desperate effort to finnish my letter. News confirmed to day that the bridge is burned over the Falling Water Creek by 15,000 rebel cavelry. This bridge is situated between Bridge Port & Chattanooga, Uncle Sam will not be a great while building a new one, but it maid our rations short for a few days. No other news to day. I found in your letter a union ticket which suits me well. Now the next thing is to get a chance to vote it. Will you dress up in Charlie Prentiss clothes & vote for me? It is a great ways for me to go to vote. Some times think that the next Presidential election will turn the tide of this war eather one way or the other. It will make it eather wor or better. I think if Abe Lincoln is elected the war may seice, but we cant tell now. You spoke in your 57 letter as though I was makeing fun of your linnen cloth. I was not. I meant what I said I think it would make good shirts espetially for those that have a good deal of scratching to do, & it is of that kind that the gray backs do not like to stay in. It must be that you do not get my letters because I have writen you a number since I have been in Atlanta. You must remember that I am a great ways from home & a letter is generally interrupted by the rebs. our R.R. is out most evry week, we have about 319 miles of rail to guard & it takes a great many troops to guard it. I am glad to hear you say that you are not much worried about me, & you have no reason to now,-- You can have all the sport with By Ballou that you wish at my expence. It does not trouble me any, & that is not all. I have not seen any very good looking ladys in the south yet, only those I use to tell you about in Kentucky-you can tell by not be alarmed for I kill nothing but rebs. You see my sheet is nearly full & I think I had better close. I have but a few months to stay & I will soon be home so keep up good spirits. I still remain your affectionate husband love to all, yours in haist

Charlie Millie

{This is an undated scrap of very thin paper which evidently was sent along with some pictures. There were some original Brady photographs in the possession of my father, and I don't know if this was to explain them or some other pictures. I do not know what happened to the photographs which my father had. Uncle Charlie had some others which he sent to Chattanooga for a memorial display and which were never returned to him. He also tried his hand at photography, and these probably referred to some of his own photos.}

I will send on a little discription of the capture of Chattanooga No 1 Rackcoon mt. Occupied by the rebes on the same side of Chatt. No. 2 where our forces lay. The river runs between No 1 & 2 pontoon bridg put up in the night. No. 4 Waldens ridg. Our army lay in 4 & five is where our army lay. No 6 Wilders battery that scared the rebs out of town I took this from the rebel works clost to the city, the right hand is up stream, you look north in to the picture. both picturs belong togeather No 1 picture belongs on the right No. 2 If you dont understand wait untill I come home

---

TOPOGRAPHICAL ENGINEER OFFICE,
HEAD-QUARTERS DEP'T OF THE CUMBERLAND.

Atlanta, October 9 th 1864.

My Dear Wife

Again it is with pleasure that I sit down to communicate to you a few lines. I am yet alive & well. I never enjoyed better health than I do now days, It has been a long time since I have received a letter from you & I think it is on account of our communication being cut off & I think it is doubtful about you getting this very soon. You know we have a long line of railroad to watch & guard & there are so many garrillias & bushwhackers that it is almost impossable to keep the road open. The road between here & Bridgeport has been badly cut up the last 2 weeks but now we have the road clear of rebs & nearly repared. The most of the railroad bridge over the Chattahoo chee was washed away & & is repared again. We expect a through train tomorrow to bring us some mail. We have not suffered any for the want of hard tack yet. For fear you have not hurd of the full explination of the rebel raid on our rear I will tell you something about it. Gen. Hood undertook the same game that Gen. Sherman played on them but did on them. They made for a small pile rations that we had at Atlanta. We had 2 million of rations of bread & 2,000 head of cattle at that place, we saved all. Had a hard fite there, the rebels charged on us 5 times & was repulsed each time with a heavy loss. Our loss was heavy but the rebs was heaver, dont know the numbers on eather side, we burried 500 rebs & took 700 prisoners, their army is badly demoralised & Sherman after them. Gen. Sherman sent in a dispatch this morning to lookout for an attact on this place to day & night. All is quiet upto this hour (9 P.M.) with the exception of a great deal of cheering. We have received a dispatch this evening that Richmond has fallen & the boys are haveing a great time over it. I cant believe it yet because we have been fooled so many times. I hope it is true. The rebel army is in a bad fix but they still keep up good courage. Jeff Davis made a speach to his men in Macon a few days ago, telling them that they would have Atlanta back again in 30 days, but I cant see it. I look at it in this light. If Sherman couldent take Atlanta with 102,000 men a rebel force of about 30,000, how is Hood a going to take it with 10,000 against the 20th A.C. of about 17,000. I think it must look rather dubious on their part. Well I took a little walk this A.M. out the ruins of the big Iron foundery. The destruction is great. The most & best of the machinery the rebs took away to Macon, there is left an emense amount of iron there, rolled out and large quantities in the raw state, some 7 or 8 large steem boilers & as many smoke stacks standing, one large cast-iron wheele, I should judge would weigh about 10 or 12 ton & some of the heavyest Iron rollers. The ruins are smoldering yet & the iron in one pile is red hot. The works was burned when they vacuated. Only think 81 car of amunition & arms at this place was burned & blowned up, the ground just covered with fragments of shells, gun locks & barrels, sollid shot, grape & canester, the trucks of the cars scatered in evry direction, the ground towrn up & & hoisted things generally. No more to night Good night. Monday evening the 10th. The news from Richmond is confirmed this morning. (But I get no mail yet.) I expect that Lees army will make for this place now. It was worst for them to give up Atlanta than Richmond, they feel it much & we expect they will make an desperate effort to get it back again. I have no mews of interest this evening only that I have been at work hard to day & feel very tired & I am not in very good trim for writing. I have broke my darning needle & lost my fine comb what shall I do. How do you all get along at home, O, how I wish I could hear from you again & how I wish I could go home once more I am a great ways from & it is an awful job to get home if I could get a furlough, that is hard to get thir preasent time & it is very dangerous travleing now. oweing to circumstances I shall have to stick it out 11 more months, then I am a free man again, Well Roenna I will close, my eyes feel bad & so do I. (tired I mean) Love to all & you too, I hope this may find you all well Yours truly

Charlie Millie

TOPOGRAPHICAL ENGINEER OFFICE
Head-Quarters Dep't of the Cumberland.
Atlanta Oct. 15th 1864

My Dear Millie,

Your kind letter of Sept. 28th came to hand Day before yesterday & words cannot express my joy after so long a silence between you & me. It seems as though months had passed since I have received any mail from home, but not so bad as that. It makes me feel sad to hear of your illness. I cannot do anything for you when I am so from you. O I wish that I were with you to night instead of sitting here a scribbleing this slow way of talking. I am willing to trust you in the hands of your kind parents for good care, I know they will do all they can for you, I hope you will try & take good care of your health & mind your failings, & dont be carless & expose yourself. If I live, 10 1/2 months will stand me on free soil again, then I trust that we may live happy & enjoy the blessings of a free & settled country. We have seen trouble enough for the last 4 years & it will be a 4 years that will allways be remembered in America. I dont know as it will do any good to write this evening as our communication is cut & it is doubtful about the mails leaveing this place. You undoubtedly have have hurd the rebs have us in a rather tite place just now but I trust that it may not remain so a great while. We have but the 20th Corps at this place about 16,000 affective men & can hold Atlanta against 40,000 We have plenty of amunition & it is dry but supplies are scarce. Up to last Friday evening 84 mules have starved to death scince our line of communication has been cut. Last night 500 waggon loads of corn came into town from the Southeast. This morning another forrageing train about 3 miles long started out again for some more corn. As long as we have corn I dont think we shall starve. Atlanta will be held to the last. I should rather live on 1/5 rations 3 months /rather {crossed out} than to give up Atlanta to the rebels again. The government is tareing down some splended buildings & building fortifications on the ground occupied by the buildings. One large splended femail Semminary has to come down & a fort erected in its place. We have to erect our forts on all highest points. Our lines being cut, we get but little news & I can tell you but little what is going on now. The rebs have not attacted this place as we expected them to but dont know how soon they will.--I should judge by the reading of your letter that you did not enjoy the state fair very much. Millie I am sorry & I will try & be at home so as to go with you to the next one. I am still at work at my old biseness in the office & dont get tired of it yet. I dont intend to sleep cold this winter. I went to the Quarter masters yesterday & got me 2 blankets & now I have 4 good woollen blankets. Weather is nice down here now, warm pleasent days & cool nights & a few mosquetoes left. The roads are dry & dusty. I suppose you are haveing some bad fall or winter weather by this time. Well Roenna I might as well owne up first as last but I am ashamed to say it, that is I am homesick or have the blues just as you are a mind to have it. I think if I could hide myself & give vent to my feelings about one hour it would do me good. Since I received your last I have not felt contented. But that wont do for a soldier, I dont know as I have shed a tear since I left Kal. but I have felt like it many atime. I can write no more to night, good night. Sunday morning Oct. 23. Dear Millie I hope you will excuse my long silence. As the enemy has had us hemed in the last 3 weeks & the road cut I new it would be of no use to start a letter from here & perhapse it may fall in to the hands of the rebels. Now I think the road is open again, a small mail came over the road yesterday & there will be one leave today. I have done a little job which I regret very much that is I burnt up all of your letters for fear they might fall into the rebels hands. I did not do it willfully but I had rather see them burn than to go into the rebels hands. We are haveing enough to eat now Last Thursday 700 waggons loads of forrage came in which gives us a good supply for 30 days. I can tell you nothing about Gen. Sherman or Thomas army to day. I dont hear any news whatever. We had a train of cars burned between the Chattahoochee river & Marietta last wednesday. It was loaded with railroad iron & ties for repareing the track. It was burned by a party of garrillas. We are haveing all that we can do to keep open such a long line of rail. I am sorry that I cant get any money to you for your use but as it is I dare not risk it by mail or express but I will try $5 dollars I want you to let me know if you get it. I hope this letter will find you & George well as I have understood that you were sick. & all the rest. My health is good, never better, the mail will leave soon & I must hurry & get this in. How does all of you get along. I tell you I want to hear from you all The health of our Company is very poor. they are troubled with the scurvy. My love to you Millie. Take good care of your self. I dont have as much time to write as I use to. Let me hear of all the news. Love to all Yours in haist Charlie

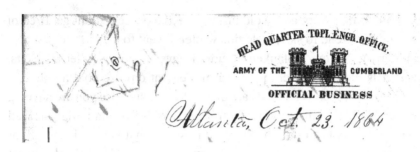

HEAD QUARTER TOPL.ENGR.OFFICE.

ARMY OF THE   CUMBERLAND

OFFICIAL BUSINESS

Atlanta, Oct 23. 1864

My Dear Wife

I am left alone in my room & the house is still except about a dozen running up & down stairs & a man tuning the piano, & a good deal of dutch jabber &c. I thought I would spend a few moments a chatting with you all at home. You say you are so fond of good long letters so I thought I would write one. This is sunday evening. I mailed you a letter this morning & enclosed in a five dollar bill & I also told you that I was well, & so I was but now I have a seveier head achake or what you are a mind to call it & have a hard cold just a comeing on caused by sleeping in damp blankits. Yesterday morning I hung my blankets out to air & I left them out untill 11 oclock last evening, conciquently I have taken cold, but that is nothing down here. Well, how do you all do this evening, & what have youall been about to day. I have to meeting most all day. with a lot of prisoners & refugees a takeing information & adding a little to my big sheat. That is the kind of meetings I go to. where I do the preaching my self. It has been uncommonly lively times here to day, a shipping off rebel prisoners & the sick & wounded to Nashville. So that there will not be so many to consume provisions. We had about 2 thousand rebels here & dont know how many sick & wounded. Col. Wharton the Chief Engr thinks so much of my information sheat that he has to fetch in all the Generals that he can find. Gen. Williams was in to see it last week. All the proof sheets are brought to me for correction. One little joke on Col. Wharton. yesterday a proof sheet was sent to him for correction. He examined it call it right, sent it back I got a hold of it & overhawled & found 17 mistakes on it. He was a little tite I guess. He is a west Pointer & has a fine education. Their I think that I have bragged enough about myself & now I will bragg about something els & something els will be about the Rail Road &c. We have a number of large piles of new T rail in this place I should think there was enough to lay 30 miles of track lots of ties plenty of cars & Engens. Now I have a better pen & I will try & write so that you can read. Atlanta is one of the largest rail road car factories in the south. The round house is about 200 ft in diameter & has stalls for 45 Engines with a large turn table in the center. We have 9 extry engines standing in there weighting for others to be captured. one train of cars is not in or out of Uncle Sams pocket. The rebels have carried off all the machinery & left nothing but the building. Now we are fixing it up & putting in machinery. The smoke stack of this building is about 100 feet high & some 8 or 10 shell holes through it. number of the collums were nocked out by our shells & a large number of buildings were burned. Atlanta suffered sevierly by our shot & shell & so did the inhabitance from hunger. You dont know how glad the people were to see our army come in. We have all of the inhabitance to feed & you can see that it takes quite a pile to feed all. We have built a large amount of brest works & forts since we came here the most of it has been done by the rebel prisoners & niggers. I am glad Uncle Sam makes them do something to pay their expences. Thats whats the matter. A large femail Seminary was torn down last week where we are building a fort & some other nice mantions has to come down for the same purpus. General Thomas is now in Nashville & it is rhumered that the Army of the Cumberland will move out there & if that is the case I shall be there too which will fetch me about 200 miles nearer home. I understand that Hood's army is very badly scatered & hard up for eatables. They are in a bad fix. they have made their braggs of takeing Atlanta back in 30 days. But I cant see it in that light. Can you? I hear good news of Sheridens giveing the rebs another dressing out & took 50 peices of atilery from them & took a large number of prisoners. That is what he tells. I would like to know if Gen. Blair is about. Why dont he procure some means for his soldiers to vote. I send you my ticket tell Father or George to slip it in the box & tell them this ticket came all the way from Atlanta to vote for Charlie Prentiss. Many of the boys of the regiment fee rather soer because they cant vote & so do I. The fact of the buisness is. I must have a vote in for Uncle Abe, People say that man wife are both one. So you can put my cloths & go up & vote for me. Well How is the weather up north by this time. Have you had any snow yet. We are just a haveing nice summer weather now & a plenty of moskeetars, but the Devels horse is played out. Dont see any of them lately. I dont think you had better send me any box this fall I will try & get along without. I am getting use to soldiers fair now & I can live on most anything. It is now 10.30 & I will stop for the night. Wednesday evening, Oct. 26th Your kind letters of 9 & 13th came to hand to day & was read with much interest. I must say that I was much surprised, when I read the contence of 13th Its a copperhead report, & if I were there I would be tempted to shoot a man that would circulate such a report. I am shure that no one has any ground to build such an infirnal lie. I am sorry for you Roenna! I am sorry that people cant let you alone. I would like to see such people of the North placed in the front ranks & be made to fight or die. but No, they they remain behind & abuse those that are unprotected. You have had a full history of all the dangers that I have undergone & you can see that I am yet alive & well. My suspition rests upon Pinney. I think him to be the rogue. What does Mrs Vahue know about me. Perhaps she never has hurd my man. If she has, what motive had to start such a yarn. I know nothing of the Vahue family only Charlie Vahue a good friend of mine & a good steady young man he is & a man that reads his bible, I think you took a wise course to trace out the story. Give Elder Wolfe my thanks for his kindness to you. I feel that I have some friends yet. Hear after when you hear such stories let them pass in one ear & out the other. Ill let you know when I get killed. You had better get a advertisement printed & stick it up in Otsego saying that Prentiss is not dead yet. I am a going to work for Uncle Sam 10 months longer and you live & well, safe & sound, in Atlanta at work hard evry day for my country & your country & the copper heads I wish were all driven out & into the Gulf of Mexico where they belong & where they ought to have been years ago. I consider that I am going as much good as most any other man. Who marks out the path for this mighty army to travel. (I think Charlie Prentiss does some of it.) Well how do you like Mrs Mabbs. I think as a family that they are nice folks. Mr. Mabbs is one of my best friends & a good sound mental man he is a christian. He received a letter from home today & this shooting scrape was in his letter, so he had to come right over & see me. He wanted to know all about the particulars. I let him read the letter. He felt very bad. I frequently draw him some pictures to send home to his little children & he thinks a good deal of them. We get togeather some times & have a sing, but as for him hearing me play on the Piano it is a mistake. I am not a player on that instrument but I make what some folks call a noise. Did you ever hear of such a thing. If you did not, I can tell you it is a very disagreeable sound to a musicul ear. Well! what about the money dicker. I do not intend to keep it a secret. I will say as I have before in your letters & that was as plain as I could explain it. I suppose you are a ware that I have rather a back handed way of explaining my self. I will try again to make you understand. The fact of the buisness is I get

$16. per. month of regular pay. That makes 16 dollars for one month. I am allowed $3.50 per month for clothing. That makes just exacly 19 dollars & fifty (50) cents for one month. I draw from the Quarter Master just 40 cents per day or $12. per month for extry duty, that makes 31 dollars & 50 cents for one month, but mind you there is 6 months extry duty cash due me now which if I had it it would swell my purse to the ammount of $73.50, This understand. Mr. Quartermaster owes me now, I get or draw from the commissary 40 cents per day or $12 per month which makes 43 dollars & 50 cents but I have to pay out my Commutation money to buy something to eat so that leaves me with only with $31.50 per. month, I have in my trowsers (let me see) I find in my burs $148. & 2 three cent stamps & one of them has to pay the frait on this letter, (148 dollars & 2 three cent stamps) Mr. Mabbs owes me 8 dollars & 25 cents borrowed Cash, a chap in company G. owes 5 dollars for an over coat. I owe the wash women 5 cents per washing, couldent make change. You owe me 5 dollars that I sent you last sunday in a letter, I have two watches one cost me 15 dollars & refused 25 dollars twice, I got it by makeing pictures on letter. The other watch cost me $10. & I have refused $35. for that. I must have $40. I cant think of any thing els in the cash line, you see that I am out of stamps most. Do you understand. (Nix for stay)~ Be patient Millie, Time is fast passing & I trust that we may see each other again & live a quiet & happy life.—There may be sometimes long intervals between my mail but I cannot help it.~ Our R.R. has been cut a long time. A large mail came through to day for the first for some time. Dont borrow any trouble. I am out of danger & have plenty to eat & to ware,--How much wheet is Father & Geo. a sowing this fall. I should like to go snucks in the sugar mill if I was at home. Ah. You have a contraband. The darkeys are a particular friend of mine. I like a good. Dont like to see them abused, if he is a good one, keep him. Give Robert my respects,--I dont know as I can invent anything for passtime for you unless you do as I do when I have nothing to do, go to makeing pictures. Yes. Yes. I just happened to think I want a nice pair of slippers to ware in the office. You work some nice uppers & get the shoemaker to bottom them & I will foot the bill. You get them made & I will contrive some way to get them. I have them if I have to go after them. Pleas tell Father that I answered his last received & should be happy to receive another. This long letter is for you, Father, Mother, Geo. & Laura, Mary, Elsie, & whats that other one's name & all the rest. Am I makeing any plans for the future? O Yes. lots of them. but my mind is not settled yet on any particular one except on a plan of a nice little Cottage which I think you will like. I cant explane it now but it will be a Gothic. I remember your birthday preasent & I have it in my possetion now but cant get it to you with safety. Its only worth $12. & I dont know as you will like it. It is a broach sleeve buttons & locket worth $4. each. I was not aware that Doct Bennett was gone. I wish I had of known of his leaveing. I shall not trouble the army when I once get out. I still remain your kind hearted, whole soul, affectionate, absent, Husband, Charlie Prentiss No more tonight.

> Head Quarters, Topl. Engr. Office
> Depart of the Cumb.
> Chattanooga Ten Nov. 3rd 1864

My Dear Millie.

I have but a few moments to write & I thought I would get down in one corner & let you know of my arrivle in Chattanooga. We commenced to move last sunday & just got in last night & evry thing is all upside under & a nasty wet rain to move in, we have had a very unpleasent time, had to ride & sleep on the deck of the cars, I am well & wet, You need not considder this much of a letter, but I thought I would tell you that I am not dead yet & when I am I will let you know. It is reported all about that Atlanta is to be vacuated but it is not so. If you hear so dont you believe it. I will as soon as I get time & settled yours in great haist My love still remains with you all—

Charlie

P.S. one word more I received a letter from Geo. just as I started from Atlanta. Direct to Chatt. &c. Charlie

TOPOGRAPHICAL ENGINEER OFFICE,
HEAD-QUARTERS DEP'T OF THE CUMBERLAND,

> Chattanooga, November 18th 1864

Dear Wife

Your good letter of the 6th inst came to hand the 16th. & it done me much good. I hope you will excuse my short letter that you have received, & takeing evrything into consideration I think that I am excusable. Excuse

me. I am in one of the worst mudholes I ever saw. & evry thing is dull
& no news, Second. My eyes are very week & it troubles me to write by
candle light. I have but very little time to myself by day light, I want to
tell you that I am superintending one of the largest maps I ever saw or you
eather, & you must know that my mind is very bisely occupied night &
day. I wouldent have a mistake on it for no price. I have my own way in
evry part of the map & it a all goes just as I say & if you live you will see
my name on title of that map. Col. Wharton has promised me a coppy of it
when compleat, I feel very much interested in the buisiness therefore I lose
no time nor chance for learning something. This is one of the best schools
I could have, I am with some of the best engineers in the United States. I
have only 6 working under my directions now, 3 draughtsman, 2 collering
maps & the one that runs the press, There will be 36 sections in the map
& we have 5 of them printed. Now dont you think that I am doing well, to
be sure my wages are small but I care not for that, I had rather be here &
work for nothing than to be in the ranks & be sick all the time. I never have
had the best health I ever had since I have been in this department. So you
must not find falt because I do not get more than I do. The idea is here with
me. A private getting up one of the largest war maps ever published, that is
what dont suit all of these big engineers, but it is just as Gen. Thomas says,
he wanted me to do it so I went at it. I have been figureing up the exact
size of the map to day & I find it to be 81 inches by 123 equal to 6 ft-9 in
x 10 ft-3 in squair. I see by your letter that you had a snow storm about
the 4 inst. & perhapse colder weather by this time, but we have wet rainy
weather & plenty of mosqetoes now. what do you think of for this time a
year. I am sorry that you had a failure in your massmeeting but I think it
has all come out right Old Abe is good for another 4 years, Tell By Ballou
that I received his note about one week after the election, & the regiment
was 139 miles from me. I was not aware that Let Baird had his discharge.
how is getting along. how is Dave pleas tell me all about the news I should
like to step in & hear you & Geo sing some of your new peices When I go
home I shall have to sing to you some of my new music such as Yankee
doodle Zip coon &c. Wouldent you like to hear me sing a little just now. I
would like to hear all about election in Otsego. I dont know what should put
it in your head that I was a comeing home now. I have to much to do just
now. I am affraid that you will have to look in vain. I shall come as soon
as I can. My last year is creping away sloly then, & then & then you will
see uer Charlie. I cant tell when boys go home when some are in Nashville

some in Louisville some in one place & some in another. I dont here you say any thing about some money that I sent you by mail. Dont you suppose a bowl of that black heifers milk would do me good, cant you send me a jug of it in a letter. I guess you will have to excuse me for the night. I am not very well just now. I was obliged to make 8 calls last night We have to use river water & it opperates like a dose of salts. I have been scarsely able to work to day & yesterday. I am better now, but feel rather week. Love to all, be sure to get your share Charlie U.S.D.

   Millie

Topl. Engr. Office
Head Quarters D.C.
Christmas Eve 24th

My Dear Millie

   Your kind letters of the Dec. 4th & 27th of November just came to hand which found me well & kicking O how glad I was to see the mail come into the office once more. I cannot tell how long since we have had amale This is a merry Chrismas eve with the boys. They bought a barrel of beer for this occation & now they are enjoying it while I amin my room chatting with you, we will have the band here to cerinade us & what a spree, hay? I thank the lord I am not of that disposition. I have the first drop to taist of yet. I will give you a history some other time of the spree I have a poor time to write now because there is so much noise. The big guns are fireing all about us & noise is plenty. Dec. 25th I wish you a merry Chrismas. I will try again & write you a letter. I had to give it up last evening on account of so much noise. My first page does not amount to much but I thought that I might as well send it along. We had quite a time in the office last night, many of the boys were tight but all went on smooth & no fuss. at 9 oclock the head quarter band came up & then we had quite a time & I had agood visit It lasted untill 12 oclock when all was quiet in the house. I went to bed & slept quietly untill morning when 3 heavy guns were fired for the city guards to rally to roll call which they have to evry sunday morning. This is the first I have writen in 2 weeks & why I have not writen I suppose you know. The road has been badly torn up for many miles & now it is all right again & the rebel army is on the retreat & makeing tracks as fast as possable for the South. I cant see for my part what the rebel army has gained by makeing that raid in our rear. They have reacently lost 2 entire

Divisions & 2 brigades besides their killed & wounded & a large number of cannon & they have lost Savannah &c. Now what have they gained. I am glad for my part that the communication is open again. The army here has been liveing on one fourth rations & now we are getting something to eat again. Tell Geo. I have the lost wallet & by discribing propperly & calling at the Topl Engr Office he can have it without the liberal reward. Now a bout those furrs. I dont see how we can afford to go to the expence of $30. or $40. for them when we have no house to live in, no teem, no waggon, no furniture. Pleas reconsider it & see if you cannot get along without a little longer untill our circumstances will admit of it. I would be very happy to accomidate you but you see we have not commence to live yet. Pleas take no offence of what I have said,--I have told you that I would be at home by the hollow days but I cannot, as I have told you before the rebels army was in the way & Col. Wharton has gone North & could not get back so as to give me a furlough. So now I cannot tell you when I can go. I have the map in a shape so that I can leave it. I will come to you as soon as I can. The mail will go out in about 30 minutes & I must hasten to get this in so that you can hear from me. I am well but sorry that I cant spend chrismas & newyears with you. Much love to you all From Your Husband

   Charlie Millie

                                Head quarters Topl Engr. Office D.C.
                                Chattanooga Tenn. Dec. 25th 1864

Dear Wife

   I have just writen & mailed you a letter, fearing that you would not be satesfied with it I concluded to write you another one. I suppose you know this is Chrismas for fear you do not know it I will put you in of it. To day is a nasty, wet, muddy day. We have not had hardly snow enough to whiten the ground but it been very cold by spells then clear off like spring. we would have all the doors & windows open & no fire. The Tenn. river is very high & the water very muddy of which we have to drink. & it is very bad for us. It phthisics us like so much salts. I cannot complain of my health for it has been very good the past year. I have not been to the docter but once since I have been in this department & that is one year the first of February. The first of last Aug I was sick. I got a dose of Caster oil which made me well & the only meadicen I have taken in the mentioned time. Perhaps you would be interested with a few details of our Chrismas Eve party. The first place was to tap the beer barrel at dark. All took a round except Charlie Prentiss then hung up the transparent lights with virious mottoes such as Welcome Chrismas eve. Union forever &c. which ade the room look very pretty. Then took another snifter, then got up a mock trial. a drunken lawyer took the table he being a very smart fellow, afforded us much fun. After the trial another round of beer, then the drunken wood sawyer, some more laughing, then another another jug of beer. So it continued untill a few minutes past & when all at once the headquarter silver cornett brass band struck up some of its sweet melodious strains at our door where we met them with our transparent motto, Welcome Chrismas eve. They cam in then we had a good time the rest of the evening, they went away at 12. Then I made for my bunk as it was Sabeth morning, thence I knew nothing untill morning, but I can tell you the beer flowed freely all the evening. Thus ended the Chrismas eve with us. It has been very quiet about the office to day. & we had a good dinner to day we bought 4 splended fowels last week for this occation when we came to examine they were so poor we did not butcher them. we had for dinner good corn starch pudding, Potatoes, beef stake, apple pie, soft cake, butter, bread, & coffee without milk. It cost us about $4. each for the supper. this all was good & I do not begrudge my money. we have a good black cook. we have 6 niggers to wait on us, to sweep, to build fires, to chop & bring in wood, to fetch water to cook &c. so we can play the gentlemen. we have 4 guards to watch about the premices evry night & to keep evrything streight, so you can see that all works like clock work except the price of eggs which is worth $1.00 per Doz. & butter the same per lb. & beer $40. per barrel. you may know that it costs us something to live if we get anything els than sow belly & hard tack, we got a barrel of Onions from the Sanitary a few days ago free gratis for nothing. we occationally get some saurkrout & pickles from there. Uncle Sam is makeing great improvements in Chattanooga. Are ditching all the streets & paveing them, covering the sidewalks with saw-dust. moveing all stores, sutlers, barber shops &c off of main street & puting up large government buildings. The big Iron works are progressing finely. Also the water works. The water works are so constructed as to carry water in evry fort & throughout the city. The water is forced up on Cameron hill (453 high) by a large steam engin, the water is taken from the river & filtered in a large well 80 ft deep & 10 ft sq. The reservoir is about 200 ft long 20 ft wide 12 ft high & made bom proof. There is a great deal of this work going on that I know nothing of. There is 100 of Citizens here in government employ & I think it would be the best thing that Geo. could do is to come down here & work at his traid (Mason) & get $60. per month & boarded on sow belly &c. untill the war is over then the draft will not trouble him I dont think the draft will trouble me. I am thankfull that most 3 years of my millitary life has passed. I am not sorry that I came out when I did & wish that I had enlisted 8 months sooner than I did. I feel anxious to hear from that letter I sent to. George. I want to know whether the name suits or not. If it does not some one els will have to try. I see you begin to reckon up the days that I am to be absent from you but I have an idea that you have not reckoned it right for I think I shall spend about 25 of these days with you before long. perhaps in less than a month. I shall try hard. Make your self as happy as you can.

Time rolles steadly on, Yours with much Love Charles H. Prentiss Chief Draughtsman

Topographical Engineer Office,

HD. QRS. DEPT. OF THE CUMBERLAND,

Chattanooga

December 14 th **186** *4*

Dear Millie

Yours of the 11 came to hand yesterday & read with much pleasure I am sorry to have to disappoint you in your expectations of seeing by New years. I dont suppose that you will lay any blaim on me for I could not help it. As I have said before, the rebel army has been between you & me & towrn up rail road for many of miles which is not in repare now, & when it is, Col. Wharton has to come here from Nashville before I can get a furlough & it will take a number of days for that to get around. However I shall get around as soon as possable for I am very anxious to see home again. I cannot tell you when I shall start It is not very safe to travel between here & Nashville for this state is full of Garillas, I hurd to day that a train was captured & $40,000 worth of Express goods was distroyed, & trains are fired upon most evry day. If I under take to go home now I will run a great risk of geting killed. The rebel army is now on their way to Huntsville

& Old Pap Thomas is after them & that leaves the rail road unguarded. We had the road most all all done once & a few trains came through which brought us some thing to eat & they have cut it again. But feer not & trust in provicance is the old saying, that is my motto. In reguard to that 36 sections map I have got my part done ready for the press. It takes about 5 days for the press to prepare the auttigraph & transfer to the stone & print one section. I am now at work on a map Nashville & vicinity which will take me about 10 days. When I get home I will explane all about the map makeing better than I can with the pen. I have been haveing the blues a few days but I have got over them now, A misunderstanding was the cause of it. It was reported that all of the detailed men & officers belonging to the 4th & 20th A.C. was to report their Regiments I belong to the 20th but come to find out the truth, all men in Convilesant Camp & Officers lofeing about are sent to their respective commands & dont mean me. If I should go to Savannah I should go in the engineer office at that place. but I did not want to go untill I got my furlough. Sabeth morning. Jan 1st 1865. A happy new year to you. My letter has had a good resting spell & now I will continue to finnish it. I hope this may be the last new years day that I will spend away from you, I have spent the day very well. I attended a meeting at a private house where I saw 10 femails & it did seem good to attend church where there was some body. They had a nice reed organ, the ministers daughter played. I began to make a noise out of my throat, they hurd it, then invited me to sing handing me the Sharon. Many thoughts ran through my mind when I saw that book. I enjoyed the meeting first rate. There was only about 15 men there, mostly citizens. This meeting was what is left of a large Presbiterean church. The minister continues to struggle on in the way of the lord & envites in soldiers. I have not hurd a Baptist surmon since I left Otsego. Dont you suppose I will be glad when I get out of this & get where I can see an englightened country again & have the privalig of going to my own church. We have some snapping cold weather the past week. As old Mr Vincent use to say Dec. had a nub on it. but to day has been a beautiful day. I think it will be useless for you to undertake to meet me at Kal. for I may be detained at Nashville for some days, we have to wride when we can ketch it on the Millitary roads & when I get under way I will travle as fas as a letter will. I dont know how it will be about some blankets for George. I will get them to him if I can but I feer that when I am caught with so many that they will be taken away from me at Nashville. I shall have to carry 2 for my own use on my back & I am not to carry a box. But you beg of me not to let anything hinder me from going home. If you will give me the power of 50,000 men I think I would walk through Old Hoods army but as it is I have to put up with it. When I do arrive in Otsego I want you should have all the stores closed, & all business stoped. Schools dismissed for one week & have the brass band to escort me through town, thats the way to do buiseness when a great man arives like me, You want to get 3 or 4 large banners suspend across the street &c. you know how I mean. Tell Geo. those Oyesters are all right, I will help him eat them but the mellons will come out minus I am thinking. I had as leave have the Oysters as anything. I think that I am good for a furlough this time for I have the Col. promise. & I dont think that he can refuse me, Dear Millie I hope you will excuse me for this time & I will tell you all when I come home. We will have a good old time if the weather is not too cold. My fingers are so cold that I can hardly write. Love to all Charlie to Millie

Our Boys are haveing some fun with 2 buck niggers that are troubleing our Cooks evry night, they have them in the Privy & a guard placed over them. They are badly scared.

CHAPTER 6

JANUARY – JUNE 1865

Topographical Engineer
Office, Hd. Qrs. Dept. of the Cumberland Chattanooga
January 14th 1865

Dear Millie

Nearly four weeks has passed since I have hurd from you. I would be very glad to know what & where the trouble is. Dec. 11 is your last date. Nothing would do me more good that just 3 words from you as I am well. Those three would would start the blues from me very quick. I think I have a good reason for them. all the rest of the boys get their mail regular & I get nothing. If you have not writen lately pleas write & tell me whether you are sick or well or what the trouble is. I feel most too bad to write much this evening for I cannot settle my mind on anything. I am well. I enjoy good health now. I have not got any furlough yet. Col. Wharton is at Nashville yet. We expect him here in about 2 weeks & then I think I can have a furlough.

Sunday 15th As I did not finnish my letter last eve I will now continue I put off writing hopeing that I might get some mail today doon. I woke this morning feeling as blue as ever. the day being very pleasent I concluded to walk about the fortifications & down to the river & elsewhere to while away the lonesome hours listning to the happy little birds. All seems like spring. The ground is quite dry & very pleasent getting about, The steemboats are buisey on the river, the river very high, higher than I ever saw it before. beyond the river the hills look pleasent & warm all nature smiles & I get no good tidings from home. After comeing in from my walk I found all of the boys reading their letters they had just received but nothing for poor Charlie, another 24 hours will soon pass when another mail will arrive which will bring me good news. I have no news to write to you only a peace rumor which is aflote but I do not believe much of it. I suppose you know as much of it as I do. The rumor is that the president has sent 3 peace commissioners to Richmond & the rebels sent 3 to washington. The presidents proposition is to abolish slavery, come back in the union & constitution as it is. This what we read in the yesterdays Nashville paper. I hope you will not think that I am going away or commit sueside because I do not get a letter. but I do feel alittle troubled, I hope it will all come out right after little. The golden sun had sunk to rest behind the westward hills, and night the sable goddess dressed with darkness hill and vale. I paused before a soldiers lone grave where towers of rocks mark the spot, crumbling from the clifts above, its massive walls with Ivy grown seem beckining me to stay and memory faithful to his trust drew back the vale of years & far adown the vista dark once more in any youth appears before me rose the vision bright of many a once loved friend and many a vow from hearts then light of love that wouldent end but where is now the soldier band that once assembled to their roll-call. Their bones bleaching in the sunny south whose merry tones in hims of prais mingled with there comrads & where are now the brave hearts who once fought so brave togeather in the fearless combats linked in brave trust, upon the stage of action each ther fulfills a part as though no danger was near. to those who have fallen for there country no trouble sorrows, care will molest them again. We'll meet on earth no more. Some have found a happy home upon the shining shoer, some stand within the sacred disk & point our erring race to liveing waters, springing forth from fountains of heavenly grace let us strive to live as christians & meet our heavenly father at his throne & render--. {The first part of the letter is written in pencil; the rest is in ink.} There I think I have spouted enough for one time & will drop the subject & talk about geese & ducks. The goose is a very useful animal but they do me no good now. I am better acquainted with the flat-foot turkey. and its a gibgobble here & a gibble gobble there & here a gobble there a gobble & here & there a gobble &c. I will enclose you another Photo, what do you think of it. I hope you excuse my writing with a pencil & will try & not do so any more. I was to lazy to get my pen & ink pleas write soon. yours with much Love Charlie

Topographical Engineer
Office Hd Qrs. Dept. of the Cumberland, Chattanooga
January 22nd 1865

Dear Millie

Yours of the 8th inst came to hand last Monday which done me much good. I was very very glad to here that you are yet alive. I did begin to think that you had forgotten to write or you was sick. You say you have your reasons for not writing. The first place the communication cut off & you expected me home, For my part I do not see hou you could expect me home when a letter cannot get over the road, & I have explaned to you repetedly why I could not get my furlough, You knew that there is a high fence between you & me & without the nescessary papers I cannot get the key to gate. I wish that I had dinied Ed Baird's statement about the furlough & it would have saved you much angsiety & trouble, & when I got ready to start I would have let you known. I wish people would let my affairs alone & attend to their own. then all would go on smoothly. You may continue to write untill I tell you to stop. The letters will not be lost, I will try to get dispatch to you before I arrive in Otsego. Now do not be in a hurry for it will do you no good. Take it cool. I shall come as soon as I possibly can. I think the time is cloos at hand when I shall receive you to my arms. I must confess that you did send me a blue letter but as blue as it was It done me a heap of good, You cannot blame me for not going home before this. I will tell you all about it when I see you. I do not want you apend so much time a cooking for me, for a little will supply me. You think that I am a big eater all the fournoon just what I would eat for dinner. So you cryed did you, I supposed that you was big enough not to cry. Lets see if you can cry when you get this letter, (My furlough is in the Generals office & approved by my Col.) now will you cry? (I expect it tomorrow) now will you cry? No, dont you do it. You say that you have been sick. I do not think it is fair to tell that much without giveing some explanation, believe me, it was a big load on my mind all the week, not knowing whether you are dead or live. do not do so again. You say that my friends are many. I dont see it, If they were my friends they would write to me. You are the only correspondant that I have now & I have one letter in 6 weeks, I will not try to write any mour just now. I have been at work all day & I am tired & sleepy. I am well. Yours with much Love. be patiant a few days Charlie

Jan. 23. Millie.

I have my furlough & transportation in my posession & I shall start tomorrow (Tues) at 1 oclock & shall try to be in /Otsego {crossed out} Kal. on Saturday next Truly yours Charlie.

I shall stop at the Cottage House in Kal.

Head-Quarters Department of the Cumberland,
Office Chief Topographical Engineers,

Nashville, Tenn., *Feb 23 d* 1865.

Dear Millie

You will find by this letter that I am in Nashville. I arrived here last evening at 5.30. Our office has not opened here yet & dont think it will. I stayed at the office last night at this place & expect to leave for Chattanooga to day at 2. P.M. I do not want to stay here, they have very poor building for the office, & it is hard work to get money to live with. I arrived safe here & am well, I do not think you had better think /you had bet {crossed out} of selling your butter down here because the boys get there butter for 50c per pound at this place. It is nearly time for me to start for Chat. & you may not expect much of a letter just now, it has rained hard since last night up to this time, Yours with much Love Charlie

Topographical Engineer
Office, Hd. Qrs. Dept. of the Cumberland
Chattanooga
February 25 1865

My Dear Wife.

Here I am again in Chattanooga at my old table & at my old traid a scribbleing to one that is so far from me & dear to me. I feel very lonesome. The weather is of that /caricture {crossed out} character it is enough to make any one homesick. It commenced to rain soon after I arrived at Nashville & it is rainning yet, we have no work to in the office to pass the time so I have nothing to do but to think over my good times the last month.

I had a very good time on my journey here, I met with no accident. landed safe in Chattanooga yesterday morning (Friday) & found all the boys at bed. I arrived here 6.30. The streems are all very high, The Cumberland has raised about 30 ft & I the Tennessee the same. Two bushwhackers undertook capture a passenger train on the Louisville & Nashvill rail road the day I came throug on that road, They done no damage to the train but lost their own lives. We had a general time at fireing big guns here & Louisville Nashville & all other large cities. all because that Charleston has fallen & for Washingtons birthday. About 25 locomotives set up a terrible howling about noon for the same purpous as the fireing the guns. Boys all very glad to see me, you aught to have seen them when they taisted the butter & Ginger snaps. it made there chops smack &c. They have partly decided to have me send for about 50 lbs of butter, so you had better hold onto it a little while untill you hear from me again,--It is very probable that we shall stay here a spell if not all summer, I had rather than to go to Nashville, That is a miserable mudy nasty dirty hole & a very poor building for an office. I am satesfied to stay here seeing that I have got here. My Col. has gone to Louisville to stay a spell. I hope I shall get some work soon & some think that I shall, we are makeing a new map of this town & fortifications, When we have some pleasent weather I will get some pictures printed for you. Cant print when the sun does not shine. I wish you would coppy off the receipt for the trochies & send it to me. Some of my friends wants to get it. (I am comeing Sister Mary etc.) Well Millie? I suppose it seems very lonely to you since I left you, I was sorry to have to do it but I could not helpt it, I felt sad when I left you but am looking ahead for a brighter time to come so that we may enjoy our selves again togeather. Be as cheerful as you can. Evry day counts one the less then & then & then I will be my own man again. I am well, I will not attempt to write a very long letter this time Pleas put my friends in mind of those Photographs I want to fill my Album. The boys all think that I have some good looking folks, Write soon, Yours with much Love Charlie

Ruch is just now smacking his chops over one of your ginger snaps. he says O how good

Head Quarters, Topl. Engineer
Office, Army of the Cumb.
Chattanooga, Mar. 3, 1865.

My Dear Millie

I will present to my trusty bird a letter to you to let you know of my good health &c. The boys have all gone to bed so I thought it would be well enough to improve a few moments a chatting with you. To begin with, we are haveing a very hard thunder shower, It lightenings very sharp. This has been a very warm day. The peepers have been tuning up their voices all day. I have also had the pleasure of listening to the sweet music of the birds which sends a cheerful thought evry vane of my person. O how happy they sing & how happy it makes me feel to hear them. Time is passing rappidly & it will soon be time for me to traverse my way northward to my native home if I am spared. I have been out a surveying to day. I commenced surveying the forts, This is such work as I like. I am doing it for Gen. Howell the Engineer inspector. He was in here yesterday. I have a plenty of work to do. There is but few of the men at work now, none but the best have any thing to do. I will say a little about the butter. Pleas send to /me Lieut. A.F. Brooks {crossed out} C.H. Prentiss 50 pounds of butter by Express as soon as you can. I will pay you 40 cents per pound. When the butter is expressed, take a receipt & send it to me also the number of pounds of butter & price of firkin & the cost of transportation to Chattanooga. Now be sure & do as I tell you. I will become responsible to you all for the money. That can of butter I brought is what sold the butter. 50 lbs is all the boys want at a time. If there should not be 50 lbs it will make any differance, I will quit for tonight. My eyes, so good bye-- Sunday morning the 4th. This is one of the Loveliest mornings I ever saw. Now I wish I were at home to attend church with you this morning, but no I must stay a little longer. The boys have been so busey that they have had no time to print any photos. they will soon get out of their hurry I think I will not get any more blankets now. The weather is getting warm & they cost $6. each now. The forest begins to look green. The weeping willow trees have leaved out & look handsome. Nature begins to smile. O, if I could have you all down here to day I think I could interest you for a while. but as it is I can do nothing gor you I wrote Hiram Rouse a letter last week. If you go there he may let you read it. How is Soph Anderson getting along I think I will write her a letter before long & cheer her up some. I hope I may hear that she is better. Tell

Dave I am looking for a letter from him when you see him & also tell him I would like that Profile of his. I have a vacint place in my Albo for it. I feel very much flattered by the boys accompliments. They say that I have some good looking folks &c. I suppose Uncle Abe takes his seat today for another 4 years. I cant think of any news to tell you only the stone river bridge is gone & we can get no mail untill wednesday next. I have had no mail since I returned from home. Pleas write often. Yours with much Love Charlie

I will enclose you $10. for butter

Head Quarters Topl. Engr.
Office, Department of the C.
Chattanooga, Mar 9, 1865

Dear Millie

Times are very dull in concequence of my not geting any mail, I have not received the first identical scrap since I returned from home, The difficulty is the water has been so high the mail could not get through. It is estimated that the water raised in the Tenn. river about 30 ft. we had hard work to save the river bridge, Had about 200 men & one steam boat to get the flood wood away from the butments. I have seen 2 buildings go down without being broken. 3 steem sawmills under water & nothing is seen of them but a few feet of the smoke stack, a number of the buildings connected with the mills are carried away, Thousands of acres was covered with water. Yesterday morning the water commenced to fall & up to this evening the water has fallen about 6 ft, 2 men were drounded last monday (soldiers), one bent of the rail road bridge at Bridgeport was carried away & the stone river bridge was also carried away. It is supposed the high water is caused by the melting of the snow on the mountains north east from this place, The night I wrote to you last I spoke of a hard thunder shower, It was a severe storm, it went in that direction, that night while I was writing the lightning struck my old bording house I showed you in the view of Lookout, It tumbled over one officer & one clark but did not hurt any one. The family has moved out.-- Well, but my own affairs, I am still at work at maps & giveing good satesfaction, Quite a large fort is building just behind our house. About 100 niggars is at work evry day. We have had some very fine weather the past week but to night some stormy out. I sent to you in last letter $10. toward payment for the butter, pleas forward the butter as soon as convieneant. It will not make any differance if you send 15 or 20 lbs more than I mentioned, It will not make any differance what it is packed in if it will keep. I suppose it might be put up in tin cans & boxed with a good solid box if you cant get a ferkin made. Dont send it in a crock. Friday Evening. I have hurd some thing to day that does not look just right. Pleas hold on to the butter untill you here from me again. It is rumered here in the office that the 20th Corps men will go to their respective commands or department, If that is the case we shall go to Savannah, There is 8 of us that will go. That will be a nice little trip, I hope it is not so, (I have been traiding gold pens & it is a very good one.) If I go I shall go in the Engineer office at that place in Sherman's army. But I think it is a false report, so do not borrow any trouble about it. Saturday morning the 11th. It seems that I am interrupted very often. Now I will try & see if I can write a little more, I had some good luck this morning. I received your No. 1 letter, but, but, but it brought tears to my eyes when I read it. How sad it is to part in such away but so it is. I should like to be with you in your room this dismal weather instead of being in Tenn. 800 miles from you. My feelings mingled with yours when I was hurled away from your sight in Kalamazoo. I wanted some hiding place to give vent to my feelings, I had none. I left you with a heart filled with grief & I feel so now. I cannot go at work with that ambition that I had before I went. Our best way is to look ahead in antipation of a better time which is not far beyond us. Let us do so & forget the past. The past cannot be recalled. What was I doing 2 weeks ago tonight, (the night you alluded to) How differant. Then we were enjoying our selves togeather with our kinds friends, then in 5 1/2 days I was 800 miles from you in the enemies country. Yes Dear Millie it seems worst for me to part now than before. It would perhaps been better for us if I had not have got a furlough nor said any thing about going home untill my time had expired. Going home only opens the old wound. I have not doubt but your room seems very lonely but there is no one dead, Now try & cheer up & put away those lonely feelings. Dry up those tears. Glad to hear that you arrived home safe. At the time you arrived home I was sitting in the Depot at Michigan City about 90 miles from you. My fair to that place 75c. Well? now about the washing machine. I suppose that we are all a going to get rich in that business (Yes I hope so) who is a makeing them & what do they cost a peice for makeing I think they will all who will try them. I dont feel sick of the bargin yet. Tell Father and Geo. if they are satesfied the machines will sell readely &

there is prospects of doing well they had better secure more territory if they it best. They can tell something about it after they have a little trial, I wish I was there to put my sholder to the wheel, I think us three could make a roll. How comes on Georges troches, I have a good supply on hand I would like to send him a plug of Navy if I could get it to him. The boys was much pleased at my return. That butter was so good they said, I put those snaps on the table, well I cannot tell you how felt or what they said, they were so good to the taist. You said you would never forget that last look of mine when I moved of in the cars. Can I ever forget when I saw that large tear that was comeing into your eyes & takeing you hand in mine & printing a parting kiss upon your lips. No I never shall. That last look is rivited in my memory for ever. Yes, Millie I will bear with in trouble & at all other times. My heart is always with you. My prayres also. But such is life & we must take it as it comes & must prepaired at all times & if by chance we should never meet on earth again we shall in heaven. My singing books are a comfort to me, but I cannot use them without bringing back the time when your voice & mine was in harmony over the same books in our quiet home. I wish they were all at home, I hope you will not make yourself sick over your greif. I have writen to Aunt Almira the last week How does my little Elsie get along. Kiss her for me. I would not find any falt of you writing Millie, I dident intend to hide your gold pen & I cannot tell you where it is. Look in the box of pens carefully then in the clock on the clock shelf next to the Door. It seems to me that I put it in the stand drawer or in the Desk Drawer & it seems to me again that Geo. borrowed it but I am not shure I did not bring it away with me but I brought the one that I carried home. I think I shall send you some Photographs in my next letter. I shall write again about next wednesday. Now about that strutting arrangement, I suppose you can do that with much trouble but be careful & not fall, Tell Geo. that I shall write to him soon also the rest. I was in hopes that there would be no draft in Otsego. I believe I will close for this time. I have lots that I want to say but have no time now to write any more. I still remain your Affectionate Husband Charlie

Bureau.
Head Quarters, Topl. En.
Office D.C. Nashville
Mar. 15 1865

My Dear lonely Wife,

Perhapse I have some good news to tell you. A General order came to head quarters to releive all detail men in this Dept. to return to their commands So of course that reached me. I went to Col. Merrill & got a good recommend & yesterday afternoon I started for Savannah & got as far as Nashville where Gen. Whipple ordered me to remain here untill he could get a dispatch to Gen. Thomas for me to remain here in this country, & go back to Huntsville & take charge of an office at that place. Now I think I shall remain here some where. But there is one thing about it. A soldier does not know one minute when he will go the next. I will not trouble you to send me any butter Do not write to me untill my fate is deturmined. I shall write very often so you may know how the cat jumps. I recived your No. 2 letter just before I left the office & I know of nothing that done me more good than that. I could not keep from sheding tears when I was mounting your pictures, Dont you beleive the boys cried when they parted, I am in a great hurry a short letter will be better than none. Yours with heaps of Love, From your most affectionate Husband

Charley

Head-Quarters Department of the Cumberland
Office Chief Topographical Engineers
Nashville, Tenn.
March 19, 1865

Dear Millie

Again I will drop you a few lines to let you know my whereabouts. I do not know where my quarters will be yet, but I think it will be in Huntsville as I expect to go there soon & take charge of an office at that place. You may write and Direct your Mail as before to Chat. If it is directed to that place I will get it in any part withing 150 miles of this place. I am well & doing nothing as useal. I feel very discontented while I have nothing to do but I hope I shall get to work some time this week. There is 5 of the boys that have gone to their regiments that might have stayed if they had have done as I did. There is nothing like being a little smart & studing a little head work. I shall save myself a very long journey by doing so, I have but little time as the mail goes out in a little while. I have been to meeting this A.M. & hurd a good sermon & some good singing. It seems like old times. The weather is very warm & streets very dusty, water is falling in the rivers & war matters go on finely, I hope you will excuse my short letters. I cant write much when I am so unsettled, I hope this may find you well. I enclose some more faces. Evry one that sees your picture wants one. I still remain Your affictionate Husband Charley

Head Quarters. Topl. Engr.
Office. D.C. Nashville
March 23. 1865

Dear Millie

It is with pleasure that I drop you few lines this morning. I am well & still remain in Nashville & doing nothing yet. Dont know how long it will remain so. I hope not a great while because I want to be doing something. We are haveing some very fine weather here, streets very dusty. I go up to the hospital once in a while to see Ed. & Ancil Baird, I do want to get away from this place very much, for this reason, the bed bugs & flees are thick enough to carry a heavy man off. When a man goes to bed at night he dont know where he will be in the morning. But what is worst than bed bugs is rats. I was interupted this morning by Capt. Rugar with a little job that kept me out of mischief today & will make this letter one day later for you. Well, what I was agoing to say about the rats, It is allmost impossable to keep any thing out of their way & to sleep They are the largest & boldest I ever saw, & the stench of the dead ones is very disagreeable on the whole Nashville is the filthyest hole I ever was in. But I will try & stand it a little while longer. Time is fast passing, & soon the day of rejoicing will soon come. The Nashville papers talks as though Jeff. Davis wanted peice. I think that he will soon get a peace. A peace of roap to hang by I reckon. Thats the way it looks to me.--I stoped in a shoe shop yesterday to get my boots taped, the man wanted $2.50 for the job, I made up my mind to put another dollar with that & go to the Quartermaster & get a new pair,--Tell Geo. that I have got one of the handsomist brest pins out, I have a chain attached to it with a pin like this {drawing of a brooch with a guard pin}.

It cost me $4.--I have 2 peaces of music which I will send you as soon as I learn it or one of them, one is Joney Schmaker which I know & the other is Just after the Battle Mother. It is good, I have found 2 very good singers down here. Al. Ruch has gone to Savannah so I cant sing with him any more. We are comeing Sister mary &c. It seems as though I have hurd that peace some where, Tell Hiram not to forget that, I have forgoten it, I seems to me like a long time since I got your last letter & I feel anxious to hear from home. It was one week last Tuesday since I got your letter. I think there is some mail in Chattanooga for me now. I hope to hear in your next that you are feeling a little better than you was the first 2 weeks after I left. I do not feel quite so lonesome as I did at first. I have wished a great many times that I had not tryed to get a furlough, for going home has only dug open an old sore. I am afraid that I have lost my skane of linnen thread. I cant find it but my fine comb is all write. I have not made any pictures since I came back. I cannot set myself to work at. My intrest for such work has gone. You seem to speak in very high turms of the Washing machines. I glad they suit, I dont think I shall trouble you any more about the butter. I hate to undertake it for it is so uncertin about getting things through quick & it may lay over some where & spoil then a dead loss. It takes about 3 months for boxes to come through. Tell Geo. that I have one of the best gold pens that he ever had in his hands. I have been offered $15.00 for it. It has cost me $6.75. This pen I intend to hang on to. I am not in very good writing trim to night so I will close hopeing to hear from you soon. I will enclose to you 2 more Photographs. How do you like them Yours with much Love Charlie

Topl. Engr. Office H. Quarters
D.C. Nashville, Tenn.
March 28, 1865

My Dear Millie

Your kind epistle of the 19 inst came to hand when I was in bed this morning. It letter No. 4. It seems that No. 3 letter has got misscarried at least it has not reached me yet. It was sent to me about 4 days ago from Chattanooga I tell you Millie, a letter does me a heap of good now days, I keep reading them so that I can nearly repeat them. I still remain in Nashville a doing nothing. My pay goes on just the same as before but

I do not feel contented unless I am doing something. I have often wish
that I was a rich man & had nothing to do but I have got over that now.
I always want something to busey myself. We are haveing very good &
encourageing news from the war Department. It does me good to hear that
Jeff Davis begins to whine. It seems that Gen. Sherman is rip & tairing
things in N.C. just as he likes. The rebs made a mistake when they made
a jump at Grant. They thought he was a sleep. He generally sleeps with
one eye open. I think their days are numbered.--In your letter you speek
of going to church. It puts me in mind of the two last sundays I have spent
in Nashville. I have hurd some good sermonds, hurd 3 last sunday. The
weather fine & pleasent except this morning it has commenced to rain.
Trees begin to look handsome. Peach trees in full bloom. While I was in
Chattanooga I sent to New York for a steel coller & I left word with M.D.
Burke to send it home to you when it came. I hear this morning that he has
sent the coller to you. So you may keep it untill I come. The money I sent
you you can use it or put it with the rest just as you like. I hope you have
not sent the butter if you have M.D. Burke will do the business right for
you. His address is the same as mine was when I was there. I have received
no letter from Hiram Rouse yet & do not think that I shall hear from that
address. There is no such a man as Capt. Merrill now. He is Col. Merrill of
the first U.S. Engineer Brig. Col. Wharton is my Commanding officer now.
I hope that he did not send his pictures in that letter. I have writen him a
letter & give him my address I think. Do I understand that he has received
my letter? Pleas tell him not to give it up so. He will hear from me again.
(We are comeing Sister mary &c.) Millie I do not clame that I have got
much the start of you, but in 2 days after I saw you I hurd robbins, meadow
larks, bluebirds, ground birds, & frog peeppers &c. sing & saw butterflys. I
do think that was a little a head of your climate but after all I will take old
Mich for my home. Enough about birds now for you have the start of me
now, I hear nothing but the noise of carts, waggons, carradges &c. which
almost deefening sometimes. This is a great buisness place, streets very
narrow. Alleys very filthy & evrything to make it very unpleasent for me.
I do not want to stay here. I do not wxpect you to do much writing if you
are not able to write. It seems to me you had better choose some other day
to write, for you seem to have a headache evry sunday. I am sorry that it
is so & would help it if I could. Perhapse if you would not use your brains
a thinking about me you would be troubled less with the headache. Tell
Mrs. Rouse that I had no time to go to the National Semitary when I was in

Chatt. & I dont know as I shall go back there again. If I do I will do what she wish to have me with great pleasure. That is write, go in on the washing machines, I expect we shall all get rich in that line. Tell Mrs. Clock that I occationally think of her kind gift. It hall disappeared except the flowers & ribben. Tell Dave if he does not write & send his Photo, he will lose a friend perhapse. I dont think that he does his duty in that respect. I rejoice to think or know that Geo. has escaped the Draft again. I think it will be the last. I hope so. (Turn over & keep a doing so) I will not have time to finnish my letter. I am off for Chattanooga this minute. Charlie

Head Quarters, Topl. Engr.
Office. D.C. Chattanooga
Tenn. March 29, 1864{5}

My Dear Millie

You can just imagin that you see me in Chattanooga in that large brick house again. Some 15 days ago I said to myself that I would take my fairwell look at old Chattanooga. But I am back again in my old room. Dont know how long I shall remain here. You can see that I cannot tell one day what I shall do the next. Yesterday noon I was busey writing a letter to you when orders came for me to pack up & go to Chatt. & in less than one hour I was on the road to said place. I was just a cungering up a long letter to you & commenced another sheet on which I had got one line writen & now that is all lost. There seems to be something wrong about my mail matters, Your No. 3. letter has not come to hand & neather has Hiram Rouse's letter. Question. Did Hiram send any Photoes? I had a very pleasent trip from Nashville & got through a live. A nice little gang of bushwhackers was captured out near Lookout mountain last Monday. A nigger who was employed in the iron works was caut carring rations to them. The good for nothing black pup had aught to swing. & perhapse he will. On my way here from Nashville I took particular notice of all that was going on along the road. The farmers was more than makeing the dirt fly, prepareing the ground for seed, Some fields I counted as many as 9 teems in one field with shovle ploughs a rooting up the ground, some planting, some sowing, repareing & makeing fences. I could see as far as the eye could reach patches of fruit trees in blossom. It did look splended, Spring is in full bloom now. I meet 18 trains of cars on my rout, which

indicates some buisiness going on out this way. There seems to be a great
stir amongst the troops. Uncle sam is drawing up on the coils of the yankee
army which will soon make the rebs black in the face & soon will begin
to look for a hole to crawl out but I feer it is two late for them now. There
is any quantity of raw troops comeing in & it is fun to see them perform.
I love to bother them. They dont know how to hault a man &c. Yes I am
glad for you that your books have come at last. The weather has been very
unpleasent to day & this evening. A fine mist has been falling all day but
it is not cold we do not have to have to have any fires. Well Millie I hope
you will be contented with a short letter this time. I feel very tired, I had
no sleep last night. I will enclose you two more Photoes, which I suppose
you want to send to your friends. I got 24 of yours & 24 of mine printed.
Is that as many friends as you have? I am well.

Yours with much Love, Good Night Charlie Millie

Topographical Engineer
Office, Hd. Qrs. Dept. of the Cumberland, Chattanooga
April 2, 1865

Dear Lonely Wife

In reply to your No. 3 letter which came to hand to day, I thought the
letter was lost but it has turned up. I would not have lost it for nothing
because it is such a good one. I have give it a good thurough reading. The
first sentance reads thus, I feel quite sad and lonely to night, Cant you
Drive away such sad & lonely feelings, try hard & make as though did not
care, (you know that I will know better) be cheerful & try and think my
being gone but think in 157 days I will be a free man & perhaps will see
me, I am sorry that you are feeling so bad & I suppose you cannot help
it. Such is the case with me some times. Dear Millie I know your feelings
& anxiety of you absent one but do not trouble you so, I know the tie of
love is strong between us. War is in our midst & we must be sepperated
for a while if not for ever as many have all ready. I hope such will not be
our lot. God do all things well & in him we must trust. In this letter you
make mention of the death of Mary Baird's little boy. Little did I think I
was seeing him for the last time when I was at home. Sad is such news.
I feel for Mrs. Baird. She has had a very hard time. She has seen a great
deal of trouble. The time will soon come when we all must part to meet

no more on earth but if we prove faithful we shall all meet again. Let us all strive to be of the number that will meet god in heaven & to dwell with him for ever, where trouble is no more,--You seem to think that the boys are mistakened, they are not, for I think I have just as good looking folks as any one. I have given away 2 of your pictures to my friends, one to Ruch & ont Gen. Benn. there is more that wants them but cant spair them, Ruch promised me one of his wife when he gets married. He & I has had some huge old chatts on mattrimonyal question, I never expect to see him again--How comes on my little lark (Elsie). Take good care of her. I want you to keep on the right side of Geo. & Laura mabee we may coax them to let us have her (maybe we wont) but I wish they would, I think a great deal of her, I have to get out my Album & look at her most evry day. Pleas tell Hiram that I have not received his letter yet. I feel that he is in dept to me yet, & when I get one from him, he will get another one from me in return, If he will direct it right it will come through safe, I am sorry the other is lost. I wonder if he sent his Photographs in it, (We are comeing Sister mary &c,) Did I write him a good letter? It seems to me you have the advantage. You get chance to read all my letters to my friends. I shall have to be carfull how I corespond with Ladies, you dont care I dont suppose.--You say you have seen Hubbard, perhaps you had better dun him for that commutation money, I dont know how much it is. Perhaps I can pick up some more Waverlys to send you,--Col. Gaw is still a pecking away at me to get me take a commission in his regiment. But I cant see it. I had rather go home & make machines & peddle &c. I received 2 letters yesterday one was your No. 5 & the other Geo. No. 0. Geo. will hear from me soon, he wrote a first rate letter, it me lots of good & so did yours. I see that this No. 5 letter is a little more cheerfull than the No. 3 letter, after all this seems to be tinted a little, but that is nature. I do not blame you any, for I am troubled that way myself some times, but I dont see what should make you dread this summer so when this is the summer that brings me home if I live. I should want to see this the most, but never mind, keep up a stiff upper lip & carry a high head as though you was going to Barnum Museum to see a mosquetoes bladder which contains 14 souls of those public speculaters who have been gougeing uncle sam out of his thousands,--You will see by this letter that I am in my old place again. I will tell you all about it. If I should have had to gone to Huntsville I should be in the same department as I am now it is a branch of this office, If I went to Sherman's army I should have wenmt into the Engr. office of that department. I will turn out for to night & finnish some other time, I am well. Yours with much Love Charlie Prentiss

April 4, I have let my letter a little while & now I will procead to business. In the first place I will speak of the doings yesterday eve. We received some glorious news from Richmond & vicinity. (I suppose you had the same) Some of our largest guns was fired (I think about 150 rounds) which made a considerable nois for one half hour. Two 32 pound guns in the the fort back of this building about 100 ft from distant. You better believe it made the windows rattle. That is the kind of music I love to hear. It put me in mind of Atlanta campaign I recon: It was very amuseing for about one half hour. The thundering of artillery was grate. All the bugles & all the drums & fifes was a going it all sorts, men all cheering &c. & you may think that there was some confusion for a little while. Now the rebels are in a bad fix. What will they do. They must yeald their communication is cut & have no means of supplying their army. The prisoners that we have taken are nearly naked. I begin to feel as though I was a going home before my time is out. What do you think, well Millie I believe I will close for this time, hoping this will find you well & all the rest, I have writen lots of letters but I get none only what comes from you at home, but that does not discourage me any. Geo may look for a letter soon Yours with a bunch of Love & beeswax, Charlie Prentiss To Millie Prentiss Yours with much Love

Topographical Engineer Office,

HD. QRS. DEPT. OF THE CUMBERLAND,

Nashville

April 16 1865.

Dear Millie

I have again turned up in Nashville. A dispatch came to me yesterday A.M. for me to report here & I did so without delay. I only had about one hour notice before I was on the way. I came through safe. I am well. I expect to go to Huntsville, La. next Sunday to take charge of the office at said place & take information. Huntsville is a very prety quiet little place. Some like Kallamazoo. I am very well satesfied with the exchange. My Address is this Charles H. Prentiss Draughtsman, Topl. Engr. Office D.C. No. 25 Collage St. Nashville Tenn. Pleas use this address untill I order it changed. From this office my mail will be brought to me by spetial messenger once or twice a week, You can breviate my address as you see I have. I have very little time to write now or I would tell you alittle about the celibration over the late Victories Yours with much Love, Charley Millie

Charles H. Prentiss Draughtsman
Hd. Qrs. Topl. Engr. Office D.C.
No. 25 Collage St Nashville
Tenn. CP
Head Quarters Topl. Engr.
Office D.C. Nashville
April 8, 1865

My Dear Millie

It is with much pleasure that I write you a few lines. I am yet in Nashville, where I expect to be untill next Monday morning at 6 oclock A.M. then I start for Decatur Alabama instead of Huntsville. I shall remain at the foresaid place perhaps a month or six weeks thence to Huntsville thence to Stevenson. I am to make a State map of Alabama or to do what I can towards it while I am in the service. Then when it becomes safe to go farther into the state I shall worke down that way, but I think the above mentioned places will last my time out. {this seems to be written over these two phrases: (there is a space between the phrases) By command of MAJ. GEN. THOMAS, Lt. Col. and Chief Topl. Eng'r. Dep't of the Cumberland.} I have all of my stock & things boxed up ready for a start. & I persuaded the Capt. to let me remain here untill monday so that I can go to church tomorrow. We have one of the best ministries that I ever hurd & have good singing. The weather is quite chilly now days. A good fire feels comfortable, what do you all think of the news now days. I begin to feel somewhat encouraged & there may such a thing as my getting home before my time is out, but I will not think much about that yet, we have fresh news here, get within 30 minutes after is is made & we know about all the movements that are made. I put out our banner in honer of yesterdays victory & I tell you it is a large one. It is about 30 ft long & in propotion other ways. We have it suspended over the street by a roap reaching from our window to the Sewanee Hotell. I did not think of writing a letter when I set down hear, if I had I should have got a decent sheet of paper. I received 2 news papers from you last night in one rapper. I am well & have enough to eat. Yours with much Love.

I still remain your obedient Servant

C.H. Prentiss Asst. Engr.

This is the way my name is signed to my papers.

Head Quarters, Topl. Engr.
Office D.C. Nashville Tenn.
April 13, 1865

Dear Millie

Your kind message of the 2nd of Apr. came to hand to day & I was more than glad to hear from you & home again. I dont know but I think it is nearly two weeks since I hurd from you except some papers that I received from you. I am well & have plenty of work to do. Your letter was accompanied with Milo Burke's letter. You need not have sent them back here, for I have no use for it. Today was the first fair day we have had since last Saturday night. It has rained almost constantly up to last night & all the streams are all swolen & many bridges are carried away, I think that I shall have to remain here about a week on that account. We have plenty of amusement here in this city such as theatres & circus we have 4 of the first & one of the latter but I do not want to trouble them. This is one of the worst places for shooting folks I ever saw (except the battlefield). There has been quite a number killed since I have been here. Whiskey is the cause of it most always. Thank God that I am not troubled that way. I have my first to taist of yet. Friday evening the 14th. I was interupted last evening & I will try again. I believe to day was Thanksgiving here. To day noon I went into the state house where there was big guns a fireing, for what I do not know. They was fired once in 15 seconds for 3/4 of an hour. There was 5 32 pound guns at the buisiness, I tell you they made things snap. The state house stands nearly in the center of the city on an elivation & it looks like a very prominant bump. There is a great deal of land covered with watter again. Some buildings in the suberbs of the city nearly under water. I saw some houses that the water was up to the eves & I dont know but they were afloat & the water is still riseing.--Tomorrow evening there is to be a grand illumination in the city in honor of our recent victories. We have one candle to each light of glass in the front of the office which will be 120 lights & a number of transparencies & mottos &c. I noticed in the paper this A.M. of an order issued by Sect. Stanton to diminish our National expences such as dischargeing all staff officers. No more amunition made, Quartermasters diminish there stock of clothing &c. What does that tell me, Does it tell me that PEICE is close at hand. What do you all think up north. The Soldiers feel so overjoyed about it that there cloths will hardly hold them--You say that you can eat eggs, if that is so you & I will sit up nights & eat eggs, & have a good old time. I am glad you have made the discoverry of meadicen to cure you. Now you want to find something to stop your head from acheing then you will be all right. The coller you may ware untill I come home. I can wear my brest pin here as well as any where I were it evry day & keep thinking of the giver. I think a heap of it tell Geo. I could not sleep without that on, You needent think you can get it away from me but you may wear it sometimes when I am at home. (It rains again to night) Tell Hyram to sing that song to you for me. Tell Mrs. Rouse I could not get a chance to go & find the grave she spoke to me about. I do not want any more thread. I hurd that Maj. Eaton was killed when I was a comeing up from Chatt. Very sad news for Mrs. Eaton. Who ever starts such stories about you, I wish they had to go in the front rank & run the risk of geting hurt &c. why cant people mind there own business, I think it must trouble them terribley, There saying so does not make it so,--I want you and Bye Ballou to keep proper distance. I am geting right away jealous of him. Yes I do know how you want to see me & I want to see you just as bad I guess, I will give you a chance to give me one of your good old huggs & maby I wont. My watch keeps good time. I have partly sold my old one & shall keep the duplex. I get $25 for it when the person get his pay. I have carried it 14 months & payed $15. for it. Yours with a big pile of Love. I am well.

Your No. 6 has come but not No. 7 Charlie to Millie

Topographical Engineer
Office, Hd. Qrs. Dept. of the Cumberland, Nashville
April 16, 1865

My Dear Millie

How great is the change since I last wrote to you. I hardly know how to express my feelings. What are we to do & what are we all a comeing to. This certainly is one of the most barberous nations on the globe. I begin to think that a person is not safe in any part of the country. I attended a Presbiterian church this A.M. & it was one of the most affective meetings I ever attended. There was scarcely a face that was not covered with a hankercheif. We had a good sermon & the music was grand. Who could help weeping I could not. Yesterday afternoon I passed up Ceder St. where I saw our Presidents portrate (life size) placed over the enterance of Col. headquarters draped in deep mourning. Tears filled my eyes. I could not look at. I never saw so many sad faces than I saw yesterday. All of the boys of this office were prepareing for the great illumination when about 10 oclock the sad news came that the President was killed. In one hour our whole building front was draped in mourning & the flag taken in & nearly covered with crape. About noon a large millitary posession pass through the streets with arms reversed accompanied with with a number of brass bands. A rebel was expressing his joy that the president was dead was stabed to the hart by one of our soldiers on the public squair. I hurd of a number that was killed in like manner, but I do not know of the whole of it to be true. All buisiness was stoped & the city in deep mourning & the same to day. Also the church I attended to day. 6 oclock P.M. I have been takeing a walk about the city. I saw on the street next to the river some 5 or 6 large steemboats standing in the st. The water is within 14 inches of being as high as it was before. They had to work all the time night & day to remove the flour, corn, hay &c to keep it from floating away. There is some houses entirely under the water, I can not get away to Huntsville or Decatur, on account of the bridges being gone, I am somewhat anxious to get away from Nashville. I do not like it here. There is to much noise to suit me. I shall go to church again & here that good man preach. He is one of the off hand preachers. He hardly looks at the bible, Thursday evening 20th Well Millie you may think that I am rather lazy about writing. I have been very buisey this week except yesterday I did not work much. We had a very large funeral in this city & the posession was a grand site, it was one hour & 55 minutes passing our office. I do not think that I will undertake to give a full discription of it. It was a very affecting sight. The posession was headed with three brass bands, then Gen. Miller & staff the post commander Then the post guards. Then Gen. Thomas & staff. Gen. Thomas was weeping when he me. he felt very bad. Then some 15 or 20 regiments each reg. headed with their field band & nearly all playimg a funeral durge then another brass band, /then a long string of hacks {crossed out} the hurse or the imitation of one, which was a splended, it was drawn /with {crossed out} by 12 span of black & white horses. the neigh wheel horse was black & the off was white. the next nigh horse was white & the off black like this {small drawing} each horse by a coldier by the haler after the herse the cavelry, then hacks, then merchants, employ mun by the goverment &c, the last of all the fire companies & machines evry thing draped in mourning. The posession went out of the city about one where they assembled for some speaches by the Gov. Gen Thomas & others. The day passed very quiet.--I received a letter from Aunt Almira day before yesterday also one from Dave. I am well. I hope this will find you well,

Love to my Millie, Charles H. Prentiss Asst. E.

Topographical Engineer Office,
Hd. Qrs. Dept. of the Cumberland, Nashville Tenn.
April 23 1865

My Dear Millie

Your kind letter of the 9th inst. (No. 7) came to hand day before yesterday also one from Wallice Stockwell with their Photos enclosed. I also received one from Dave. He claimed that he did not owe me a letter. I claimed that he did you know. He dont fool me, I had not received a letter since last summer sometime & I had sent him 3 or 4. I have answered his letter also. Last evening I wrote a letter to Sophie. I have not answered Aunt Almiras yet but will soon. it beats all letters I ever received. it is now 19 minutes to one oclock & I can just imagin you all getting ready to church except Mother, Geo. & Laura & Elsie & the little one. Did I guess right? The weather is fine but cool. I did not go to church to day but think I shall this evening. I have a headache to day that makes me feel rather dul

& stupid. I have worked very hard this last week & concluded that I would rest to day & write a letter to you I have received your No. 3 letter but have not received any from Hyram Rouse yet. I expect I will have to write another before he will write again. I am glad he did not send his pictures in that letter but tell him I am looking for them evry day. In regard to your pictures I think you will find market for them. I have disposed of about 4 doz. of my own & they still keep a calling for them. I find enough that wants my picture & I think they are all good friends. It seem that you did know enough to take the hint about the 2 cent stamp but I did not send it for a hint. The way it hapened I had just been buying a lot of 2 cent stamps & had them out to tair up ready for use & put them in my wallet. I left out one so I thought I would put it in your letter & let you use it. If you have not got the papers handy you need not send them while I am in Nashville. I have all that I want to read here but when I get out of Nashville I shall not have any to read only what I buy at 15 cents apeice. I hope your new Docter will prove to be as good as Doct. Hopkins for such men are scarse. When I get home I expect I shall be sick again. I never had any better health than I have had while I have been in this office. If father & Geo. are puting seed in the ground tell them not to the beans in wrong end up, if they do they may have to dig them out & put them in right. Tell Father I will excuse him from writeing but I do like to read his letters first rate. Also Mother too. I suppose that you & Geo. can write for them. but never mind I will not trouble you to write a great while longer. I am a comeing home in a few weeks if I live & have my life spaired & dont get killed & nothing happens to me more than I know of &c. If you want to go out to Uncle Orrins why dont you go. You have money enough I suppose to pay your fair & I think you have time to spair. Go if you want to.--I am glad to hear that the neighbors puting in lots of sugar cane for I want to go in to the buiseness stout next fall. Also into the washing machine buiseness. I want to get rich if there is any such a thing as geting rich. Well Millie! there is but 19 weeks for me to surve when my time will be out then you & I will have one good time I reckon. You must try & buisey yourself the best you can. The words is spoken now forever even to my heart I have bound & naught can on earth to sever the chain so strongly thrown around us & rolling years shall come to test the bonds of love we have made years ago but time shall only find them blest & harmless they pass by. True merits formed the links rivets them in heaven--I am usely well except a headache & I hope this may find you well & all the rest. Perhaps you do not like my stile of writing I only thought I would try to chang my hand alittle & see how it would go. Tell Elsie I often think of the promised candy & if I dont forget it I will bring her some. Also I will fetch all the babys some. I think I have writen about all I can think of. one of the boys just came in & says that Johnson & surrendered his army to Sherman. I hope it is so, dont you. Love to all & you two loves, I still remain your unworthy old man Charlie Prentiss Asst Topl. Engr. Look through to the light & turn over & keep doing so

Topographical Engineer
Office, Hd. Qrs. Dept. of the Cumberland, Nashville Tenn.
April 25, 1865

My Dear Millie

Seeing that I have got Geo. letter Done I will make a begining on one for you. I do not intend to write much more to night as it is 10 oclock & my bed time. I will not abuse you as I did Geo. for I dont think you can endure as much abuse as he can, I received your No. * letter with Georges letter yesterday & I must confess I had a good time a reading them. They were two of the best letters I have got in a long time. You can see by the heading of Geo. letter that it made me feel good, I dont know but I went a little too far with the joke but I guess he will understand the joke, I feel about the same to night. I am well. & are haveing a good time a writeing all alone by myself, I have nothing very interesting to write & I will have to fill my sheet with nonsense as I did the other one.

Wed. evening 26th. I have just come in to have a good chat with you & in come a lot of the boys to bother me & I will postpone this evening & make another begining some other time, as I have plenty of time evenings when the boys are all gone. When they are all here I might as well try to write in a threshing machain while in in motion. good night. Fri evening the 28th. Now I will try again. I am stil alive & well. I feel very tired to night. I have been to work hard on my map. It is a very slow job & it requires a great deal of brain work to make all points meat. It is one of the largest jobs I ever undertook & do. It must be that they have a great deal of confidance in me to put me in such a job. The scale of the map is one mile to 1/4 inch & evry mans name & house is put on evry church, mill & shop &c has to distinctly made on that scale. Just imagine one mile squair out doors is all put inj side of one quarter inch squair on paper. I think you must lay to bed late if letters will find you in bed, I shant allow that when I get home, then you will wish I would have not come home. You must improve the time while I am gone, Dont you suppose I would like to have just been a mouse in the wall or in the room. You needent be surprised if I should / come {crossed out} go home & ketch you in bed & asleep. I will come some game over you all if you do not keep your doors locked nights. You may tell Geo. I have not coaxed him for his babys yet. I let you do the coaxing & for I know you are better at that than I am. keep cool (Yes I wonder why you dread the summer. Yes. Yes. Yes. I know all about it now. I dont say any more hem &c) (only one a year) Our city is still in deep mourning for the death of our cheif majistrate. It is one of the worst things that hapened to the rebels, I find the old soldiers have no mercy for a rebel now. They must come to terms.--I feel sorry for Uncle Henry Clark he has hard time of it. I dont know what the man will do, It will be hard for him to part with his little ones. Millie? if you think you can get one of his children & you can have my consent. I am willing to give it a good home. I will leave it all with you. You have the most care of it & you can do as you like. I repeat it, I will give you my consent. I am of the same opinion that you are about bringing up children. I prefer those of our relation than those that are no connection then we know what we have got. I think I will begin to look for peace. seeing that Gen. Joe Johnson has surrendered his whole army encluding all the territory from North Carolina to the Chattahoochee riv. Prospects looks bright & nearly all the fighting is over. Nearly all the soldiers are nearly wild with joy thinking they will soon get a chance to return to their homes. The same here. Love to all. Charlie

Head Quarters Topl. Engr.
Office D.C. Nashville X a c
April 30, 1865 sunday evening

My Dear Wife

I have just finnished a letter to Aunt Almira & now it comes your turn. The old saying is honest folks pay their debts. I guess I am one of that kind, I have all of my letter debts paid & I dont want for the intrest to run up

a great sum. I have {from here on the letter is written in red ink} writen
a letter nearly evry day the last week or 2 that is when I can get alone.
This red ink writeing is commenced on evening of the 2nd of may. I had
just commenced this letter when 5 or 6 of the boys came in then I could
not write for the noise, I received your No. 9 letter last Sat. It was read &
contence layed away in my memmory. I sent you a waverly this morning.
It contains a very good peice of Music, Pleas sing it while I listen. You
asked me if I hurd you sing that other music, It seems to me that I did hear
a noise a few days ago, Pleas sing a little louder, We are comeing Sister
Mary is a brag word down here, It is sung the same as Hy & Dave sings
it. I am affraid u will not have a chance 2 address me My absent Husband.
much longer. I think that peice is the same as declaired. Dont u? Now here
comes in a lot of strangers to bother me. {The rest of the letter is in black
ink.} Wed. eve. I am well. There seems to be a great deal of excitement
amongst the soldiers about this place. They seem to think they soon will
be mustered out. The hospitals are being payed off & mustered out. The 4th
Corps is here & are expecting to go out soon, all detailed men aside from
Department Head Quarters are ordered to their commands. I hear the 14th
& 20 Corps are on their way to Washington or Alexandria to wait untill
disposed of. I have no idea when I shall get out. I dare not think much about
it for fear I shall get disappointed. I hope my turn will come soon for I am
tired of this kind of life. Keep still. A rat is sticking his head through the
floor and stairing me in the face about one foot from me & a lot more a
running about the room. We kill lots of them but that dont help the mater
any for there are so many. I dont think you all can grumble much for not
getting much mail. I keep you well supplied. I sent you a paper yesterday &
shall send you another with this in the morning. I have done some painting
on one of the pictures I call that a very good design. It represents the nation
in mourning. The Godess of Liberty weeping over President coffin pleas
take good care of that paper--I have not made but one picture since I came
from home. I have got off the notion of it. I have enough to do--I hardly
expect to go to all the places I have here to fore mentioned. They want to
keep me, but when I hear the regiment is mustered out Tennessee will not
hold me long & the map of Alabama can go. I am looseing all intrest in the
business.--O yes, I have plenty to eat now but it costs me a nice little sum
to get it. Only $20.00 per month what do you think of that. Do not forget
to give me an introduction to the new steers, I am sorry the dog is killed.
Who do you suppose did it, I understand you are peiceing a new quilt, Is

it for me or is it for you. for they say what is yours is mine & what is mine is my own. I have 2 nice bed quilts, 2 very old goverment blankets. & they want washing. I have use them nearly 2 years & never washed them. The niggers want a dollar for washing them. I cant see the dollar. I dont see as Aunt Almiras proposition will do me any good for I might as well start from Mich. to go to York state as from here. I expect to get mustered out here on my discription roll at this place. I must say she wrote me a splended letter. I send it to you. I dont know as I have any thing more to write so I bid you all good night. Charlie

Hd. Qrs. Topl. Engineer
Office, D.C. Nashville x a c
May 7, 1865

My Dear Millie

Your kind letter of the 25th of Apr. (No. 10) Came to hand yesterday & read with intrest, I should judg by the reading of your letter that you feel some as I do in regard to war matter. I thing this rebelion is nearly played out, many of the rebs complain like a dog with a sore head, & willing to come back on any terms. Hundreds are standing in the street front of the Provost Marshals office evry day a takeing the oath. I begin to feel impatient about getting home. I dont think that $300. per. month would hire me to stay here after my time is out, at any rate I will not stay in this shebang all summer. I have had inspection this morning, then after inspection I went skirmishing. I kill some less than a quart of bed bugs on my bunk. I lay untill 2 oclock last night a fighting them & got wounded a number of times, You see they are to much for me. They are armed to the teeth, I swore vengence on then, so this morning I got the turpentine bottle & went at them. Without jokeing I think I killed not less than 500. I use up nearly a quart of turpentine. Nothing is better to kill them than this liquid. Just as soon as the gass is turned down the bugs will come out of there hideing places in the wall by Divisions & Corps & charge on our bunks & they do not fail to take them. It is very often I see them out on company drill on our drafting tables, What do you think of the bed bug story. Will it come in eith the Kalamazoo stories, I have no news to write you this evening only that I am well as useal, I suppose that is good news for you. That is the news I look for first in your letters. You seem to talk very encourageing about the washing machines. That is what suits me. I hope soon to get home to open a staveing business, If we can seel 3 machines a day it will not take long to get rich.--We have had an extreamly warm day to day, Why does the doting Father feed his daughter on beans. We are comeing Sister Mary. O. I got a letter Hiram Day before yesterday & answered it, You must see that letter & read what I have said. maybe you will be jelous of me but I was only jokeing. I think I have answered your question in your No. 8. I sayed you have my concent & you can do just as you like. If I had Uncle Henrys address I would write to him. When you write to him tell him I am all right & doing what I can towards my Country. Pleas give him my address & ask him to write to me & I will answer him directly. I have not been to church to day. the reason why I have worked hard all the week so I concluded to sleep to day.--Do you /have {crossed out} find any bugs in your bedstead. Has the Mosquetoes come yet. They do not trouble us here untill about Sept. then they come by the droves--I would very gladly except your invitation & give you a call but my business is so urgent that it would be almost impossible for me make you a visit just at preasent.--I thought there was something wrong with the numbers of my letters. I sent some away & forgot to note the number. It is just as well now. My eyes pain me to night writing by gass light. I am useing my eyes most to much for my own good now days. i dont know as they get any worst than they were when I was at home. I hope this will find you all well & kicking. I still remain your affectionate Husband

C.H. Prentiss Millie Butternut Grove

Head Quarters Topl. Engr.
Office D.C. Nashville Tenn
May 13. 1865

My Dear Millie

I suppose you will expect a few lines from me this morning. I can tell you that I have not done much to day, I have felt sad lonely & homesick since I heard that you was sick, I cannot sontent myself or settle my mind on my work, I hope to hear soon that you are well. I have expected to hear that you are sick this some time back for when you write you would speak of not feeling well. I hope you will come out all right soon, try & take good care of your self for when I get home I dont want to find you sick. The soldiers do not talk any thing but mustering out now days & there is all kinds of rumors about it, so I do not know what to think, Sometimes I think I will get mustered out in a month then again I dont think so. I shall not have to go to my regiment & at least the officers tell me so. I have my disscription roll & can get mustered out on that when the regiment is mustered out. I am thankfull that my time is so near gone after all a week seems like a month. I dont know as I shall go down to Huntsville if I can get red of it. I have quite a lot of work to do here yet. 2 of the boys have gone from here & 3 more are going soon. All detailed men aside from department head quarters are ordered to there commands, most all the government works have stoped & it seems a considerable like civil life again. The city is full of parolled rebel prisoners & seem to be very well satesfied. I tell you it makes me feel sad to see the ladies meet them on the streets, say a few words to one another then silent in tears. The lady enquires after her friend, her brother, her husband or her father, his reply is he is dead. This being the first time they could hear from them. Soon our soldiers will return to their homes, but many will be left behind never to return. How glad I am that I have escaped all the dangers & death & if nothing hapens I shall soon be on my home. O how I wish that day would come, for I want to see you. I want to hear from you now very much & know how you are. I am very glad you have a good place to stay & have good care. I am well as useal, I have worked very hard the last 3 or 4 weeks & I am a going to ask for to be excused from duty for a few days. I am confined to much of the time & it begins to ware on me some. Day before yesterday evening I payed a visit to the grave of President James K. Polk. There is a very nice monument over the grave. He is burried in the dooryard of His residence I also saw the lady they call Mrs J.K. Polk but I am not shure that she is his wife. A number of us boys are trying to go out to see President Jacksons or Harrisons (I have forgot which) old residence called the hermitage. It is about 8 miles up the Cumberland river. Well Millie I hope you will get well soon. I cannot do anything for you while I am way down here but I wish I could. Live True to your faith & if death should overtake you, you will be prepaired to meet our Heavenly Father & give an good account of yourself. Such is my aim, you have my prayers evry day. & when we are done with the worlk I hope we shall join each others in prase in heaven. Pleas have some one write often for you & let me know how you are, Pleas except lots of Love

from your unworthy Husband Good bye C.H. Prentiss Millie

Head Quarters, Topl. Engr.
Office, D.C. Nashville,
Tenn. May 14, 1865

Millie.

I feel as though I wanted to say a few words to you as I am here all alone & the room is quiet, I mailed a letter to you this morning but that does not satesfy me, I sent to you yesterday morning a Waverly & two peices of music. I thought if you was sick & able to read, you would be very glad to get the Waverly. I will try & furnish you with reading matter while you are sick. I have been to meeting this fournoon & heard an exilent sermon & some good singing. The minister is a northan man man & is union to the backbone. He preached President Lincoln's funeral sermon & had large attendence. I have been haveing a good time this afternoon I got out my bundle of your old letters & red them all over, They are just as good as new or nearly so, only they do not tell me how you are now, I suppose you have heard that Jeff Davis & his crew are our prisoners, That is the news we get this morning. I should like to be there & help take care of some of the gold, I guess that he will find that pulling hemp or cotten will be his occupation the rest of his days also a number of others. This war is what you may call over, Curby Smith is about to surender & I think that is all of the rebel army. Uncle Samuel has so many troops that it will take a long time pay off & muster them all out. It cannot come quick enough for me. Five minutes notice is all the time I want to get ready to go home in. I want to get home where I can have freedom & have what I want to eat & not pay out all that I earn to get a deacent liveing. It costs me some months $20.00 per month to eat. Dont you think I have a inward (as Elsie calls it) to supply. This office office is dwindleing out very fast. The Chattanooga office has all moved up here & many of the boys are leaveing I am thinking that my state map of Ala. will come out rather slim. I have made a good begining for some one. A fellow about my size cant be hiered to stay & finnish it. I think I shall try & make a riffle. A fellow told me this morning that I could get mustered out by sending in my application to the Ajt Gen. Office. I will find out if it is so or not. I dont hardly think I can. I do know of a way that I can get my discharge in a short time, that is to play off sick & go to the hospital, but they dont come that on me. My Supper is ready & you must excuse me for a while, will you come & Dine with me. We have for supper tea bread & butter & molases & some dishes. Monday evening. I wil again continue my scribbleing this evening. We are some expecting Jeff Davis to pass through here tomorrow & if he does I mean to get a squint at him. I expect the streets will be so crouded that it will be almost impossable to get any where near him. I would give more to see him than I would a circies. I forgot to tell you in another letter that I had a mess of strawberries a week ago today we paid one dollar a quart for them. The weather has been very hot to day. Do you have hot weather yet. I am swetting like a butcher while I write now. O, how I would like to hear from you this evening But no, that cant be I can do no better than to guess how you are. If you are not able to write I wish you would get some one to write just a few lines for you, as often as twice a week at any rate. I am well to night, I have one diseas settled on me & I am afraid it will ruin me that is lazyness, I have not done a half days work to day. Since the talk has been about mustering out it is all most impossible for me to keep my mind on my work. Pleas tell Geo. that I wish he would write & let me know how he has made out about the traid I am anxious to know whether I am in debt $1,500. or not. I forgot to tell him that I was satesfied with the proposition he made to Nelson. I think I should be satesfied to get 1,000 to 1,200 dollars for the farm. 1,000 dollars down for the farm is (I think) is somewhere near what the farm is worth, but I will leave it entirely to Father & George. Geo requested an immediate answer from his letter & I had hardly time to think much about it, I think if Geo. does make a rap {sic} with Fred Nelson that we must not alter our calculations in reguard to the cane mill if there is a good crop of cane a growing in the neighbourhood. I think that will pay us well, also the intrist of the washing machines must be kept up.--I received a letter from Dave Anderson to day. There is not much news a float here now, & the City is very quiet, most all public works have stoped & are sending off all citizens employees, 2 leave this office tomorrow. I think this office will soon be broken up entirely. I am sure I do not care how soon. The sooner it brakes up the sooner I go home that whats the matter. There is only 10 left here now. The Capt. in charge of this office told me last night that he expected evry day that all of us men (employed in this office) would be called away to be mustered out. that looks rather favorable dont it? I am affraid I shant be sorry. When this office is broken up there will be another sivil engineer office started in this place where they want to hire me. No sir--ee dont get this chap down here to be shot at any more. some of these old rebs woul just as soon shoot a man as to look at him, you dont ketch me out without a pistle in my pocket. We generly have a lot of them lying around in the office, I do not go out much nights, so I feel very safe, I do not wish to have you understand that I am in gread danger, not so, but if I was to be out nights in some secluded place there would be danger. I cannot go where I choose & feel safe, say for instnace, take a walk out in the country or in the woods or in some back streets or in the suburbs of the city. There is where the danger is. Well Millie I think this will do for this time. I hope this may find you well & enjoying your self better than when I last heard from you. Yours with much Love Charlie Millie

Hd. Qrs. Topl. Engr. Office
D.C. Nashville, Tenn.
May 20, 1865

My Dear Millie,

I received your much welcomed letter to day (No. 11) & I rejoiced to hear that you are so that you can write a little to your absent Husband, I have felt much greaved the last week knowing that you was sick. My thoughts have been with you day & night wondering wheather you was getting worst or better. I am happy to know that you are better & I hope you will be carefull & get well again, I hope our lives will be spared to meet each other again & enjoy the blessings of a home life, I know this is a world of trouble & pain, & it stands us in hand ever to be ready, I will expict a very lengthy letter from you at preasent, while you are feeble, The most I want is to see a few word /of you {crossed out} writen by your own fermilyer hand, you dont know how I felt when I saw your hand writing on that last envelop, when I saw that it seemed as though I knew all there was in side. that seem to tell me you are better. I feel so glad that you have such good care & such a good place to stay, I hope it may allways be so. I feel somewhat troubled about you throat, I am afraid it will trouble you about singing. I hope not for I calculated on takeing lots of comefort a singing with you if we live. I do not doubt that you wanted to have me near you when you are sick. When I was in the hospital it seemed as thought I would give all I had if I only had you with me. What is it that Mother says? dont want to see me, I have done nothiing, she must be mistakened in the person. I dont know but I look like myself yet, I have not been drink any thing but cumberland water, & that looks as though it has been used to mop floors with. It is nearly half mud, but that has nothing to do with my picturs, if that does not suit you I will send you another some these days, Well I am not mustered out yet & cannot tell when I can, I am waiting patiently for the time to come, They are still mustering out hospital men, There is a good many joining the hospital now days but I do not go to the hospital unless I am obliged too I dont want the name "hospital" writen on my discharge papers, do you? Uncle sam will do what is right, It was hinted here to day that Bragg was captured & that Curby Smith had surrendered. I hardly think it is true, When I am sure that the regiment is mustered out I shall apply for a releif & go to Detroit & get mustered out forth with. This will be my game, we have been haveing some very hard rains the last 3 days, Well you have the joke on me shure enough. I was not aware that I had made such blunders a numbering my letters, I will try & do better here after. I received another letter Hiram & Julia Rouse, she seems to have trouble, she says that her two sisters are very sick & one is not expected to live. I know it is a sad thing to have death visit a family. I do not know now wheather I have seen them or not I have done very little work this week. I have not been very well, yesterday I did not work, but I did to day I am well to night. I have a sort of a lazy streek this week, why, because I begin to think about going home, thats why. I will try & write a letter to mother before long. I would like to hear from Geo. & know how he made out with the traid. I will not undertake to write a very lengthy letter to night on account of my eyes. They trouble me as much as ever. This lettern contains lots of love for you. I still remain your affectionate Husband

Millie Charlie

I am much obliged to you for the Egle C

Head-Quarters Department of the Cumberland,
OFFICE CHIEF TOPOGRAPHICAL ENGINEERS,

Nashville, Tenn., May 25, 1865.

My Dear Millie

It is a great pleasure for me to address you a few lines this evening. I am yet alive & well, I have not received any letter from you this week but I expect one tomorrow. I do not hear anything about getting my discharge yet but I keep hopeing. They have not got through mustering out hospital troops yet. I was toled to day that they were paying off the 4th A.C. & sending them to their respective states, I hope this may be true, but I am affraid it is not I hear all kinds of stories nowdays. We are haveing some very wet weather now, the river is very muddy which makes it very bad for us, A great many are haveing the ague & I think it is because of the filthy water we use & the wet weather, I have not had the ague yet but I am afraid I shall, The river is up again & on the river banks are 200,000 barrels of salt which is under water. Millie? it is 10 oclock & I have made a beginning & I may get a letter tomorrow to answer Sat eve, May 27 Millie, I did not finnish my letter yesterday evening as I entended too, I had a job to do for Gen. Thomas. It was a survey of the Andersonville prison grounds & fortifications, he wanted by 8 oclock, to send to Washington. I got it done. I received your No. 12 letter this A.M. I tell you I rejoice to hear of your getting along better. The letter seemed to put new life into me, but I feel very bad about your throat, for I was expecting to have some very good times a singing with you, I am in hopes you will get over it, you must do all you can & get it cured, I have some more good music for you, I tell you what it is, I have got in to the first class choir in this city. There is none byt the best singers that sing there, (that is a big word for me) They are most all Boston singers & the leader is the richest man in the city & his lady is one of the best organ players I ever heard,--I was out this morning for a walk & I meet Mrs. J.K. Polk. she is a good old rebel, I hope you will eat fast & get fat again before I get home for I shall not want to see you so poor for you know I am a great hand for fat calves, I suppose you will have the fated calf ready when I come or when the prodigles son returns. That will be a great treat, I hope it will not be long before we shall enjoy a good feast togeather I feel that my time is near when I shall be welcomed home & hearts made glad, O! wont that be a happy meeting. To know that I have come home to stay The Old wheels of time does not roll fast enough in this case. I have got lots of good rheumers you spell this word to day but I will

Dutch Gap.

not puzzle your brains with them for fear they are not true but you must continue to write (if you are able) untill I tell you to stop, I will try & let you know a few days before hand when I shall come & not come unawairs this time, Pleas do not expect me to soon, I will let you know when there is a prospects for me to get mustered out,-- I am a looking for a letter from Geo. evry day, I am anxious to hear about the traid. I have received Hirames letter & paper & answered it. Hiram is a good boy, I believe he likes to

write to Soldiers, He agrees to write as often as I do. Hello here, what have I done, I guess Sister Mary has come at last see the music fly out of his mouth dead cats &c.-- Well Millie I will not worry any more about you as long as you are in good health. You could have keept it from me if you wanted to for no one has spoke in their letters a word about your being sick. I am glad you are well again I hope you will keep so. Capt. Rugar has been gone the last 2 weeks & has arrived to day. I am glad. I have been very lonesome since he was gone. The boys all love him. he is a good man. A christian. A reformed Drunkard & has served 4 years in the army. I hope this will find you well Yours as ever, Charlie, Dutch Gap Millie

Head Quarters, Topl. Engr.
Office D.C. Nashville 10, a, c
May 29 /65

Dear Millie

You may not write any more now, wait untill you hear from me again. I am going to Washington soon, you will hear from me soon again. I suppose you will understand what this means &c. Truly yours Charlie

Hd. Qrs. Department
of the Cumberland,
Topographical Engineer Office Nashville, Tenn.
June 3 1865.

Dear Wife.

Good news. You may look for me home in about 10 days from Date. I sent in my papers yesterday. I am to be mustered out to day at 10 oclcok at this city. I dont know as you will hear from me again before I arrive home. I am well, Do not be impatient. Yours in great haist Charlie

Epilogue

Following the war, Charlie and Roenna never did live in their own house on his farm in Pine Creek. His wartime injury made it impossible for him to farm. About 1869 he opened a planing mill in company with Bartlett Nevins of Otsego, and took over D.M. Hall's sash and blind shop. He ran these for several years. Charlie and Roenna moved to Otsego and built a house, which he designed, on the corner of Court and Fair Streets. Charlie also drew the plans for the Methodist Church in Otsego, a building which is still in use. Later, after the mill was destroyed by fire and rebuilt, he sold it and opened a paint, wallpaper, and art supply store in Otsego and conducted business there for many years. This store became headquarters for his Civil War cronies, and they used to gather there to re-fight engagements and reminisce. My father remembered being an interested spectator at many of these sessions when he was a boy.

Roenna died in 1908. Charlie lived until 1924, a beloved granduncle to my father and his sister.